UNSETTLING EXILES

UNSETTLING EXILES

CHINESE MIGRANTS IN
HONG KONG
and the
SOUTHERN PERIPHERY
DURING THE COLD WAR

ANGELINA Y. CHIN

Columbia University Press
New York

Columbia University Press
Publishers Since 1893
New York   Chichester, West Sussex
cup.columbia.edu
Copyright © 2023 Columbia University Press
All rights reserved

Library of Congress Cataloging-in-Publication Data
Names: Chin, Angelina Y., author.
Title: Unsettling exiles : Chinese migrants in Hong Kong and the Southern Periphery during the Cold War / Angelina Y. Chin.
Other titles: Chinese migrants in Hong Kong and the Southern Periphery during the Cold War
Description: New York City : Columbia University Press, 2023. | Includes bibliographical references and index.
Identifiers: LCCN 2022040565 (print) | LCCN 2022040566 (ebook) | ISBN 9780231209984 (hardback) | ISBN 9780231209991 (trade paperback) | ISBN 9780231558211 (ebook)
Subjects: LCSH: Chinese—China—Hong Kong—History—20th century. | Refugees—China—Hong Kong—History—20th century. | Cold War. | Identity politics—China—Hong Kong. | Hong Kong (China)—Social conditions. | Cold War. | Chinese diaspora. | National characteristics, Chinese. | Hong Kong (China)—History—20th century.
Classification: LCC DS796.H75 C4345 2023 (print) | LCC DS796.H75 (ebook) | DDC 951.2505—dc23/eng/20220823
LC record available at https://lccn.loc.gov/2022040565
LC ebook record available at https://lccn.loc.gov/2022040566

Cover image: Sampans and Shenzhen's skyline in Lau Fau Shan, with hanging strings symbolizing unsettledness. Photo by Angelina Y. Chin in 2017.

Cover design: Chang Jae Lee

FOR HEUNG KONG YAN

CONTENTS

Acknowledgments ix
A Note on Transliteration xv

INTRODUCTION
—
1

1. "REFUGEES" OR "UNDESIRABLES": THE FATE OF CHINESE ESCAPEES IN THE 1950S AND 1960S
—
21

2. THE THIRD FORCE AND THE CULTURE OF DISSENT IN HONG KONG
—
58

3. CULTURAL REVOLUTION AT SEA: DEAD BODIES AND KIDNAPPING IN THE HONG KONG SEA TERRITORIES
—
97

4. THE UNWANTED IN LIMBO: WAS HONG KONG A REFUGE OR A DUMPING GROUND?

133

5. THE THREE ESCAPEES

168

6. COMMEMORATING THE BIG ESCAPE: THE QUESTION OF MEMORIES

226

EPILOGUE

253

Glossary of Chinese Characters   259
Notes   263
Bibliography   285
Index   293

ACKNOWLEDGMENTS

I would like to start by thanking Gail Hershatter and Emily Honig for their encouragement and advice over the years. The UCSC East Asian History Program provided me a nurturing environment, and I am thankful to all the professors and graduate students in that program. In the past few years, I have developed a close friendship with Cathryn Clayton, our *da shijie*. During the Covid years, we spent many hours on Zoom discussing each other's drafts, and she convinced me that my concept of the Southern Periphery is not ridiculous.

I was flattered when James (Woody) Watson, one of the pioneer scholars on Hong Kong, wrote to me and said that he enjoyed my article and wanted to read more. He has made me believe that my research is important and worth continuing. I am also very indebted to Antonia Chao for showing me why a book about migration is worth writing and, more important, for introducing me to a few of the main subjects of this book. Shelly Chan has inspired to think about Hong Kong in a diasporic framework and given me helpful comments on some of the chapters.

This project would not have been possible without the following interlocutors: Chair Sai Ying, Albert Cheung, Cheung Tak Foo, Jennifer Chiang, Freda Cho, Ip Cheung, Fish Ip, Nicholas Kwok, Agnes Lam, Wai Ha Lam, Lao Zhengwu, Mong Kok Gou Wu Tun, Benedictus Ng, Shuk Ying, Tam Man-Kei, Abby Wan, Lennon Wong, Leo Yiu, Xiao Yujing, and a few who would want to stay anonymous. I was saddened to learn about the passing of Wan Yue Ming, Wang Qing-quan, and Zhou Qingjun before I finished the project.

This project was supported by the Chiang Ching-kuo foundation and the Pomona College Faculty Research Grants.

Besides funding, my home institution, Pomona College, has been very generous in many ways. My colleagues in the History Department—Gina Brown-Pettay, Pey-Yi Chu, Gary Kates, Arash Khazeni, Sid Lemelle, Preston McBride, April Mayes, Char Miller, Tomás Summers Sandoval, Miguel Tinker Salas, Victor Silverman, Ousmane Traoré, Ken Wolf, and Sam Yamashita—have been very supportive and understanding throughout these years. Helena Wall has read drafts of this project and given me useful feedback. The Ena Thompson Lectureship funds have helped me invite guest speakers to give stimulating talks on China, Hong Kong, and Taiwan. I also benefited from the fellowship and the writing workshops organized by Kevin Dettmar and Gretchen Rognlien of Pomona College Humanities Studio. The 2021–2022 fellows—Colin Beck, Heidi Haddad, Esther Hernández-Medina, Joti Rockwell, Tony Jin, Luke Meares, Laila Ruffin, Alice Shinn, Ruby Simon, Nick Yi, M. Bilal Nasir, and Nikia Robert—have helped me refine my arguments.

The following students at Pomona and other Claremont Colleges were instrumental in the research process: Don Chen, Eugine Choo, Laurel Hilliker, Kelly Ho, Justin Hsu, John Kim, Jonathan Lee, Justin Lee, Ruiqi Li, Marcus Liu, Mingda Liu, Kathy Lu, Raymond Lu, Agnes Mok, Patrick Oh, Wei Jun Mun, Zelin (Jacob) Wang, Jacob Waldor, Jessica Ning Tan, Elaine Yu, and Lily Zhang. Many of them spent many hours translating and organizing my archival materials. The work was so tedious that it has persuaded most of them not to become historians! Many of these research assistantships would not have been possible without the financial support of the Pomona's Summer Undergraduate Research Program (SURP). I would also like to thank Chris Rand for sponsoring many of these projects.

Claremont and the 5C community have been my home base even before this project started. I want to thank Pey-Yi Chu, Ted Laird, Claire Li, and Seo Young Park for the friendship, meals, outings, and laughter, as well as Allan Barr, Emily Chao, Eileen Cheng, Vin de Silva, Anne Dwyer, David Elliot, Peter Flueckiger, Zayn Kassam, Terril Jones, Kyoko Kurita, Tom Le, Karin Mak, Lisa Maldonado, Georgia Mickey, Lynne Miyake,

Aya Nakagoshi, Zhiru Ng, Albert Park, Chang Tan, and Chelsea Wang for being there when I needed help.

The Claremont Colleges Library has a very special place in this project. I am especially grateful for the assistance provided by Ayat Agah, Grace Chen, Lisa Crane, Ashley Larson, Carrie Marsh, Myles Mykulic, Adam Rosenkranz, Sean Stanley, and Xiuying Zou in the library and the Special Collections. Through the librarians, I was introduced to Claremont's former mayor, Peter Yao, who took me out to delicious meals and spent hours telling me how his parents, Norman Gan-chao Yao and Anne Lee Yao, took the whole family from China to Hong Kong and then to Claremont in the 1950s. Some of the photos included in this book were taken by Norman Yao, who worked as a photographer for the U.S. Consulate in Hong Kong and then for the Claremont Colleges. Peter's mother, Anne Lee Yao, was the first Asian American woman librarian in the Claremont Colleges Library.

Thanks also are due to staff members who have assisted me over the years in various archives and libraries, including the University Service Center and Special Collections at the Chinese University of Hong Kong, the Hong Kong Central Library, the Public Records Office of Hong Kong, Guangzhou Municipal Archives, Guangdong Provincial Archives, the Institute of Modern History Archives, the Academia Historica, the KMT Archives, the National Central Library (Taiwan) and the National Taiwan Library, and the National Archives in the UK.

I have been lucky to be able to visit many places to conduct my research and participate in scholarly activities. In Taipei, I would like to express my gratitude to Max Ko-wu Huang, Lien Ling-ling, Lin Siu-chuan, and Yu Chien-ming at the Institute of Modern History at Academic Sinica, who facilitated my research trips there. During those trips to Taiwan, Ding Naifei, Shirley Lai, Amie Elizabeth Parry, Teri Silvio, Yen-ling Tsai, Andy Wang, and Shawn Wu made me feel so at ease that I am seriously considering moving to Taiwan after I retire. The Berkeley Summer Research Institute held by You-tien Hsing, Wen-hsin Yeh and Robert Weller in 2012 inspired me to think about some of the fundamental ideas of this project. At the workshop, I particularly benefited from friendship with Mike Liu, Chih-Chieh Tang, and Shao-hua Liu. I also learned a great deal from a conference that one of the participants, Jenn-Hwan Wang, organized at National Chengchi University a few months later. Ip Hung-yok kindly invited me to another conference on mid-twentieth-century China at the Academia Sinica in Taiwan in 2015. I am also grateful to have participated in the Hong Kong History Project Conference and the Society for Hong Kong Studies Conference in 2019.

I have been thinking about this project for about a decade, and throughout the years I have also benefited from conversations with many scholars and friends, including John Carroll, Carolyn Cartier, YC Chen, Hsiao-wen Cheng, Howard Chiang, Ching Cheong, Maybo Ching, Ian Chong, Grace Chou, Katherine Chu, Robert Chung, Alexander Day, Evan Dawley, Harriet Evans, Xiaofei Gao, Andrea Goldman, Linda Grove, Peter Hamilton, Hatta Tomoko, Hasegawa Kazumi, Hasegawa Kenji, He Bixiao, Todd Henry, Hirano Keiko, Denise Ho, Madeline Hsu, Calvin Hui, Ito Ruri, Maria Jaschok, Joan Judge, Kawamoto Kanae, Belinda Kong, Paul Krietman, Tong Lam, Fabio Lanza, Yvonne Leung, Lo Sze-Ping, David Luesink, Suzanne Miers, Jeremy Murray, Ohashi Fumie, Osamu Nagase, Glen Peterson, Lisa Rofel, Leo Shin, Sing Ming, Elizabeth Sinn, Helen Siu, Alan Smart, Wayne Soon, Michael Szonyi, Jia Tan, Priscilla Tse, Jeffrey Wasserstrom, Yiching Wu, Ka-ming Wu, Dominic Yang, Yau Ching, Yi Sumei, Ray Yep, Hon-ming Yip, Kenneth Yung, and many others whom I have forgotten to include here.

In California, several Hong Kong friends make sure that I don't forget how to speak Cantonese. Ching Kwan Lee has always been a wonderful mentor and friend. Her leadership in promoting Hong Kong studies is vital in bringing more awareness to the city in this critical time. I am always happy when I am in the company of Wai Kit Choi, Charles Lam, Gabriel Law, Hakwan Lau, Bellette Lee, Ka-yuet Liu, Winnie Man, Kwai Ng, and Eddy U. Thank you for the friendship.

I am grateful to Caelyn Cobb at Columbia University Press. Caelyn has been a huge supporter of this project since she read my proposal. She has always been accommodating and patient with me throughout the process. My appreciation also goes to Monique Briones, Marisa Lastres, Gregory McNamee, and the rest of the production team at Columbia. I also want to express my gratitude to the two anonymous reviewers who gave me generous feedback and suggestions. Gregory Epp and Robert Fullilove helped me with some of the early editing, and Guoping Huang created the maps.

I always exploit my friends for my needs. This book is no exception. I am indebted to Yan Yan (Seven) Chan, who helped me with research and illustrations. Thanks also goes to Harriet Cheng, who took me to Sha Ling and the border area between Shenzhen and Hong Kong. Other important friends, including Brian Chan, Dorothy Cheung, Choi Wan Cheung, Conal Ho, Jude Hui, Ho Lai Yin, Ho Lai Heung, Lucetta Kam, Mary Ann King, Anson Mak, David Moses, Joanne Poon, Xiaoping Sun, Wendy Tam, and Gar Yin Tsang, have given me tremendous support throughout the years. I am forever indebted to Gemma Gonzales and Ho Lai Hing, who spent many years helping my family but left the world too soon to have much time at home with their loved ones. I am also very grateful to my family—my late father, James; my mother, Julia; my brothers, Victor and Sammy; my sister-in-law, Angie; Auntie Gladys Fong; and my late uncle Jack Yang and my auntie Joanna Yang. Revelinda Perez and Ana Retana relieved me from my duties in the households. My pets, Pee Wee, Momo, Boopie, Twinkee, and Jiji, have taught me that every little thing counts.

Finally, I want to thank my beloved Heung Kong Yan for showing much wisdom, compassion, and courage during the time of crisis. Even though we may be far apart, our hearts are always connected.

A NOTE ON TRANSLITERATION

For most of the Chinese terms, personal names, and place names throughout this book, I use *hanyu pinyin* as the default transcription system for easier cross-referencing. For individuals who use Cantonese or other dialects or languages as their main language of communication, I render in their preferred Cantonese or other dialectic romanization. This is the case with well-known people such as Chiang Ching-kuo, Lee Teng-hui, and Tsai Ing-wen. For place names in Taiwan, I use their official spellings whenever available. I use Kuomintang or KMT instead of Guomindang (GMD) for the Nationalist Party. For individuals who have moved from mainland China to Taiwan through Hong Kong or Macau, I use *pinyin* to romanize their names because the official transliteration of their names used in Taiwan is not known. Most place names in Hong Kong and Macau are given in their official English or Portuguese spellings or as they were spelled in the original documents.

For certain colloquial expressions in Cantonese, I sometimes use my own transliteration in keeping with the sound in which they were expressed.

For some of the authors' names, I follow the authors' preferences when provided; otherwise, I use *hanyu pinyin*.

A glossary of Chinese characters is provided at the back of the book, although it does not include some of the names and pen names that appear in the chapters to protect the anonymity of the individuals.

UNSETTLING EXILES

INTRODUCTION

During and after the Chinese Civil War (1945–1949), many people fled to Hong Kong from the mainland (figure I.1). Hundreds of thousands of them settled down in squatter settlements in Kowloon District, south of the mountain called Lion Rock (figure I.2). Lion Rock since then has become an important cultural symbol representing the postwar development of Hong Kong and the common challenges that lower-class people faced. This sense of identification was reinforced by a popular drama series and its theme song, which shares the same title: "At the Foot of Lion Rock" (Shizi Shanxia). Both the series and the theme song depict the daily lives of these people in the 1970s. In many television dramas and movies in the 1980s and 1990s, the great exodus was interpreted as an episode of the history of hardship endured by immigrants.

The phrase "Lion Rock Spirit" was coined to describe the core values of Hong Kongers—including perseverance, courage, honesty, and diligence—developed in the decades following the influx of poor immigrants. It is perceived as the quality that helped many of them succeed in transforming themselves into members of the middle or upper class and the city into first an industrial powerhouse and then later an international financial hub.

Instead of following this trend and writing a place-based history that celebrates the struggle of settlers and the myth of the Lion Rock, my project seeks to tell a less easily celebrated but more complex and accurate version of Hong Kong—a space not inhabited only by settlers who

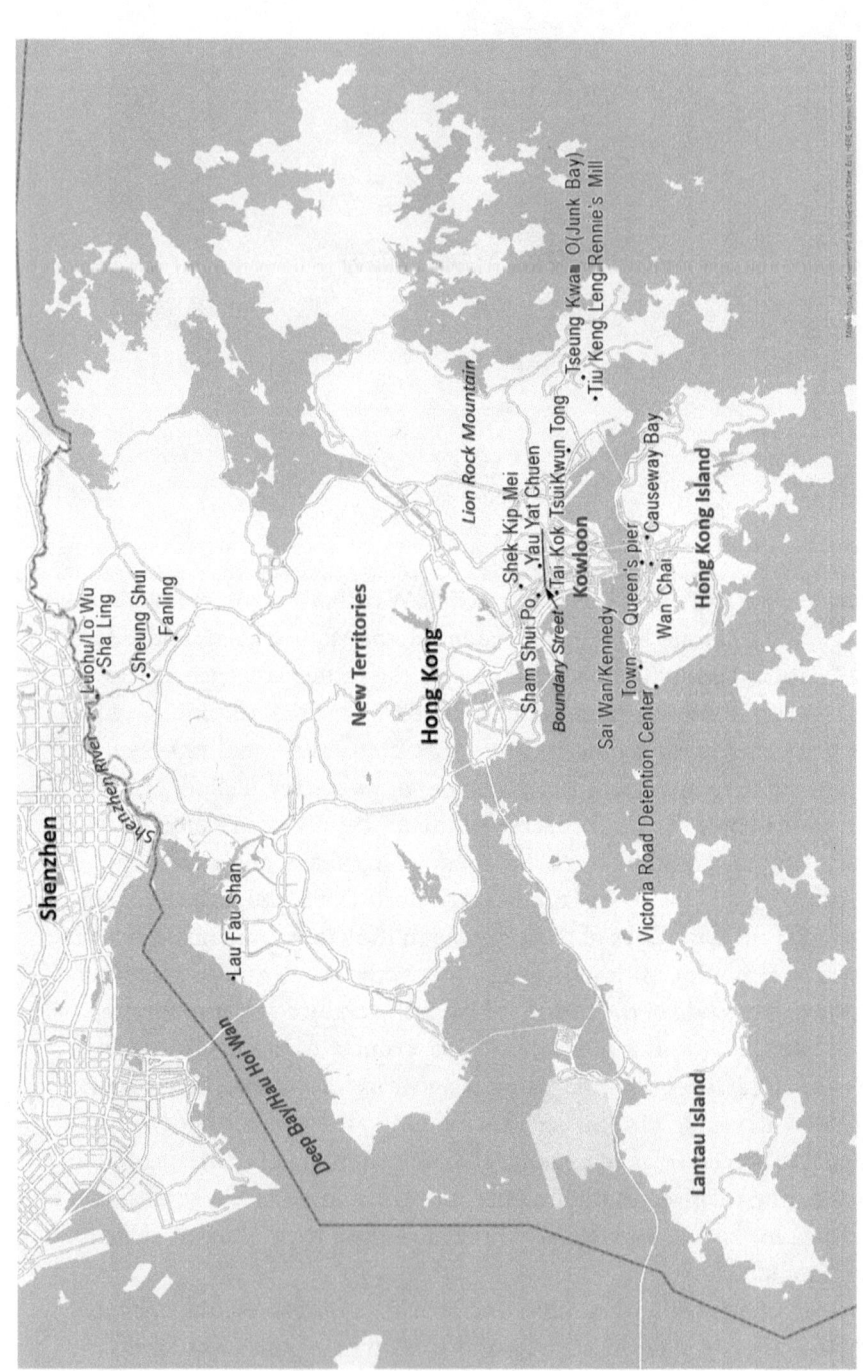

FIGURE 1.1 Hong Kong.

Map created by Guoping Huang.

FIGURE I.2 Lion Rock Mountain with a protest banner calling for true universal suffrage in Hong Kong during the Umbrella Movement in 2014.

Photo by Pasu Au Yeung on December 29, 2014, CC BY 2.0, via Wikimedia Commons.

later became Hong Kongers but also by various types of exiled people in transit, including political critics, people who were caught between the People's Republic of China (PRC) and the Republic of China (ROC), people who were taking temporary refuge, intellectuals hoping to explore political alternatives, victims of abduction, as well as people who were not welcome anywhere else. Not all of these people desired to settle in Hong Kong, and not all of them were allowed to settle. Some of them treated Hong Kong as a peripheral space connected to the Free World on the opposite side of the "Bamboo curtain"; others used Hong Kong as a hideout while waiting for a regime change in the mainland so that they could return; some wanted to leave but were stranded there for their rest of their lives. In other words, Hong Kong was a dwelling place for people whose sense of home and belonging was uncertain.

In an article published in a magazine in mainland China in 1948, an author with the penname Hu Guang wrote about the kinds of people who took refuge in Hong Kong when China was in the midst of civil war and what Hong Kong meant to them:

> The British colony, Hong Kong, has a very important meaning in the political lives of Chinese people today. Many people see it as a paradise

of democracy and freedom and aspire to go there. But, to some others, it is an eyesore, or a thorn stuck in the skin that they want badly to pull out. In this beautiful island in the Southern Sea, there are more than a hundred of the most active, most famous people from China, including political leaders, writers, scholars, cartoonists, journalists and young students.... Most of them are exiles who were not allowed to stay in the motherland, or they do not want to stay within the territories governed by the [Communist] authorities. They are always dissatisfied with the reality. In this place, they can enjoy the freedom that cannot be attained in the mainland. Some have been working hard quietly, others running around and calling out slogans, but all are doing their best to achieve their dreams. Looking around the world, there appear to be no other nations other than our Chinese Republic (*Zhonghua Minguo*) that would build such an important political and cultural center outside of the nation.[1]

In an article published in the same year, another author, Cao Lin, made a similar observation that Hong Kong had turned into a "refuge" (*binansuo*) for "important people in despair" (*shiyi yaoren*) from China: "For the ones who came from China, each of them has a title, and each of them came for a good reason. But if we look at them as a whole, they mostly came to just lay low for a while; they may do some business, or try other things. But there is only one ultimate goal—that is, to run for their lives."[2] In addition to the political dissidents and people who were active in the cultural circles mentioned by the previous author, Cao added that there were also economic elites from major Chinese cities such as Shanghai who left China for Hong Kong with their families and wealth because they were pessimistic about Communist rule.

These two descriptions in 1948 challenged the common perception that Hong Kong was a politically neutral city where Chinese immigrants during and after World War II settled down and became the first generation of "Hong Kongers." Their depictions show that for some people in transit, their dwelling in Hong Kong was incidental. The subjects of this book include escapees, migrants, squatters, and deportees who spent time in Hong Kong in the 1950s–1970s. These people were all caught in the whirlwind that rose from the seeds of political turmoil sustained by the Chinese Communist Party (CCP), the Nationalist Party/Kuomintang

(KMT), the local governments, and the Cold War; moreover, they were often marginal to the two main political parties that represented China.

The myth of Lion Rock was founded on the struggles of the lower-class people settling in the city and starting new lives. The people who were in transit or those who lived on the fringes of Hong Kong society were not part of the Lion Rock narrative because they never quite settled down. Thousands who arrived in Hong Kong faced deportation or had to stay in a refugee camp in a remote area because of language and cultural barriers. A number of them stayed in Hong Kong temporarily but were transferred to Taiwan, the United States, Southeast Asia, or elsewhere. The rest were stranded in Hong Kong despite preferring other destinations.

One's residential status was further complicated by the different criteria of citizenship set by the political regimes of recipient territories. By crossing the border and leaving China proper, these people had become stateless citizens in exile because the regimes of the territories they were entering were not always ready to accept them as immigrants. When these people in transit were in Hong Kong, their residential statuses were defined by their political affiliations, class backgrounds, and places of origin. These statuses in turn often determined their destinies and treatment in society. The ones labeled as refugees were depicted in popular discourse and newspapers as people who had no home to which they could return. There were also people whom the Hong Kong authorities regarded as undesirable because of either their political activities or the threat they might pose to the social order of the city. While these migrants or travelers moved from one territory to another, it was unclear to them which of the main governments—the PRC state, the ROC government in Taiwan, or the Hong Kong government—was responsible for them or could protect them from political threats or persecution.

This book focuses on three processes of the Cold War that profoundly altered the destinies and identities of the Chinese people who decided to leave the PRC after 1949: The first process was the exoduses in the 1950s–1970s to the territories at the edge of the PRC that I will call the Southern Periphery; the second was the enforcement of borders by the political regimes in the Southern Periphery that determined where these people should go and how long they could stay; the third one was the influence of political and popular discourses about exiles that solidified the local attachment and political views of the people who continued to live in Hong Kong until the 2010s.

THE SOUTHERN PERIPHERY AS A FRAMEWORK

In this book, I will use Hong Kong to tell a history of China that has been neglected by situating Hong Kong in the larger Southern Periphery, where individual lives and notions of citizenship, home, and borders were constantly challenged by the effects of policies and political campaigns of the PRC, local regimes, and the Cold War. I use the term Southern Periphery to refer to the vast territory at the southern frontier of the PRC beyond its administrative border. The population in the Southern Periphery was predominantly ethnic Chinese, and it continued to play an important part in the geopolitics of China even though its people had moved away from the PRC after 1949. In terms of administrative regions, one could say that the Southern Periphery roughly encompasses Hong Kong, Taiwan, and Macau. The PRC regime claimed these territories in the Southern Periphery to be part of China; the people who had settled down in the Southern Periphery may have conflicted sense of belongings toward their local regimes and the PRC; and many people who were in transit left the PRC but still considered themselves living in the political imaginary of China.

The differences between Hong Kong, Taiwan, and Macau in the Southern Periphery on the one hand, and China proper on the other lie partly in their experience of colonialism. They had not shared the same political jurisdictions as mainland China since the late nineteenth century. Taiwan was ceded to Japan by the Treaty of Shimonoseki in 1895. The KMT occupied Taiwan and moved its Republic of China regime there after 1949. Hong Kong Island was ceded to the British in 1842 with the signing of the Treaty of Nanjing (Nanking) after the First Opium War. The area was extended over the next few decades to what is now known as Hong Kong. In 1898, Britain was granted an additional ninety-nine years of rule over Hong Kong under the Second Convention of Peking. In 1984, after years of negotiations, the British and the Chinese signed a formal agreement approving the 1997 turnover of the island. Macau was leased to Portugal as a trading post in 1557. In 1887, it gained perpetual colonial rights in the Treaty of Peking. It was returned to China in 1999.[3]

Historically, locations in China under strong colonial influence have served as refuges for political dissidents. The Southern Periphery also shared this characteristic. For example, the number of refugees to Hong Kong and Macau rose to its peak during the 1950s and 1960s following their displacement by the Chinese Civil War and political persecution by the CCP. In Taiwan, the retreat of the Japanese colonial regime in 1945 left a political vacuum that allowed the KMT to take refuge there. When colonialism ended in Taiwan in 1945 and in Hong Kong and Macau in the late 1990s, the people in these territories experienced a rupture of the way of life that they had been used to, and their feelings toward their homeland were tainted by their past engagements with the PRC and the uneven political and economic development due to their colonial past.

More recently, scholars have used a variety of frameworks to study the politics and the network among southern China, Hong Kong, Macau, and Taiwan. Political scientists tend to focus on cross-strait relations, but this framework mainly deals with the historical and contemporary tensions between the PRC and the ROC and does not include Hong Kong.[4] Other frameworks such as Zhong-Gang (China–Hong Kong), Gang-Tai (Hong Kong–Taiwan), or Gang-Ao (Hong Kong–Macau) may be useful in learning about Hong Kong's relations with its neighbors, but they do not fully explain the political and social implications of the Cold War on Hong Kong, Taiwan, Macau, and China. The framework of the Southern Periphery can be useful not merely to describe the diplomatic relations between these political entities, but more important, to understand how the Cold War dynamics and the political turmoil in mainland China impacted the circuits of people and political discourses across these territories and shaped the identities of Chinese people outside of the PRC's southern borders.

Although most of the events detailed in the chapters happened in Hong Kong, this book uses the Southern Periphery instead of Hong Kong as its main geographical framework (except chapter 6) because, in doing so, it destabilizes the popular perception that Hong Kong was a unique colonial city devoid of regional politics. In most existing Chinese-language and English-language scholarly works on the modern and contemporary history of Hong Kong or China, Hong Kong has been treated as a colonial city separate from mainland China since the Opium War. As I will explain, even though many people who left or intended to leave China imagined Hong Kong to be the exit to the Free World, the flow of people and political discourse during the Cold War did not stop at Hong Kong's sea borders but bled into neighboring territories such as Taiwan and Macau as well. Situating Hong Kong in the Southern Periphery allows us to see such movements beyond the administrative borders of the city.

This book discusses how the colonial regime enacted policies that restricted immigration and residency beginning since 1950, as well as how people in the colonial city began to imagine the city as the home in the 1960s, but the reframing of the region as the Southern Periphery expands the scope and places emphasis on the political and cultural influences of the larger environment surrounding Hong Kong.

CHINA AS HOMELAND?

The Southern Periphery can also be used to counter the popular framework of Greater China, used by pro-unification scholars and politicians even today to refer to the PRC, Hong Kong, Macau, Taiwan, and other disputed territories in the South China Sea. This framework was first created by the CCP in the 1990s to cultivate a sense of belonging among people who have spread across Hong Kong, Macau, and Taiwan. It is the party-state's wish to build a Greater China through reintegrating with these territories and sustaining coterminous economic growth that would benefit residents in the mainland and the territories that were once colonized by foreign governments. In addition, the Greater China framework was endorsed not only by PRC nationalists in mainland China but also by people who live outside of the PRC but still identify as Chinese. Some of them may want to sustain a global community of ethnic Chinese people promoting traditional Chinese culture, while others are strong advocates of Chinese national reunification.

In the past two decades, scholars of Chinese migration studies and Sinophone studies, such as Wang Gungwu, Ien Ang, and Shu-mei Shih, have launched critiques on the concepts of Cultural China, challenging the Sinocentricism and romanticization of Chinese emigrants' relationship with the Chinese homeland.[5] Building on these works, my book interrogates the concept of "center." What is common among the various case studies of exiles examined in the book—refugees, so-called Third Force intellectuals, victims of abduction, deportees, defectors—is that they remained in a state of precarity after their initial displacement and continued to be marginalized by the PRC and the ROC. Being "peripheral" does not refer only to one's physical location, but it also alludes to the status of statelessness and nonbelonging. In this sense, there were two "centers" of China asserting political legitimacy, the PRC regime in mainland China and the ROC regime in Taiwan. In addition, Hong Kong and Macau were under British and Portuguese colonialism, and their future destinies were not yet clear in the 1950s–1970s. Chinese citizenship was more of a cultural concept and nationalism could mean contested loyalties to different party-states. My selection of the terms "periphery" and "center(s)" is deliberate, for the stories I will tell are precisely about how the people living in the margins have coped with the two dominant Chinese states.

Unlike other Chinese migrants who settled abroad and might have had the option of immersing themselves in their new homes, the people who fled to the Southern Periphery were displaced right outside the border of the PRC; this positionality put them into continued close engagement with the homeland.[6] Diaspora is a useful concept to understand the conditions of the people dwelling in the Southern Periphery in the second half of the twentieth century, even though these migrants did not settle in a place far from home. In fact, it was the relatively close distance that allowed them to maintain a collective memory of their homeland and continue to regard their homeland as their true home to which they would eventually return.[7]

Many of the people dwelling in the Southern Periphery were emotionally attached to China and were loyal to a Chinese party-state that they saw as legitimate, but the ways in which they interpreted China differed. To some KMT supporters, their idea of China or homeland could mean a lost Republican China that had collapsed after the Communist takeover of the mainland. Other KMT loyalists believed that their homeland was where the exiled KMT government was located, even though they might have never been to the island of Taiwan previously. China could also mean an imaginary China waiting to be rebuilt after the KMT or other anticommunist forces took back the country from the CCP. When this idea became too remote, some eventually began to use home to refer to the place of their resettlement, whether Hong Kong, Macau, Taiwan, or other overseas Chinese communities.

The term "Free China" or "Free World" was commonly used in anti-CCP propaganda, and it could better capture the migrants' imagination of their permanent destination at the time of crossing the border of the PRC. However, the term may perpetuate the idealization of the conditions outside the borders of the PRC, and it does not reflect the reality at that time, especially when most people who successfully crossed the border continued to be subjugated to discrimination and marginalization by the KMT and even the colonial regimes of Hong Kong and Macau. The people intended to leave the PRC in the 1950s and 1960s wanted to get out of the country, and to most of them, Hong Kong and Macau were two of the more reachable destinations because they shared borders with the mainland. After stepping across the border, some may feel a sense of temporary relief, but soon after they may be overwhelmed by the uncertain future once again.

It was not Hong Kong or Macau that these Chinese people longed for, but the idea that they were outside the PRC. While the territories in the Southern Periphery were seen as part of what was known to be Free China in Cold War terms, people's freedom of movement and freedom to be politically active were not guaranteed by the respective governing regimes of the places where they resided. Instead, such freedoms often were constrained depending on the regimes' political agenda in relation to the changing circumstances of the Cold War.

THE SOUTHERN PERIPHERY AND THE COLD WAR

In the post–World War II era, the struggle between the KMT and the CCP to be the legitimate Chinese state soon turned into a full-fledged civil war that led to the CCP's taking over China. After 1949, the conflict became entangled with the Cold War and was spread to other East Asian regions as well. As China entered the Korean War in October 1950 after North Korea invaded South Korea, U.S. leaders saw the need to demonstrate a firm commitment to defend against aggressive Communist expansion and regarded the PRC as a threat to U.S. interests in Asia. As a result, the United States opted to maintain formal diplomatic ties with the ROC in Taiwan, which eventually led to the establishment of the U.S.-Taiwan Security Treaty in 1954 that incorporated Taiwan into the U.S.-led collective security alliance in East Asia.[8] During the Cold War new meanings about citizenship were formulated and through the process the ROC regime in Taiwan emerged as a new "center" to counter the PRC regime as the legitimate state of China.

In mainland China, most people decided to go into exile because of the social conditions of the PRC under Mao. However, the social history of the PRC was seldom analyzed together with the Cold War. As Cold War scholars such as Covell Meyskens and Jeremy Friedman have argued, the Chinese political campaigns such as the Great Leap Forward and the Cultural Revolution were not directly related to the Cold War; they believe instead that the PRC's expansive foreign policy in the Mao years mainly pertained to its competition with the Soviet Union for leadership among newly independent states.[9] The exiles in the 1960s and 1970s, the floating bodies and kidnappings, as well as some of the deportation cases are often depicted as the spillover of the Cultural Revolution on Hong Kong, but they are also indicative of the escalating Cold War in China and its Southern Periphery. A lesser-known effect of the Cold War tension in Chinese politics was the KMT's shaming of these incidents in Hong Kong as CCP brutality and the sense of terror evoked among the people who were living in the margins of both regimes. These incidents challenge dominant interpretations of the Cold War that the internal social turmoil had diverted the CCP's attention from the global politics at the time. Rather, the Cold War and the political development in mainland China were closely intertwined.

One important theme of this book is the idea of *fangong* that circulated in the Southern Periphery. *Fangong* can refer to the anticommunist/anti-CCP sentiments, or sometimes it could mean a counterattack against the CCP regime in the mainland. Even though the KMT ruled only Taiwan after 1949, it continued to cultivate *fangong* sentiments across the Southern Periphery as well. In Hong Kong, for example, much of the residents' *fangong* sentiments were influenced by KMT newspapers and propaganda materials. For the people who left mainland China, some anticipated a war against the CCP to retake China. Nevertheless, even that kind of loyalty changed through mutual distrust or personal circumstances. Some of the exiled people from mainland China who were *fangong* eventually became disillusioned with the KMT because of the White Terror and the persecution of people who were critical of Chiang Kai-shek or the KMT. Following a diverse range of people who transited or dwelled in the Southern Periphery, this book transcends the common Cold War binary oppositions between the PRC and the ROC; instead, it analyzes the effects of the Cold War through the experiences of the people who faced multiple challenges in an unfamiliar environment while being marginalized by both the KMT and the CCP.

THE CHANGING STATUS OF HONG KONG SINCE THE COLD WAR

This book starts with the Southern Periphery but ends with Hong Kong in the 2010s. I argue that the enforcement of borders in the PRC, the ROC, and Hong Kong as well as the flow of information in Hong Kong during and after the Cold War generated a sense of belonging among the people who continued to live in Hong Kong after the 1970s. Hong Kong played a special role in the Southern Periphery: it was physically connected to mainland China and served as a gateway for those who wanted to move further away, and ideologically the colonial regime was more closely linked to the so-called Free World. As such, Hong Kong was caught between the two Chinese regimes. As historians such as Chi-Kwan Mark, John Carroll, and Priscilla Roberts have argued, Hong Kong played a significant role in the Cold War, both politically and economically.[10] With the founding of the People's Republic, the colonial British government opened unofficial relations with the CCP. The British government did not want its colony to be grounds for anticommunist insurgency, but the U.S. and ROC governments perceived Hong Kong as the passageway for people fleeing the Communist regime to the other side of the Bamboo Curtain. If we imagine Hong Kong as a passageway to the outside world, the other constituents of the Southern Periphery were the extensions of this transit zone, except many people ended up dwelling in it permanently.[11]

Moreover, as the Southern Periphery became the nexus for many Cold War geopolitical circulations, Hong Kong became an important stage for propaganda warfare between the CCP and the KMT in the 1950s, which reached its height in the 1960s during the Cultural Revolution. The CCP and the KMT each used newspapers and magazines operating in Hong Kong to attack the rival regime. Reports and commentaries of mass killing and kidnapping by CCP agents in the Guangdong region and the territorial waters of Hong Kong generated anxiety among readers in Hong Kong, especially because it was right at the doorstep of the PRC.

In addition, Hong Kong also served as a base for people to cultivate political ideas that were not tolerated by the two parties. Dozens of intellectuals dissatisfied with both the CCP and the KMT came together and published magazines and spread ideas about democracy and constitutional government in Hong Kong in the 1950s. Hong Kong's location between the PRC and the ROC and the neutral stand of its colonial government helped foster this kind of alternative political culture for the people who resided there as well as in Taiwan and abroad. The U.S. State Department was also active in Hong Kong in the 1950s, sponsoring Third Force magazines and interviewing people who escaped from China and recruiting them to work for the Central Intelligence Agency. Hong Kong, central to the Southern Periphery, was an important battlefield in the East Asia front of the Cold War.

In relation to contemporary politics of Hong Kong, the political identity of people in Hong Kong today was built not only on the successful story of struggle by lower-class immigrants under British colonial capitalism but was also founded on fear, despair, and disillusionment with the two Chinese party-states. Even after Hong Kong's return to the mainland in 1997, the excitement of "homecoming" to the motherland did not increase for the majority of the local residents despite the propaganda of the Hong Kong and the PRC governments; quite the contrary, the sense of frustration and helplessness grew among Hong Kong residents as their local democratic advancement was stalled by the CCP. This can partly be attributed to the lack of decolonization when the end of British colonialism did not come with a return of sovereignty to the local people; rather, power was transferred to another, more authoritarian state. Or perhaps the financial benefits that were supposed to come with reintegration were less alluring than they appeared. Furthermore, the collective trauma evoked by the narratives of exile, dislocation, and abandonment in the 1950s–1970s that have appeared in public discourses has strengthened the local identity of the people in Hong Kong after the handover.

BORDERS

This book also challenges our perception of the national borders of China. Foremost, the definitions of borders need to be scrutinized. A border can mean an actual physical barrier, whether a set of artificial barbed wire fences or the natural waters that surround a place. But the function of a border also goes beyond political separation. It defines the space in which residents within a particular border form communities and identities. It makes a community imaginable. A border legitimizes citizenship and the right of abode for people within the border. Communities and states also use borders to separate out people who are not welcome into "their" territories; for example, through refugee and immigration policies, polities engineer their citizenry into one that is desirable for governance. In the case of the Southern Periphery, the border has become an important barrier to prevent undesirable mainlanders from entry. At the same time, those who try to cross the borders are scrutinized and their statuses are constantly redefined by the state(s).

During the Cold War, the three political regimes—the PRC, the Hong Kong authorities, and the ROC—intentionally marked those borders through migration and deportation policies to differentiate themselves from one another in the 1950s–1970s. Hong Kong had always been one of the most desired destinations of migrants from China, and many people had moved back and forth across the Hong Kong–China border before the Civil War. Nevertheless, the influx in the late 1940s was unprecedented and brought a huge burden to the colonial government. In 1955, the head of the UN mission to Hong Kong, Edvard Hambro, wrote about this in his report *The Problem of the Chinese Refugees in Hong Kong*:

> The phenomenon of Chinese people streaming into Hong Kong in times of stress and danger, and of the surge back again when the situation calms down, is nothing new in the history of the Colony.... But the influx after the civil war has been of unprecedented size and has led to considerable overcrowding of Hong Kong. There has been a widespread belief that hundreds of thousands of these Chinese people are living not only in poverty, but in misery and on the verge of starvation; and it has been suggested that a great number of them are political refugees.[12]

As a result, new policies were set up in 1950 to restrict the number of migrants who were allowed to cross the China–Hong Kong border at Lo Wu (Shenzhen). Despite these restrictions, it has been estimated that more than two million people crossed the border from China to Hong Kong between 1950 and 1980. Once they stepped across the border, they became stateless people at the mercy of the Hong Kong government. However, doing so also placed them at the edge of the nation and provided some of them with new vantage points from which to look at China.

In PRC discourse, sometimes they were traitors who escaped to the enemy's territory; at other times, they were just exercising their rights to live in Hong Kong, which the PRC state claimed as part of China. The PRC side of the border was always heavily guarded, though, except for a brief period in 1962 when people were allowed to leave because of the severity of the Great Famine. For the rest of the period, people caught attempting to cross the border were heavily punished, sometimes by death. The ROC regime, on the other hand, maintained a very strict policy that allowed loyalists to enter the island of Taiwan only as political refugees from China because they wanted to sustain the morale of the citizens so that they could be mobilized to retake the mainland.

Besides administrative borders that divided political entities, unmarked borders within a state also played a role in separating and uniting people. In the Southern Periphery, sometimes the people who live near the Shenzhen–Hong Kong border are seen as lesser citizens than those in the city center. The touch-base policy implemented in 1974 allowed immigrants from mainland China who reached the urban areas and met their relatives to register for a Hong Kong identity card, but those who were intercepted in the "closed area" near the border would be repatriated back to the mainland immediately. The Hong Kong government was intentionally vague about what defined urban areas. It would seem as though the border was set not between Shenzhen and Hong Kong, but between urban areas and nonurban ones.

Even though discussions of Chinese migrants leaving the mainland tend to focus on the border-crossing activities between Shenzhen and Hong Kong, water borders were also important in the Southern Periphery. Some people went to Hong Kong by crossing the seas to the east and west of Hong Kong. Including other border-crossing activities such as these allows us to conceptualize borders as sites of connections. For example, the sea between China and Hong Kong was the location of kidnapping and interactions. The movements of Chinese people across the various borders of Hong Kong, Macau, and Taiwan also complicate our previous understanding of the "free world," as it was known in Cold War parlance, and of the people who circulated in the Southern Periphery. Some people first went to Macau before they sneaked into Hong Kong and then took a ferry to Taiwan. Another case that reveals the ambiguity of the border is the cross-border kidnappings that happened in Lau Fau Shan and at sea in the late 1960s. Even though the victims were residents of Hong Kong, the government was unwilling to exercise its sovereignty over people living in these border regions, because doing so might result in undesirable conflicts with the PRC authorities.

The border issue has remained relevant since the handover of Hong Kong to China. In December 2015, Lee Bo, one of the booksellers at Causeway Bay Bookstore, a Hong Kong bookstore that traded books that were considered sensitive and banned in mainland China, was allegedly abducted by PRC Public Security officers and taken across the border to Shenzhen. There was no official record of him having crossed the border. Several other booksellers were also detained on the mainland, having been arrested outside of Hong Kong's jurisdiction. Although Lee Bo and the Chinese authorities later denied the claim that he was abducted, the case caused a great deal of local and international controversy about cross-border PRC law enforcement by mainland officials in Hong Kong and the security of the residents and travelers in Hong Kong.

In 2019, the Hong Kong government proposed an Extradition Bill that would have allowed anyone suspected of committing a crime to be detained and taken across the border to China for trial. The proposed law caused grave concern among the residents in Hong Kong because they had always believed that the border was there to protect their lives and freedom as guaranteed by the Basic Law of Hong Kong. The bill was ultimately withdrawn after the massive protests in 2019, but the enactment of the Beijing-imposed National Security Law in May 2020 reignited the anxieties of the people of Hong Kong that anyone charged with violating this law could be extradited to the mainland for trial and imprisonment. China's claims of cross-border legal enforcement authority and jurisdiction may appear to be new inventions by the PRC to tighten control over Hong Kong, but people had been subject to kidnapping, deportation, or repatriation across the various borders of the Southern Periphery long before the territories were returned to China.

THE PLAN OF THE BOOK

This book will begin with the refugee and immigration discourses and policies from 1949 to 1980 in Hong Kong and Taiwan and then turn to particular sets of exiled people to understand how they, together with the larger population of Hong Kong, were affected by the politics and stories about exiles and the homeland. Then it will return to Hong Kong at the end to explore the implications of this history on the contemporary politics of China and the Southern Periphery.

Chapter 1 studies the involvement of the Kuomintang, the Hong Kong government, the United Nations, and other international organizations in discussing and settling the refugees who escaped to Hong Kong. Hong Kong and Taiwan had their own priorities when it came to dealing with this issue on the ground. The solution for the refugees remained ambiguous in Taiwan because the KMT was not ready to accept them, for security and financial reasons. The KMT used Hong Kong as a zone where refugees were screened so that only the desirable ones could move to Taiwan. The Hong Kong government, meanwhile, viewed them as a burden to the city and avoided using the term "refugees" because it wanted to neutralize the political affiliations of the refugees who stayed in Hong Kong. In the Southern Periphery, the use of the term "refugees" was politicized, and they were depicted as victims of Communism or as anticommunist fighters.

Chapter 2 focuses on another group of stateless people that Hong Kong hosted: the self-proclaimed members of the Third Force, a little-known political movement located in Hong Kong during the Cold War. Formed primarily by exiled Chinese intellectuals who were not committed to the KMT but wanted to reach out to the United States for support to fight against the CCP in the late 1940s, the Third Force relied on the peripheral location of Hong Kong and its overseas connections, using limited funds to operate publications and arrange meetings. Members of the Third Force shared a sense of disillusionment with both the CCP and the KMT and perceived Hong Kong as a refuge where they could organize dissident political activities and articulate their visions for a better China. Essays written by the Third Force leaders reveal that Hong Kong functioned as an international production center for cultural and political critiques of China. The critiques made in these magazines also reveal how people who were in limbo in Hong Kong used the city as a space to imagine a future democratic China.

Chapter 3 examines sensational reports among KMT-affiliated print media on border-crossing activities in Hong Kong territorial waters in the 1960s—in particular, the discovery of bodies along the coastlines of Hong Kong and Macau of people who were believed to be victims of the Cultural Revolution, and alleged cross-border kidnappings of oyster farmers in the peripheral coastal district of Lau Fau Shan of Hong Kong by CCP members from the mainland. These reports generated a sense of terror in Hong Kong about the Communist regime. These media representations were examples of political propaganda in Hong Kong at the time and reinforced the public impression that mainland China was under a totalitarian regime and was no longer a home to which people in Hong Kong could return. The stories of dead bodies and kidnapping generated a collective trauma that made returning to the "homeland" impossible.

Chapter 4 uses three stories to show how Hong Kong and Taiwan constructed "desirable" citizenry through the practice of expulsion and the denial of entry. The first story is about a fake KMT general, Lam Yin Chang, who survived in Hong Kong by pretending to be a British general's savior to gain the trust of various politicians and community members. The second story is about the famous couple, Fu Che and Shek Hwei, who were active in the 1967 riots and were later arrested by the Hong

Kong police. The Hong Kong authorities intended to deport them back to mainland China, but the two were not allowed to enter China through the Lo Wu Border. The third case looks at ten KMT prisoners of war who participated in the Civil War and were released by the CCP in the 1970s; some passed through Hong Kong but were trapped in the city because the KMT refused to take them back to Taiwan, suspecting them of being undercover agents for the CCP. These examples reveal that Hong Kong was at times carved out by both the CCP and the KMT as a dumping ground for various "undesirables" who were regarded as unqualified for citizenship.

Chapter 5 examines three "escapees" who left mainland China in 1962 through the April 4 policy. One of them, Ip Cheung, stayed in Hong Kong. He did not participate in politics but remained critical of the CCP two decades after the handover of Hong Kong. The other two, Xiao Yujing and Lao Zhengwu, eventually went to Taiwan and were groomed to be anticommunist fighters (*fangong yishi*). They became strong advocates of the Chiang Ching-kuo regime. They spent a little time in Hong Kong or Macau but went to Taiwan soon after. They still believed in the notion of the Republic of China and hoped for its restoration on the mainland. How did the differences in their routes affect the political affiliations and consciousness of these migrants? The chapter will explore the connections between Taiwan and Hong Kong and the meanings of home, nation, and belonging to the people who were floating between peripheral regions during the period of intense conflict during the Cold War through studying the oral histories of those three men who left China in 1962. The two *fangong yishi* featured in chapter 5 were clear examples of how people successfully migrated to Taiwan but remained peripheral to the ROC regime.

Chapter 6 focuses on the rewriting of histories and memories in both state and popular discourses, and it highlights the effect of the collective trauma on the sense of belonging on the people who remained in Hong Kong. In the two decades since Hong Kong was returned to China, the journey across the border from China to Hong Kong has served as a major source of inspiration for a plethora of PRC government-sponsored documentary and fictional representations. A new narrative around border crossing before Deng Xiaoping's economic reform was invented, rationalizing the desires of the people who wanted to go to Hong Kong at a time when most people in China suffered from poverty and political instability. In it, the state is actively the homeland in order to lure back those who left, ensuring that loyal returnees will receive the benefits of prosperity, comfort, and stability. This last chapter will also delineate the recent push in Hong Kong for autonomy and independence and explain why a construction of a diasporic history of the Southern Periphery is necessary to help us understand the political currents in Hong Kong today.

1

"REFUGEES" OR "UNDESIRABLES"

The Fate of Chinese Escapees in the 1950s and 1960s

I took the train from Wuchang on the Beijing–Hong Kong railway. I didn't end up buying merchandise, because it was easier to travel light. If asked, I would say that I was going to Guangzhou to buy paper, but actually, we weren't interrogated, even though I had rehearsed my lines. I was 19 at the time and had never traveled far from home. I rode a rickshaw to the train station. The four of us traveling together split up and each sat in a different car. We refrained from speaking with each other.... We alighted the train at Shenzhen. Before arriving, we had found a guide who would meet us in Shenzhen and take us to Hong Kong. At the border, the border guards stuck a knife into my luggage to check what I had.... The guards didn't speak. They checked my luggage and gestured for me to pass. They were lenient during the new year. There were people on the other side who knew we were headed to the city and offered to guide us for a fee. They knew because we flashed a hand signal at them. They knew we wanted to go to Eastern Hospital in Hong Kong, which was run by the KMT.[1]

In this way, escapee Wang Qing-quan describes his journey to Hong Kong. It was 1950. The border was still open for crossing, and people could still cross through the official checkpoint without a permit. He was afraid that he would be detained or sent back home at the border, but things went smoothly. Wang was among the many "political refugees" who later resided in the Rennie's Mill Refugee Camp. Soon after his crossing, the border was closed, and it became much harder for people to flee to Hong Kong.

This chapter examines how, in response to the rising number of people fleeing the PRC into the Southern Periphery, the ROC and the Hong Kong governments refined the criteria for immigration in the 1950s and 1960s through their articulations of who should be counted as "refugees."[2] This process made movement across the Southern Periphery more difficult and shaped the meanings of citizenship in both Hong Kong and Taiwan in the following decades. From the beginning, the term "refugees" generally referred to people who were victims of the CCP and was frequently invoked in a wide range of *fangong*/anticommunist discourses in the Chinese Civil War and Cold War contexts. The Hong Kong and ROC governments, as well as international agencies like the United Nations High Commissioner for Refugees (UNHCR), and Aid Refugee Chinese Intellectuals (ARCI), discussed the issue of refugees and set up different qualifications for people to enter and stay in Hong Kong, Taiwan, or the United States. Although these were part of what was called the "Free World," people could not just enter and freely leave these territories. The immigration and refugee policies were never just about saving the victims and assisting them to build a new life in the host territories but were instruments for the states to socially engineer their citizenry during the Cold War.

In the early 1930s, the population of Hong Kong was about 850,000. When Guangzhou fell to the hands of the Japanese during World War II, hundreds of thousands of people went to Hong Kong. The population of Hong Kong on the eve of the Japanese occupation in December 1941 was around 1.6 million. As a result of the influx, the Hong Kong government attempted to introduce its first Immigration Control Ordinance in the early 1940s. The ordinance gave permissions to Hong Kong officials to refuse entry to anyone without relevant travel documents or permits. However, the law was not effectively enforced.[3] About a million Chinese residents of Hong Kong left for the mainland and thousands left for Macau after Japan occupied Hong Kong in December 1941.[4] Japan's occupation of Hong Kong lasted for three years and eight months (figure 1.1).[5] It has been estimated that the number of people who went to Hong Kong from mainland China in the few years

FIGURE 1.1 The Lo Wu Bridge at the Hong Kong–Shenzhen border in 1938, during the Japanese occupation.

after Japan's defeat in 1945 far exceeded the number who had left during the occupation.[6]

In the late 1940s, when the Chinese Communist Party (CCP) began to take over the vast territories of China, it was quite lenient toward the people who wanted to leave the country. CCP leaders perhaps believed that if dissidents could leave the country, the state could manage the rest of the population better. Therefore, Chinese were allowed to cross the border into Hong Kong till the late 1940s. As a result of the open-border policy, the colony's population rose from 600,000 to 1.8 million in 1947.[7]

Many who came to Hong Kong after World War II and before 1950 were not from Guangdong Province and therefore lacked familiarity with Hong Kong and Cantonese culture. A large majority were business and intellectual elites who brought with them their assets and skills. The main motivation for their departure was their "aversion to communism" and fear of losing everything if they stayed in China.[8] A number of textile entrepreneurs came from Shanghai, and the textile factories they established became an important foundation for Hong Kong's later industrial takeoff.⁹ The cultural workers who came included writers, filmmakers, painters, and musicians from major cities such as Shanghai and Guangzhou. Intellectual elites took up academic posts in Hong Kong and took advantage of the freedom to continue the promotion of Chinese literature and culture. Some set up presses and taught Chinese language and literature in Hong Kong.¹⁰ A few of these intellectuals later joined the Third Force movement and published magazines in the 1950s and 1960s, which will be the focus of chapter 2. Since these early migrants brought capital and expertise with them, they became the economic and cultural elites in Hong Kong.

The movement of people continued after the closing of the border in 1950, when restrictions were implemented. The population in 1951 was known to be around 2.5 million.¹¹ In closing the border, the Hong Kong government set up a physical barrier right inside the northern rim of the New Territories, along the Shenzhen River in 1950. Over the next few years, a series of surveillance posts were also set up along the border; the Frontier Closed Area (FCA) was established as a buffer zone to keep out migrants from China and prevent other illegal activities.¹²

On April 28, 1950, the Hong Kong government introduced a quota system that allowed only fifty people a day to enter Hong Kong from the mainland. In the mainland as well, anyone entering and leaving Guangdong Province had to carry a permit issued by the Public Security Authorities. While natives of Guangdong Province could still enter Hong Kong relatively freely, people who were not from Guangdong Province had to obtain an additional entry permit or reentry visa issued by the Hong Kong Immigration Office or the British authorities in Beijing or Shanghai to legally enter Hong Kong.¹³ The issuance of these permits was extremely restrictive. The closing of the border and creation of the quota system made it much harder for ordinary Chinese to enter Hong Kong through legal means. In 1950, the introduction of immigration control in Hong Kong prompted a formal protest on May 8 by the Foreign Ministry of the PRC to the British government, denouncing the new measure as "an unreasonable and unfriendly act towards the PRC and its people."¹⁴ This reflected the PRC government's view that Chinese people should have the right to enter and leave Hong Kong because it considered the city to be part of China. As more people tried to leave the mainland and the migration was getting more international attention, however, the PRC government began to restrict people from leaving to avoid embarrassment.

Despite the difficulty, however, many Chinese still risked their lives by coming to Hong Kong without permission. In those years, when people wanted to get out of China, they had to prepare far ahead for their trip. First, to travel away from the locality where one held a household registration, one had to seek a "mainland transit pass" from the Public Security Bureau. Once that was obtained, emigrants would make their way from their hometowns to Shenzhen by any affordable means. From Shenzhen, some made a land crossing into Hong Kong. There were barbed wire fences and steep hills along the land border, and many escapees became lost or suffered injuries during the journey. During periods of strict restrictions, PRC officials patrolled the border and arrested anyone who tried to cross it.[15] After political or natural disasters, large numbers of people would wait in Shenzhen to make the land crossing. They also had to avoid encountering British Gurkha soldiers who would capture anyone they found crossing the border.[16]

The guarded border and the difficult hill paths were not the only dangers, for there were also plainclothes police stationed in various parts of the New Territories along the popular travel routes. People coming in from the mainland without documentation could still be arrested in the New Territories and sent back to China. Only when they reached the city center of Kowloon were they safe. Others crossed the waters separating Shenzhen and Hong Kong by sampans or even by swimming for days, or they sneaked through the land borders by climbing over barbed wire and running through forests in the dark. Many escapees drowned because of the strong currents or boat accidents.[17]

After restrictions on entry were in place, the experiences of those who arrived in Hong Kong varied depending on how immigration policies treated them. They also dwelled in Hong Kong for different lengths of time: some stayed permanently and made Hong Kong their new home, while others moved on after a short stay of a few weeks or months that left little impression on them. Today, popular literature and media depict the Chinese who made these dangerous journeys to Hong Kong after 1949 as hardworking souls determined to start life anew in Hong Kong, the majority of whom contributed greatly to Hong Kong's rapid industrialization in the 1960s–1980s. In reality, many who came to Hong Kong did not intend to remain in Hong Kong. Some hoped to join families or friends in Taiwan; others wanted to wait for the CCP to collapse so they could return home. Many were in limbo upon arriving in Hong Kong and did not have a true sense of belonging. It was by mere chance that some of these migrants ended up staying in Hong Kong permanently and consequently provided labor during the territory's economic takeoff.

In the early to mid-1950s, Hong Kong and the ROC governments' attitude toward and treatment of escapees from mainland China were heavily influenced by the Cold War and UN rhetoric of refugees, which were founded on anticommunist ideologies. However, the legitimacy of the PRC government and the conflicting interests among the international powers have made UN intervention difficult.

THE INTERNATIONAL POLITICIZATION OF CHINESE "REFUGEES"

In international diplomacy, "refugees" is a category distinct from general migrants, because refugee status applies to persons who have escaped their original homeland out of real or possible future political persecution.[18] A state's acknowledgment of a person as a refugee means that it agrees that such persecution is unjust, and the act of allowing entry or granting residency reflects a political stand that could cause tension with the state of the refugee's homeland. It is often unclear whether a refugee's stay is to be temporary or permanent. Lenient refugee and immigration policies on the part of a receiving state may encourage more people to come there to seek refuge.

The Cold War added new political meaning to the term "refugees" because it began to be used to refer to people who escaped from Communist regimes to the other side of the Iron Curtain. "Refugees" in the post–World War II international context became an important propaganda symbol for the UN, as well as the United States and its supporting allies in the Cold War in their attempt to contain communism. Headquartered in Geneva, Switzerland, the Office of the United Nations High Commissioner for Refugees was established on December 14, 1950, with the goals of protecting and supporting refugees at the request of a government or the United Nations and assisting in their return or resettlement. The 1951 United Nations Convention relating to the Status of Refugees defined a refugee as a person who, "owing to a well-founded fear of being persecuted for reasons of race, religion, nationality, membership of a particular social group, or political opinion, is outside the country of his nationality, and is unable to or, owing to such fear, is unwilling to avail himself of the protection of that country." Initially, the UNHCR was mainly concerned about refugees escaping from the Soviet bloc but not ones escaping from China.[19]

In the Southern Periphery, the CCP, the KMT, and the Hong Kong government each had its own interpretation of the people fleeing mainland China to Hong Kong and Macau. The topic of refugees was a sensitive one with implications of political instability or persecution in China. Therefore, each of the three regimes chose its words carefully in making sure its interpretation stayed consistent with its state discourse about national sovereignty over its people. Their choice to use or forgo the term showed how they viewed the relationship between the state and the people. From the 1950s to the early 1980s, in PRC propaganda, Hong Kong and Macau were portrayed as decadent cities under the influence of colonialism. Internally, the CCP put anyone who attempted but failed to flee the PRC on trial on charges of counterrevolutionary activity or treason (*panguo toudi*). According to such logic, anyone desiring to live under capitalism was understood as having betrayed the PRC's socialist ideals. Rhetorically, the PRC insisted to the world that residents in China had the right to reside in Hong Kong or Macau and should not be deported back to China for whatever reason. It refused to acknowledge the existence of any "refugees" in Hong Kong because such admission would indicate that people were discontented with the regime.[20] Nevertheless, in reality, the CCP initiated border controls in 1951. After that, anyone wanting to enter or leave the PRC was required to have a permit issued by the Public Security Bureau.[21] Those who did not have permits were subject to arrest if found trying to cross the border.

Meanwhile, official KMT discourse in Taiwan used the term *zainan tongbao*—defined as "fellow citizens who are victims of a disaster"—or *zaibao/nanbao* to refer to people who fled the Communist regime. To deal with the problems of *zainan tongbao*, the Free China Relief Association

(FCRA) was created on April 4, 1950, as a nonprofit philanthropic organization to deal with relief and resettlement of Chinese refugees, with offices in Hong Kong and Macau to help new arrivals.

The association was tasked with assisting refugees fleeing the mainland, as well as promoting the values of Free China on behalf of the ROC. To the KMT government and its affiliated FCRA, the escape of so many Chinese to capitalist Hong Kong was "illustrative of the tyranny of the People's Republic, and the plight of these anti-communist refugees should be a concern of the Free World."[22] The KMT also emphasized the CCP's takeover of China as a disaster. The implication of this term is that all people who left China became one category—victims of the Communist regime. A 1952 government document defined refugees and their relatives (*nanbao nanshu*) as "anyone whose family member was killed by the [Communist] thieves (*fei*), or were individually or collectively tortured, their labor exploited, their possessions taken away, or their emotions abused should be seen as refugees (*nanbao*) and their immediate families dependents of refugees (*nanshu*)."[23] The FCRA's idea that the people who fled to Hong Kong were victims of Communist oppression fit well into the 1951 UN refugee convention's definition of a refugee as someone having a "fear of persecution."[24]

The UNHCR in the early 1950s wanted to extend its mandate on refugees beyond the European context and began looking for other crises in Asia. With the influx of escapees from Communist China, Hong Kong naturally became the exemplary case. Nevertheless, the attempt to put Hong Kong on the UNHCR's agenda faced resistance from the Hong Kong and British governments. Since the United Kingdom was one of the few countries that recognized the PRC's legitimacy, the British government under Winston Churchill was wary that raising the refugee issue in Hong Kong might anger the CCP.[25]

The people who escaped from the PRC in the 1950s–1970s and settled down in Hong Kong usually described their background as having run away from a disaster (*zounan*). Occasionally, they would say they sneaked across the border (*toudu*); however, mostly they only described their predicament and seldom identified as "refugees (*nanmin*)" per se. In the first decade after the establishment of the PRC, the Hong Kong government expected most of the people who crossed the Lo Wu border into Hong Kong to go back to China or otherwise leave the colony. Government officials also avoided using the term "refugees," and until the late 1950s, they regarded the bulk of the population as sojourners who had fled the mainland for temporary refuge from wars, revolutions, and economic disasters.[26] As a result, "refugees" were almost nonexistent in government documents because the Hong Kong government either expected them to leave or mixed them with the larger population of lower-class people.

In the early 1950s, the Hong Kong government did not provide assistance to persons fleeing China, partly in order "not to encourage any more of China's 400 millions ... to come begging for free lodging and free food."[27] It also feared that the UNHCR's singling out of a particular immigrant group as "refugees," who were assigned privileged status and who required special treatment when the great majority of the colony's Chinese population was experiencing similarly desperate circumstances, would politicize the issue at the international level without actually solving the social and economic crisis.

After discussion in meetings with the UN General Assembly, the UNHCR decided to investigate on the colony's refugee situation with the help of the Hong Kong authorities. The UNHCR approached the Ford Foundation and obtained a grant of $50,000 to send a mission to Hong Kong. The UNHCR's intended purpose was to use the investigation as a means to seek support for expanding its mandate in Asia.

The mission, headed by Edvard Hambro, conducted a qualitative study on the issue of people crossing the border from China into Hong Kong with the help of various departments of the Hong Kong government. The mission began its research in Hong Kong on April 28, 1954, and finished its work three months later on August 1. The dilemma the Hambro mission faced was whether the "refugees" in Hong Kong met the two conditions: first, they had to "have fled their country of citizenship for political reasons or be unwilling to return to their country of citizenship for political reasons;" and second, they had to be "unable or unwilling to avail [themselves] of the protection of [their] national government because of a 'well-founded fear of persecution' by their national government."[28]

For the first condition, the mission calculated there were 385,000 individual "refugees" who did not want to go back to China for political reasons. Of these, roughly 100,000 were "refugees sur place"—that is, Chinese citizens who were already in Hong Kong at the founding of the PRC and were "unwilling to return on account of their political status or beliefs."

In addition, there were 282,000 dependents who were refugees "in the social sense" but not in the strict "legal sense" because they were born in Hong Kong and thus did not "flee their country of citizenship for political reasons" as indicated in the definition.[29] If both groups were counted, the total number of refugees was 667,000, or 29.6 percent of the colonial population of 2.25 million. But it was unclear whether they constituted "political refugees" from the PRC because it was hard to determine who, if any of them, "possessed a 'well-founded' fear of persecution," given that some may have become convinced they would be doomed if they had to live under communism but there was no evidence of actual persecution. It was also hard to differentiate between those who had fled for political reasons from the rest who may have migrated for a combination of reasons. In conclusion, Hambro expressed that "from a strictly legal point of view the Chinese refugees may fall outside the High Commissioner's mandate," but from a broader humanitarian perspective, he could not see any difference between these Chinese migrants in Hong Kong and refugees in other parts of the world.

For the second condition, the phrase "national government" proved controversial because technically the ROC was the legitimate Chinese government in the United Nations, but the UK at that time recognized the PRC as the legitimate government of China. Thus, it was unclear whether these migrants could be counted as "refugees" according to UN's definition if they were persecuted by an illegitimate government. Arguably, those who left the mainland could seek the protection of the UN-recognized ROC government. But if they were defined as "refugees," it would be a source of embarrassment to the ROC government because of the implication that the PRC regime was the legitimate government of China.

In the end, whether the majority of the people who recently crossed the border to Hong Kong met the two conditions remained ambiguous. Therefore, the mandate was not extended to the escapees in Hong Kong. Hambro's report was submitted to UNHCR on November 15, 1954.

Because the UN failed to influence Britain or the United States on the issue of expanding the mandate, the UNHCR took only an advisory role in Hong Kong. By 1954, the UN decided that emphasis should be placed on the possibilities of outside resettlement and not on relief schemes within the colony.[30] In February 1957, owing to the continuous efforts of the Free China Relief Association, the UN Association in Hong Kong, and various international charitable organizations, the Chinese refugee problem was brought to the agenda of the United Nation Refugee Fund Executive Committee at its fourth session. Finally, in November of that year, the General Assembly voted to allow the UNHCR to raise funds from member states to assist the Chinese refugees in Hong Kong, mostly for resettlement.[31] Overall, the UN's humanitarian definition of "refugees" did not have a direct impact on Hong Kong's immigration policies, but the way Hambro associated "refugees" with poor immigrants in Hong Kong influenced the Hong Kong government's policy on squatters in the 1950s and 1960s, as we will see later in this chapter.

In the Southern Periphery, the statuses and meanings of "refugees" became politically charged because of the Cold War and the tensions between the CCP and the KMT. The CCP attempted to deny the existence of refugees, admitting only that those who attempted to flee the country were traitors to the Communist ideals, whereas the United States, along with Taiwan and other allies, treated all people who fled the PRC after 1949 as "political refugees" who had to flee because of political persecution by the CCP. The international discourse of refugees was filled with anti-Communist rhetoric. The UN had a stake in expanding its scope of power but was lukewarm owing to the complication of regional politics. Hong Kong and the UK, wanting to appease the CCP, both focused only on economic migrants.

As we will see in the following section, whether one satisfied a particular set of criteria of "refugee" would have tremendous effects on where and how they were treated and settled by the authorities. By the mid-1950s, the Hong Kong government had realized that the UN was not useful, and the colonial government had to find other means to solve the crisis. Nevertheless, the early contesting definitions of "refugees" and the characterization of the CCP as an inhumane, victimizing party-state continued to shape the policies in the Southern Periphery.

SETTLING THE MIGRANTS WHO "LANDED" IN HONG KONG

The United States, Hong Kong, and Taiwan created criteria of citizenship through their respective refugee policies and programs that aimed at resettling Chinese escapees from the early 1950s through the 1970s. The divergent paths of escapees from Communist China were determined by how well they satisfied the various criteria of naturalized citizenship set by the KMT, the Hong Kong government, the UN, and other U.S.-sponsored organizations. Each of these programs categorized the Chinese escapees differently according to their political agendas: the ARCI called them "exiled intellectuals," emphasizing their education background; the U.S. government mostly grouped them as "immigrants" who were expected to contribute to U.S. society; the ROC government in Taiwan used the term "political refugees" to highlight their flight from the CCP; and the Hong Kong government mostly referred those who settled in Hong Kong as "squatters" to neutralize the political reasons for their migration. The terminologies also impacted the destinies of the escapees—those who went to the United States and Hong Kong were generally less active in the politics of China after they settled down, whereas those labeled as "political refugees" by the ROC and Hong Kong governments tended to have more complicated relationships with both the CCP and the KMT.

OVERSEAS RESETTLEMENTS THROUGH THE ARCI AND THE U.S. REFUGEE ACT OF 1953

The Aid Refugee Chinese Intellectuals (ARCI) organization was responsible for most cases of Chinese escapees who wanted to resettle abroad. The ARCI was formed by U.S. Representative Walter Judd (R-MN) and Chinese American lobbyist Ernest Moy in February 1952, and its network of supporters was drawn from the uppermost circles of the U.S. political, military, and business establishment, most of whom had close connections with the Nationalist government. It received most of its funding covertly from the Department of State.[32]

The ARCI had four goals: to aid in the "resettlement and rehabilitation of refugee Chinese intellectuals," to "distribute aid without discrimination," to "increase public awareness of the 'oppressed and imperiled people in Asia,'" and to "raise and disperse the funds necessary to achieve these goals."[33] The four aims were intertwined, as part of a larger effort to help the people oppressed by the PRC government and to raise consciousness in other territories of the fight against the CCP.

Since the ARCI was mostly interested in doing propaganda, it was less concerned with the ordinary people who escaped from mainland China to Hong Kong. It aimed at "identifying and aiding educated, anti-communist Chinese refugees" in Hong Kong who had the potential to play a leading role in the propaganda effort. It especially targeted "high-value defectors" with "insider knowledge of communist states" who could provide the American consulate general in Hong Kong with valuable information on the PRC regime and the latest developments in their homeland.[34] Between 1952 and 1956, the ARCI carried out registrations among those who qualified as exiled intellectuals in Hong Kong and Macau. Those who were approved were sent to Taiwan, the United States, or Southeast Asia to study or work for anticommunist agencies.[35]

The Hong Kong office registered people who wanted to resettle abroad, developed programs to assist them with finding residence and employment, and filed their applications when their visas were approved.[36] Even though the ARCI also sponsored anticommunist publications and higher education institutes, the Hong Kong government warned the organization that it should focus on the resettlement of escapees overseas and that because the ARCI was "vulnerable to Chinese Communist propaganda attacks," it would be "most desirable if no publicity were given in Hong Kong to the fact the US is supporting ARCI."[37] The Hong Kong government's attitude was consistent with its effort to maintain political neutrality.

By August 1952, the ARCI had collected a variety of resettlement applications from around 15,000 Chinese in Hong Kong. Some sources indicate that more than 40 percent of the applicants were former KMT military and police officers, most of whom sought to resettle in Taiwan Only a quarter of the total applicants fitted the ARCI's definition of "intellectuals," however.[38] Allegedly the Hong Kong office tried to include as many people as possible so some applicants who had only a secondary school education passed the initial screening.

The original plan was for Hong Kong to send as many of its 25,000 qualified applicants as possible to Taiwan to aid Chiang Kai-shek's fight against the Communists and the effort to retake the mainland. While the Hong Kong office processed the paperwork, the Taiwan office negotiated with the Nationalist government for documentation and security clearances for those who were accepted to relocate to Taiwan and helped them find jobs and accommodations.³⁹

However, Taiwan was not willing to receive a large number of escapees for fear that spies may infiltrate the island. Many applications were rejected when screened by the Security Bureau as applicants were suspected of being Communist agents. Taiwan also had a shortage of white-collar and professional jobs, so it could not take in too many immigrants with professional skills. Those in whom the regime was most interested were technicians and industrial workers whose expertise would be useful. In addition, there were subsets of the ARCI's special leadership programs that provided job training for several hundred prescreened registrants in Hong Kong for later employment in the Nationalist military and public administrative offices in Taiwan.⁴⁰

In the end, about fourteen thousand registrants successfully went to Taiwan, of whom three thousand obtained jobs and clearance from the Security Bureau. The rest found a way to survive on their own, with or without the help of relatives and friends. Some relied on the ARCI only for travel funds and other resettlement expenses while finding other means to make their way to Taiwan.⁴¹ The Taiwan office shut down in mid-1956.

Although many wanted to go to Taiwan, ultimately the majority of the applicants had to stay in Hong Kong because they did not pass the screening process. The ARCI also contacted Southeast Asian countries and Australia for help in resettling these applicants. However, most of these countries were lukewarm about Chinese escapees, in part because these countries did not want to offend the Beijing government by accepting such immigrants as refugees.⁴²

In her book *The Good Immigrants*, Madeline Hsu explores how refugee relief programs in the United States transformed Chinese into "welcome and valued immigrants with shared political and economic values."⁴³ The Refugee Act of 1953 provided a channel for those who wanted to immigrate to the United States. It prioritized those who shared anticommunist sentiments and had the potential to contribute to American society. The law provided entry for more than 200,000 refugees who had been displaced by Communist regimes around the world. Because the United States already had an immigration quota system based on national origins, this was an emergency measure to raise the quota for people who met the criteria of "refugees." The Refugee Act of 1953 could be considered the country's second refugee resettlement law, following the Displaced Persons Act of 1948, which mainly targeted agricultural workers and "professional or highly skilled persons."[44] Both the Refugee Act of 1953 and the Displaced Persons Act of 1948 were part of the postwar immigration policies in the postwar period. The people who were allowed to enter were expected to contribute to U.S. society in the future.

The Displaced Persons Act did not extend to Asian refugees but allowed people who were already in the United States by April 1, 1948, to change their status to immigrants. The emphasis on skills and professional background in the Displaced Persons Act shows that a standard of desired qualifications was already in place before the issue of Chinese refugees arose. Both laws reflect a new direction in the State Department toward "mobility and exchanges as a means of fostering American friendships with newly strategic global partners."[45]

The Refugee Act of 1953 had similar criteria to the Displaced Persons Act but also worked in coordination with the ARCI. The applicants had to demonstrate their anticommunist bona fides and preferably had received some college education and would be able to find a U.S. sponsor to prearrange employment in the United States.

The immigration form that was given to applicants after passage of the Refugee Act included a few questions related to political persecution and affiliation. One asked: "What was the nature of the persecution or fear of persecution, if any, which caused you to flee or escape from your former home and which caused your inability to return?" Norman Yao, an applicant who worked as a photographer at the U.S. consulate general of Hong Kong at that time, gave this answer (figures 1.2 and 1.3):

1) Being educated for 16 years in American Missionary schools, I fully enjoy a democratic living.
2) I inherited plenty of estates and lands in my own village, the communists would blend [sic; hereafter brand] me as a "landlord."
3) My wife joined U.S.I.S. [United States Information Services] in Canton [Guangzhou], China since 1947, we would be [branded] as "spies" provided we remained in Canton.
4) We devoted working in U.S.I.S. and American Consulate General, Hong Kong since 1949, the Red would [brand] us as "Anti-revolutionists"

provided we remained at or returned to Canton or anywhere in China.⁴⁶

Yao's background of studying in a missionary school and having a family label of "landlord" made him vulnerable in China. In addition, he claimed that his and his wife's work at the USIS and the American consulate general might subject him to persecution if he returned to China. Although he did not say whether his life would be in danger if he remained in Hong Kong, his fear was sufficient to warrant protection and the right to migrate to the United States. In answer to the question, "What was the nature of the natural calamity or military operation, if any, which caused you to leave your former home, and which caused your inability to return?" Yao gave a one-word response: "Communism." In addition to submitting the application documents, Yao was required to find guarantors in the United States who could promise to provide a job for him upon his arrival. He was able to find such a guarantor through a church, and his transition to the United States was facilitated by other church members in California.⁴⁷ Yao's and his wife's anticommunist background, together with his professional career and church network, made them ideal candidates to transfer to the United States.

Overall, the Refugee's Act's criteria resonate with the ARCI's original intentions of settling elites. As Ernest Moy expressed at the founding of the ARCI, the Chinese escapees stranded in Hong Kong would be useful to the United States because they were "professionals and technically trained, English speaking, [and] anti-Communist Chinese."⁴⁸ The Chinese immigrants would thus be able to sustain themselves without burdening the U.S. economy or welfare system and have a positive impact on the United States. Subsequent amendments increased the number of Chinese visas to accommodate the escapees temporarily staying in Hong Kong.⁴⁹

After 1956, the ARCI still had an office but was no longer registering new applicants. Thousands were left on the books after the 1953 Refugee Relief Act expired, and the organization was still trying to get them visas to go to the United States. Some people had longstanding applications on file. Congress passed Public Law 85–316 in 1957 authorizing redistribution of the unused refugee visas. Possession of technical or professional skills and experience of political persecution remained the top prerequisites for

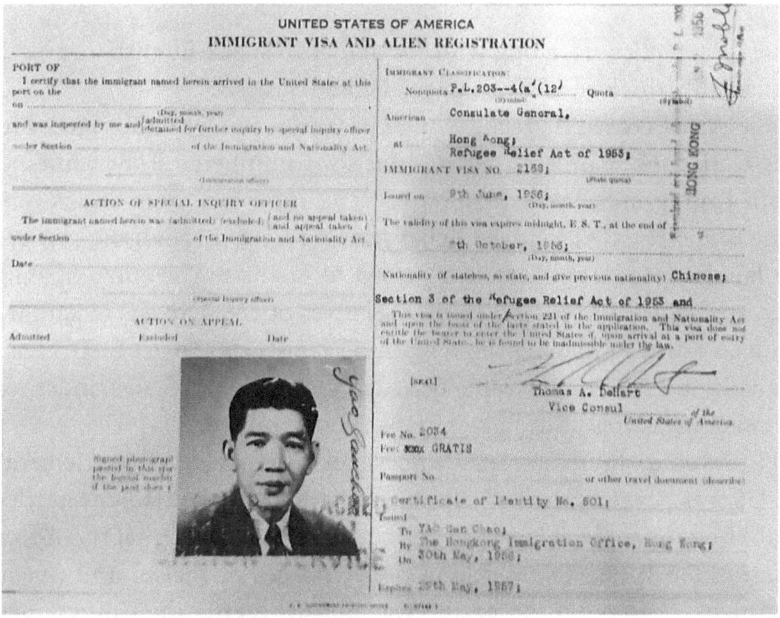

UNITED STATES OF AMERICA
IMMIGRANT VISA AND ALIEN REGISTRATION

PORT OF
I certify that the immigrant named herein arrived in the United States at this port on the

Immigrant Classification
P.L.203--4(a)(12)
Quota

American Consulate General,
at Hong Kong;
Refugee Relief Act of 1953;
IMMIGRANT VISA NO. 2169;
Issued on 9th June, 1956;

ACTION OF SPECIAL INQUIRY OFFICER

The validity of this visa expires midnight, E. S. T., at the end of
9th October, 1956;

Nationality (if stateless, so state, and give previous nationality) Chinese;
Section 3 of the Refugee Relief Act of 1953 and

ACTION ON APPEAL
Admitted Excluded Date

[SEAL]
Thomas A. Dellart
Vice Consul
of the United States of America.

Fee No. 2034
Fee: GRATIS
Passport No.
Certificate of Identity No. 501;
To YAO Gan Chao;
By The Hongkong Immigration Office, Hong Kong;
On 30th May, 1956;
Expires 29th May, 1957;

HONG KONG

FIGURE 1.2 Norman Yao's U.S. immigration application.

Norman Gan-chao and Anne Lee Yao Collection, Box 1, Folder 1, Courtesy of Special Collections, Claremont Colleges Library.

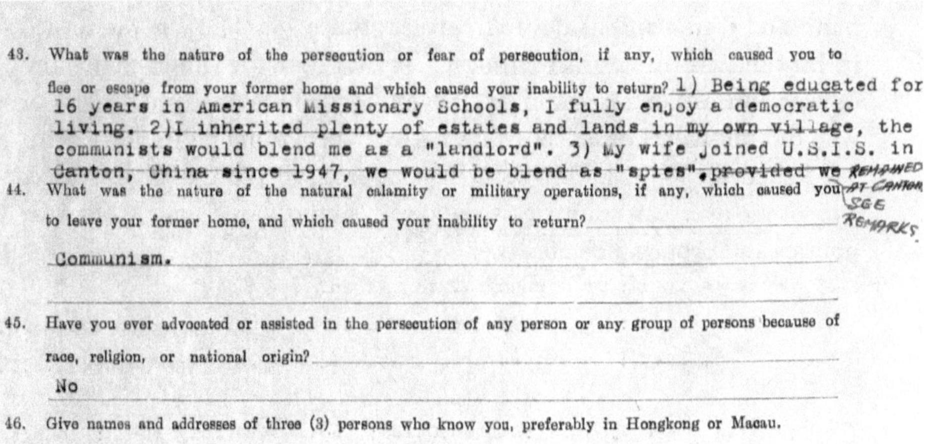

43. What was the nature of the persecution or fear of persecution, if any, which caused you to flee or escape from your former home and which caused your inability to return? 1) Being educated for 16 years in American Missionary Schools, I fully enjoy a democratic living. 2)I inherited plenty of estates and lands in my own village, the communists would blend me as a "landlord". 3) My wife joined U.S.I.S. in Canton, China since 1947, we would be blend as "spies", provided we REMAINED AT CANTON SEE REMARKS

44. What was the nature of the natural calamity or military operations, if any, which caused you to leave your former home, and which caused your inability to return?

Communism.

45. Have you ever advocated or assisted in the persecution of any person or any group of persons because of race, religion, or national origin?

No

46. Give names and addresses of three (3) persons who know you, preferably in Hongkong or Macau.

FIGURE 1.3 Norman Yao's U.S. immigration application. There were questions on "the nature of the persecution or fear of persecution" as well as "the nature of the natural calamity or military operations . . . which caused you to leave your former home."

Norman Gan-chao and Anne Lee Yao Collection, Box 1, Folder 1, Courtesy of Special Collections, Claremont Colleges Library.

these visa applicants, along with the ability to speak English and having sponsorship or close relatives in the United States.[50]

The ARCI ceased its Hong Kong operations in December 1960. From 1944 until 1960, Chinese quota admissions numbered 8,781 while nonquota immigrants totaled 23,433. Of the nonquota admissions, 6,862 came under the 1953 Refugee Relief Act and 3,514 through the 1957 refugee law. In 1962, a new act was passed to facilitate the entry of skilled alien specialists and permit certain relatives of U.S. citizens to gain legal status as a way of helping the remaining registrants to get their visas. A total of 2,500 ARCI registrants resettled in the United States under refugee relief measures undertaken in 1953, 1957, and 1962.[51]

However, as the historian Laura Madokoro argues, "resettlement to the US was never a priority." Although the Refugee Relief Act resettled a total of 5,701 people, it "represented the bare minimum that the Administration felt it had to resettle to deny charges of racism and unequal treatment."[52] The main intention was not to resettle the Chinese being stranded in Hong Kong but to protect the United States against accusations of racism.

The ARCI's agenda in Hong Kong was also instrumental in helping Chinese resettle in Taiwan and in Southeast Asian countries. Taiwan's strict immigration policy reflected its suspicion toward people who fled mainland China and its desire to protect those who had already settled in Taiwan. The "undesirable" immigrants, for both the United States and Taiwan, were those who did not vehemently condemn communism or who did not have needed skills. The ARCI's program and the 1953 Refugee Relief Act show that the resettlement programs in the United States and other overseas countries were deeply intertwined with Cold War politics and propaganda efforts.

RENNIE'S MILL REFUGEE CAMP AND THE TRANSFER OF "POLITICAL REFUGEES"

The only people in transit whom the Hong Kong governments officially classified as "(political) refugees" were those who claimed to have a KMT affiliation. This designation is important because these were politically active individuals who claimed they were persecuted by the CCP regime.

Nevertheless, since the Hong Kong government wanted to maintain political neutrality vis-à-vis the Nationalists and Communists, it saw these "refugees" as outsiders to Hong Kong society and perceived their political leanings toward the KMT as a threat to the social harmony of the territory. The Hong Kong government's policies toward this group of migrants was twofold: ideally, they should be sent to Taiwan to be reunited with the KMT, and if that fell through, they should be separated from the rest of the population.[53] As for Taiwan, even though the issue of Chinese refugees in Hong Kong and Macau generated heated debates in the Legislative Yuan and some politicians and activists argued that most should be admitted for humanitarian reasons, the numbers who were given permission to immigrate to Taiwan remained low because of security and economic concerns.

The first wave of "political refugees" were KMT soldiers who got sick or were injured during the Chinese Civil War and decided to go to Hong Kong to seek medical attention. About 600 such soldiers were originally hospitalized in Guangzhou.[54] In November 1949, the Hong Kong police directed 148 starving and exhausted Nationalist soldiers and their families who were "scattered throughout the streets of Sai Wan (or Western District) and Kennedy Town—sheltering themselves beneath the verandahs of nearby houses to the Tung Wah Hospital."[55] By the end of the month, 1,682 people were accepted at Tung Wah, and by December 16, the number reached 2,731.[56] Soon after, many people of similar backgrounds who learned about Tung Wah accepting KMT soldiers also flocked to the hospital. The number continued to rise, reaching 5,000 in 1950.[57]

In their languages and places of origin, these migrants were distinct from the majority of the Chinese escapees who came later. As historian Dominic Yang describes, "Unlike the rest of the mainland exodus, a considerable number of the Nationalist refugees hailed from the northern provinces. They could not speak Cantonese and lacked the indigenous communal and familial networks, which Governor [Alexander] Grantham considered important social safety nets in assisting newcomers in Hong Kong."[58] The majority of them wanted to go to Taiwan, but many had neither the financial means nor the political connections to do so.

The Hong Kong government, worried that the influx of Chinese escapees would explode the colony's economic and social infrastructure, tried to find other ways to resettle them elsewhere. The Hong Kong government also tried to hand the KMT-affiliated migrants to Taiwan to avoid further controversy over extending protection to these enemies of the PRC.[59] Nevertheless, things did not go as expected, because just as it responded to the ARCI, the KMT government maintained a strict immigration standard toward those it termed "political refugees."[60] For example, in January 1950, the Hong Kong government sent more than a hundred KMT soldiers and their families to Taiwan aboard the Hiram Ferry, but most of them were returned to Hong Kong because they lacked the right documentation. The next month, the Hong Kong government tried again to transport KMT soldiers and their families to Taiwan on the Kweiyang Ferry, but only 34 of 946 were allowed entrance.[61] The ROC government refused to accept these migrants in part because Taiwan's economy was in a depression at that time and could not accommodate too many new immigrants. Politically, the KMT regime also was highly suspicious of these "refugees" being spies working for the CCP. Furthermore, a large number of the former soldiers had serious injuries and would require long-term medical care—entailing a burden for the strapped ROC government.[62]

The Hong Kong government along with British diplomats complained to the KMT government about this issue. To appease them, the KMT government finally let around five hundred refugees enter later that year After that, Taiwan tightened its policy again. The Hong Kong government also attempted to send some of these "political refugees" back to China across the Lo Wu Bridge or through Hainan, but the mainland authorities rejected them as "traitors." To appeal to the mainland authorities, Governor Grantham of Hong Kong proposed to the PRC that it would give ten Hong Kong dollars for each refugee expatriated back to Tianjin or Qinghai. However, the PRC government ignored Graham's overture and later rejected the offer.[63] From the beginning, these "political refugees" were not welcome in both Taiwan and mainland China and had to stay in limbo in Hong Kong.

Then, in March, the Social Welfare Office decided to move the 1,889 people temporarily to Jubilee Fort on Mount Davis, a British military stronghold on the western end of Hong Kong Island.[64] A more permanent solution had to be found because the conditions of the Mount Davis camp were dilapidated and the residents were forced to live in tents.[65] More importantly, the number of "political refugees" continued to grow to over 8,200.⁶⁶ Meanwhile, there was a clash in June 1950 between Nationalist refugees and pro-CCP residents in the colony that was widely reported in the local media. This conflict further reinforced the image of the "political refugees" as troublemakers in Hong Kong. To avoid more political scrutiny by the public or the mainland government and to prevent other social disturbances they might create, the Hong Kong government decided to relocate them to a more remote place.

The initial site chosen was Silver Mine Bay on Lantau Island. The landowners and farmers of Silver Mine Bay protested strongly against setting up a refugee camp near their properties providing evidence that at least some long-term residents did not welcome the "political refugees" affiliated with the KMT. The Hong Kong government finally selected Rennie's Mill as a permanent site for the settlements.⁶⁷ Rennie's Mill was named after Canadian businessman named Alfred Herbert Rennie, who established the Hong Kong Milling Company at Junk Bay in 1907 and killed himself there later after his business failed. Junk Bay is known in Cantonese as "Tseung Kwan O," located in the eastern mouth of the Victorian harbor, far removed from the urban areas. On June 26, 1950, the Social Welfare Office shipped several thousand refugees to Rennie's Mill. According to welfare office records, office there were more than 6,800 "inmates listed in the official registry in 1950 as well as about 5,000 people waiting to be registered."⁶⁸ The policy of letting these "political refugees" stay proved to be controversial. Although free food and housing were made available to these migrants in particular, the Rennie's Mill Refugee Camp also developed a reputation as a place where anyone could go and seek refuge.⁶⁹ Indeed, so many new arrivals who had heard about the camp went there by the summer of 1951 that its population swelled to around twenty thousand.⁷⁰

Until 1952, the ROC government did not have a specific policy for the refugees residing at Rennie's Mill. Many inmates in Rennie's Mill Refugee Camp initially thought that it would take just one to two years before Taiwan would take them in; however, for most of them this never happened. They submitted articles to newspapers and magazines expressing their wishes to go to Taiwan, sometimes even suggesting that the ROC government could require them to serve in the military if it had any suspicions as to their backgrounds.⁷¹

Among politicians and intellectual elites in Taiwan and overseas, complaints arose about the KMT's lukewarm attitude toward the "political refugees." Critics argued that the KMT had a responsibility to shelter these people who had escaped from China. One of them blasted the KMT regime for forsaking its obligation to the Rennie's Mill inmates, saying that to reject their transfer to Taiwan was as bad as giving them a death sentence.[72]

In an article published in the *Hong Kong Times* on June 28, 1950, about the problem of refugees in Hong Kong, the Control Yuan in Taiwan expressed its opinion that the refugees who escaped to Hong Kong were the "Heroes (*yimin*) of China."[73] The author also expressed that intellectuals should be prioritized in the rescue effort, because they were people who held "firm nationalistic consciousness and deep patriotic thoughts" and understood their duties of this time (*shidai renwu*)."[74] Along the same line, Lei Zhen (Lei Chen), one of Chiang Kai-shek's advisers, argued that the people in Rennie's Mill were military and civilian officials and therefore transferring them to Taiwan could motivate Chinese people overseas and uplift the spirit of the government. He also believed that the young and strong should be given priority.

Some Legislative Yuan members who were sympathetic to the Rennie's Mill inmates also wanted to revise the original terms permitting entry. Some believed that letting the pro-KMT refugees in Hong Kong migrate to Taiwan served the essential function of anticommunist propaganda to win the hearts of people in mainland China, and they further believed that these people could be important resources for the war against the Communists.[75] Debates about the criteria of transfer were heated in the Legislative Yuan in 1950, with some members suggesting that students, youths, bureaucrats, and teachers be included in the scope of rescue because they all could contribute to international propaganda and help fulfill the plan of retaking China. Another issue discussed during the meetings was whether those who were accepted into Taiwan could just live there as ordinary citizens or should be required to actively participate in the military or economic production. These discussions, which lasted till the end of 1950, reflect that while some intellectuals and politicians were more sympathetic than others to the plight of inmates at Rennie's Mill, they also expected the migrants to contribute to the anticommunist effort if they were allowed to immigrate to Taiwan. Finally, the new "Application Guidelines for the Refugees of Rennie's Mill to Enter Taiwan" (Bianli Xianggang Diaojingling Nanbao Rujing Banfa) were passed by the different departments in the Taiwan government in

December 1950 in response to suggestions by members of the Legislative Yuan. The guidelines gave priority to the Rennie's Mill inmates who held food ration tickets. Those without food ration tickets who held residential permits had to wait for a year before they could apply. The logic behind this differentiation was that refugees with food ration tickets had been sent to Rennie's Mill by the Social Welfare Office and thus had a more legitimate status. Those who did not have food ration tickets mostly had gone to Rennie's Mill of their own accord because they lacked any other means of survival. Furthermore, inmates who were suspected of having affiliations with the Third Force or had shown signs of being critical of the KMT were barred from going to Taiwan.[76]

In the summer of 1952, the FCRA was informed that the Social Welfare Office of Hong Kong intended to end food rationing at the Rennie's Mill camp the following year in an effort to disperse the camp's inhabitants. The move by British authorities created a vacuum of authority, which the FCRA filled. Since the food-rationing system was canceled, the young and the strong were given priority to enter Taiwan.[77] Between April 14 and 17, the Central Reform Committee of the KMT met to debate and decide on a proposal called "Suggestions for Resolving the Issue of Refugees in Hong Kong and Macau" (Jiejue Gang'ao nanbao chuli yijian). Its recommendation was to select refugees from the age of eighteen to thirty-five to form a guerrilla group of three thousand to five thousand fighters to be sent to mainland China to battle the Communists.[78] No definite resolution on the matter was forthcoming, but the committee's suggestion may have been taken into consideration, since 1,128 adults were transferred to Taiwan the following year.[79] Thereafter the number of transfers was reduced and only a few hundred were permitted to enter Taiwan each year.

Nevertheless, the application procedures to immigrate to Taiwan remained complicated. Applicants had first to submit the application and the guarantors' letters to the internal committees within Rennie's Mill; then, after the first screening, the guarantor in Taiwan had to send the application to the FCRA, and the FCRA would send it to the Security Bureau to do further screening.[80] Wang Qing-quan, who is quoted at the beginning of this chapter, was one of the first inmates at Rennie's Mill. He stayed in Hong Kong for a year and eight months, most of that time in Rennie's Mill. He eventually left for Taiwan in 1952. The reason he could leave was he was able to find a relative whose husband happened to be a military general of the KMT to serve as his guarantor. Those applicants without guarantors often found themselves rejected. Finding a guarantor was not an easy task either, as Wang said: "[The wife of the guarantor] was concerned for me and told her husband she would not come to Taiwan if I could not either. The husband of course was hesitant to be my guarantor, due to the strict punishment for guarantors if the applicant was found violating the rules.... He was hesitant to sponsor me because it was dangerous. The KMT was suspicious of communist infiltrators." Because Wang was nineteen or twenty at the time and had been enrolled in the Hubei Branch of the Zhongnan Military and Politics University (Zhongnan Junzheng Daxue Hubei Fenxue) before his escape, he was admitted to the Junior College of Administration, and after that the Taiwan College of Law and Business, and eventually National Taipei University upon his arrival in Taiwan. He also became a reservist in the military. Wang's successful transition owed partly to the luck of finding a high-ranking KMT military officer to be his guarantor, and partly to his educational background and young age.

According to Chih-Yen Lin, the author of *The Price of Freedom*, a book about the history of the Rennie's Mill Refugee Camp, the total number of people who transferred from Hong Kong to Taiwan from 1950 to 1961 was 18,873, most of whom were inmates in Rennie's Mill (figure 1.4).[81] Supplementing this information, an Immigration Department study in 1970 documents that between 1953 and 1969, the number of transferees to Taiwan decreased year by year. In the early 1950s, about five to six hundred people transferred each year, but by 1961, the number dropped to 175. Rennie's Mill became an open camp after 1962, and the formal transfer of its residents to Taiwan practically ceased. Overall, only a portion of Rennie's Mill inmates were able to go to Taiwan. Preference was consistently given to people who demonstrated anticommunist qualities and loyalty to the KMT.

THE GREAT EXODUS OF 1962 AND THE APRIL 4 POLICY

In the Great Exodus of 1962, some people who escaped to Hong Kong and Macau were recommended by FCRA officials to move to Taiwan.

FIGURE 1.4 Rennie's Mill in 1955.

While the policies for Rennie's Mill reflected the default criteria for transferring to Taiwan, the escapees who went to the FCRA in 1962 were granted special permission to transfer to Taiwan within weeks. The April 4 policy was meant to showcase how the ROC regime not only rescued political victims who defected but also helped them excel in society. For this reason, those who were selected were mostly young people with the most potential to eventually contribute to society. Most of these migrants were single, with a small number moving with their families.

The April 4 policy was a response to the Great Exodus to Hong Kong, also known as the May Exodus of 1962 (Liu Er Da Tao Gang/Wu Yue Da Tao Gang), a huge influx of people entering Hong Kong and Macau mostly in the first half of 1962, spurred by the failure of the Great Leap Forward policy and the resulting widespread famine in the Guangdong region. A more immediate cause for the increase in escapees arriving in Hong Kong were the widespread rumors in Guangdong that British authorities in Hong Kong were planning to open the border around the time of the Queen's Official Birthday in mid-June, and to guarantee that people who could enter Hong Kong by that date would not be repatriated. Those who believed the rumor rushed to the areas near the border hoping to try their luck. At first, people mainly came from Bao'an County and Dongguan County, but soon rumors (later proven to be false) spread to Huiyang, Haifeng, and counties farther away.[82]

As crowds began to gather in Guangzhou Train Station and at the Shenzhen border, in April 1962, Governor Tao Zhu of Guangdong ordered the border guards to stop patrolling the PRC side of the border. The PRC police or border patrols did not stop the Chinese from leaving even when they did not carry proper documents as they would normally do.[83] This caused around 150,000 refugees to cross the Shenzhen River into Hong Kong over the next two months.[84] Yet, the Hong Kong side of the border was still closed. In the next six weeks, 62,400 border-crossers were arrested and repatriated by the Hong Kong authorities, while another 60,000 crossed undetected.[85] Most of those arrested were then sent back to the mainland by trucks after being detained in camps. Those who hid in farmlands and mountains in the New Territories of Hong Kong evaded arrest. Dissatisfied with the repatriation policy, crowds in the New Territories who were sympathetic to the escapees' plight stopped the trucks from taking the immigrants to the border point at Lo Wu.

Some of the escapees who arrived in Hong Kong and Macau during these two months were invited to transfer to Taiwan at the FCRA. This policy to relieve the pressure of the influx of people in Hong Kong was called the April 4 policy (also known as the April 4 program). The FCRA also saw this as a chance to advertise to the world how those they called "returnees" were treated in Taiwan. The publications of the FCRA thereafter included sections featuring beneficiaries of the April 4 policy attending vocational training and educational opportunities in Taiwan. This small group of people captured media attention, and a few became well-known representatives of the anticommunist fighters (*fangong yishi*). Two of these figures will be featured in chapter 5.

The escapees who made it to the FCRA in Hong Kong and Macau in 1962 were interviewed, and those who were fit and motivated were invited to go to Taiwan. Most of these escapees went to the FCRA on their own. According to two people who later moved to Taiwan, they were also interviewed by representatives from the U.S. Central Intelligence Agency during their visits to the FCRA. It is unclear how many went to the United States during this period, but like those who went through ARCI sponsorship, those who were invited by the CIA had to not only be explicitly anticommunist and fairly well educated, but also have some knowledge of the CCP and be able to provide intelligence.

On April 4, 1962, Executive Yuan leader and vice president Chen Cheng of the ROC government ordered the transfer of 771 people from Hong Kong and Macau to Taiwan. Through an arrangement by the FCRA, a total of eleven Sichuan ferries carried these *nanbao* in May and June. While priorities were given to single young individuals, some went with their family members, with the youngest being an infant. They were given the following opportunities depending on their age and wishes: (1) arranged employment; (2) education; (3) assisted living (for the elderly or young children); (4) cohabitation with relatives; and (5) opportunity to seek employment on their own. Those in their late teens or twenties who wanted to continue their education would be sent to the Overseas Chinese Preparation School or the Overseas Chinese Secondary School to prepare for the University Entrance (Liankao) Exam. Those who did not want to have their employment or education arranged received monthly stipends of around 3,000 TWD. The emphasis of the program was on training the beneficiaries to be productive citizens in Taiwan.

The Overseas Chinese Preparation School was aimed at helping youths who received inadequate education in mainland China. Lao Zhengwu and Xiao Yujing (two of the main subjects of chapter 5) benefited from the education program since their subpar secondary school education in mainland China would not have prepared them to enter university. The April 4 policy and its education program gave priority to those in their late teens and early twenties like Lao and Xiao. After a year of study, the students then would take the University Entrance exam. For this exam, the *nanbao* from the April 4 policy belonged to one of the special categories—"veterans," "soldiers," "indigenous people," "students from the peripheries (of China)," "children of diplomats," "students from overseas," and "April 4 policy recipients"—and received extra credit in their total scores on the exam; some universities gave these categories a special quota for acceptance.[86] An FCRA publication announced that fifty-eight people from the April 4 policy enrolled in the Overseas Chinese Preparation School, fifty-four of whom eventually graduated. Out of the forty-eight who were accepted by universities, about half got into Taiwan University, the rest went to National Chengchi University and National Chenggong University. Besides tuition, they were also given subsidies for food, books, and uniforms.[87]

The April 4 policy formally ended in August 1963 with the students entering the university of their choice, but the stipend program continued. On January 25, 1984, Lianhe Bao published a report on a visit by FCRA Vice Chairman Fang Zhi (Fang Chih) to the beneficiaries of the April 4 policy. He remarked that only fifteen of the elderly were still receiving stipends from the FCRA, indicating that the April 4 policy was largely successful.

Overall, the escapees covered by the April 4 policy received many benefits. Even though some expressed regret that the KMT did not fully trust them because they were under police surveillance, and some of them were not allowed to take high government positions because of this distrust, most were grateful for the opportunities created by the Kuomintang. Unlike the other immigrants, they did not have to go through several levels of screening before entering Taiwan. The procedures were much shorter and simpler than for the long-term residents of Rennie's Mill.

On May 23, 1962, the CCP decided to close the border once again to prevent the flow of migrants into Hong Kong.[88] It resorted to very stern measures, including shoot-to-kill orders for border guards against anyone trying to cross the border without permission. The April 4 policy proved to be a onetime opportunity for fairly easy and quick processing for escapees trying to get to Taiwan, as Taiwan's resettlement policy also became stricter after that policy ended in June 1962. The leniency of the April 4 policy should be seen as an exception to the overall strict regulation of immigration from China through Hong Kong. Even so, the policy favored young people who were interested in receiving education or professional training. It reflected Taiwan's interest still in using these retraining programs as part of its state propaganda to boast that it was helping the refugees oppressed by the mainland government.

THE INTEGRATION OF "SQUATTERS" IN HONG KONG IN THE 1960S

Since the closing of the border, the Hong Kong government seldom used the term "refugees" in its official documents in order to downplay the political nature of their migration, especially because the UN defined refugees as migrants escaping political persecution. In the early 1950s, the government did not have a policy for Chinese in transit because they were expected to return to China. The political affiliations of these new members of Hong Kong society were rarely highlighted except when they became a point of concern, such as during the clash between pro-CCP trade unionists and KMT soldiers near Mount Davis in 1950 that led to the establishment of the Rennie's Mill Refugee Camp. In extreme cases, the undesirable residents would be deported. By the early 1960s, the problem of "illegal immigrants" had been mostly excised from the discourse of refugees. To maintain the support of Hong Kong residents in general, the government focused on community building and economic relief for the lower class.

In the 1950s, even as the Hong Kong government worked to send a portion of the escapees to Taiwan, the United States, and other countries, many of them still ended up staying in Hong Kong. In 1964, one member of the British Parliament described the escapees in Hong Kong in the previous decade:

> Hong Kong is very largely populated by Cantonese and, therefore, when these people eventually get to the Island of Hong Kong they do not want to be told that they can go on to Formosa, which is quite a long way—from their point of view almost unget-at-able—and they know very little about it. These people say, "No, we will not go. We have our own relations and friends in Hong Kong, and if we can get there and occasionally slip back to the mainland to see those relatives that we have left behind we would infinitely prefer it." Therefore, about 90 per cent of the people who are trying to get away from the mainland do not want to go further than Hong Kong.[89]

While the number of the people who wanted to stay in Hong Kong is debatable, this description captures the sentiments of at least some of the escapees who had relatives there and who felt more familiar with the culture of the city, given that the main language used was Cantonese and that most of these people came from the Cantonese-speaking Guangdong region.

The Hong Kong government from the beginning used the term "squatters" to refer to the majority of the escapees who made it to Hong

Kong, because "squatters" gives the impression that they might leave once the political situation in China became more stable. The "squatters" in the early 1950s lived in makeshift wooden huts in hillside areas, like the rest of the colony's poor population (figure 1.5). This attitude of deemphasizing the existence of escapees from China was made clear when Governor Grantham said in 1952 that he did not want to turn Hong Kong "into a glorified soup kitchen for refugees from all over China."[90] The escapees who found their way to the city were mostly tolerated, but the level of welfare provided was kept to a minimum, so that they would not be motivated to stay if or when the political turbulence stopped.

However, when a major fire broke out on December 25, 1953, on Shek Kip Mei hillside where many escapees lived, 53,000 people were left homeless and the government had to respond to the situation by providing low-cost housing to resettle those who were displaced. In addition, fires also occurred in other squatter settlements in Hong Kong between 1950 and 1954 causing around 100,000 people to lose their homes (figure 1.6).[91]

FIGURE 1.5 Wooden huts in Kowloon, Hong Kong in 1955.

Photo by Norman Yao. Norman Gan-chao and Anne Lee Yao Collection, Box 2, Folder 4, Courtesy of Special Collections, Claremont Colleges Library.

FIGURE 1.6 Mother and child looking at the debris after the fire on December 25, 1955.

Photo by Norman Yao. Norman Gan-chao and Anne Lee Yao Collection, Box 2, Folder 8, Courtesy of Special Collections, Claremont Colleges Library.

After the fire, the governor launched a public housing program and introduced the Shek Kip Mei Low-Cost Housing Estate for displaced residents and any residents still living in makeshift houses. This policy was symbolic because the residents no longer lived in such houses and had begun to settle in permanent public housing. As anthropologist Alan Smart argues, the drastic consequence of the fire also forced the Hong Kong government to reconsider its overall social welfare policy toward the poor and new immigrants. In 1954, it created the Public Housing Authority to resettle an average of 75,000 squatters annually for the next several years.[92]

The Hong Kong government's new policy of integrating the "squatters" was in part the result of the inability of the UNHCR and other international organizations to solve the issue. By the mid-1950s, the Hong Kong government decided it had to take the issue into its own hands. The solution it came up with was an attempt to depoliticize the Chinese escapees and turn the "squatters" issue into a class problem.[93]

In 1956, in its annual report, the Hong Kong government called this "a problem of people," noting the consequences of excess population on finance, housing, education, medical services, social welfare, industry, commerce, and even political relations and the law. At this time, the government was looking for a lasting solution for the city's problems with the lower class and began to see these newly arrived Chinese as permanent settlers. The government enacted policies after 1956 aimed at improving the housing conditions of these people rather than just offering temporary relief.[94] From then on, the discourse of social welfare for lower-class residents replaced the former emphasis on "squatters."

In September 1960, the Hong Kong government took a further step toward depoliticizing the escapees. Colonial Secretary Claude Bramall Burgess said the government was "making a decision to put the word 'refugee' out of the dictionary." He said that the aim of the migrants was to "join their family, clansmen and people of their own race, language and dialect in Hong Kong, and that they do not in many cases desire to go further afield."[95] This indicates a shift in policy toward allowing migrants to stay and become members of the society, instead of waiting for the member states of the UN to resettle them.

From the early 1960s, the term "illegal immigrants" was invoked by the government to exclude the newcomers during times of massive influx. As historian Chi-Kwan Mark writes, the new categorization of "illegal immigrants" had become "a mechanism for inclusion and exclusion."[96] It was also around this time that we see the refugee policies elsewhere besides Hong Kong changing. The Refugee Relief Program in the

United States formally ended in the late 1950s, and the Rennie's Mill Refugee Camp opened after 1962. While international attention on the "Chinese refugee" issue was fading, the Hong Kong government decided that the policy of social integration was a better alternative to either repatriation or massive onward emigration.[97]

As has been noted, some of the people who arrived in Hong Kong during the Great Exodus of 1962 participated in the April 4 policy and went to Taiwan; others stayed in Hong Kong and became the squatters. After that spike in migration, the solidification of the two categories, "Hong Kong residents" and "illegal immigrants," proceeded through several changes in government structure and policy. First, in 1962, a special branch of the police force was formed to enforce the government's policy to "apprehend as many as possible of those people who seek to enter Hong Kong illegally and to repatriate them to their countries of domicile."[98] Second, starting in 1963, the colonial government began to repatriate "illegal immigrants" caught in the border area, but a limited number of entry permits were issued to a small number of escapees who had particular individual circumstances. Third in 1967, the Hong Kong government decided not to report the escapees who were found in the city but only required them to report to the authorities so that arrangement could be made for them to stay.[99] While to the escapees, which group they belonged to was just a matter of luck, to the public in Hong Kong, a clear line of citizenship was being drawn: escapees who succeeded in entering the urban area of Hong Kong or who were already present as squatters could eventually become legitimate residents; whereas those who were caught while crossing the border were cast as "illegal immigrants" and were forced to repatriate to mainland China. This new policy gave a sense of belonging to those who had arrived in Hong Kong earlier, since it offered them a possibility of staying in the colony indefinitely. The divide between "squatters" and "illegal immigrants" was thus not one founded on political ideology or class status, but on one's fortunes in entering the city and gaining needed support from relatives or friends in Hong Kong.

While in the 1950s till early 1960s, there was considerable international intervention in the treatment of escapees in Hong Kong, during the period that followed the Hong Kong government's immigration policies took an inward turn. This change may have had to do with the decrease of international pressure in politicizing the migrants as victims of communism. By not having a separate category of "squatters" or "refugees," the government successfully further defused the political sensitivity of the escapees. This reflects a change in the Hong Kong government's overall approach and a reduction of the Cold War's influence on Hong Kong's immigration policies. By the mid-1960s, the government used deportation primarily as a way to remove undesirable people residing in Hong Kong temporarily, as will be shown in chapter 4.

The Chinese people who arrived in the United States, Taiwan, or Hong Kong in the 1950s and 1960s may have come from the same origin as escapees from mainland China. In the process of sorting and evaluating the escapees, categories such as "political refugees," "exiled intellectuals," "immigrants," and "squatters," were redefined to make sure that those who were permitted to enter fit into a given state's idea of citizenship. While the United States wanted immigrants who could contribute to the country, Taiwan wanted KMT loyalists who could help in the cause of retaking China. The Hong Kong government did not want the escapees to stay in the first decade and later began to accept those who were there to stay except the troublemakers.

PERMANENT RESIDENCY AND THE TOUCH-BASE POLICY, 1972–1974

Because of the cost of providing housing, facilities and education to immigrants, the Hong Kong government moved to further restrict their entry. The goal of differentiating between legitimate and illegal immigrants was furthered by the ID card policy and the touch-base policy in the first half of the 1970s. Three levels of citizenship were created among Hong Kong residents. At the highest level were "Hong Kong permanent residents" who enjoyed full citizenship; in the second tier were "Hong Kong residents" who were newly arrived in Hong Kong and who enjoyed some rights and benefits; on the lowest rung were the illegal immigrants who would be repatriated back to China.

Those who successfully reached Hong Kong and avoided arrest in the New Territories were allowed to stay and register. The system of permanent residency started on April 1, 1972. Anyone who lived in Hong Kong continuously for seven years could receive the Hong Kong permanent ID. "Permanent residents" enjoyed more government benefits, especially in terms of social welfare, housing, and education. To differentiate "permanent residents" from "residents," those in the latter category had a green stamp on their IDs. After being in Hong Kong continuously for seven years, they could exchange their ID for a permanent resident ID with a black stamp.[100] The "green stamp" was used to refer to immigrants from China. The differential treatment in terms of residential status and the ID system helped to build up the sense of local belonging among the permanent residents and gave the residents with green stamps a sense of legitimacy. This new system shows that the government had begun to acknowledge that the majority of the former escapees were there to stay.

In 1973, illegal immigration jumped from an annual average of 3,000 per year to 20,800 that year and continued to rise. This increase happened during the midst of the Cultural Revolution as urban youths were being sent to the countryside. The touch-base policy (*dilei zhengce*), formally enacted in November 1974, allowed immigrants from mainland China who reached the urban areas (south of Boundary Street in Kowloon) to register for an identification card. Those who did not cross that line were subject to arrest and repatriation. Along with this policy, the Hong Kong authorities also tightened patrols in the New Territories, such that fewer migrants made it to the urban areas. This policy reflected the ambivalence of the government toward these escapees, most of whom were from the Guangdong region.[101] On the one hand, the Hong Kong government wished to be tolerant toward those escapees who were not given a chance to become legitimate citizens, to keep them from being exploited as illegal immigrants or workers; at the same time, their labor could also mitigate the growing labor shortage in secondary industries. On the other hand, the government's tolerance only encouraged people who were in mainland China to keep trying to sneak into Hong Kong, and many risked their lives to try to get to the urban areas of the city. This policy was relatively successful in the first few years, and the number of illegal immigrants dropped to about 10,000 per year. Annual legal immigration remained at 19,000–25,000.[102]

However, Deng Xiaoping's economic reforms introduced a new incentive to go to Hong Kong because the stark contrast between Hong Kong's prosperity and the poverty in China became apparent when some of the coastal areas of the country were opened up and more Chinese had the opportunities to receive information from beyond the border. Between 1978 and 1980, about 46,000 illegal immigrants arrived in Hong Kong, and half succeeded in "touching base." The touch-base policy failed to halt the influx of illegal immigrants once again. In October 1980, the governor estimated that one of every five individuals who set out from China reached Hong Kong and "touched base." This created a heavy burden on transportation facilities and social services. The government enacted a new policy to require repatriation of any illegal immigrant in any part of the city. Anyone arriving in Hong Kong on or before October 24, 1980, was required to register for a Hong Kong identity card during a three-day grace period. All Hong Kong residents had to carry their HKID cards after this policy went into effect. Immigrants who arrived illegally thereafter would be sent back immediately.[103]

THE LIMITS OF FREEDOM

China's Southern Periphery played a special role in Cold War politics after 1949 because many Chinese took refuge there after escaping from Communist rule. Refugee and immigration policies became both an issue of Cold War diplomacy as well as a tool of government propaganda. When the escapees reached the territories in the Southern Periphery, the various states weighed in and evaluated their qualifications for resettlement. At the same time, in this space people who fled from China began to rethink how they wanted to connect with China in the future. Their entering Hong Kong became a symbol of defiance in the Cold War. However, the restrictive policies imposed by the various states show that these displaced people who chose to "vote with their feet" were not necessarily welcome in the Free World. Their paths thereafter depended on how well they fit into a given state's idea of citizens. Those who were allowed to move to the United States or to countries in Southeast Asia through the ARCI and the US Refugee Act of 1953 were usually highly educated and had an anticommunist background. While the majority of these refugees became integrated into society either in the United States or in Southeast Asia, some continued to be active in connecting with the Third Force in

Hong Kong and other overseas alliances, as will be discussed in chapter 2. In contrast, KMT affiliates and sympathizers either volunteered to go or were sent to Rennie's Mill Refugee Camp, many hoping to join the KMT and contribute to its cause. Only a minority of them ended up in Taiwan because the KMT enforced a very strict immigration policy and anyone who criticized the KMT or was suspected of being a spy was not allowed entry. Those who continued to be stranded in Rennie's Mill either left the camp or stayed until its demolition. Politically neutral arrivals tended to stay in Hong Kong and became less involved in national politics. Such policies also induced Hong Kong and Taiwan respectively to each develop its own distinctive political culture and character. Ironically, the refugee discourses and immigration policies of each region made it more challenging for people to move away from where they were dwelling or back to the mainland. Through the varied categorizations of refugees and enactment of differing immigration requirements by the governments in Communist China, Nationalist Taiwan, British Hong Kong, and the United States, the ideas of a proper Chinese citizen became legitimated, differentiated, and diffused across the Southern Periphery and beyond.

2

THE THIRD FORCE AND THE CULTURE OF DISSENT IN HONG KONG

Conventional historical narratives of China's Cold War experience focus on two actors: the Chinese Communist Party (CCP) and the Kuomintang (KMT). Chinese politics in the 1950s and 1960s, however, was more vibrant and complex than most historians have assumed if we expand the geopolitical landscape to the Southern Periphery. During this time, a small group of diasporic intellectuals, who called themselves the Third Force, were also striving to reunite China by offering a third option outside of the CCP and the KMT.¹ Mostly based in Hong Kong with a network of a few dozen core members living or moving between Taiwan, North America, and Southeast Asia, the Third Force emerged as an attempt at articulating visions for a democratic China with a constitutional government. As such, they were both *fangong* (anti-CCP) and anti-KMT. Chen Zhengmao, a scholar based in Taiwan who studies the Third Force, says it represents a kind of political culture of the Chinese democratic intelligentsia.² This group of intellectuals, having escaped from the mainland after 1949, created study groups and publications that sought to unify Chinese democratic activists in Hong Kong and overseas for the goals of national reunification and democratic reform. The existence of the Third Force showed that the KMT was not the only anti-CCP force in the Southern Periphery, and the anti-CCP sentiments were not always merely products of KMT propaganda. Moreover, the network of the Third Force in Hong Kong and beyond is a good illustration that the landscape of the peripheral democratic movement was boundless. While many of the core members were in Hong Kong physically at least temporarily, key figures also had the mobility to move to Taiwan, other parts of East Asia, or the United States when they felt it necessary to do so. Moving farther away from mainland China did not stop their dreams of reconstructing their homeland.

In chapter 1, we saw that the Hong Kong government tried to prevent immigrants with strong political inclinations from settling as permanent residents in the city in the 1950s. Yet some political activists, as we will see, continued to carve out space in Hong Kong and engage in political discussions about what they wanted China to become despite the constraints. In this context, Hong Kong served as a contingent base where they united with other diasporic Chinese in Taiwan and overseas. It did not need to be Hong Kong, though; some people suggested Taiwan or the United States as the new base after the Hong Kong government tightened the restrictions on political organizing. At the same time, the Third Force magazines provided a virtual space for people who may have lacked a sense of belonging in Hong Kong or overseas to voice their discontentment and wishes.

Since the Umbrella Movement in 2014, interest in the history of Hong Kong's democratization has been strong. Most academic works on Hong Kong refer to the early 1980s when preparation for the 1984 Joint Declaration signed by the UK and the PRC began as the moment when Hong Kong residents began to think seriously about local politics and their future relationship with China. Before then, Hong Kong only had what sociologist Ming Sing calls a "parochial political culture," characterized by a sense of powerlessness and "lack of knowledge and commitment to democracy."[3] Citing the political scientist, Stephan Hoadley, Sing explains that one contributing factor to this "parochial political culture" could be the traumatic events that these Hong Kong people or their families had experienced:

> The historical mayhem of riots, rebellion, civil war, and Japanese attacks on China in the past two centuries stimulated a strong inner yearning among the Hong Kong Chinese for political stability. The Chinese migrants treated Hong Kong as a lifeboat affording relative stability, disinterested justice, and a good economic prospect in the rough sea of

China. Those who had got into the lifeboat did not want to rock it. Political activities were frowned upon and could hardly flourish in such a context.[4]

This characterization of the new immigrants who arrived after World War II needs to be challenged. Not only can we find evidence of "strong knowledge and commitment to democracy" in Hong Kong since the early 1950s (three decades prior to the Joint Declaration), but the traumatic events that many individuals in Hong Kong went through in the 1940s and 1950s, specifically the takeover of China by the CCP and their migration from mainland China, only solidified their yearnings for a place with a more democratic political system than those of the CCP and the KMT. The Third Force movement, particularly in its early stages, showed that there was much concern over how to build a democratic political entity in China among the exiled people in Hong Kong in the first two decades after World War II.

In the first stage of the Third Force Movement, we can find two kinds of diasporic consciousness through the Third Force publications in the from 1950 to around 1958. One was expressed in the political discussions among the activists who founded and wrote for the Third Force magazines; the other was more about a sense of homelessness articulated by the readers who were mostly less educated and socially established than the regular writers. The founders of the Third Force magazines, as we will explore, wanted to find a third way to reunify China in the early 1950s. For their part, non-elite escapees from China voiced diasporic sentiments about being in limbo in Hong Kong. Most of the latter did not write in detail about governance and constitutional democracy as elaborated by the Third Force leaders. They were much more affected by the social circumstances of being marginalized by Hong Kong society. Overall, the writings in the first stage indicate that the people who arrived in Hong Kong after they left China did not feel at ease in Hong Kong, and some were waiting for a chance to launch a counterattack.

Core members of the Third Force changed their stances in the second stage of the Third Force Movement, after direct subsidies by the United States were reduced in the mid-1950s and tighter restrictions on political organizations were imposed by the Hong Kong government. Some of the leaders of the Third Force remained politically active, but most of them looked to compromise with Chiang Kai-shek's government rather than creating a separate political force in Hong Kong. While some still hoped to have an overseas-led alternative movement, the majority aimed at further democratizing the KMT regime in Taiwan as the forefront of the anticommunist movement. This change coincides with the changing immigration policy of Hong Kong. As people who arrived in Hong Kong in the 1950s and early 1960s began to settle in to become permanent Hong Kong residents, their wishes of retaking China or returning to their homeland faded away.

The turning point of the Third Force Movement in the late 1950s was indicative of how the exiled Chinese people in Hong Kong imagined their status in the colony as well as their homeland—China. While in the early days, some believed that Hong Kong had a role to play in the mission of retaking China, by the 1960s, Hong Kong slowly disappeared as a significant site of political organizing for these anti-CCP activists. The yearning for a more democratic government and the critical attitude toward the two parties became an important political legacy in Hong Kong in the decades after the Third Force movement faded away.

THE FIRST STAGE, 1949-1958

THE FORMATION OF THE THIRD FORCE

The Third Force movement in Hong Kong originated in a critical political culture during the Republican era. Most leaders of the Third Force were already involved on the political scene in the 1920s and 1930s—some as members of such minor parties as the China Youth Party or the China Democratic Socialist Party, and some serving in the KMT as high-ranking officials, or both. These minor parties later became known as "The Third Force" in the Republican era because they looked for alternatives to the leadership of the KMT and the CCP. Three leaders of the post-1949 Third Force movement were influential players in these minor parties: Li Huang, Zuo Shunsheng, and Zhang Junmai (Carson Chang).

Li Huang and Zuo Shunsheng were leaders of the China Youth Party. Li Huang formed the China Youth Party in December 1923 in Paris with other overseas Chinese students. The party moved to Shanghai the following year and was active in the International Settlement. Zuo Shunsheng, who was a magazine editor active in the Shanghai intelligentsia, joined them and later became the head of the organization. As the political scientist Edmund Fung says, the China Youth Party provided a "framework for cooperation with the ruling party" and "opened up the possibility of changing the political system by working within it."[5] Most of its members were intellectuals who shared ideas about liberal democracy. Its main platform was to have a competitive multiparty system, freedom of the press and assembly, as well as a representative constitutional government. Many of these goals continued to be objectives of the later Third Force movement. From 1937, the China Youth Party attempted to align with the KMT to fight against Japan and joined the People's Political Council held by the KMT in Chongqing. During this period, some China Youth Party members also served in the KMT government.

Zhang Junmai, another leader who played an important role in international networking after 1949, studied in Japan and graduated from Waseda University in Tokyo in 1909. While in Japan, he was active in the overseas Chinese intellectual circle and was influenced by Liang Qichao's ideas of constitutional monarchy. After returning to China Zhang attended the Imperial Examination for returned students and was subsequently made a Han Lin Scholar and then became the editor-in-chief of the *Peking-Tientsin Shih Pao* in Tianjin. He later served a secretary of the Ministry of Industry and Commerce briefly after the 1911 revolution. He then went to study in Europe from 1919 to 1921, where he became enamored with German social democracy. During that time abroad, he wrote about how proletarian dictatorship is emphatically not suitable for China and declared that communism should not be the solution for his country.[6] After he went back to China, he was appointed chief of the Foreign Affairs Bureau at Hangzhou, Zhejiang Province and later became general manager of the China Times, Shanghai. It was during those years in Shanghai that he organized the China Democratic Socialist Party.

Together with other minor parties, the China Democratic Socialist Party and the China Youth Party formed a coalition called the League of Democratic Political Groups—later known as the China Democratic

League (Zhongguo Minzhu Tongmeng)—in 1941 to mediate the chasm between the CCP and the KMT. This alliance conceived of their political agenda as the middle faction, as Wan Lijuan, author of a dissertation about the Third Force, describes: "In politics, [the League] follows English or American models of democratic politics; in economics, it seeks to develop a national capitalist economy; in theory, it adopts a liberal attitude; in behavior, it has a peaceful, reformist stance."[7] The league attempted to form a coalition with the KMT and joined the ROC Congress in 1946. Ultimately, however, these minor parties were not able to gain more political power or negotiate with the KMT in reforming a multiparty national government because China had been torn apart by the war with Japan and the KMT used this as an excuse to extend the period of political tutelage As the CCP began to take over China, many of the members of the minor parties left China and went to Hong Kong or abroad in the late 1940s as it became clear that the CCP would succeed. Nevertheless, some of their ideas were carried on by the leaders of the Third Force in the 1950s and 1960s.[8]

After 1949, Zuo Shunsheng and other exiled intellectuals arrived in Hong Kong and founded the Union Press, which published the first Third Force publications.[9] Others, such as Zhang Junmai and Li Huang, moved abroad and attempted to find support by networking internationally with U.S. and European politicians. During their time with the Third Force, both Zhang and Li acted as liaisons to U.S. officials, and Zhang attempted to use his connections to procure additional U.S. support. Zhang was quite well known about the U.S. political circles and the Third Force magazines were able to get financial backing in the first stage of the movement partly due to his effort.

The Third Force leaders also were in close contact with a few prominent KMT critics in Taiwan. The critics in Taiwan technically were not part of the overseas Third Force movement in the 1950s because they lived in Taiwan and were subject to the KMT's political repression, but their criticisms of the two parties may be similar to those made by the Third Force leaders in Hong Kong and overseas. Lei Zhen (Lei Chen) was a prominent critic of the KMT. Before moving to Taiwan with the KMT, Lei held many important party and government positions, including as deputy and secretary-general of the National Assembly that created the ROC Constitution. He was already active with opposition parties, mediating the entrance of the China Youth Party and the China Democratic Socialist Party into the ROC Congress in 1946. Even after 1949, he served as a national policy adviser to the president on Taiwan's policy on the Rennie's Mill Refugee Camp. He was later persecuted for his critical views, and his case became an important example of the KMT's authoritarianism and lack of democracy for the Third Force magazines.

Nevertheless, the first Third Force organizations in 1950s Hong Kong were not started by these leaders of the minor parties but by military generals. The pioneer of the Third Force in Hong Kong was Li Zongren. Unlike the other leaders who were intellectuals and minor-party members, Li served in the KMT government and was a general during World War II. In April 1948, he was elected vice president of China by the National Assembly under Chiang Kai-shek. In January 1949, he became the acting president of the Republic of China after Chiang resigned the presidency for not stopping the CCP's advance.

Three months later, when Nanjing fell to Communist forces, Li further withdrew the government to Guangzhou. At around the same time, he had a fallout with Chiang Kai-shek because he wanted to negotiate with the Communists and Chiang refused. Then, on August 15, 1949, after discussion with employees from the U.S. Embassy, Li Zongren created a Third Force in Hong Kong and established the Great Freedom and Democracy Alliance (Ziyou Minzhu Da Tongmeng). At the start of September, the alliance secretly held its first meeting in Guangzhou.[10] At the beginning of October, the alliance moved from Guangzhou to Hong Kong and added more members. The cadres met every week and decided to operate a propaganda publication called *Da Dao*. The founding members donated HK$20,000 as startup funds.

At the same time, another group in Hong Kong headed by Zhang Fakui, a former military commander who had worked for Chiang Kai-shek but later broke with him, also developed with endorsement from the U.S. politician James McClure Henry. The two "Third Force" groups decided to join forces to procure U.S. support for the movement. Soon after, other leaders from China Youth Party and China Democratic Socialist Party also joined the Third Force movement, including Li Huang, Zuo Shunsheng, and Zhang Junmai.[11] It was then renamed the Struggle for Freedom and Democracy Alliance (Zhongguo Ziyou Minzhu Zhandou Tongmeng). The group had some two hundred to three hundred members, and in its proclamation it laid out the political objectives of the Third Force movement in Hong Kong.[12] At the start of the Korean War, the U.S. government's stance shifted from tacit encouragement to outright economic aid, and in turn Third Force organizations began popping up in earnest. The alliance was established as a major attempt to unify the rather disparate Third Force. However, it struggled with a lack of confidence in its effectiveness overseas.[13]

As the Hong Kong administration acted to restrict its movements because of the fear of too much U.S. political influence in the colony, the Great Freedom and Democracy Alliance soon ceased to exist, along with *Da Dao*. Some of the core members of the China Youth Party formed another organization, Democratic China Forum, and started the publication *Duli Luntan* (Independent Forum) to take the place of *Da Dao*. Over the next few years, other publications identified with the Third Force also were launched.[14]

Among all the publications, *Ziyou Zhenxian* (Freedom Front; see figure 2.1), *Zhongguo Zhisheng* (Voices of China), and *Lianhe Pinglun* (United Voice Weekly; see figure 2.2) probably were the most important because of their readership and prominent editorship. The three magazines also represented the two waves of the movement: the 1949–1958 period in which the founders of *Ziyou Zhenxian* and *Zhongguo Zhisheng* tried to advocate for the Independent China Movement, and the 1959–1964 period in which opposing the CCP, preserving the values of democracy and freedom as stated in the Constitution of the Republic of China, and criticizing Chiang became the three main directives, as elaborated in *Lianhe Pinglun*.[15]

Scholars who have examined the Third Force emphasize its connections with foreign political forces or characterize it as an anticommunist movement sponsored by the U.S. government.[16] Financially, the U.S. government did help foster this anti-CCP political culture in Hong Kong. Because of its anticommunist agenda after World War II, the United States sponsored a number of these publications financially for about a decade.[17] Some of these publications were also associated with the ARCI office in Hong Kong. The U.S. State Department and some of the U.S. politicians, together with the leaders of the Third Force, saw its transnational nature, with a main base in Hong Kong and a wide network of overseas connections, as a crucial asset.[18] These advocates saw the Third

FIGURE 2.1 Cover of *Ziyou Zhenxian* (Freedom Front) 2, no. 7, July 16, 1950.

Force not only as a force for democracy but also as a tool against the CCP in China. The U.S. State Department arranged for escapees in Hong Kong to receive military and intelligence training in Okinawa, the Philippines, and Saipan, and some are believed to have participated in intelligence work in mainland China. Culturally, it supported the Third Force magazines and publishers such as the Union Press and the Freedom Press as its main propaganda efforts against communism in East Asia. However, the military aspect of the Third Force was rarely mentioned in Third Force publications.

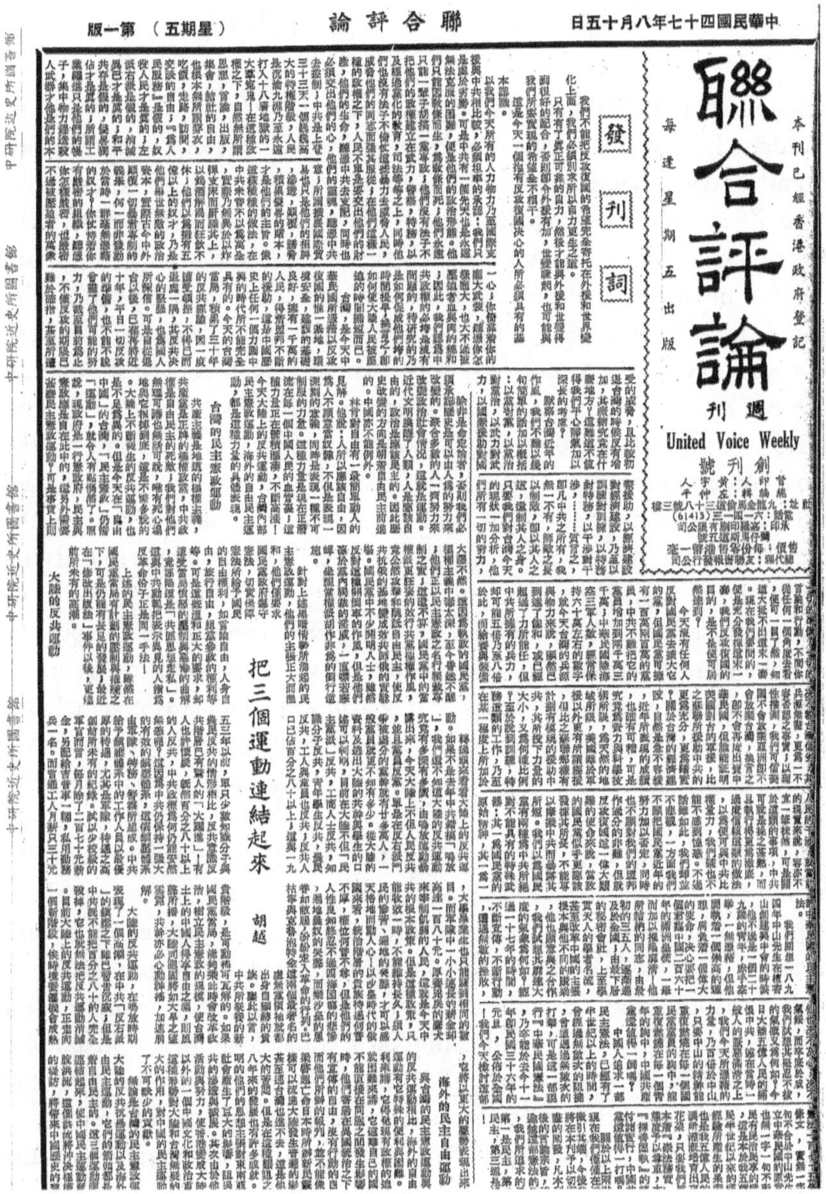

中華民國四十七年八月十五日　聯合評論　（星期五）第一版

本刊已經香港政府登記

聯合評論

週刊

United Voice Weekly

創刊號

每逢星期五出版

發刊詞

台灣的民主憲政運動

把三個運動連結起來

胡越

海外的民主自由運動

大陸的反共運動

FIGURE 2.2 Cover of the inaugural issue of *Lianhe Pinglun*, August 15, 1958.

ZIYOU ZHENXIAN (FREEDOM FRONT) AND THE THIRD FORCE

In 1949, when Li Zongren was in Guangzhou serving as acting ROC president, he gave the China Youth Party and China Democratic Socialist Party 20,000 yuan, which the China Youth Party used to establish *Ziyou Zhenxian*. The magazine also received substantial support from U.S. diplomat Phillip Jessup through the Asia Foundation.[19] The main goal for most Third Force publications was to mobilize people who shared the intent of reunifying and democratizing China. *Ziyou Zhenxian* was no exception. Created on December 3, 1949, and shut down in June 1958, *Ziyou Zhenxian* was clear on the Third Force's definition and agenda. In the first few issues, authors were eager to lay out plans for the Third Force. One author, Zhang Yizhi, said that the goals could be divided into short term, medium term, and long term. For the near future, the objective should focus on taking down the CCP regime and reunifying China (figure 2.3). After achieving that, the agenda should proceed to its medium-term goal: to establish democracy and freedom for the people. Last, the ultimate goal should be to establish world peace through eradicating authoritarianism in the world. *Ziyou Zhenxian* was a vehicle for achieving these goals. Besides seeking an alternate path between the two parties, the Third Force also attempted to "create a new road between capitalism and socialism."[20]

Ziyou Zhenxian's editors explained that the Third Force movement's fundamental ideals lay in "political democracy," "economic equality," and "cultural freedom."[21] They hoped to form an independent anticommunist force outside of the KMT that could take up the responsibility of retaking China and rebuilding a new China that could achieve their societal ideals, which included democracy, equal economic distribution, and freedom in all walks of life.[22] Most writers also shared the view that both the KMT and the CCP were unacceptable as a governing regime of China because of their authoritarian nature and lack of tolerance for dissenting views.[23]

The editors of *Ziyou Zhenxian* also admitted that the movement was still in its early stages. In the third issue, they reviewed the development of the Third Force movement and the status of *Ziyou Zhenxian* since its establishment:

FIGURE 2.3 A riddle by Yu Tian published in *Freedom Front*, June 4, 1952. The answer is *Lian He Qing Gong* (Unite to exterminate the communists!).

Our first issue discussed the past discourse [on democratic movement] and analyzed the term "Third Force," affirming its existence and forecasting its development in the future. This time period can be called the gestation period. In our second issue, many readers and writers responded to the Third Force movement, enthusiastically discussing the Third Force's mission, responsibility, and other questions like organization and leadership. This time period can be called the period of discussion and debate. From today forward, the Third Force must move forward to the period of theorization and actions.[24]

A letter written by a former civil servant in Shanghai who escaped to Hong Kong in 1951 praised *Ziyou Zhenxian* for having very practical content regarding actions and organization beyond just abstract ideas, which were useful to people in Hong Kong who were uncertain about their future. In reply, the editors said that the Third Force movement was established to promote democracy and freedom and to fight against totalitarianism.[25] However, the editors' reply shows that even after almost two years of operation, the Third Force leadership on the cultural front lacked a formal organization and still remained at the stage of discussion and networking. It functioned more as a forum for former escapees to share sentiments about China and Hong Kong than as an action group ready to engage in warfare with the PRC.

As for reactions to the Third Force, at the beginning the KMT wanted to build a united front with the movement and tried to co-opt it. The KMT at first harbored hopes of cooperation with the Third Force toward the common goal of overthrowing the CCP. The KMT sent Lei Zhen to Hong Kong twice to gather information and attempt to unite the Third Force with the KMT, but to no avail. By the end of 1951, the KMT's attitude shifted. As reflected in *Ziyou Zhenxian*, many contributors remained critical of the KMT and its authoritarian rule, refusing to collaborate the KMT to fight against the CCP. The KMT instead began plotting ways to sabotage and suppress the movement, including infiltrating it with special operatives.[26] In the Central Reform Committee meeting on April 30, 1951, the KMT had decided to take on a new approach of "bundle" (*lianhe*), "divide" (*fenhua*), and "crack down" (*daji*), meaning that it would no longer tolerate views critical of the KMT. After that, the KMT tried to isolate those Third Force members who were unwilling to show loyalty to the KMT.[27] This approach could be one reason why from that point until the end of the first stage of the Third Force movement most publications, including *Ziyou Zhenxian*, remained hostile and critical of Chiang Kai-shek's regime and the editors did not consider joining the KMT as an option.

NON-ELITE WRITERS IN THE EARLY STAGE OF THE THIRD FORCE

Most of the scholarship of the Third Force focuses on its leadership and the role of the United States in sponsoring their activities. But the renowned intellectuals who served as editors and regular writers for Third Force publications were not the only participants in the movement. While the intellectuals mostly wrote about what their future China should look like, the individuals who best illustrate the particular kind of diasporic consciousness that took root in Hong Kong were the nameless exiled contributors who wrote about their restlessness, dislocation, and mixed sense of belonging toward Hong Kong. These people yearned to live in the Free World and were easily persuaded by the Cold War rhetoric about Communist China. They were also dislocated by the political turmoil in China as well as the Cold War. Through their articulations, we can see a deep concern for democracy and a vision for Hong Kong as the base of an anticommunist reunification movement. Even though the original intention of most Third Force publications was to discuss strategies for an anticommunist reunification movement, the editors also received requests from readers to provide a space for their contributions. *Ziyou Zhenxian*, along with *Zhongguo Zhisheng*, included a section for readers' letters. Many of these submissions were written by recent escapees and migrants from mainland China. The following is a letter written by a reader who expresses a thrill upon discovering that *Ziyou Zhenxian* would soon arrive in Hong Kong:

> Recently I came to this small island (*xiaodao*) from the mainland. Even though I can breathe in the sea breeze of freedom, my lifeless heart had an iron door that was tightly locked. Luckily, one day I found Freedom Front. How strange! Only after flipping through a few pages, it seemed as though my eyes were pulled by some magnetic force. They are glued to it, and I can't get them off [the magazine]. After a few more glimpses, it was as if the sky has cleared after the rain. The frustration in my heart was suddenly all gone. Just like that, it was as if I were an old boat in the ocean discovering the lighthouse. Actually, [*Ziyou Zhenxian*] has given me a great deal of courage and hope. Before I had thought that I would be enslaved for the rest of my life. Who knew that there is actually a new world (*xin tiandi*) outside all of this!"[28]

Like this writer, many readers of Third Force magazines published in the early 1950s found a new purpose in life. Submitting articles or letters to *Ziyou Zhenxian* and other Third Force magazines became an important way to vent their frustrations over being in a foreign place. While the elites had used the publications to organize their political campaign against the CCP, the nonelite contributors who had just arrived in Hong Kong used the magazines as platforms to express their anxieties surrounding the uncertainty of their lives and China's future.

The sense of community created through letter exchanges and article submissions was especially important for the people residing in Rennie's Mill Refugee Camp. As mentioned in chapter 1, the Hong Kong government originally planned to place these refugees in the camp temporarily before transferring them to Taiwan, but owing to the KMT's suspicions of migrants and the overflow of applications, ultimately only a small number of the inmates were eventually allowed to enter Taiwan.[29] From 1949 to the early 1960s, migrants who escaped from Communist China and did not have relatives in Hong Kong went to Rennie's Mill for refuge, only to find that it was very difficult to obtain the entry permit to Taiwan. Moreover, the KMT-sponsored FCRA maintained strict censorship within the camp. As a result, some residents became very disillusioned with the KMT. Their writings can be found in the Letters sections of these magazines. They mostly used pen names for fear of being identified. Most of these authors do not appear to have had direct connections with the leaders because they belonged to a different social class in Hong Kong and to distinctive social circles. From their writings, we can see that their concerns were quite unlike those of the Third Force leaders and editors of the magazines.

The young inmates in Rennie's Mill were often thirsty for materials that discussed Chinese politics in a critical way. As Li Minde, a camp resident, said in a letter published in *Zhongguo Zhisheng*, "Hong Kong is the window of democracy (*minzhu de chuangkou*) where you can find many different kinds of publications with a variety of viewpoints. But in Rennie's Mill we can only find *Xianggang Shibao* [The Hong Kong Times] and *Ziyouren* [two publications in Hong Kong that contain some critiques of the KMT but were more moderate than most Third Force publications]. The first few issues of Voices of China were sold here, but soon after that they could not be found anymore."[30]

Most of the inmates of Rennie's Mill in the early 1950s could work outside the camp in the daytime, so they did have access to other publications, but they were not allowed to read or distribute them publicly inside the camp. Li was upset mainly because he did not expect the KMT would go so far as to restrict people's freedom in the refugee camp. In contrast, Hong Kong at large was to him "a place of freedom" where all kinds of viewpoints were allowed.

Li's article also reveals his dissatisfaction with being in Rennie's Mill. He mentions that if refugees wanted to apply to go to Taiwan, their cases would be handed over to special agents from Taiwan for evaluation. According to Li, these agents often judged the refugees' applications based on their moods and likings. They were even sometimes bribed by inmates with a few cups of milk or other material rewards. If a special agent of the KMT learned about an inmate's complaint, the inmate with the grievance would be labeled "Third Force" and later reported to the authorities at the camp. He would be blacklisted and lose all chance of going to Taiwan for the rest of his life.[31]

Historian Dominic Yang, who has written about Rennie's Mill, also mentions the infiltration of special agents inside the camp. According to Yang, these agents purportedly paid residents to report on so-called disloyal actions, such as supporting the Third Force, thus poisoning the atmosphere within the camp with suspicion. Because of the close surveillance, residents of Rennie's Mill had to select carefully what they read—if caught reading *Ziyou Zhenxian*, *Duli Luntan*, or *Zhongguo Zhisheng*, they would certainly be accused of having Third Force sympathies.[32]

A number of residents eventually left Rennie's Mill because of political suppression. One of them, Zhang Kun, said he chose to leave despite financial difficulties because he "loved freedom and could not tolerate the inhumane kind of life" in the camp.[33]

It is through the Third Force magazines that we have a glimpse of the lives of the lower-class escapees from China. Besides complaining about the tight political control inside the camp, some articles and letters published in *Ziyou Zhenxian* and *Zhongguo Zhisheng* indicate a gradual loss of faith in the ability of the KMT to lead the reunification campaign. One article says:

> The struggle against the CCP is no small matter. Before, Hong Kong people only rely on other people to fulfill this dream. But because of the international situation it is being put off again and again. Now that three years have passed, people's feelings have changed. Those who care about the international situation would at least realize that this anti-communist

struggle is the duty of every single individual. Before, people put too much hope on Taiwan to take up the mission. Now, it has proven that what Taiwan can take up is just so pathetically little.[34]

This critique of the ROC government for not helping the escapees from mainland China residing in Hong Kong touched on a consistent theme that transcended the boundary between the elite editors and the lower class writers in these Third Force magazines.

Disappointment with the KMT led many new migrants to reexamine their existence in Hong Kong. A number of writers express a sense of being stranded in what they saw as a border zone between the PRC and Taiwan. As one explained: "Because [Hong Kong] is located between the mainland and Taiwan, on the one hand its free atmosphere makes many people feel warm and fuzzy, but on the other hand a foreign place is ultimate not somewhere one feels belonged. For many people, all they can think about is: when is this life of vagrancy going to end?" Another letter echoed this frustration: "We cannot go back to the mainland, and we cannot enter Taiwan, then should we jump into the sea and drown ourselves?"[35]

Many authors in similar situations used the term *gudao*—meaning a lonely/isolated island—in referring to Hong Kong. *Gudao* was also used to refer to the International Settlement in Shanghai between 1937 and 1941, where business and culture flourished despite the Japanese occupation of the surrounding areas. By calling Hong Kong a "*gudao*," the writers highlighted the city's political isolation since the Communists took over the mainland, as well as their own sense of loneliness. At the same time, *gudao* reminded readers that Hong Kong was the opposite of Taiwan, which was known as "*baodao*," the island of treasure.

If read carefully, the articles indicate a shift in diasporic consciousness among the writers for the Third Force in around 1952, as many Chinese became more disillusioned with the KMT and the possibility of settling in Taiwan. Some writers thus adjusted their attitude toward Hong Kong, as the author of an essay about Hong Kong since 1949 published that year writes:

Three years ago, many people in Hong Kong wanted to return to China, because they heard from others that the CCP was not that bad, so this made those who had stayed in Hong Kong for an extended period of time yearn to go back to check out the situations. Today, people in Hong Kong would only go back to the mainland if the CCP is ousted, or else they would rather stay on this poor lonely island (*gudao*). This is a change of heart. If we take this as a joke then it may just be a kind of wishful thinking. But if we are serious about it, then we can say that the change of mind is the binnacle pointing to a new direction of our times (*shidai fangxiang de luopanzhen*).[36]

The "new direction" here could mean the determination to wait for regime change in China or the willingness to settle in Hong Kong. It is more likely the latter, as the author continues to elaborate on the sense of disillusionment shared by many KMT supporters who had originally hoped to go to Taiwan: "The loyal subjects from the mainland had different views than the people in Hong Kong; all they wanted was to go to Taiwan, but their good intention was rejected. In the past three years, how many people with dreams, ambitions and willingness to sacrifice for the nation and for the people were locked out of the 'treasure island' of Taiwan!" Finally, the author concludes that Taiwan may not be the ideal destination after all, even for anticommunists: "Now, after three years, people are planning long term; there are very few who want to go to Taiwan at all. This is a 180-degree change from three years ago. They are right, if you are anti-Communist, it doesn't matter where you are."[37]

When these new immigrants discussed Hong Kong in optimistic terms, they often called the city the "window of democracy" (*minzhu zhi chuang*). It is a term that had appeared in publications since the 1940s, when the Civil War broke out. As a metaphor for Hong Kong, it symbolized the differences between the colonial city and the mainland under Communist rule. Some migrants took this imagination further, claiming that Hong Kong could eventually democratize the mainland. For example, a self-proclaimed exiled youth wrote:

We are a group of exiled youth who escaped from China. To pursue our dreams and recover our freedom, we had to leave our home sorrowfully, give up our education, and go through a great deal of hardship to get away from the brutal Communist rule and come to Hong Kong. In this remaining land of freedom we hope to find a group of young friends who are rational and ambitious to form a convention of Chinese youths. We will use our passion to water the budding flowers of democracy and freedom, so that these flowers will also blossom all over China and let the fragrance of the winter rain wash away the bloodshed in the mainland."[38]

Hong Kong, to this author, had the potential to be the base where aspiring Chinese youths gathered and from which they could eventually democratize China. These writers, who also used pseudonyms like those who submitted letters, may not have been Rennie's Mill inmates, since their writings were directed much more at the lofty goal of retaking China. Rennie's Mill inmates tended to be more concerned about their own personal future. Along the same lines, a student named Li Hao at United College wrote a letter to the Youth Forum of the *Zhongguo Zhisheng* saying: "Since the CCP swept across Mainland China, the new force of democracy and freedom (*minzhu ziyou de liliang*) has gradually lightened up the pinball-sized city of Hong Kong (*xianggang danwan zhidi*). This of course symbolizes that China will have unlimited hope. This is also something that we all feel fortunate to have." The same author also called for an expansion of the Youth Forum section in the publication so that readers in Hong Kong could network with other youths in the city and in other countries to discuss social issues.[39]

Some more ambitious activists wanted to take this beyond the Third Force publications. In the special issue on the third anniversary of *Zhongguo Zhisheng*, a contributor, probably a woman activist in the movement, wrote:

> We cannot deny that the special environment of Hong Kong has made many young women silent and ignorant in politics. How many young women are lured by materialism, wallowing in the luxury of nightlife, forgetting the nation? And how many young women, restrained and oppressed by family and society, do not dare to talk about politics? This has made women today lazy (*lansan*), degenerate (*duoluo*) and apathetic (*mamu*).

The author then articulated what she thought Hong Kong had to offer: "Hong Kong is situated outside the bamboo curtains of Taiwan and the mainland. Only here can we find the fresh air of freedom! Only here can we do what we have always wanted to do." Furthermore, the author believed that it was in Hong Kong that young women could improve themselves and enhance the Third Force movement: "We have to fight for social welfare for women, so that women who are in exile in Hong Kong can have a place to settle. We also should set up education and vocational trainings for women, so that women can develop physically and mentally, use their abilities fully, and give their best to the movement."[40]

Before 1952, many escapees from China were hoping to go to Taiwan. After that, they saw Hong Kong as a place to settle down and carry on their activism. Their perception of Hong Kong was affected by the political attitude of the ROC regime in Taiwan and whether they had a chance of moving elsewhere. Overall, the attitudes of new migrants' sense of home in the early 1950s were unstable. We can see that more and more writers blamed the KMT for their stranded existence, while the more optimistic ones praised Hong Kong as a place of democracy and freedom that had surpassed Taiwan under KMT rule. The most radical ones were eager to transform the city to become a powerhouse for the democratization of China. There was also a strong emphasis on what young people (*qingnian*) could do in the future. However, none of these writers seem to have been connected to the editorial boards of the publications. Although some of them identified as "students" and "intellectuals," they were mostly poor and had to take low-paying jobs, such as custodial or factory work, to survive. From their writings, we see most of these young people slowly developing a sense of affinity toward Hong Kong, but ultimate goal was to join a bigger force beyond what they could find in Hong Kong to retake China.

THE SECOND STAGE, 1958-1963

LIANHE PINGLUN (UNITED VOICE WEEKLY)

Even though in the early 1950s the Third Force enjoyed significant U.S. support, the intensification of the Cold War following the Korean War prompted the U.S. government to shift most of its funding to the KMT regime in Taiwan in the mid-1950s.[41] The removal of financial support by the United States was arguably the most important factor in the shift of direction in the Third Force movement. It was a time when there was a competition in using education as a means to attract students. In 1953, the PRC government also attempted to entice Chinese youth in Southeast Asia to return to China. In response to this, the board of Yale-China decided to invest in a campaign to promote educational opportunity. The Ford Foundation also believed that supporting education was the best means of combating the appeal of communism.[42] Following this trend, the State Department began to direct most of its funds to education for overseas Chinese. As a result of this shift, funding for the Third Force movement was cut significantly. Some historians even argue that the Third Force failed by 1954 because of the pullout of U.S. support.[43] Before long, *Ziyou Zhenxian* was forced to cease publication.[44]

Although *Ziyou Zhenxian* was disbanded because of the lack of foreign support, some Third Force leaders continued to use their own money to start other publications, such as *Lianhe Pinglun*, which was operated in a different funding model than *Ziyou Zhenxian*. Because they lacked outside financial support, the founders of the *Lianhe Pinglun*, such as Zuo Shunsheng, were forced to reach deep into their own pockets to fund printing and distribution. Its early funding came from a monthly donation of HK$700 by Zhang Fakui, HK$500 from both the Independent Press and the Union Press, and also funds from other founders—Zuo Shunsheng, Li Huang, Huang Yuren, Luo Yongyang, Liu Yulue, and Leng Jingji—some of whom were active in the previous stage of the Third Force movement. Others joined anew after a long hiatus from politics. Like other publications in this stage of the Third Force movement, *Lianhe Pinglun* was beset by financial constraints; in 1957, the Independent Press stopped its financial support because of decreased aid from the United States, and in 1963 the Union Press also completely cut off its funds.[45]

The change in the Third Force movement in Hong Kong may also have to do with the colonial government's trend of neutralizing the residents' political affiliations in Hong Kong beginning around 1956–1957. The Hong Kong authorities placed stricter restrictions on political organizations and activities and began to emphasize a stance of political neutrality. In terms of readership, like *Ziyou Zhenxian* and other Third Force publications in the first stage of the movement, *Lianhe Pinglun* was still read by overseas Chinese in America and was translated into English by the American consulate in Hong Kong for the U.S. State Department.[46] Nevertheless, there were fewer non-elite contributors in *Lianhe Pinglun*, and as time progressed, fewer readers' voices were heard in the later issues.

The content of *Lianhe Pinglun* was also affected by the withdrawal of U.S. funding. The lack of U.S. support affected how the Third Force positioned itself. While condemnation of totalitarianism continued to be the most prevalent theme throughout the *Lianhe Pinglun*'s run, leaders of the Third Force in the second stage were split on how the movement should proceed as they became steadily warier of the U.S. State Department's motives, some even going so far as to say the United States had become an obstacle to their vision of national reunification.

Lianhe Pinglun was launched in the midst of the Anti-Rightist Campaign on the mainland in 1957–1959 as a reaction against the Hundred Flowers Campaign, which had encouraged pluralism and even criticism of the government. The anti-rightists purged about 300,000 Chinese, most of whom were critics or intellectuals whom the Communist Party deemed to have rightist or capitalist tendencies or who opposed party policies such as land reform and collectivization.

Like the first stage, the editors of the publications still felt that the crucial, fatal weakness of the CCP was manifested in the totalitarian nature of the regime that had been built on the back of the Chinese people. In the introductory remarks published in *Lianhe Pinglun*'s first issue, the editors stated:

> [The CCP] has no other option but to construct the regime on military might, police, special operatives, and education that has been molded according to the party.... Under this kind of regime, people not only have to hand over their property and lives, and allow the CCP to allocate things, but at the same time they must also hand over their hearts, their souls, and allow the CCP to control them.[47]

Some contributors argued that the CCP would not be sustainable in the long run, because it did not have the people's mandate. For example, one anonymous contributor remarked that there had been widespread disappointment and a decrease in support among youths for the CCP since it took power. The author believed that a totalitarian regime requires a passionate nationalism to bolster its power and enable it to continue its reign; thus the decrease in support showed that there was a lack of enthusiasm for the country that had put the regime's survival at stake.[48] After the Anti-Rightist Campaign began, a number of articles pointed to the widespread public dissatisfaction and internal strife as indicators of the regime's volatility. One critic named Na Lan said the campaign exposed the weakness of the CCP—not only was it suffering from deteriorating party discipline and cohesion but there was also a staggering loss of faith among the people in the party ideology. Even though the Anti-Rightist Campaign and other purges had made further outright protests difficult, Na Lan believed that citizens had already found other more passive means to undermine the state, such as deliberately spoiling crop yields.[49]

Another critic with the penname of Tian Xin contended that despite the tight control the party still maintained over the mainland populace, the lack of structural integrity at the top, as reflected in in the Anti-Rightist Campaign, marked a significant weakness that could lead to the CCP's downfall.[50] These writings indicate that many people who wrote for *Lianhe Pinglun* continued to believe that public support was necessary to a political regime's sustainability.

Building on that idea about public support, many also viewed democracy to be of the utmost importance in a modern society. As one author remarks, "modern civilization has roused people; people should be free, and politics should be democratic. Therefore, the direction in which history is changing is toward freedom and democracy. China cannot be an exception."[51] Even among authors who did not express such optimistic sentiments so explicitly, there was a shared belief in the need for democracy in the struggle to reunify the country. In nearly every article discussing fighting back against the CCP, democracy was considered an essential part of the equation. The exiled elites who contributed to the Third Force magazines believed that democracy was the foundation to a modern society and continued to characterize the CCP as authoritarian, and that was the main reason they believed it was illegitimate and needed to be removed from power.

While most *Lianhe Pinglun* contributors still supported the overarching anti-CCP stand and called for democratizing China, signs of insecurity intensified after the decrease of U.S. support. About two years after the establishment of the second stage of the Third Force movement, as revealed in the debates over how to go about fighting against the CCP, Third Force leaders became divided over where the base of the movement should be, overseas or Taiwan. The discussion about the base of the movement illustrates that while most of the leaders were still using Hong Kong as a location to write and publish, the landscape of the Chinese democratic movement that started in the Southern Periphery was actually global.

BUILDING A NEW BASE FROM OVERSEAS?

Decreased support from the United States also meant that Third Force leaders had to find new ways to sustain the movement politically. The most obvious political entity to rely on was the KMT. However, the more radical contributors of *Lianhe Pinglun* were disillusioned with the KMT that the party was concerned only about expanding the party while failing to capitalize on opportunities to reunify the country and they believed that they needed to build a new base for a counterattack on their own merits.

Xie Yufa, one of the regular writers of *Lianhe Pinglun*, who moved from Hong Kong to the United States in 1958, focused on the role of overseas Chinese.[52] He was confident in the organizing power of overseas Chinese students. In a 1961 article, Xie argued that overseas Chinese had developed a strong sense of national identity and home that derived from the diasporic sentiment of "having a home but not being able to go back" (*youjia gui bude*). In this article, he demonstrated deep disappointment with the KMT and believed that overseas students shared his view that the ROC regime was failing their expectations of retaking China. He wrote: "if the national government actually launches a counterattack but is completely defeated, we would rather have the CCP annex Taiwan than suffer the current half-dead, half-alive state of Taiwan." In Xie's eyes, the PRC was a disaster waiting for the straw that will break the camel's back, and therefore he did not see any reason why the KMT would not take action.[53] These students in exile would be perfect candidates to be the new leaders of the Third Force. Xie returned repeatedly to the idea of a revolution led by overseas Chinese in later issues. During the few years he lived in the United States, he saw the international community of diasporic Chinese gradually gaining more awareness of the Third Force, and he felt buoyed by this increase in attention. He viewed the movement as unstoppable and, indeed, as the only real force left after the hopes for the KMT in Taiwan and Hong Kong had diminished. He contended that some Chinese students studying in the United States had started joining anti-CCP activities, forming secret connections with compatriots still in mainland China. He had confidence that such overseas students would rise to the occasion when the time arrived to reclaim China.[54]

This view, although not very popular among Third Force leaders and writers, was echoed by some overseas students. Ouyang Fang, apparently a student activist studying abroad, wrote an open letter about building a communal fellowship among like-minded overseas Chinese: "We who reside overseas and struggle for ideals are not at all lonely, because even though we in this young group have never met, justice and ideals act as an amorphous, powerful current that has long since allowed us to closely connect."[55]

Third Force leader Huang Yuren also believed that Chinese students abroad in the United States could lead the anti-CCP democratic reunification movement.[56] He provided several reasons for that. First, the student exchange programs with the United States had concentrated the most outstanding members of the young generation of Chinese. Second, he argued that because the United States was the leader of the Free World and home to the UN headquarters, Chinese exchange students in the United States enjoyed geographical advantages and convenience in promoting foreign awareness and striving for international sympathy. Third, because these students had already been living in a successful democracy, they would be more ready to respond to any setbacks. To Huang, if there was to be an overseas Chinese alliance, Chinese students in America must be at the forefront. While Huang and other writers who saw the potential Chinese students in the United States were distrustful of the KMT and the U.S. government, they believed that overseas Chinese students were more intellectually and politically equipped to lead the anticommunist movement than the people residing in Hong Kong.

One major factor that made these Third Force activists decide to break away from the KMT was its reliance on the United States and the signing of the Sino-American Mutual Defense Treaty in 1954, which some activists believed had prevented the ROC government from initiating military actions against the PRC. A number of authors began to question the role of the United States as being a hindrance for the KMT to launch a military campaign against the PRC. In an article responding to recent moves by the ROC legislature in 1962 to consider amending the Sino-American Mutual Defense Treaty, the author, Xu Ziyou, said that if the treaty was amended, then one concrete barrier obstructing national reunification would be removed. Furthermore, Xu argued that the KMT would no longer be able to hide behind the United States as an excuse to keep from fighting back against the CCP. To Xu, the KMT was not trustworthy and might still find other excuses for maintaining the status quo even if the amendments were passed.[57] Another article published in the same year expressed similar concerns about the ROC's inaction. The author argued that the problem of U.S. aid posed a paradox for the ROC: Without U.S. aid, the ROC was not strong enough to reunify the country, but acceptance of U.S. aid brought with it many political implications, chief among them an expectation that the ROC could not move unilaterally without consent from the United States. The pact with the United States created a significant restriction on the ROC's freedom to launch a counterattack.[58] In the end, the mutual security treaty was not amended and stayed in force until the 1970s. Overall, there was a consensus among the more radical contributors of *Lianhe Pinglun* who insisted on an independent Third Force movement that a military campaign was necessary if the ultimate goal was to reunify China. These examples show that even in the midst of the Cold War in the late 1950s and early 1960s, there were people in the Southern Periphery voicing *fangong*/anti-CCP opinions not in line with the rhetoric of the KMT and even challenged the leadership role of the United States in fighting against the CCP. To them, the *fangong* movement was a local one among Chinese people in China and overseas, and it should be disentangled with the global Cold War.

RECONCILING WITH THE KMT?

Nevertheless, the arguments for military mobilization led by overseas Chinese largely fell flat. The prospects of turning the Third Force into a party that could surpass the KMT also became increasingly bleak because of the improvement of the relationship between the United States and the ROC. By 1958, the more practical individuals among the Third Force leadership began to realize that crafting a truly independent alternate path was no longer feasible.[59] The majority of Third Force authors instead argued vigorously in favor of a KMT-directed counterattack against the CCP, likely viewing it as their best, most realistic option.

By the late 1950s, the majority of the Third Force intellectuals started to harbor hopes of becoming part of the ROC political landscape. Consequently, some Third Force leaders took as their motto "Politically opposing the mainland, democratically reforming Taiwan" (*zhengzhi fangong dalu, minzhugaizao Taiwan*). The decision to choose to work beside the KMT rather than against it marked a clear departure from the past.[60] The author viewed prospects for national reunification as very promising: "I believe Taiwan will before long become a base that will use true freedom and democracy to rouse people domestically and abroad to cause the CCP to disintegrate, to fight back, and to reunify the country . . . so I am still very optimistic for the future of the democratic movement, and I am still very confident in the future of the ROC."[61]

A major criticism of the KMT was its lack of determination to fight a war with the CCP. The more hawkish members of the Third Force wanted the KMT to launch a military campaign against the PRC because they held that overthrowing the CCP regime should be the number-one priority. Liu Yulue established himself most notably in articles that provided detailed plans for KMT military action. Critical of the United States, he believed that the KMT must move to reunify the country using an approach that "relies on one's own strengths" (*zili gengsheng*) rather than wait for international support.[62] His later article built on this conclusion to frame a specific opportunity the KMT could use to gain a foothold on the mainland. In an article explaining how Taiwan should launch a military campaign, he advocated what he called a "partial counterattack" (*jubu fangong*) in deference to Taiwan's military reality. He suggested mobilizing only one-third of the 600,000 troops available in a concentrated strike strategy so that even if it suffered losses, it would not wipe out the military completely.[63] In another article, Liu suggested the KMT could take advantage of the mainland's many minority communities' marginalization and their lack of strong allegiance to the PRC. He aimed to send the KMT's air force and navy to the peripheral regions to provide the minority communities with military aid so that they could also join the fight against the CCP.[64] Liu clearly believed that the people in China were on the side of the KMT and that the widespread resentment against the CCP after the Anti-Rightist Campaign could serve as an opportunity for the KMT to network with oppressed groups in the PRC to achieve its reunification goal.

The majority of the *Lianhe Pinglun* editors and contributors wanted to reconcile with the KMT. They expressed dismay at the faults of the KMT and Chiang's rule but also acknowledged that, given the circumstances, the KMT was their best option. As one author summed up this sense of pragmatism: "Taiwan is the Republic of China's only base for counterattack and national reunification" (*fangong fuguo de weiyi jidi*).[65] Shifting from his earlier stand about seeking a third path, Li Huang alluded to the idea of the Republic of China in his article "No One Is as Patriotic as Me." Li seemed conflicted as he explicitly referenced the Third Force throughout the piece and identified himself with that movement, but at the end of the article, he concluded that since after all these years of turmoil the beloved Republic of China was still led by a legitimate government, the KMT, it might be the best and most feasible solution to have a national reunification under a reformed KMT government instead of toppling it and starting from scratch.[66]

Nevertheless, there was one caveat—the KMT needed to undergo political reform. In the issues between 1960 and 1963, a number of writers launched complaints about the KMT. The main complaints included the KMT's lack of determination to achieve national reunification and its authoritarian rule.[67] One regular contributor, Li Yansheng, leveled some heavy accusations at Taiwan, viewing the KMT administration as ineffectual and power-hungry. He argued that although Chiang Kai-shek had been announcing grand plans for national reunification since the Civil War began, nothing had come to fruition after ten years. For that reason, Li Yansheng no longer had much faith in the KMT and believed that Chiang was strengthening his grip on power under the guise of preparing Taiwan to mount a counterattack. In Li Yansheng's words, "Fighting back against the mainland is the best excuse to justify Mr. Chiang's desire for reelection as president."[68] He believed Chiang was more interested in personal power in Taiwan than in national reunification. Most other writers were less harsh on Chiang and the KMT than Li Yansheng was, but as the publication continued, the writers' calls for Taiwan to democratize grew in intensity.

As a prerequisite for retaking China, Zuo Shunsheng, who continued to play a leading role in the second stage of the Third Force movement, advocated for the KMT to undergo political reform in order to further unify the people. A key concern of Zuo Shunsheng's revolved around the suppression of opposition parties under the KMT, which resonated with critiques made by the China Youth Party a few decades earlier. In an article he wrote in 1958, Zuo mused over the lack of strong opposition parties in the Republican era, taking a historical view of Chinese history after the fall of the Qing dynasty. To Zuo, a major obstacle to the KMT's democratization was Chiang Kai-shek's multiple presidential terms.[69] Other *Lianhe Pinglun* writers also believed that political reform of the KMT was a prerequisite to any expedition against the CCP. Li Jinye, an occasional contributor, argued that democratization of the ROC was necessary for national reunification. In one article, Li Jinye argued that the fates of both the CCP and KMT rested in their respective modes of governance—the CCP's international isolation stemmed from the regime's refusal to respect human rights, whereas the crux of the KMT's failures in fighting the CCP lay in its lack of democracy.[70] Another author expounded on the feeling that Chiang would need to change to meet the demands of the people, declaring, "I believe that through free speech's rousing and supervision of the masses, there will ultimately come a day when the Taipei establishment will undergo a great awakening."[71]

The case of Lei Zhen (Lei Chen) became another rallying point for the writers of *Lianhe Pinglun* to come together. Lei Zhen was a cofounder and editor of *Ziyou Zhongguo* (Free China Journal), a KMT-sponsored publication created to serve as a forum for free thought and discussion around opposition to the PRC, which soon also became quite critical of the KMT. Lei was expelled from the Kuomintang in 1954 as a result. In 1960, he founded the China Democratic Party with other politicians. In September of the same year, Lei Zhen and other staff members of *Ziyou Zhongguo* were arrested on charges of fomenting rebellion. He was sentenced to ten years' imprisonment, and the publication was shut down. In the eyes of many Third Force leaders, the plight of Lei Zhen represented an assault on the freedom of speech, an ominous precedent for an undemocratic future, and a symbol of the KMT's disastrous mismanagement of the ROC. Contributors to *Lianhe Pinglun* viewed the arrest as an attack on freedom of speech and a major setback in the democratization of the ROC.[72] One author linked the arrest of Lei and others to a concerted effort to weaken opposition parties, saying the case "brazenly ravage[d] newly emerging opposition parties, and it is one-hundred percent a political issue."[73] Zuo also weighed in and said that people should "unite in protest of the KMT's mismanagement of Taiwan and its increasingly authoritarian policies."[74] Li Huang saw a parallel between the CCP and the KMT, accusing the KMT of using the same heavy-handed tactics to oppress the populace.[75] A year later, Li continued to cite the Lei Zhen case in condemning the KMT government's inability to extend freedom of speech to opponents of the regime.[76] The articles the contributors wrote document the changing sentiments toward the KMT regime. While by 1963, most still believed the KMT should lead the reunification movement, they increasingly called for democratization of the regime, citing infringements of freedom of speech and Chiang Kai-shek's authoritarianism as the most urgent issues in need of reform. These voices show that even though the participants in the second stage of the Third Force believed that a compromise was inevitable, they still laid out the prerequisite of democratic political reform before the KMT could take the lead in the anti-CCP movement. They had no illusions that the KMT represented Free China. The writings by these Third Force activists demonstrate that the Cold War was more than just a contest between the CCP and the KMT and it was during this volatile period that many intellectuals saw publications as a platform to remonstrate the KMT or share ideas about what their ideal government model should be.

NARRATIVES ABOUT ESCAPING CHINA

While the two major Third Force publications in the early 1950s provided a platform for new immigrants to voice their frustrations and hopes in the host city, such outlets almost completely vanished by the late 1950s, when most Third Force editors began to think that an anticommunist movement independent of the KMT leadership was no longer feasible. Unlike the earlier publications, *Lianhe Pinglun* did not appear to accommodate viewpoints that dwelled on the psychological ambivalence of exile and the growing attachment of some to the physical space of Hong Kong. There are also differences in terms of how "migrants" were represented. Illegal migration from China became a featured issue in *Lianhe Pinglun* between 1958 and 1962.

Ziyou Zhenxian and *Zhongguo Zhisheng* each had a section featuring readers' contributions, but *Lianhe Pinglun* did not provide much opportunity for its readers to submit articles expressing themselves. Those who wrote for the magazine were mostly its editors or intellectuals with strong political ambitions. Even though there were some testimonies purportedly written and submitted by refugees, the narratives about refugees were formulaic and mainly served to tarnish the reputation of the CCP. There were almost no articles or letters written by residents of Rennie's Mill. The letters to the editors were less about daily challenges facing a new environment. Seldom do we find autobiographical writings by migrants struggling to adapt to the city, let alone transform it. Instead, detailed stories about the perilous escape from the mainland to Hong Kong were prominently featured. Like many propagandistic narratives, the main messages of these stories were the triumph of freedom or the brutality of the CCP. By the early 1960s, the Third Force movement, as represented by the contents of the *Lianhe Pinglun*, had entirely removed itself from the reality of Hong Kong. Most of the writings about the experiences of the escapees were critiques of the worsening political crisis in the mainland and the lack of humanitarian measures aiding the escapees.

A topic to which Hu Yue returned repeatedly was that of exiled students from the mainland. Hu Yue saw these youth activists as the lifeblood of the Third Force, representing a dangerous weakening in the CCP's totalitarian rule, and Hu argued that the Third Force must prioritize aid to these escaped youth.[77] Amid another rush of migration to Hong Kong a few years later, Hu Yue painted these young refugees in shining, hopeful strokes: "The compatriots who fled to Hong Kong, particularly our young friends, magnanimously let out a roar condemning the CCP, entering the anti-CCP national reunification ranks even before their lives have settled and the new environment has become familiar to them."[78]

The wave that arrived Hong Kong in 1958–59 seemed mostly to comprise people fleeing the constraints of the Anti-Rightist Campaign and

CCP dogma. They complained of the CCP's reign of terror, with its totalitarian policies and purges. In their eyes, the CCP simply did not care about the welfare of its people, as demonstrated by the poverty and starvation spreading among the masses.[79]

One student who had survived the journey complained about the lack of information from the outside world, stating that the only media reports they were allowed to read had been sanitized by the party. The student wrote, "Honestly, among the mainland's young students, virtually every single one dreams of Hong Kong and dreams of freedom; the moment they have an opportunity, they will flee the mainland controlled by the CCP toward the free heaven." After characterizing Hong Kong as heaven on earth, however, the student concludes by stating his/her ultimate objective, which is not Hong Kong but rather Taiwan: "I hope that those classmates who are now still in the mainland suffering hardship will be able to escape; everybody can together return to our motherland, the Republic of China, and achieve freedom and happiness."[80] In this account, Hong Kong still represented a place of democracy and freedom, but it was only an "exit" to the Free World rather than a place to dwell. In contrast, Taiwan, or the imaginary future homeland of the Republic of China, was depicted as the happy destination of their journey. Unlike the letters and articles written in the early 1950s, however, these narratives were not concerned about the escapees' psychological well-being after they arrived in Hong Kong. Their descriptions of the past sound more strategic and practical and probably were published because of their propaganda value.

Articles written by the editors on exiled students who fled to Hong Kong in 1958 usually carried a propagandistic tone. In an article describing the plight of the young escapees who wanted to continue their education in Hong Kong, Hu Yue began by exulting the high numbers of young people who had recently fled to Hong Kong, holding these students up as proof that the CCP was losing control over the people. However, Hu urged the KMT to implement concrete policies that would distribute immediate aid to these students. Hu then drew up detailed recommendations for different kinds of students, arguing that the work of procuring assistance for exiled students, especially economic aid, allowed them to stay in Hong Kong, thus striking a heavy blow against the CCP by depleting the regime of the young generation. Furthermore,

Hu noted that special agents sent by the CCP were already in the city searching for these students and attempting to convince or force them to return to the mainland, so it was urgent for the KMT to reach them first.[81]

The exodus of 1962 was much more diverse than the earlier migrations, and more people fled China out of economic necessity than from ideological disagreement. Most accounts about the exodus published in *Lianho Pinglun* followed a storyline like this: the author first talked about the hardships of living in the PRC, then the decision to escape, followed by several failed attempts, and finally success reaching the "paradise" of Hong Kong. For example, one author who may have been a youth leader in the KMT described his process of successfully fleeing mainland China. Although he himself had already left China, in 1950 he returned in order to help his family leave as well. Unfortunately, he was under surveillance by the CCP, and after an intense interrogation, he was made to sign a confession and was imprisoned. After several years, he managed to make his way to Guangzhou and then to Shenzhen, at which point he attempted to cross the Hong Kong–China border. He was caught three times, once by CCP forces and twice by British patrols, but on the fourth try he managed to get through undetected because he was given shelter by farmers. After this very long detailed story of escape, he exclaims that at long last he was able to "conclude [his] thirteen years of hell on earth and embark on the bright path to happiness."[82] In this context, Hong Kong was depicted merely as the "exit" from hell rather than a place to dwell. To these writers, Hong Kong served as a window to the Free World, not a base for political organization.

The entrance of a large number of refugees also set off renewed criticisms directed at the CCP regime. According to most accounts written by escapees who successfully crossed the border, the situation in the mainland had catastrophically declined, leading to true desperation. People were leaving "under threat of death."[83] Some articles served as summaries of the main events that were occurring in mainland China, providing context for the sudden rush of people fleeing China into Hong Kong. Others pieced together testimonies given by the famine refugees, pointing to several different concrete shifts that had rendered staying in the mainland untenable, including people's resulting loss of faith in the CCP as a governing party, shortages of seeds and crop failures, massive deaths from starvation, and steep unemployment.[84]

Zuo Shunsheng saw in the flood of refugees not a group of suffering compatriots, but instead a mass of pawns in a nefarious CCP scheme—meant to overcrowd Hong Kong until it reached a crisis point when "its social order will immediately turn into chaos."[85]

Besides attacking the CCP, contributors to *Lianhe Pinglun* also used the exodus to pressure Taiwan to adopt a more open policy toward refugees. Li Huang wrote a letter accusing Gu Zhenggang, a KMT official in charge of the political refugees from the mainland, of hypocrisy: Hong Kong had recently turned away six escapees from the mainland who came by boat, sending them back home, and in response Gu Zhenggang released a statement condemning Hong Kong for its actions. However, only a year prior, a similar event had unfolded in Taiwan, in which a young Hong Kong citizen, who for whatever reason had been unable to depart with the KMT to Taiwan, repeatedly attempted to enter Taiwan but was caught and deported both times. Li used this example to attack Taiwan's policy excluding most political refugees and concluded that if Taiwan did not shelter them from mainland China, their only escape would be death.[86] He condemned Taiwan for neglecting its responsibility to take in these escapees, remarking the KMT should treat people fleeing from the mainland as ROC citizens and accept them.[87] Such stories about escapees were not genuinely voices of people who were in limbo, but propaganda broadsides criticizing both the CCP and the KMT.

THE INSIGNIFICANCE OF HONG KONG

Unlike the first stage of the Third Force where many writers actively discussed the importance of Hong Kong, few second-stage writers even mentioned where they were located, and neither did they discuss Hong Kong as a location for political organization. The Third Force leaders' own physical location did not matter. Moreover, Hong Kong's significance was largely dismissed in the writings of the second stage, even though *Lianhe Pinglun* and other Third Force magazines were still based there. This lack of reference may reflect the social atmosphere in Hong Kong after the crackdown of the pro-KMT riots in 1956 and the tightening of control over political organizing in Hong Kong that followed. While Hong Kong after 1956 was still a place where such publications could exist without much suppression, it was not seen as a site with potential for political organizing.

One article that explicitly discussed Hong Kong's role in the Third Force movement was written by Huang Yuren.[88] Huang denied the possibility of Hong Kong activists serving the central role of leading the anti-CCP democratic national reunification movement. He remarked, "According to ten years of on the spot experience, I believe Hong Kong can only bear the responsibility of an outpost (*qianshaozhan*), but it is not capable of transforming into a center for mobilization (*fadong de zhongxin*)."[89] It sounds as though Huang had given up on Hong Kong as a base for the movement against Communist China. Or, perhaps, like most Third Force leaders, he never considered Hong Kong a significant place, even though he had spent much of his time there.

The editor/writer who was most enthusiastic about the potential of Hong Kong as a base for the Third Force was Sun Baogang. In 1954–1955, Sun tried to form a political group called the Association for the Study of Democratic Socialism in Hong Kong, but it was banned by the government after a lengthy correspondence between the colonial government and the British Parliament. A letter written by the colonial government states: "Under the Societies Ordinance of H[ong] K[ong], societies ... of more than 10 persons ... must apply [to] obtain registration before they may lawfully function. Sun [Baogang]'s society is likely to be incompatible with peace and good order in the Colony."[90] After the association was banned, Sun took a bleak view of democracy in Hong Kong, as reflected in an essay published in 1963, in which he wrote: "The self-rule movement in Hong Kong" would be doomed like the "democratization movement in China." He said, "China has undergone decades of democracy movement, but we still don't see democracy anywhere; Hong Kong also has been talking about self-governance [*zizhi*] for many years, but we don't really see any signs of it."[91] What he meant by self-governance was for Legislative Council members and Executive Council members to be elected by the people, through a form of universal suffrage. He had been an observer of Hong Kong politics in since the early 1950s, and his later writing shows that his hope for Hong Kong being a democratic city was diminishing.

Nor was Sun Baogang optimistic about the two Chinese party-states. In several of his essays, Sun criticized both the PRC and ROC for their "pseudo-democracy." He believed that true democracy should originate from the political consciousness of the people, and a top-down reform from the government would not suffice. Shifting back to his analysis of Hong Kong, he expressed that the people in Hong Kong at that time still did not have a strong political consciousness, implying that they were not ready for a full democracy.

Sun continued to write about Hong Kong over the next few years. He was especially critical of the tightening of political control by the colonial government. He said:

> There is a very popular saying in Hong Kong ... that Hong Kong is a window of democracy into the Far East. Is this not an enormous joke? Hong Kong is England's colony, the Hong Kong government has absolute power; whatever the Hong Kong government wants, all of Hong Kong people must obey; the Hong Kong government answers to the British government, not to the people of Hong Kong.

The fundamental problem, Sun believed, was that the colonial government did not allow political parties, without which, according to Sun, Hong Kong would not achieve self-governance or democracy. He continued: "We who live in Hong Kong seem to be very free, but in theory, or in spirit, we are captive slaves (*nuli*) who are not free."[92] Regardless of his pessimistic viewpoints, the title of the article, "Let's Discuss Hong Kong's Democratic Self-Governance," was provocative at that time and appears to be his last reflection on the possibility of making Hong Kong the base of a democratization movement. Even though readers' renderings of Hong Kong as a "land of freedom" or revolutionary powerhouse that had filled Third Force publications in the movement's first stage eventually faded by the mid-1960s, this article provides a hint that some people continued to envision an alternative, significant political future for Hong Kong.[93]

THE THIRD FORCE'S LAST BREATH

Despite the shift in elites' views, some readers still looked to the Third Force to bring them hope. For example, one reader who had just fled from China submitted a letter to the editor in 1962 exclaiming, "I escaped from the mainland to find the Third Force." Responding to these readers' high hopes, a flurry of other published pieces rushed to trumpet the unity of the Third Force community. One author emphasized the intimate nature of the Third Force's transnational network, writing, "We who reside overseas and struggle for dreams are not at all lonely, because even though we in this young group have never met, justice (*zhengyi*) and visions (*lixiang*) act as an amorphous, powerful current that has long since allowed us to closely connect."[94] Another author remarked that the Third Force is "growing in the people's flesh and bones" because "it is beloved and welcomed by the people." The author also spoke of the role of recent escapees, saying that "in recent months, many resolute people who escaped from mainland China into Hong Kong did not flee to Hong Kong just for the sake of escaping, but to go outside of China to look for 'the Third Force.'"[95] In an open letter to these recently arrived escapees from mainland China, Hu Yue praised those who dropped everything to join the fight against communism:

> The 100,000 compatriots who fled the mainland not only critically attacked the CCP's political propaganda system, they also inspired confidence in the anti-CCP (*fangong*) camp, adding a troop of youthful, fresh-faced activists to the Chinese who are struggling for freedom. The compatriots who fled to Hong Kong, particularly our young friends, selflessly let out a roar condemning the CCP, joining the anti-CCP national reunification ranks even before their lives have settled and the new environment has become familiar to them.[96]

Nevertheless, Hu Yue praised only those migrants who enthusiastically supported the anti-CCP cause; anyone who continued to dwell on their discomfort in Hong Kong was seen as a weakling. For Hu, the objective was no longer to form a third path for reunification, but to unite with the KMT and overseas Chinese to fight against the CCP.

Other Third Force leaders also weighed in on the issue of what should be prioritized in the national reunification campaign. Liu Yulue wrote a quasi-advice column for young intellectual activists recently arrived in Hong Kong. He instructed readers to take cues from Sun Yat-sen's determination and single-minded persistence in overthrowing the imperial system. He told the exiled youth that, like Sun's determination, they also should take "overthrowing the CCP regime as the prerequisite for national unification and reconstruction (*fuguo jian'guo*); [because] without first overthrowing it, *everything else is out of the question*."[97] Witnessing the dwindling strength of the Third Force, Liu Yulue and other leaders believed that the *fangong*/anti-CCP movement needed to be streamlined and that there should be only one united force that takes overthrowing the CCP regime as their first priority.

Zuo Shunsheng' s final contribution to *Lianhe Pinglun* came in the form of an explanation for its ceasing publication. At this point, he is no longer warning of potential dangers, but rather reflecting on the mission of the Third Force and the fifteen years that have passed since the PRC-ROC split. He rails against the passivity of the KMT and its investment in maintaining the status quo, against the control the United States exerts over Taiwan because of the mutual security treaty, and finally, against the Third Force itself: "From start to end [we] have never been able to change a single aspect of the current political situation, and to go even further, we have not had a bit of use; consequently, we might as well shut down this newspaper."[98] Overall, the Third Force remained a loose alliance formed by intellectuals and never transformed itself into a political party. The leaders performed the role of social commentators but, ultimately, were unable to remain independent of the dynamics of power on the Chinese front of the Cold War.

CONCLUSION

The Third Force movement gradually died down after *Lianhe Pinglun* folded as a result of financial problems and its organizers' diminishing faith in its mission. The scholar, Chen Zhengmao, believes that ineffective leadership and poor organization crippled the movement.[99]

Some leaders rejoined the KMT or even served as important advisers over the next two decades. Others moved abroad and gave up their campaign. It is difficult to determine the whereabouts of the lesser-known writers who contributed to the earlier Third Force publications. Many might have dropped their identity as "exiled students/youths" and assimilated into Hong Kong society.

On the surface, the Third Force just disappeared without achieving much. Its stance was vague beyond purporting to be a third path superior to the CCP and the KMT. As the author Chen Zhengmao said, "Simply calling oneself a force for democracy and freedom is not enough to give an organization a concrete framework and direction."[100] Nevertheless, they represented a concerted effort to find strategies to challenge the CCP and the KMT in the Southern Periphery and beyond. The activists in the Third Force movement were not satisfied with either the CCP or the KMT but were at the same time marginalized by them. This movement also played an important role in cultivating ideas about democratic ideals and constitutional government among Chinese people outside of the PRC border. The Cold War was also a moment when Chinese intellectuals began to ponder what they really wanted for a free "homeland." More important, Third Force publications created a virtual space for migrants to exchange ideas about their identities and communities. Through these magazines, people from different social backgrounds shared their sense of loneliness being stranded and expressed about their ambivalence about home and belonging. The base of the movement was in Hong Kong, but the network was in the broader region of the Southern Periphery and beyond. In their writings, we can see that during the 1950s–1970s, national loyalty and party loyalty were conflicted, and how one could contribute to the nationalistic cause depended on where one was located physically and politically.

Furthermore, to understand the emergence of political consciousness in Hong Kong, we need to dig deeper into history beyond the conventional narrative that Hong Kong identity was formed in the 1970s when the settlers began to develop a sense of belonging in the city. Revisiting developments in the 1950s and 1960s and examining the Third Force movement that connected people in Hong Kong and overseas helps us reflect on how much Hong Kong's political aspirations actually originated from the diasporic consciousness of the exiled people who did not at all feel at ease on this "lonely island." They believed that there was a Free China outside of the PRC border, but in reality they continued to live on the margins physically and politically.

3

CULTURAL REVOLUTION AT SEA

Dead Bodies and Kidnapping in the
Hong Kong Sea Territories

In 2019, during the massive protests in Hong Kong, more than a hundred dead bodies were discovered in Hong Kong waters over the course of a few weeks. News reports stated that the number of corpses exceeded the total number recovered from the sea in Hong Kong in a decade. The dead were mostly treated as suicides, and the bodies were quickly cremated by the police. However, speculation abounded about the identities of the deceased. Because there were Hong Kong residents reportedly missing during the yearlong protests, many people suspected that the floating corpses were those of Hong Kong residents who had been tortured and killed by the police in the detention center in San Uk Leng or in police stations. There were also rumors that some protesters were captured and secretively sent to detention centers in mainland China. Some people also believe that MTR train passengers were killed on August 31, 2019, during a police raid at Prince Edward Station, because the police closed the station for several hours, and some people who had been seen being arrested reportedly remained missing after the raid.[1] One such case involved the discovery of a naked floating body on September 22, 2019, near Yau Tong, in the vicinity of Tseung Kwan O, also known as the Junk Bay, where the former Rennie Mill was located. It was proven on October 11 that the body was that of a fifteen-year-old girl named Chan Yan Lam, who had been missing since September 19, 2019. The police told the public that Chan committed suicide by jumping into the sea after walking barefoot from her school to the shore while taking off all her clothes. The press found out that Chan was a competitive swimmer, and many people found it unconvincing that she would choose to drown herself. Since she had participated in the Anti-Extradition Bill protests since June, her mysterious death raised speculations that she might have been murdered by the police.[2]

The discovery of dead bodies in the sea and the reports of missing people reminded people of the corpses discovered in the territorial waters of Hong Kong between the 1950s and 1970s. *Fangong*/anticommunist feelings developed from the trauma and fear that people experienced and witnessed in Hong Kong during those decades. On the surface, these stories were just about the people who worked in the sea and their uncomfortable work environment—every day the fishermen and oystermen might run into floating corpses, or they risked their lives to work in the sea—but they also reminded the population at large the precarity of being on the fringes of Hong Kong or China, because they may be detained and sent back to China. At the same time, the colonial Hong Kong government would not protect them. In the Southern Periphery, stories about missing people and crimes at sea were particular to Hong Kong because they were mediated by pro-KMT newspapers and publications to provoke anticommunist emotions among the people who lived in or transited through Hong Kong. Thus, Hong Kong served as a stage where real-life horror was played out for propaganda causes. In contrast, these stories seldom appeared in newspapers in Macau, where KMT newspapers did not have a strong presence.

Since the Hong Kong government closed the Shenzhen border in 1950, people began to find alternate routes to cross the borders to evade arrest. Because of the heavily patrolled land border on both sides, some people chose to travel by water. Sampan boats were hired for passage to Hong Kong or Macau along various water routes on both the western and eastern sides of Hong Kong. Some escapees attempted to swim with improvised flotation devices. The water routes were no easier than the land route, however. Water currents were at times fierce, and many people drowned and were unaccounted for. After arriving on the shores of Hong Kong—whether on the west coast of Lau Fau Shan or the east coast of Sai Kung—travelers on the water, like those who crossed by land, also had to find their way to the city.

The coast of Hong Kong occasions a sense of peripherality both among the people who work at sea as well as the population in Hong Kong at large. Oceans or seas are often depicted as a type of natural border separating territories. Yet, the waters surrounding Hong Kong not only divided China and Hong Kong; they have also been sites of horror. They were popular routes of escape for people fleeing the PRC from the 1950s to the early 1980s. Moreover, the water, especially the lower Pearl River connected to the sea territories of Hong Kong, historically, was a convenient place to discard the unwanted. Sometimes corpses were thrown into the Pearl River and washed ashore in Hong Kong or Macau. At the same time, the sea was a worksite for fishermen, oystermen, and other people in coastal communities on both sides of the border. For members of these communities who needed to go out to sea to make a living, border crossing was a daily activity, not a one-time event. The sea thus became prime locations for crimes including kidnapping, robberies, and murders because the areas were not actively patrolled by governments on either side.

The examples of dead and missing bodies highlight the precarious situation on the border of mainland China, in particular in 1968, at the height of the Cultural Revolution, where killings and other crimes were rampant in the territorial waters near Hong Kong. While Hong Kong was not the epicenter of the factional struggles in southern China, the people in Hong Kong experienced the Cultural Revolution in a distinctive way—they were reading news reports of dead bodies and missing people daily; some traveled regularly to the mainland to visit relatives and brought back to Hong Kong horrific stories about the rampages they had witnessed in mainland China. In contrast to their counterparts who resettled in other countries or even in Taiwan, such horrific stories were so ubiquitous and close to home that there was nowhere for the people in Hong Kong to hide. Being right outside the border of mainland China also added a sense of familiarity to the trauma they were experiencing. It reminded those former escapees of what they had gone through before they reached Hong Kong in the not too distant past; the victims of the crimes could also be their loved ones.

Accounts of dead and missing bodies meant a great deal for the people in Hong Kong, surviving on the Southern Periphery, some of whom had recently fled to the colony themselves after having experienced political turmoil in mainland China, in particular during the early years of the Cultural Revolution, when armed struggles were most severe in the Guangdong and Guangxi regions. The movements of people between Shenzhen and Hong Kong show that China's upheavals bled into Hong Kong territories and became part of Hong Kong's collective memory. The horror that Hong Kong residents witnessed during the Cultural Revolution only confirmed their fear about the PRC regime's use of terror. The accounts of these horrific incidents of people dying or being kidnapped were mostly told through pro-KMT publications, which formed the core component of the anticommunist discourse in the Southern Periphery that became integral to the diasporic consciousness of Chinese who settled in Hong Kong. By recounting stories about horrific crimes committed by alleged CCP members, these pro-KMT newspapers perpetuated the Cold War rhetoric of the brutal Communist regime on the other side of the Bamboo Curtain.

The people whose livelihood depended on the sea such as fishermen and oystermen faced an additional sense of alienation because of their ambiguous relationship with the colonial state in Hong Kong. While the fishermen and oystermen in Lau Fau Shan were Hong Kong residents, they did not receive much protection from the Hong Kong government, especially when they were in the sea. Their lives were not prioritized by the state, and their status as residents of Hong Kong made no difference to their precarious existence as they were constantly harassed by fellow fishermen and self-proclaimed commune members from mainland China. Thus, the fishermen and oystermen who worked along the seacoasts were the epitomes of the peripheral existence of people in Hong Kong.

The corpses belonged either to migrants who died while escaping from the mainland to Hong Kong or to individuals who were killed in the PRC for various political reasons. By the mid-1960s, stories of dead bodies at sea had become a familiar narrative among the residents of Hong Kong. Then, in the summer of 1968, a large number of dead bodies were found almost every day in Hong Kong's sea territories. Unlike before, these bodies were identified as belonging to Red Guards who were killed in armed struggles in Guangdong during the Cultural Revolution. The reports of these discoveries by rightist newspapers generated a "red scare" in Hong Kong and later became a familiar narrative about the CCP's brutality.

Then there was a spate of missing bodies, kidnappings, and other crimes on the west coast of Hong Kong in the late 1960s, followed by the killing of three oystermen from Hong Kong in 1970 by self-proclaimed people's commune (*renmin gongshe*) members.[3] These incidents heightened Hong Kong residents' fear of the CCP and of what the Cultural Revolution had unleashed, as we will see. The killings and the crimes show how the Cultural Revolution created a sense of fear and solidified the opposition to any interference by Communists in Hong Kong society that continued till the 2020s.

DEAD BODIES

Between the early 1950s and the mid-1960s, many pro-KMT newspapers as well as publications by the KMT-sponsored Free China Relief Association (FCRA) reported large numbers of dead bodies found along the seacoasts of Hong Kong. However, besides a few photos of the corpses taken by reporters, not many details typically accompanied these reports concerning the backgrounds of these victims. The anticommunist media portrayed the dead as fellow countrymen who had been victims of great disasters (*zainan tongbao*) under the CCP. The reports of dead bodies mysteriously turning up in the sea provoked frightened speculation about the brutality of the CCP in mass murdering innocent people.

One speculation that the pro-KMT newspapers advanced to explain the rising numbers of dead bodies floating in the Hong Kong sea territories was that the people had been shot dead by the People's Liberation Army or other mainland authorities because they posed a threat or because they wanted to leave the PRC. The earliest report of floating bodies was in 1952. Daya Bay, located along the southeast coast of China and best known for the nuclear plant built there in the 1980s, was at that time the site of a national military facility. In the spring of 1952, the construction of that facility was just being completed. Not long after the construction work ended, one day in March, Hong Kong fishermen discovered more than fifty male bodies in the sea in close proximity to the base. Some of the bodies were tied together, while others floated alone. Residents of one of the islands in Daya Bay told the fishermen that they suspected that construction workers had been killed by the Communist army because of worry within the CCP that they might leak secrets regarding the construction of the facility when they returned home. No further elaboration on the case was forthcoming. The discovery was not widely reported and appeared only once in *Wah Kiu Yih Pao*.[4]

After that time, there were intermittent reports of dead bodies found in Hong Kong, Macau, or neighboring sea territories. Another example of a report of a dead body occurred on July 28, 1956, when the corpse of a man dressed in an old PLA uniform and riddled with gunshot wounds was found near Macau. This body was reportedly first spotted in the sea near Coloane, Macau. A few hours later, a body with gunshot wounds was found in the international waters (*gonghai*) between Macau and Hong Kong, and the report says it was identified as the same body spotted earlier near Coloane. When the reporter questioned residents in Macau, many said they believed the man was shot during an attempted escape.[5]

Most newspapers that reported on the dead bodies were pro-KMT ones. They generally did not investigate the identities of the dead bodies or double-check the causes of these deaths. These reports appeared on the front page but not always as the lead story. It seems the photos of the dead bodies captured attention, but apparently there was not enough curiosity or perhaps insufficient information to prompt a more thorough investigation into these cases.

Other speculations posited that the bodies belonged to escapees who had drowned while swimming or taking boats across the eastern or western sea territories of Hong Kong. At that time, the British colonial government of Hong Kong was perceived as more stable than the Portuguese colonial government of Macau, but many people who wanted to leave China went to Macau first—because it had a more lenient entry policy—and then used Macau as a stepping-stone to go to Hong Kong. Those living in Macau at that time had to apply for an entry permit from the authorities to legally move to Hong Kong, but because of strict limits on the number of permits and the lengthy application process, some decided to take a chance and sneak into Hong Kong by boat. In a news report on August 21, 1957, titled "Forty Bodies Were Found near Waglan Island," *Wah Kiu Yat Po* noted that the dead included males and females of all ages. It was speculated that the victims had tried to escape to Hong

Kong by boat and had capsized. The bodies were first discovered by a fishing boat near Waglan Island, located southeast of Hong Kong Island. When the fishermen lowered their net, they discovered more than thirty dead bodies. This discovery was verified by other fishing boats nearby. However, a day later the incident was denied by the Marine and Water Bureau of Macau and nine travel agencies. (All vessels, including those used for human smuggling, technically had to register with a travel agency, but none of them had reported having received notice of an accident.) The bureau claimed that no relatives had filed a missing person's report with the police. The travel agencies also denied that any boats registered with them had capsized.[6]

When escapees made it into the news, it was usually because an accident had occurred and escapees had been killed. In the more serious boat accidents, all the people traveling on the boat died and the place of origin of the boat would be unknown.

Sometimes reporters made guesses about victims based on the materials they had with them. For example, a boat sank near the Hong Kong island, and more than twenty dead bodies were found on Chai Wan beach at 8:00 a.m. on November 28, 1962. A *Kung Sheung Daily News* article the next day, entitled "Piles of Bodies Floating on the Sea, Horrific Scene Unbearable to the Eyes" (*haimian fushi diedie canbu rendu*), reported that the dead were believed to be escapees who used a boat to take them from China to Hong Kong. Unfortunately, the boat had an accident and all the passengers died. They all were carrying "mainland travel identifications" (*tongxingzheng*), perhaps implying that they had all intended to escape from the mainland.[7] Another newspaper report on the same incident stated that six of the dead were women over fifty. The reporter remarked that it was the worst accident of human smuggling (*qushe*) ever seen. Also noted was that "many carried pieces of scratch paper with the addresses of their relatives" living in Hong Kong. These documents and notes found on the bodies of the dead were evidence that they were escapees who had been killed while crossing the border by sea. Moreover, a few ex-escapees I interviewed noted that in the 1960s men tended to escape by swimming and women tended to escape by boat.[8] Perhaps that is the reason why this boat carried so many women.

In the following days, rescue efforts continued, and more bodies and some survivors were found. A follow-up report stated that thirty-one bodies were found in total and that most were women and children. The sister of one of the victims was interviewed. She said that her sister had arrived in Macau the year before and had decided to take the boat with her eldest child to sneak into Hong Kong. Both the mother and child died in the accident.[9] Such a case shows that despite most dead bodies' identities were not known, sometimes it was possible to know the origins and relatives of these dead bodies. In this case, the body was not a nameless, unknown person, but a Hong Kong resident's sister. Yet, the interviewee just happened to have known about the victim's plan to escape to Hong Kong and could go look for the body. Thus, the horror permeated through these reports did not come from an experience of alienation, but also from an experience of familiarity.

Even though many children participated in these perilous journeys, there was little discussion in newspapers about what should be done. Most of the pro-KMT newspaper reports and even the editorials did not take a humanitarian stand and simply reported the facts of the events or criticized the CCP as a brutal regime that forced many people to leave China. The purpose of these reports was to enforce the negative image of the CCP in people's minds in Hong Kong. This goal seemed to be largely successful, as memoirs and journalistic writings on the illegal migration from the mainland to Hong Kong published in the 2000s still discuss the great details of the horror of dead bodies in the 1950s–1970s.

Some of the escapees did not originally intend to escape by illegal means. They wanted to apply for entry permits from Macau or China, but they were not able to do so and decided to try their luck by hiring a boat or swimming by themselves. A news report in 1962 told the story of a woman who was found drowned near Mui Wo, Lantau Island. The newspaper reported that she had taken a boat to come to Hong Kong. Her husband and her eldest son had gone to Hong Kong from Shanghai a few years prior to her journey. She had then applied to emigrate through legal means, but the permit had not been issued after a long period of waiting. The report claims that the woman was particularly anxious, since she was told that her husband had married another woman in Hong Kong. Their marital crisis triggered the woman's decision to go to Macau and then to take a boat to Hong Kong.[10] The report evoked a sense of sadness, but it did not elaborate on the details. This case seems to contradict the general assertion in these pro-KMT publications that it was political persecution that caused all these deaths; even though she was unable to travel legally because the CCP did not issue a permit, the main reason she wanted to leave was marital trouble, not political persecution.

The dead bodies found in the sea surrounding Hong Kong from the 1950s to the late 1960s were depicted largely as evidence of the CCP's oppression of the Chinese people. The stories of these escapees were told only indirectly through their relatives or the documents that were found on their persons. The stories were mostly unsensational, and most readers understood the dire situation and treated such disasters as common phenomena. In the interviews I conducted in the 2010s, almost all of the interviewers who fled to Hong Kong in the 1960s mentioned the accounts of dead bodies they had read about, but the timing of those accounts was almost always vague, mostly to contrast with their fortunate experience of arriving safely in their destinations of escape.[11] The stories of dead bodies were timeless legends, reminding the escapees who successfully reached Hong Kong about the perilous journeys they had taken to flee mainland China and confirmed their frightened speculation about the brutality of the CCP in mass-murdering discontented people and even innocent workers.

1968 AND THE CULTURAL REVOLUTION

The political context and the characteristics of bodies had a dramatic change in year of 1968. Beginning in the third week in June 1968, fishermen and the marine police forces discovered a few to dozens of dead bodies along the western seacoast of Hong Kong and the eastern side of Macau every day for the next two months. For the first few days, people in Hong Kong did not know where these dead bodies came from. Gradually they found out that they were from the Pearl River floating down to the sea.

In the summer of 1968, the struggles between different factions in the Guangdong region intensified. In his book *Collective Killings in Rural China during the Cultural Revolution* (2011), Yang Su describes the mass killings in the Chinese provinces of Guangdong and Guangxi at that time. He argues that the mass killings took place when the party-state began to demobilize mass organizations.

Before Su's book, most previous studies of the Cultural Revolution focused on urban Red Guards. However, as Su says, the Cultural Revolution was not just an urban phenomenon. According to Yang Su, between 400,000 and 3,000,000 people were systematically exterminated in rural villages.[12] There were two major causes of deaths. One was factional struggles (*wudou*), which were especially intense in Guangdong and Guangxi. In late 1967, the mass movements had been underway for more than a year. Local governments had been dismantled, and the masses had been loosed to form organizations and alliances to contest for power. Many of them formed revolutionary committees, which would then conduct violent armed purges of "revisionists." These armed struggles were a response to Mao, who insisted that the "revisionists" needed to be eliminated from the party. Many of these factional struggles resulted in multiple deaths. The second major cause of deaths was wholesale executions that took place in rural communities. These executions were initiated by the local leaders of revolutionary committees. Unlike the armed struggles, in these executions the local leaders identified who the class enemies were. The situation in both provinces was chaotic, leading to more and more people leaving China for Hong Kong.[13]

A report on floating bodies published by the Free China Relief Association also supports Su's claim that the reason why there were so many deaths at sea was the factional struggles and political persecution in the Guangdong and Guangxi regions.[14] In an article about mass killing during the Cultural Revolution, the historian Yongyi Song found reports that cited the Guangxi Revolutionary Committee Preparation Group and Guangxi Provincial Military District as committing collective killings of the rival mass faction and of "class enemies" throughout the whole province.[15] According to the research of another Chinese scholar, Wu Ruoyu, 60,061 people were subjected to violent "struggle sessions" or arrested, and 7,199 died after July 3 in Nanning Special District.[16] By the end of July, about 84,000–100,000 people were killed, most of whom were civilians from the rival mass faction and "class enemies."[17] The extent of the deaths was not known in mainland China until years after the Cultural Revolution. Nevertheless, through snippets of the reports on dead bodies, the people in Hong Kong learned about these stories of atrocities, albeit not in great detail.

A letter addressed to the ROC Ministry of Foreign Affairs (*waijiaobu*) in Hong Kong on July 10, 1968, stated: "In the past few days, there have been countless dead bodies of mainland people [*dalu tongbao*] floating in the water, from the mouth of the Pearl River to Hong Kong and Macau. Over the past seventeen days up to July 10, sixty bodies in all were found, including thirty-four discovered within the sea boundaries of Hong Kong and twenty-six within the sea boundaries of Macau."[18] The flow of dead bodies did not end in mid-July. Between June 22 and the end of August, more than a hundred bodies were found in the waters off Hong Kong. The bodies found that summer were concentrated in the western sea territories of Hong Kong, and most were found by fishermen. Some turned up on the coast of the western New Territories, such as at Sai Kong and Lau Fau Shan, or on the beaches of the outlying islands, such as Lantau and Tsing Yi.

An article titled "Observing Mainland China and Taiwan from Hong Kong" (*You Xianggang kan Dalu, Taiwan*), published in *Kung Sheung Daily News* on October 15, 1968, states:

> The mainland is their homeland, so everyone has an inseparable relationship with China like skin and flesh. Since the Communist Party took over China nineteen years ago, many people not only feel that they have a home to which they cannot return but also cannot escape from the torture of humanity. In the Big Exodus in 1962, thousands of people crossed over the rivers and mountains to escape to Hong Kong. Many Hong Kong residents ran around to help them out. The hardship was unimaginable. Before they could catch their breath, the Mao faction started the Red Guards Movement, and the relatives of the migrants were the first victims. Family members of many were publicly humiliated, and some could not bear the persecution and committed suicide. The Hong Kong migrants saw these disasters, they could not find anyone to help them, and they cried until their tears were dried up. From then on, the mainland has had many violent armed struggles and people have died. It was unbearable to hear the news. But before they could calm down and dry their tears, they witnessed floating bodies coming to Hong Kong nonstop. These corpses were all tied up, with scars and wounds all over their bodies. Their facial features were unrecognizable. Many Hong Kong migrants were fearful and sad and tried to confirm that none of the dead were their loved ones. From these incidents, we can see how deep a grudge the Hong Kong migrants hold against the Mao regime and how much they worry about the chaos in the mainland, as

well as how anxious they are while waiting for Taiwan to save the country.¹⁹

The author situated the influx of dead bodies within the context of Hong Kong's ties with the mainland and argued that political events in the mainland, mainly the Cultural Revolution and the violent armed struggles in Guangdong, had been taking a toll on Hong Kong residents' emotional health. The reports of deaths generated a great deal of anxiety about the safety of their relatives in China. The author also alluded to Taiwan as the only possible savior for Hong Kong residents.

Although this commentary was written about a decade later than the peak of the Third Force when people wanted to restore the rule of the Republic of China, the sentiment that the KMT government was the legitimate government of China had not changed. Many people hoped for the KMT government in Taiwan to save them. This kind of yearning was not just common among the intelligentsia or the Third Force activists but had also become part of the greater political consciousness of some of the general population living in Hong Kong. By the time the Cultural Revolution, the pro-KMT newspapers' propaganda effort in creating a sense of terror had taken effect on the people, but continued yearning for Taiwan to come to their rescue by some of the people dwelling in Hong Kong might have been more than these publications had bargained for.

The bodies that were found in the summer of 1968 were concentrated in the western sea territories of Hong Kong. Many fishermen who worked in Lau Fau Shan, Yuen Long, found bodies while they were out at sea. Some of the dead bodies floated to the outlying islands to the west of the Hong Kong sea territories. A number of them reached Macau (figure 3.1).

The locations of the bodies are good indicators that they floated from the part of the Pearl River (Zhujiang), which flows through Guangdong Province. From some of the newspaper reports that tried to trace the origins of the dead bodies in June and July 1968, we learn that there was severe flooding in Guangdong, inundating areas such as Zhaoqing, Sanshui, Xinhui, Taishan, Nanhai, Zhongshan, and Dongguan, causing river water to gush into the sea territories of Hong Kong and Macau. The armed struggles were most serious in Guangzhou and Zhaoqing areas.²⁰ In a letter written to the British colonial office, Governor Trench of Hong

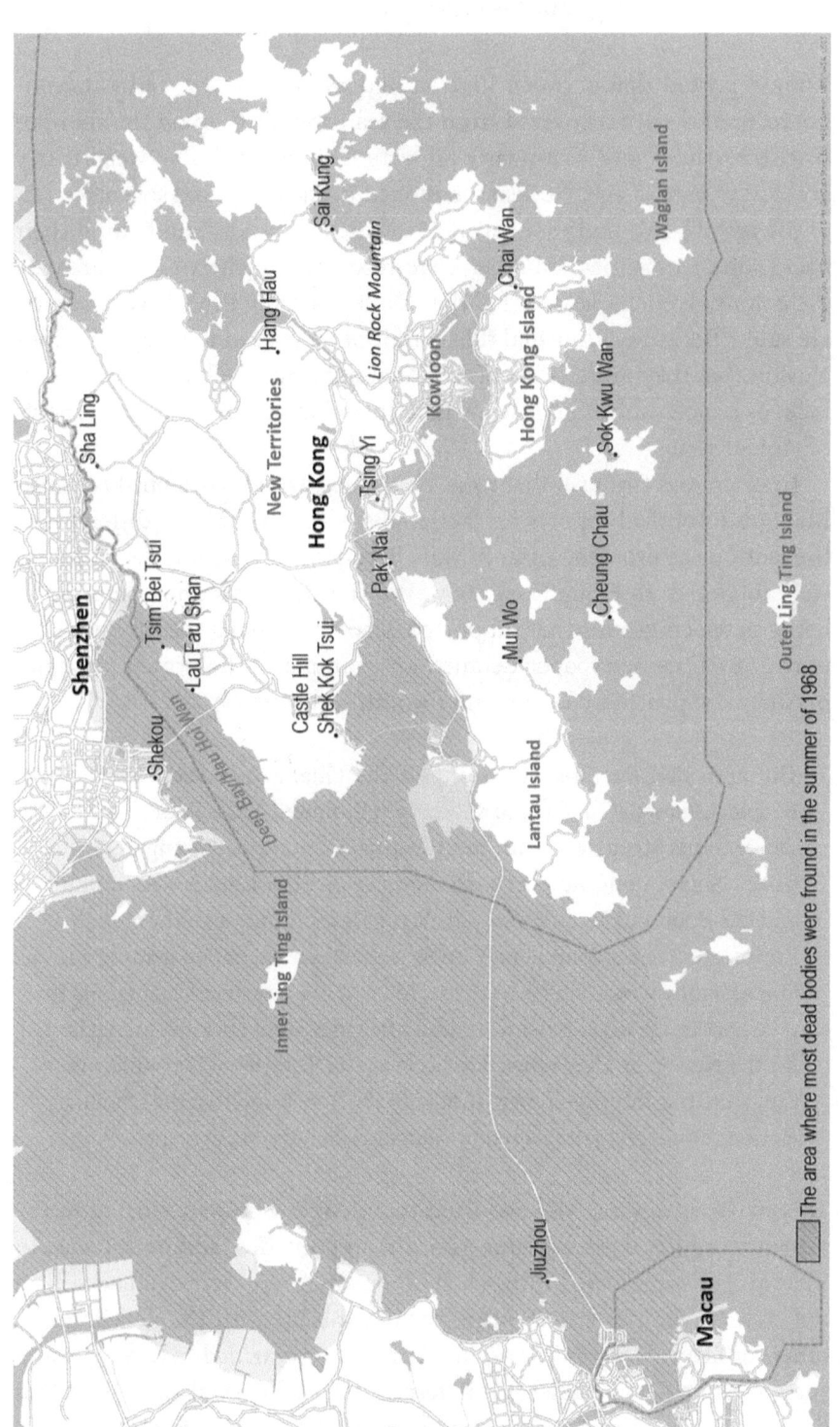

FIGURE 3.1 Map of the area where floating bodies were found in 1968.
Map created by Guoping Huang.

Kong reported that between June 22 and 28, twenty-two badly decomposed bodies were recovered from the sea or washed up on the shore in British territory and that nearly all were Chinese males between thirty and forty years of age. He also mentioned in the letter that seventeen out of the twenty-two bodies recovered had their hands bound behind their backs. Since most of the bodies were recovered in the western areas of the colony, Trench guessed that they came from the Pearl River Estuary. He said, "Because of unusual tide condition, it is hard to escape the conclusion that they are victims of factional fighting in [Guangdong] Province, or conceivably [Guangxi], where there have been persistent reports of violent struggles."[21]

In mainland China at that time, no groups would self-identify as anti-Mao, and political reports on factionalism also would not differentiate the factions as pro-Mao or anti-Mao, because no "anti-Mao" sentiments were tolerated. In Hong Kong, however, the strife was often depicted as being between groups that supported Mao and groups that did not support Mao. One newspaper detailed an example of the armed struggles between the pro-Mao faction and the anti-Mao faction:

> The anti-Mao factions, consisting of the Guangzhou Suburban Poor People Alliance (Guangzhou shijiao pin lianmeng), the Poor and Middle Peasants Struggle Committee of Shipai Commune (Guangzhou Shijiaoqu Shipai gongshe pinxia zhongnong geming zaofan weiyuanhui) and the Poor and Middle Peasants Struggle Committee of the Conghua Prefecture (Guangdongsheng Conghua xian pin xia zhong geming zaofanpai lianhe weiyuanhui), were told to go to northeastern Guangdong to take part in the flood relief work. But after they went back to Guangzhou for the New Year, they refused to leave again. They felt it was unfair that they were the only ones sent to deal with the floods and that the Dongfeng faction (Dongfengpai) favored by Mao did not have to participate.[22]

This newspaper story also reported that people who participated in the armed struggles used machine guns, hand grenades, and poison gas. In Zhaoqing, people were killing each other, and there were dead bodies on the streets. The newspaper also speculated that, with the flooding and other unfavorable conditions in China, many armed refugees would rush to Hong Kong. Such critical description of factionalism was seldom depicted in mainland newspapers because most propaganda materials downplayed any discord within the country. This kind of detailed description of factional struggles was characteristic of Hong Kong reporting of the Cultural Revolution, and thus engendered a particular kind of terror specific to the residents in Hong Kong.

One report published on June 25, 1968, in *Kung Sheung Evening News* describes the conditions of the bodies: "Since some of these floating bodies have both arms tied up, and others have wounds all over their bodies, it is fair to say that these bodies were either victims of violent armed struggles or they were executed by the Communist Party." The author speculated that because of the large number of deaths near the rivers and because the local people neglected to bury them, "for convenience sake, they just threw the bodies into the rivers." The rising water then carried many of the bodies down the Pearl River to Hong Kong and Macau territories. The author also commented: "The horrendous scene of floating corpses not only was obscene to the eyes of Chinese and foreigners but also affected the psychology of the leftists as well. Because of that, the Communist newspapers have never mentioned the discovery of bodies."[23] In the same report, the author also notes that CCP officials in Guangdong were "sending out vessels to salvage dead bodies on the Pearl River" to prevent more corpses from floating into Hong Kong and Macau. The bodies of the mainland Chinese washing up on Hong Kong's shore also meant that there was a lack of closure for their families were unaware of their deaths or were unable to bury or mourn them. As such, these bodies connected Hong Kong and the PRC in a topography of distanced or imagined grief, both of which were generated by the Cold War tensions and the Cultural Revolution.

A report published in *Kung Sheung Daily News* on June 27, 1968, titled "Dead Bodies Rolling in from the Mainland" (*Dalu fushi gungunlai*), describes the condition of the corpses discovered in the sea or along the coastline:

> Ninety percent of corpses discovered on the sea are incomplete and unrecognizable. They have no names on them, and nobody knows who their parents, siblings, and other relatives are. The only truth we know about them is that most of these victims are youths. They are tied up with ropes, and some are even blindfolded. This is evidence that they were killed and discarded in the sea. As to their clothes, there are some in Communist military uniforms and some in "liberation outfits," and

others just look like regular civilians. This indicates that they died during the factional struggle, and the culprit behind all these murders is the greatest evil Mao Zedong!"[24]

Another account described the bodies found the previous day: "One was a girl about fourteen or fifteen years of age. She had a rope on her neck. They all had bruises. Some were dismembered and some had wounds all over their bodies. Some were blindfolded with towels. It's unclear whether they were executed because they tried to escape, or whether they belonged to the Mao camp or anti-Mao camp."[25]

In most of the newspaper reports, the dead bodies were discovered in PLA uniforms (*jiefang zhuang*) or had no clothes on the upper parts of the bodies, with their limbs tied up at the back (*wuhua dabang*). Occasionally, they also wore Mao badges.[26] The majority of them were men in their thirties. The women who were found wore flowery outfits.[27] On average, eight or nine bodies were discovered each day between late June and mid-July. The police tried to search for bodies by using boats and helicopters.[28] The newspapers that published these discoveries tended to be rightist newspapers, and they used the reports to critique Mao and his policies. Such reports tended not to be found in mainland newspapers.

To many of those who had experienced escape from China and who perhaps had witnessed fellow refugees dying on the journey, these reports reinforced their traumatic memories of fleeing the PRC. This trauma was centered not so much on actual physical abuses such as arbitrary imprisonment or torture (although some did experience such things) but rather on the psychological threat that people felt and the sufferings of others that they witnessed. The journeys of those who made attempts to escape to Hong Kong illegally were driven by and filled with the fear of dying, and yet even for those who had survived the journey, media reports continued to haunt them with tales of those who were less fortunate.

HONG KONG TRAVELERS

While information about the Cultural Revolution in China remained scarce in Hong Kong, travelers who had recently returned from China brought news. Reporters often went to train stations seeking travelers to interview. In 1967, *Kung Sheung Evening News* interviewed a traveler preparing to go back to China at the Tsim Sha Tsui Station. The title of this article was "Hearing That All His Family Members Were Killed, an Overseas Chinese Risks His Life to Go Back to His Hometown to Visit Relatives" (*Wen jiaren bei sha jin bengang yiwei huaqiao maosi huixiang tanqin*).

The traveler said, "One relative from mainland to Hong Kong told me that all my family members in China were beaten to death or died in the armed struggle, but I don't know if it's true or not, but after seeing so many corpses in Hong Kong and Macau, I am very worried, and I must go back to my hometown to check it out." The article mentions that his parents and wife were in China and he was by himself in Hong Kong. The relative who purportedly informed him about this was an elderly woman and was unable to provide more details on the deaths. The man told the reporter that his family might have been killed because they were suspected of hiding surplus food in their house.[29] Many people in Hong Kong wanted to check on their hometowns and other relatives after hearing about the armed struggles in South China as well as about the bodies floating in the sea.

Accounts written by people who came back from the mainland were featured in newspapers. Journalists wanted to find out more about what had been happening in China, and the returning travelers became the witnesses of the Cultural Revolution, according to *Kung Sheung Evening News*:

> A couple coming back from one of the further provinces in China started complaining in the train. He said, "I won't ever go back again in my life. What kind of country is that? It's a shame to five hundred years of propriety and culture (*liyi zhi bang*). It's so chaotic. Younger brothers use knives to stab brothers. Grandchildren hit their grandfathers with sticks. How can this be called 'the model of revolution?'" He pointed to a pile of messy, old clothing and exclaimed: "This pile of clothing would be unwanted if you left it on the street in Hong Kong, but I wanted to bring it back to my relatives who have no clothes to wear. However, the officers at the border said this is all Western clothing, full of imperialistic flavor, [the people in China] cannot wear them. Then [the officers] took out another pile of Chinese-style clothing, and said 'the government'

ordered no outside clothing is allowed in the 'motherland.' Okay, then I would just leave [my bag of clothes] there then. Who would expect that before I stepped into the train back to Hong Kong, they were calling for me [from the platform] to take it back. I would just let it go if they had only made a mess of my tidy clothes, but they did not stop there and tried to charge me 6 *kuai* RMB as a 'safekeeping' fee. I would have to face detention if I did not want to pay. This kind of theft (*gualong*) is too much, how can I not be upset?"[30]

Other tales were even more horrific, revealing the devastating state of armed struggles in Guangdong and the rest of China. A widow who came back from Guangzhou revealed her experience after a family visit. Her younger brother went through a great ordeal to escape from Beijing to Guangzhou. The brother had been studying at Beijing University, but he said the campus was burned down and classes were canceled; because he did not want to join in the Red Guard activities, he had no choice but to escape back to Guangzhou. The brother also mentioned that, while he was escaping from Beijing to Wuhan and then to Guangdong, he witnessed armed struggles (*wudou*) everywhere: "They were much more severe than in Guangzhou. For example, in Wuhan, public transit was destroyed, and there was looting and killing in the cities everywhere, and there were dead bodies all over the streets."[31] Some of these accounts were later proven to be false when the truth came out; for example, Beijing University's campus was not burned down. However, it was the lack of information that made these accounts believable and that generated so much fear among readers in Hong Kong.

In a newspaper article on travelers returning from mainland China, the reporter interviewed a few people who saw or heard about what had been happening in China at that time. A young woman said the problem of floating bodies in Hong Kong was not so serious, since she had witnessed twenty people being thrown into the river at once somewhere in China. In the same report, a cook also testified to the reporter that he had witnessed a massacre on the street and heard sounds of bombs in Guangzhou. He heard that one bomb landed in a residential district and more than ten houses collapsed and many people lost their limbs. The reporter also interviewed an old woman from Heshan who said her sixteen-year-old grandson was recruited to participate in "corpse-retrieving groups" (*laoshituan*) to look for dead bodies in the river. The reporter talked to a traveler who claimed that several hundred photos of members of the anti-Mao groups were put up in main intersections and train stations by the pro-Mao faction; once these "suspects" were caught, they would be executed on the spot. Finally, there was a story about another traveler from the mainland to Hong Kong who said: "A few days ago, Nanhai residents were salvaging a piece of cedar in the ocean, but, after pulling it out of the water, they found out that seven bodies were nailed to the underside."[32]

The crossing of the sea border highlights the ambiguous identities of some of the "people" who crossed the seas. Many people died in the violent armed struggles between factions in the Guangdong region during the Cultural Revolution. Their bodies were discarded in the rivers and then floated to Hong Kong. These former Communist Red Guards or activists went through a transformation as their bodies crossed the border into the Hong Kong sea territories—from CCP activists to grotesque propaganda objects the KMT deployed to emphasize the misery of the people under the CCP in mainland China. The people who were found dead in Hong Kong territories were often not identified. Their true identities and their pasts were lost permanently during their sea journeys.

These accounts contributed to a period of terror in Hong Kong. This is also part of the Cultural Revolution experience, but from the perspective of the people who witnessed the events in China and told their stories in Hong Kong. Hong Kong became a window through which people beyond the borders of the PRC gained some access to what was happening during the Cultural Revolution on the mainland through a particular lens—both directly through the dead bodies that were discovered and indirectly through the reports of the escapees' background and journeys. However, much of the information was presented in a particular interpretative framework that shaped the narrative about the PRC regime being a murderous one. It was a distinctively Hong Kong narrative, since any kind of critical interpretation of such events was prohibited in the PRC at that time. The sense of loss and fear was a collective trauma for people residing in Hong Kong because it brought back memories of the horrific escape journeys that they or their loved ones had gone through. The bodies floating in the sea territories also reminded that the danger might be imminent.

SHA LING CEMETERY

We do not know much about how the Hong Kong government dealt with the large number of unidentified bodies found in the sea. A few newspaper reports mention that they were buried in Sha Ling Cemetery near the Shenzhen border (figure 3.2).[33] A pamphlet published by the Free China Relief Association states: "One body was found every day on average. They were all buried in Sha Ling and their identities were unverified."[34] The tombstones bear no names, just a number engraved on each one (figure 3.3). The identities of those buried there remain a permanent mystery. Their only records are the brief description in the police file and the number assigned to each of them.

FIGURE 3.2 Shaling public cemetery in 2017.
Photo by Angelina Y. Chin.

FIGURE 3.3 Shaling public cemetery in 2017. No names were engraved on many of the gravestones, only numbers.

Photo by Angelina Y. Chin.

In writings about people who died while escaping from China, we see conflicting feelings toward their homeland. An essay published in the editorial section of *Kung Sheung Evening News* in June 1968 expressed the belief that these homeless souls should at least get a proper place of burial and not be sunk to the bottom of the ocean. He suggested that the burial site could face the Zhujiang and that a tombstone reading "Gazing at the homeland" (*wangxiangtai*) could be constructed for it, to comfort the dead in looking back toward China. His suggestion to the government was to find land for a mass burial and to record the clothing, characteristics, and age of the dead on the tombstones. The author further suggested that, after creating tombstones for these floating bodies in the sea, the Hong Kong authorities could ask Tung Wah Hospital to hold a ritual commemorating them twice a year.[35]

Some escapees felt differently about their homeland. One note found on a dead body read, "If I encounter ill fortune and die, please don't tell my family in my hometown. Please bury my body in a land of freedom!"[36]

The people who were critical of the CCP did not miss any chance to mock the regime. One satirical commentary remarked that the CCP should claim all the floating bodies because if the "barefoot doctors" could resurrect people by chanting from Mao's Little Red Book, as was rumored, then they could do the same to these dead bodies. After the dead ones were revived, they could be put on trial and then shot in front of the public. That way the CCP could display the remains to the public and ensure that no one would dare to escape to Hong Kong anymore.[37] The author who suggested the special tombstones suggested the Hong Kong authorities should use the floating bodies to prove Mao's crimes to the world. Further, the organizations and individuals concerned about the matter should request that Hong Kong authorities designate the third Sunday of June as a Day of Commemoration (*aisi jinian ri*), because, he argued, most people in Hong Kong "tended to be forgetful and would not remember the Communist disaster (*gonghuo*) if there was no such reminder."[38]

Corpses continued to float into Hong Kong long after the Cultural Revolution violence ended, until the early 1980s. For example, in 1970, between November 2 and 12, Hong Kong buried more than forty bodies. They were found in Lau Fau Shan, Tsim Bei Shan, and Pak Nai. Unlike the bound corpses in 1968, most of these bodies were in their early twenties, with lifebuoys and other floating objects attached to them and no obvious wounds or scars on their bodies. The news report on this incident expressed the view that "the refugees from the Communist regime worked like slaves for a long time." Not only did they not have enough to eat or wear, but they also had to attend meetings every night, and they all felt that life was meaningless. As a result, every refugee had wanted to escape this abyss and enjoy freedom.[39]

Another article published in the same month reported that the cooperatives in Guangdong near the border had stopped selling balls to prevent people from using them as instruments of escape. It said that customers would need to get permission from their units to buy basketballs and volleyballs. Those who tried to escape were so desperate that they even bought Ping-Pong balls as flotation devices if there were no other balls available.[40]

A newspaper reported that from January to November 1970, 323 bodies were found. The Hong Kong government usually tried to determine the identity of each dead person and then decide whether the body should be cremated. The rest of the unidentified bodies were buried in a mass grave near a hill at the border.[41]

For the people who died while crossing the sea to Hong Kong, their citizenship was ambiguous or perhaps irrelevant. Pro-KMT media portrayed them as freedom fighters who yearned to live in the Free World. Their bodies were cremated and interred in mass burials in Hong Kong, but their deaths were not counted in the colony's official death registry because their identities remained unknown.

The migrants who escaped from China and ended up in Hong Kong chose to leave because life in China was difficult. After they came to Hong Kong, these narratives about dead bodies caused them to realize that the PRC was also not hesitant to kill or abandon them. The dead bodies were uncanny reminders through which the public in Hong Kong was subjected to a kind of emotional violence that was psychologically damaging as traumatic spectacle. The media coverage and the propaganda materials containing gruesome details and images added to the terror of the acts themselves.

In the other parts of the Southern Periphery, there were much fewer accounts of floating bodies. Dead bodies were reportedly found on Macau's sea coasts in Hong Kong newspapers, but they were not reported in their counterparts in Macau. Stories about people dying while crossing the sea to Taiwan sometimes appeared in Taiwan newspapers, but they were much more scattered and did not evoke the same level of fright.

FISHERMEN

Chinese fishermen and other people whose livelihoods depended on the sea had many direct encounters with escapees and dead bodies (figure 3.4). They were usually the first to discover the bodies. The newspapers in the 1960s also reported the toll the large number of corpses took on the lives and psychological health of the fishermen. According to one report, one woman was thrown into the sea because she allegedly had helped escapees from China sneak into Hong Kong. Her sampan was first surrounded by more than ten mainland junk boats. Then, the people

FIGURE 3.4 Fishermen in Hong Kong in the mid-1950s.
Photo by Norman Yao.

on those junk boats yelled at her, calling her "a traitor of the nation" (*maiguozei*). One motorboat crashed into her boat, causing the woman to fall into the water and drown.[42] Some fishermen believed they would be putting other detained fishermen at risk if they continued to help escapees enter Hong Kong. An article titled "Corpses Rolled into the Mouth of the Pearl River" (*Shiyong Zhujiang kou*) describes the horror felt by fishermen from Hong Kong who witnessed the floating bodies; many avoided them as fast as they could.[43] Another article claims that because the vicinity of Kou Chau was filled with corpses, fishermen were afraid to cast their nets there. In the same article, a fisherman said that even more bodies were found near the Inner and Outer Ling Ting Islands. He said, "Sometimes there were dozens of bodies floating and sinking. Some of the bodies were bundled together in groups of three or five, others were just floating by themselves. On average, there was one body every few feet in the water, so the fishermen couldn't lower their nets to catch."[44]

Even for those fishermen who did not help the escapees, their livelihood was negatively impacted by the surge of dead bodies in the sea.

Fishermen on the Chinese side of the sea border were affected too.[45] The Communist army in Zhongshan reportedly offered a reward of 10 yuan for each corpse retrieved from the sea. However, since there were so many of them, the reward was said to have been reduced to 2 yuan per corpse.[46] Many of these fishermen arrived in Hong Kong. Because they lived in their boats, taking their boats to Hong Kong seemed to be an easy way to escape. One newspaper did a one-page feature on them:

> The lives of the fishermen were decent until the arrival of the CCP. Ever since the CCP took over China, however, the fishermen have become slaves; besides being poor, their lives have no protections. The most vivid example is the nineteen fishing boats and the over two hundred fishermen and their families escaping to Hong Kong together. The size of the group is almost unprecedented. Even though they were ordered to leave Hong Kong's territorial waters, ten of the fishing boats and over a hundred fishers persisted and tried to enter Cheung Chau three times. Now they are detained by the police. It is said that they have violated the immigration law. They would rather die in Hong Kong than return to the mainland.
>
> The [KMT government] should settle them in Taiwan. This is their responsibility. Since Mao, Lin, and their followers started the so-called "Cultural Revolution," China has fallen into total chaos, the organization of the CCP is gradually paralyzing. The cadres and militants are distrustful of one another, and this indicates that the regime is divided and decentered. The citizens surviving under the cruelty of the regime are all yearning for alternative leaders. This is our best chance of starting the restoration movement in twenty years. The government should wait no longer.[47]

This sentiment of the writer reflects that many people in Hong Kong were still thinking of a restoration of China by the KMT even in the late 1960s. They were still hoping that the KMT would come to their rescue as they faced the imminent threat posed by the CCP. The collective imagination of Free China was prominent, and going to Taiwan was the first step of that dream for the people dwelling in the Southern Periphery.

FIGURE 3.5 Lau Fau Shan.
Photo by Angelina Y. Chin.

The sea territories also exposed the precariousness of people who worked on the sea. In their occupation, many fishermen and oystermen traveled constantly back and forth between the sea territories of mainland China and Hong Kong. Enforcement of the law across such large expanses of water was all but impossible. Even though many people technically had their homes in Lau Fau Shan (figure 3.5), their rights to government protection were regularly put into question because they lived on the fringes of Hong Kong's borders.

The marginal status of people working on the sea gave the Communist communes near Shenzhen an opening to take advantage of those who lacked proper citizenship status in Hong Kong. Some self-claimed Communist commune members set up an outpost near Lau Fau Shan and forced fishermen to go there for indoctrination. Sometimes they even kidnapped them or forced them to surrender their catches and to attend study sessions in Shekou. Later, when the mainland oyster farmers were not doing so well in their oyster catches, they stole oysters from Hong Kong oyster farmers to compensate for their losses.

MISSING BODIES AND KIDNAPPING

During the 1960s, there were also rampant kidnappings of politically active people in Macau. The "123 incident" on December 3, 1966, which marked the beginning of de facto Chinese control of Macau, was a significant date for the Southern Periphery because after that Macau was considered particularly unsafe for Hong Kongers who supported the KMT. After the incident, the Portuguese retained only nominal control of Macau and the real power lay with pro-Beijing businessmen. It became much easier for CCP agents to conduct their work in Macau, and political dissidents or KMT members who could not be legally arrested or easily kidnapped in Hong Kong were abducted when they traveled to Macau.

According to an article published in *Kung Sheung Daily News* in 1968, the CCP set up a bureau for agents to control the Macanese government. The bureau allegedly sent out dozens of "action squads" (*xingdongxiaozu*) to kidnap people "with questionable backgrounds" or those who were suspected of anticommunist activities. Members of the squads stationed themselves in the Hong Kong ferry terminal and followed such people, then kidnapped them when they had a chance.[48] The details of some of the kidnappings were reported by the Hong Kong KMT office to the Foreign Affairs Office:

> One was a lecturer in the Linguistics Department of Hong Kong University, Chen Zhe. Chen went to Macau to look at some antique paintings. He checked out of his hotel on the second day and disappeared after that. The second person was a KMT officer in Nanjing, but now working in Rennie's Mill conducting relief work for Chinese refugees

and students. Weng disappeared after he took the ferry to Macau on April 12. His son is in the military in Taiwan and serving in Jinmen. His sister lives in the US. The third person lived in Hong Kong and made a living by selling goods from Taiwan.[49]

Similar kidnapping incidents also happened in Hong Kong, especially during the height of the Cultural Revolution in the late 1960s. On July 1, 1968, fifty fishermen were kidnapped by Communists from mainland China.[50] They were subjected to a public hearing in the theater in Shekou, on the mainland, then taken away from the coast of Bak Lai, Sha Kiu.[51] According to a report to the ROC Ministry of Foreign Affairs, the CCP officers said they took the fishermen to mainland China to have a meeting and that the fishermen would be returned in three days.[52] The same report contained the information that ten people had been arrested by the mainland Chinese police in Shekou, Guangdong, and sent to Shenzhen. It was unclear whether these arrested individuals were trying to escape to Hong Kong.

From the point of view of the residents of Hong Kong, such incidents of people being taken away were considered to be a form of kidnapping or abduction. However, from the point of view of the mainland authorities, these incidents may be seen as lawful detention, especially if they authorized the acts, because the PRC government always claimed Hong Kong as part of China. Whether it was kidnapping or detention depends on the perspective. What complicates this further is that the people who conducted these cross-border activities were self-claimed Communist commune members. They could be pirates committing crimes in the name of the CCP. There is little information about them in official records. Thus, whether they were legitimate agents of the PRC authorities or the CCP was questionable. Since most of the following accounts were reported from the perspective of people residing in Hong Kong, I will use "kidnapping" to refer to these acts.

The Hong Kong colonial government sent police vessels from Hau Hoi Wan near Shekou to find out more about the kidnappings and arrests. After being detained for six days, forty-seven of the fishermen were released back to Lau Fau Shan. One fisherman, Huang Kai, in his thirties, was beaten and suffered severe injuries. The exact number of kidnapping victims was not clear, but, according to the report in *Zhen Bao*, there were still five boats and twenty-three fishermen in custody on the mainland.⁵³

Teng Chai On, president of Lau Fau Shan Business Association, revealed that five of the kidnapped men had been taken to the second floor of Shekou Theater. Their wives and children were left on their boats. Some of the wives were asked to meet their husbands in Shekou, but they refused, worrying that they themselves would be abducted as well. It was reported that the fishermen were indicted on three charges: (1) helping illegal immigrants to enter the territories of Hong Kong; (2) entering PRC territories while fishing; and (3) fishing (in the PRC's sea territories) without approved fishing licenses from the commune.⁵⁴ Another newspaper article revealed that in order to get a license from the commune, each fishing boat would have to pay monthly dues of 600–700 catties (approximately 800–925 pounds) of fish and attend philosophy classes at the Shekou commune (*renmingongshe*). One sixty-five-year-old fisherman testified that he was put on trial and brainwashed. He was also forced to kowtow to the cadres and repent that he stole fish from them (*guidi koutou ren tou yu*). The fisherman was enraged by the public humiliation, since he had never been accused of stealing before. He declared that he would not go out to sea again unless the Hong Kong authority could guarantee his safety.

Another forty-seven-year-old fisherman, also from Lau Fau Shan, testified that every time he went to Shekou to have meetings at the commune, he would see a leader on stage reciting from Mao's Little Red Book, and that leader would demand that the crowd follow him. The fisherman expressed that he was "almost bored to death" every time because he was illiterate. He often went to the toilet as an excuse to sneak out of the meetings.

The Hong Kong Fishing Industry and Commercial General petitioned the Hong Kong government for assistance to address the kidnapping threat and to set up preventive measures for the future. In a letter sent to the Legislative Council and the governor of Hong Kong, the association claimed that from April 1967 to July 1968 the militants from the communes in the PRC had entered Lau Fau Shan three times and had taken away fishermen and boats.⁵⁵ The government did send a telegram to the Guangdong government and received a response. It explains what the PRC authorities viewed as an intrusion by Hong Kong fishermen:

The frequent sneaking into our oyster farms to undermine production by some fishermen from the Hong Kong side had aroused indignation among the local fishermen, especially as some of the intruders have carried out sabotage activities against China and helped bad elements to escape to Hong Kong. This time most of the transgressing fishermen were released after they had admitted their mistakes and guaranteed not to commit again such activities endangering the socialist cause of their motherland. As to the few who are still under detention, some of them have been found to be US–Chiang Kai-shek agents who have been conspiring sabotage activities against China; some are either pirates or political prisoners or criminals. The relevant Department of the Chinese government certainly has the right to put them under trial according to the law of the Chinese government.[56]

Beginning in the early 1960s, the PRC government set a policy for mainland fishermen that included raising the level of production by 60 percent and increasing the tax that they had to pay after they reached their catch quota. Many fishermen were said to have escaped to Hong Kong after the decree.[57] This continuation of this policy probably put fishermen living in the PRC under a great deal of pressure and forced them to resort to the kidnapping of Hong Kong fishermen.

One article published on July 2 in *Kung Sheung Daily News* discussed the reasons for kidnapping. According to rumors the fishermen in Lau Fau Shan had heard, one possible reason why the Communist Chinese sent ships that crossed the sea border to kidnap Hong Kong fishing boats was the income of the fisheries in Shekou had dropped significantly due to a decrease of fishermen working the sea. The members of the communes would "use extreme measures including strategies of pirates to force the fishermen from Hong Kong to join their 'communes,' so that they could continue to do whatever they want [to the fishermen from Hong Kong] and drain their blood and sweat." The article then explained that the reason this was happening specifically to the people of Lau Fau Shan was that the proximity of where they worked to Shekou. According to the analysis of the writer, this kind of piracy was not ordered by the CCP in Beijing, because it rarely happened in other areas besides Hau Hoi Wan, a sea territory that was neglected by the Hong Kong government. Within the CCP, some members pretended not to know about such crimes; others colluded with the kidnappers and took a share of the profits from the robberies.

The author continued to suggest several tactics to stop these cross-border crimes from happening. The first step was to press the colonial government to protest to Beijing to stop intrusion by the fisheries in Guangdong into Hong Kong territories, as well as to compensate for losses and to guarantee that similar incidents would not occur. The CCP should also be held accountable for the pirates' behavior.

The second step would be for the Hong Kong government to increase marine police patrols in the Hau Hoi Wan area and stop all illegal activities by boats from the mainland at all costs. Third, if a strong protest to the Beijing government did not achieve a satisfactory result, the Hong Kong government should restrict Chinese cargo ships from entering Hong Kong or detain their vessels in response.

The writer of this article believed the Hong Kong government had the responsibility to guarantee the safety of workers in the fisheries, because if they could not go to work out of fear, their income would be negatively affected, and it would also reduce the supply of seafood in Hong Kong.[58]

For the next two years, kidnappings continued. In newspaper editorials, commentators wrote about their frustration with the incompetence of the Hong Kong government in stopping the crimes. One editorial stated that it was not effective for the government to send out a statement demanding the release of the people or even to ask for help from the British government, because the Chinese Communists were unreasonable robbers. As a last resort, the writer suggested, the government should arrest all suspected Communist agents in Hong Kong or simply deport them back to the mainland as punishment.[59] These crimes in the sea were usually reported by pro-KMT newspapers in Hong Kong. Besides reporting the incidents, they condemned the CCP for its brutality and the Hong Kong government for its incompetence in protecting its citizens.

THE 1970 LAU FAU SHAN INCIDENT

Fishermen reported that at about 5:30 p.m. on September 1, 1970, a fishing junk dropped anchor near an oyster bed at Pak Nai on the Hong Kong shore of Deep Bay, two miles from Lau Fau Shan. According to the witnesses, as reported in the *South China Morning Post*, about twenty men from the junk boarded two sampans, sailed closer to the oyster bed, and forced the eight oyster farmers working there to board their boat. As soon as they had all boarded the junk, it sailed off toward China.[60] The eight men who were abducted were Tsang Ngau, forty-five, owner of an oyster farm; his two sons, Tsang Ping-lam and Tsang Cho-hing, both in their twenties; four oyster farm laborers, Ng Sai-lo, Tang Lo, Tang Wah-yau, and Wong Fu; and an unidentified fisherman.[61]

Three of the fishermen were later found to have been killed during their capture. Tsang Ngau was first shot and then stabbed to death because he resisted. His older son, Ping Nam, attempted to escape by swimming furiously to the shore. He was then reportedly "shot in the chest, beaten with poles, and had both his hands chopped off at the wrist" and was "disemboweled" before he died. The younger son, Cho-hing, was "severely beaten with wooden poles on a sampan and dumped on the pier" when the kidnappers' vessel reached the Chinese side of Deep Bay. He was later taken to a stone hut, where he died the following day. Their bodies were left on a shore in the New Territories, Hong Kong, as a warning to others and then later cremated.[62]

There was a rumor that the oystermen were captured for two reasons: first, they had stolen oysters planted by the Chinese communes in the vicinity for fattening; second, they upset the Chinese communes because they adamantly refused to attend Communist propaganda sessions in a Hang Hau village shack set up by the communes.[63] Chen (Yen-fook), a twenty-year-old oyster farmer who had escaped from China in 1968 by swimming across the bay to Lau Fau Shan, did not go out to sea that day because he was sick. He told the reporter that he would have met the same fate had he been well.[64]

Four of the kidnap victims abducted on September 1 were released by their captors a few days later. The oystermen were brought back in their sampans, towed by a Communist motorized junk, and released off Lau Fau Shan in Deep Bay.[65]

The *South China Morning Post* included excerpts from several newspapers warning the Hong Kong government that tolerance and appeasement of intruders violating Hong Kong's territorial borders to abduct people could further embolden Maoist elements. The forcible abduction of Lau Fau Shan oyster farmers was an act of "open defiance of the Hong

Kong government," observed the *Hong Kong Times*. The newspaper warned that the continuation of such a policy of tolerance and appeasement would "amount to encouraging the Maoist elements to carry out more nefarious activities." It urged the government to "strengthen border defenses and provide adequate protection for the oyster farmers near the border," adding that the kidnapping was an outrageous violation of Hong Kong's territorial jurisdiction and that a strong protest to the relevant Chinese authorities was called for. Other newspapers feared that the abductions at Lau Fau Shan could make the people of Hong Kong to lose confidence in the maintenance of law and order within the colonial city's territories. Overall, newspapers reported on this incident hoped the government would act to reassure the people in the New Territories that law and order would be upheld.

The *Express* said the government must shoulder the responsibility for permitting the Communists to intrude into Hong Kong's territory and forcibly abduct people. It also raised concerns about the detention and beating of people in a hut purportedly permitted only to be used for studying Mao's philosophy.[66]

The Hong Kong Fishing Industry and Commercial General Association chairman, Ng Lam-wai, called on the Hong Kong government to strengthen security measures in Deep Bay to prevent the recurrence of a similar incident. He added: "A representation on the incident serves no useful purpose.... Only a strong protest can make Peking restrain the criminal activities of the militiamen in Shekou." Ng further pointed out that the abduction of Tsang and his two sons took place in the colony's territorial waters and constituted a breach of international law.[67]

The people of Lau Fau Shan rallied at the Governor's House to protest against the government's failure to provide adequate protection for oyster farmers in the Deep Bay area. One told a reporter for the *South China Morning Post*:

> All this talk about additional police launches and military helicopters to protect the people of Lau Fau Shan is useless. I personally made a check along the coastline. There were no police launches in Deep Bay itself. There were two police launches today, but they were outside the area. As I mentioned before a police launch stood by doing nothing during 1968 and watched some 61 fishermen being abducted. And the kidnappers

were civilians, they were not even in uniform.... The recent killing of the three members of the Tsang family by the communists was murder. Murder is a crime. What is the Government going to do about it? You cannot repay the Tsang family by giving them relief.... Even our business has been affected. We are afraid to go to sea because of the danger.[68]

Meanwhile, the association planned to contact the Taiwan government to send the widow of Tsang Ngau and her family to Taiwan for resettlement.[69]

One newspaper said the government must shoulder the responsibility for the freedom with which Communists were able to intrude into Hong Kong's territory and forcibly abduct people.[70] Despite the protests and critiques in the media, there was not much change in government policy regarding the sea territories. However, as the Cultural Revolution moved to another stage, cases of cross-border kidnapping dwindled over the next few years—or at least they no longer appeared in the newspapers.

CONCLUSION

The Tsang Ngau case and other kidnappings exposed the ambiguities of the residential status of people who worked at sea. Law enforcement in the sea territories was difficult, and coverage was sparse. The right to government protection for Hong Kong residents who worked on the fringes of the colony's sea borders were perennially in question. There were numerous cases of kidnapping both in the sea territories and near the land border in the 1960s and 1970s. These cases make clear that the Hong Kong government was not to be counted on for protection in areas outside the city center. Even though the majority of Hong Kong's population did not live or work on the sea, it made them worry about their own safety because there did not seem to be any effective countermeasures against such crimes even within Hong Kong's jurisdiction.

In addition, territorial waters are a distinctive geographical category. Unlike land borders, the definition of sea borders is often ambiguous. The jurisdiction over the sea shared by Hong Kong and China was unclear. Moreover, because many fishermen and oystermen frequently traveled back and forth between the sea territories of mainland China and Hong Kong, there was no documentation of their actual whereabouts. The sea became a ghostly space where people might disappear without a trace or reappear as dead bodies, and no one could protect them. It was a space where the dead, the living, and the missing all blended into each other. Dead and missing bodies were particularly horrifying, not just because of the number and the way they are discovered, but because the living imbue them with all the dread and fear they had had about the PRC regime all along.

To many of those who had escaped China and even seen fellow refugees die in the attempt, reports of dead bodies and kidnappings reinforced their traumatic memories of running away from the CCP. The journeys of those who made attempts to escape to Hong Kong were driven by and filled with the fear of dying, and yet even those who had survived the journey continued to be haunted by reminders in the media about those who had been less fortunate.

During the Cultural Revolution, terror was present in daily life for Hong Kong residents in general and for people in the fisheries in particular. Horror stories of the sea, such as the floating bodies and the kidnappings in Hong Kong territorial waters, triggered new fearful imaginings about what the CCP was doing to its people beyond its nominally closed border. In these horror stories, the CCP was portrayed as nothing but an agent of death, with dead bodies washing up on shore and CCP agents invading Hong Kong waters to kidnap and gruesomely kill fishermen and oystermen. At the same time, the entire population of Hong Kong was traumatized either by their memories of escape and or their concern for their families back home, or both.

These stories were being publicized by mostly pro-KMT newspapers, and many of them had an anti-CCP propagandistic flavor. These traumatic memories about dead and missing bodies and the fear toward the CCP mostly pertained only to the people in Hong Kong, however. The discovery of dead bodies and incidents of kidnapping were seldom reported in Macau newspapers even though there was evidence of both in Hong Kong newspaper reports and government documents. In Taiwan, some newspapers and publications may contain some of these accounts, but those residing in Taiwan consuming these stories were not equally impacted because of the island's detachment from the PRC physically and politically.

The case of the floating bodies in Hong Kong in 2019 made many people fear that protesters had been killed after being arrested. The lack of transparency about treatment of protesters in custody is not unlike what the people of Hong Kong experienced during the Cultural Revolution. People died out of sight, and the truth about their fates remained unknown.

4

THE UNWANTED IN LIMBO

Was Hong Kong a Refuge or a Dumping Ground?

In the previous chapter, we learned that kidnappings at sea and the discoveries of floating bodies of those who died while fleeing the mainland or were killed during the Cultural Revolution traumatized the residents of Hong Kong and shaped their views toward the Chinese Communist Party. Using the cases of deportation as examples, we will see in this chapter that Hong Kong served as an important stage for Cold War propaganda warfare between the CCP and the KMT. The Hong Kong government and the KMT in Taiwan used immigration and refugee policies to divide the migrants from China into categories and allowed only "desirable" escapees to enter and live in their territories. Indeed, Hong Kong and Taiwan used each other as dumping grounds in casting out unwanted elements in their societies. Throughout the 1950s–1970s, while the Hong Kong authorities used the deportation ordinance to expel political activists from Hong Kong, Taiwan did not want to admit anyone whose political status was in doubt.

The exclusion of these individuals from territories that claimed to be part of the "Free World" or "Free China" exposes the KMT and its Cold War allies to the charge of hypocrisy. People who left Communist China were not free; their movements and even their existence in these territories continued to be restricted. More important, the Cold War generated anxieties for the governing regimes and the people transiting through the Southern Periphery. On the one hand, the KMT, the Hong Kong government and the PRC authorities wanted to police their administrative borders so that only desirable people could enter or stay in their territories; on the other hand, the discussions and decisions about who was desirable or undesirable reveal the mistrust, suspicion, uncertainty, and ambivalence that the regimes and the media felt about the intentions and backgrounds of the people who expressed their desires to move or to stay.

The subject of deportations during the Cold War is similar to a recent hotly debated topic in Hong Kong that prompted massive antigovernment protests in 2019, the Extradition Bill. The bill, which would have allowed for criminal suspects to be extradited to mainland China, prompted outrage when it was introduced in April 2019 because critics feared that, if passed, the law could subject Hong Kong citizens to arbitrary detention and unfair trials in mainland China. Hundreds of thousands of people took to the streets, and the bill was eventually withdrawn. Nevertheless, under the Beijing-imposed National Security Law passed on June 30, 2020, suspects in Hong Kong who are charged with violating this law may be subject to extradition to mainland Chinese courts for trial.

In her commentary on the Extradition Bill, former legislator Margaret Ng Ngoi-yee made the argument that the chief executive, Carrie Lam, is "duty bound not to send anyone in Hong Kong into a place where you cannot guarantee that this person will have the minimum protection of a fair trial."[1] However, the policy of sending "suspects" outside of the territory of Hong Kong is nothing new. Hong Kong authorities have a history of sending people to places where they cannot guarantee the person will have the minimum protection of a fair trial.

As early as the 1940s, certain people in Hong Kong were coded as "undesirable" residents or aliens subject to immigration control: "vagabonds or bad characters without visible means of subsistence"; "persons who . . . become a source of danger to the peace, order, and good government of the colony"; and the "large proportion of the immigrant population which is either incapable of being absorbed into useful occupation for any length of time or has no such desire."[2]

In 1949, at a time when there were many immigrants from mainland China arriving in Hong Kong, there was discussion on whether to modify the definition of "suspected undesirable" in the Deportation of Aliens

Ordinance as too ambiguous and hard to implement. The government decided that the ordinance should be used only in emergency situations but agreed that the power of the ordinance could be expanded without approval from the legislature if there were a "deterioration in the security situation" that required it.[3]

In the early 1950s, the Deportation of Aliens Ordinance (CH 240) was revised to meet the conditions of Hong Kong at that time and the definition of "undesirables" came to include any person who:

(a) does not have the means of subsistence and is diseased, maimed, blind, idiot, lunatic or decrepit and may be hindered by his state from earning a livelihood; or
(b) is unable to show that he has in his possession the means of decently supporting himself and his dependents, if any, until he obtains a livelihood; or
(c) is a person likely to become a vagrant, beggar or a charge upon any public or private charitable institution; or
(d) is a person suffering from a contagious disease which is loathsome or dangerous; or
(e) has been removed from any country or state by the government authorities of any such country or state for any reason whatever; or
(f) is suspected of being likely to promote sedition or to cause a disturbance of the public tranquility.[4]

The ordinance targeted people who were weak, sick, and deemed "unproductive." Subsection (f) was often used to target people who were active in politics or who were Triad members. In the 1950s–1970s, the Hong Kong government tried to maintain political neutrality so that it would not offend the regime in mainland China while upholding the democratic ideals of Great Britain. The form of the deportation ordinance was borrowed from Great Britain at a time when the country wanted to prevent certain people from becoming permanent residents. In Hong Kong, the people perceived as threatening to its political neutrality, regardless of their political stance, could be suspected of "being likely ... to cause a disturbance of the public tranquility." The ordinance also specified that people who were not British citizens or who had not lived in Hong Kong for more than ten years (termed "Hong Kong belongers") as "aliens" could be subject to deportation, but not people who had lived in Hong Kong for a longer period of time. The law created a double standard for residents, with those who were born or had been in Hong Kong for a sufficient period considered permanent residents and those who did not fulfill these requirements being treated as people in transit with no definitive rights to stay.[5]

Three deportation cases show how Hong Kong and Taiwan attempted to "remove" or disallow the entry of "undesirables." These three cases show that the difficulty of policing administrative boundaries because it is hard to know the truths about the people who entered or left a territory. Because there was so much unknown about the other side of the Bamboo Curtain, the background of the people who originated from outside were always in doubt. The first case is the deportation of a man who fraudulently claimed to be a KMT general throughout the 1950s. Between the 1950s and 1970s, numerous people who disrupted the harmony of Hong Kong society, including Triad members and people who committed crimes in Hong Kong, were deported to Macau, Taiwan, and other territories. The protagonist of this case, Lam Yin Chang, later ended up as one of these deportees. In 1962, he was deported from Hong Kong to Macau, which refused him entry, and then to Taiwan, along with two high-profile homicide suspects, for fraudulent dealings and causing community tensions. The archival materials suggest the strength of the KMT network in Hong Kong both within prestigious circles and among the Triads and ethnic gangs. It also shows that how the Hong Kong government saw people with KMT affiliations as a threat especially in the 1950s and early 1960s, when it maintained a political neutral stand. The second case is the deportation of a pro-CCP couple, Fu Che and Shek Hwei, who were famous movie stars in the 1960s but also were active in promoting propaganda in Hong Kong. They were first detained in a concentration camp for their political activities during the 1967 riots. In 1968, the Hong Kong government tried to send them to the PRC, but the deportation was not successful. This case was widely reported in newspapers because of the couple's celebrity; these reports, by both KMT- and CCP-affiliated newspapers, show how the media in Hong Kong furthered propaganda efforts for both political parties. Like the dead and missing bodies in the last chapter, this case reveals how the Cultural Revolution bled into Hong Kong and traumatized the population in the late 1960s. Unlike the first two cases, the third case in this chapter is a "homecoming" story and a denial of entry rather than a deportation. Ten KMT POWs who were released by the PRC in 1975 tried to "return" to Taiwan because they believed the KMT was their state. However, they were not given entry permits after staying in Hong Kong for a few months. This case reveals that while Hong Kong was able to deport political activists or people who had committed crimes to Taiwan, Taiwan also had its own strategy of abandoning "undesirable" people in Hong Kong.

These three cases were chosen because of the complexities of their experiences and affiliations. The first and second cases show that people who were affiliated with the KMT or the CCP were not welcomed in Hong Kong because of the Hong Kong government's desire to maintain the neutrality of the city. The second and third cases show that "repatriation" efforts to both the PRC and ROC sometimes failed, leaving these exiles in limbo in Hong Kong. Together, these cases reveal that while the Hong Kong government wanted to send self-identified Chinese patriots back to whichever regime the individuals claimed to belong, the PRC and the ROC did not extend a welcome to these exiled patriots because their trustworthiness and loyalty were open to doubt.

It also exposes the complexities of Chinese people's citizenship in the Southern Periphery. On the one hand, the various states seem to have clear definitions of what constituted undesirable based on political neutrality or loyalty; on the other hand, there were fears that the individuals may have intentions that were different than what they appeared to be. The ambiguities of these people show us that not just the physical borders in the Southern Periphery were porous, but also that people's political loyalty and affiliations could also cut across those borders. It also raises the question about whether any migrant can be trusted by any political regime.

CASE 1: LAM YIN CHANG

Born in 1917 or 1918 in Guangdong Province, China, to a poor seaman, Lam Yin Chang did not have any schooling and spent most of his childhood working as a ball boy at a club tennis court next to the residence of famed KMT general Heung Hon Ping in Guangzhou.[6] In the late 1930s, when the war between China and Japan broke out, Lam decided to join his distant cousin Lam Cham, who was on the KMT Military Council in Chongqing.

Throughout his later days in Hong Kong, Lam claimed to have been "a regimental comer in Burma in 1941–42," where he was responsible for the rescue of Francis Festing, a senior British Army officer who later became the commander of British forces in Hong Kong in 1945–46 and again in 1949. During his time in the Burma-Yunnan region, General Festing and his troops were cut off by the Japanese. At one point, a story began to circulate among the British and Chinese troops that Festing passed out in the middle of a battle and was rescued by a Chinese military official.[7] Lam later identified himself as that officer.

In actuality, however, Lam was only a "temporary and very junior officer of the KMT engaged in recruitment in the On Shun [Anshun] area of Kwei Chau [Guizhou] Province." Shortly after he resigned and was discharged from the military, he became "the manager of a truckers' café" near the border of Burma and Yunnan for three years from 1940 to 1943, selling fish and rice to military personnel active in the war. It was probably during that time that he heard the story of General Festing and decided to turn himself into a hero.[8]

In 1947, two years after Japan surrendered, Lam was back in Guangzhou and was "initiated into the Hung Fat Shan Chung Yee Tong, the official KMT Triad society later generally known as the 14 Society." Since the early 1950s, the "14 Society" was known in Hong Kong as the "14K Triad Society." The 14K was also known to consist of former KMT members who had become active in organized crime since the early 1950s.[9]

Sometime in 1950, Lam Yin Chang went to Hong Kong, where he became the disciple of two well-known figures who would later be deported to Taiwan. After he had settled in Hong Kong, Lam started impersonating a high-ranking KMT general and claimed to be the rescuer of General Festing. With medals and a military uniform jacket borrowed from acquaintances who had served in the military, Lam went to a studio to have a professional photograph taken in the summer of 1957.[10] As a result of his adopted "identity," Lam was able to obtain high status in the political and upper-class circle of Hong Kong in the following decade.

Lam's link to Festing also helped him con businessmen into fraudulent deals.[11] In 1958, apparently because of his reputation as a KMT general, Lam talked to Leung Kwai Fong, the adviser to the Committee of the Guangdong Tongxiang (Native-Place) Association, at Rennie's Mill Refugee Camp. He might have earned the trust of the officials at Rennie's Mill because of his alleged KMT affiliation. He offered to raise funds toward the cost of constructing a new building for the association. Lam later managed to raise HK$10,000 and was elected as the honorary president of the association as a result. It later emerged that Lam collected money far in excess of that sum and pocketed the remaining funds. Despite that, by then Lam had gained a considerable following in the community of Rennie's Mill and successfully ousted committee members opposed to him and replaced them with members of his clique. The trust he gained at Rennie's Mill shows that people with high status in the KMT had much power within the camp and in Hong Kong.

The reputation of being a KMT general also helped him with Buddhist leaders in Hong Kong. In 1959, Lam Yin Chang made an impression when he visited the Chuk Lam Monastery in Tsuen Wan, in the New Territories.[12] The head monks wished to obtain permission from the government to construct a small temple and asked Lam to use his political influence on their behalf. Whether all former reputable KMT generals had this kind of special access to the government is not known, but it was a common public perception that they were highly influential people in Hong Kong political circles. Per Lam's request, Lam was given HK$1,000 to "entertain officials," and then later another HK$2,500 to erect a *pai lau* (a traditional Chinese style archway or gateway as the main entrance of a hall or monastery). Lam did not build the *pai lau* and later informed the monastery treasurer that he wanted another HK$10,000 urgently, since "although he had hundreds of thousands in the bank it was tied up in business deals." The monks gave him HK$10,000 against three promissory notes. When the money was not paid back, the treasurer presented the checks to the Bank of Canton, but they were rejected. There are no further details in the case about whether Lam would really have had the ability to help the monastery to obtain the building permit even if he had wanted to, but it does not seem likely that he did.

More important in terms of his political influence as a "KMT general," Lam on multiple occasions attempted to secure the release of Triad members and KMT-affiliated people between 1957 and 1959. The first one Lam tried to rescue was the chairman of the Mong Kok Kaifong Association, Suen Koon Ching. After World War II, traditional mutual aid organizations were set up with the help of the Secretariat for Chinese Affairs, particularly the Social Welfare Council, with the intention of developing nongovernmental civil society and serving the residents of specific neighborhoods (*kaifong*). The main purpose was to provide low-cost or free services in such areas as education and health care to the local residents, many of whom were escapees who had just arrived from China. Suen was scheduled to be deported for suspicion of connecting to the Triad. Using his faux reputation as a KMT general, Lam asked the police to release him. The result of the petition is unknown, but likely it was rejected.

In 1958, Lam asked the police to release Kong Wing Wah, the alleged leader of the Green Gang, who was due to be deported. His deportation was suspended, though Kong was later expelled from Hong Kong for operating a worldwide heroin trafficking ring. Lam also requested the release of two suspected Triad members, Tai Kai Hon and Pang Chi Fai. It was noted in Lam's deportation case that the presiding official believed that Lam might be useful for the Special Branch of the police because of his seemingly wide connections with the KMT and the Triads. The Triads in Hong Kong were known to have links to the KMT in Taiwan. Before the formation of the Independent Commission Against Corruption in the 1970s, Triad crimes were rampant in Hong Kong, and the police may have used Lam's connections to get to more senior KMT leaders, or else Lam may have bribed the police to suspend the KMT members' deportation.

By summer 1962, Lam moved to Fanling, a town in the New Territories, and began to involve himself in the politics of the district. The Fanling Rural Committee, a powerful organization in the district at that time, was divided into two groups. One group was headed by Pang Fu Wah and was made up of Cantonese members, many of whom were ex-Nationalist soldiers with 14K Triad connections. The other group consisted of Hakka residents. Lam identified with the former and was scheming to take over the leadership. He was able to gain the trust of the high-ranking members because they believed that Lam had sufficient political clout to eliminate the Hakka leaders and could help them solidify their power in the committee. Lam was rumored to have pocketed funds from the people in Fanling, and his involvement with the Fanling Rural Committee began to attract the attention of the police.[13]

The planning of the New Year's Fair of 1963, a popular event among local residents, resulted in controversy. Lam invited members of the Fanling community to a dinner dedicated to the deceased KMT officers once (purportedly) under his command in late 1962. There he announced he would open an amusement park featuring a gambling stall at the fair. At the dinner, Lam met Chan Kam Hei, a businessman impressed by Lam's tale of influence. After some negotiations, Chan and his friends gave Lam HK$6,000 in January 1963 as part of an investment in the amusement park. Later, when Chan approached Lam to inquire about the deal, he was told it was canceled. Lam used the same tactic to cheat other influential residents of Fanling, one of whom was Tung Kei.[14] His dispute with Tung turned out to be detrimental.

ARREST

Lam's fraudulent and other criminal activities were brought to light when he filed several complaints about his neighbors and a few police officers. On December 26, 1962, in a letter addressed to the assistant commissioner of police, Lam complained that Tung Kei, with whom he had a dispute over money, was threatening his life and requested police protection. The letter was forwarded to the Criminal Investigation Department New Territories the next day. Lam called on the assistant commissioner of police in the New Territories the following day and handed him two typewritten letters, one repeating his allegations against Tung Kei and requesting a full inquiry, the other making fresh allegations listing a number of persons who were said to have damaged Lam's reputation by declaring that he was not an ex-general, including two police officers who were involved in his case. He condemned the policemen for being "British spies" and demanded an investigation of the two officers, whom Lam accused of receiving money from "vice establishments."

Eventually, the police were fed up with Lam and noted that "Lam gave the impression of being drunk and his attitude to the Deputy Commissioner was loud-mouthed and aggressive." After a fight in a local market, the police arrested Lam and charged him with disorderly conduct. Lam pleaded guilty through his legal adviser and apologized for his bad language in the court, explaining "that as an old military man he had a quick temper." He was discharged for that particular offense but was later brought to the Victoria Road Detention Centre for a special hearing. Since the people who were held at Victoria Road Detention Centre were mostly future deportees, it seems clear that the authorities had already decided to remove Lam from Hong Kong.

At his hearing, it was decided that Lam was disruptive to the order of Hong Kong and must be deported. The concluding statement made explicit that his claim to be a general as a fraud: "Lam Yin Chang ha[d] lived so long with his "Major General" pose that he ha[d] become deluded and now believe[d] in it himself." It also described the potential harm Lam could bring to Hong Kong society, in particular to Fanling, where he resided. The official who presided over the hearing also weighed in on the social disturbances Lam fostered among the ethnic groups in Fanling and on his negative effect on the police force. The decision of the committee was to issue a "deportation order for life" against Lam under section 3(1)(c) of the ordinance.

DEPORTATION

Lam's case was reported in major newspapers when his deportation was announced. However, most reports treated the story of Lam as a facetious tabloid scandal rather than a serious news event. The reports focus on how he had managed to impersonate the KMT general and cheated money from all kinds of people for so many years. They were not so concerned about the process of the trial and deportation, as most readers were not interested in knowing what punishment the convicted received, as long as they were out of sight. Those who wrote about Lam were much amused by his acts. One commentary summarized his pattern of financial cheating: "[Sometimes] he claimed to be omnipotent and said anything can be done using just his name, and he took in substantial amount of money from that"; at other times, "he persuaded others to do business with him, and then swallowed other people's share." He also sometimes "issue[d] promissory checks to borrow money, pledging to give benefits to the lenders in the future."¹⁵ Other newspaper articles focused on how he posed as a general for so long and what led to his arrest.

The initial plan was to deport Lam to Taiwan within two weeks. However, for reasons not recorded in the case file, he was instead deported to Macau on August 24, 1963, four days after the hearing. When he reached Macau, he was told to return to Hong Kong because the Macanese authorities considered him to be "unwelcome" too. This was not the first time deported people from Hong Kong were rejected by Macau.¹⁶ Like Hong Kong, the authorities in Macau also did not want the city to be infiltrated by KMT agents.

In October, it was reported that the Hong Kong authorities planned to deport him again. Before the final destination of deportation was announced, some newspapers speculated that he would be sent to Macau again. At that time, Taiwan was only briefly mentioned as an option, but according to *Kung Sheung Evening News*, his wife indicated that Lam still preferred to go to Macau because it was closer to Hong Kong, which would enable his relatives to visit more easily. The family still hoped that Macau would reaccept him.¹⁷ This purported preference of Lam and his family shows that to some residents in the Southern Periphery, physical distance was more important than differences in jurisdiction, but the regimes had their own concerns about regional security. In the end, Lam was deported to Taiwan on October 15, 1963, despite his family's protest.¹⁸

IMPLICATIONS OF LAM'S CASE

Most of these deportees went through hearings inside the detention center rather than an open court trial. Journalists asked legal experts to examine the legality of the controversial process. One international law expert held that there should be a formal court dealing with such deportation cases.¹⁹ Upon careful examination, the legality of the hearing process and decision seems arbitrary. There were no due processes for these cases, and the decisions were made by the official in the detention center.

The official reason for Lam's deportation was apparently the disharmony he had caused in Hong Kong society. However, the immediate trigger that led to his arrest finally was the complaint he filed against two police officers, which had angered the police force. If Lam had not reported them, perhaps the police would have tolerated his misdeeds for a while longer, as they had done for many years despite his impersonation of the KMT general.

From the testimony of the hearing and the newspaper reports, Lam did not seem to have strong political convictions. However, in the hearing, testimony proved that his presence disrupted peace and order in Hong Kong. The most notable disharmony he had caused was the conflict between the Cantonese clan and Hakka clan in Fanling District. Ethnic tensions between ethnic clans had long existed before Lam's arrival in Fanling, and they probably did not disappear after Lam left. It is doubtful that Lam was the cause of the ethnic unrest in Fanling.

A more likely potential disharmony that made Lam "undesirable" in Hong Kong was his involvement with the Triads and the KMT. From his story, we learn that he had deep connections with the KMT and its affiliated Triads and the Green Gang. His reputation among KMT circles came from being the apocryphal figure who had saved Francis Festing, the British general, during World War II, but his ability to gain trust and monetary support in Hong Kong society at large came from his fake identity as a KMT general and the subsequent connections to the 14K Triads and the powerful local cliques in Fanling.

Lam's story sheds light on the active role the KMT played in Hong Kong society in the 1950s and early 1960s, as well as the deep ties it shared with the 14K Triad groups. From his case and the other deportation cases it mentioned, it is apparent that the extensive networks of KMT and the 14K had been a problem of colonial security. The solution the Hong Kong government applied to the problems of the Triads was to deport known members to Taiwan rather than send them to prisons in Hong Kong, probably because those who were sentenced to jail in Hong Kong would eventually return to society and could continue to be a problem. During the 1950s and early 1960s, a large number of KMT affiliated people were deported to Taiwan. The KMT's infiltration in Hong Kong society posed a threat to the carefully constructed political neutrality of Hong Kong.

Another factor that made Lam "undesirable" in the city was his alleged bad character, as reflected in his attempts to defraud citizens. It is unclear how "attempted" crimes were taken into consideration in regard to the verdict, since most of the fraudulent schemes seem ultimately to have failed. The testimonies of the alleged fraud victims were used to prove Lam's dubious character, in addition to his fake persona as a KMT general. The hearing record also includes the testimony given by Lam's chauffeur, who provided further proof of Lam's disreputable character. The driver, Peter Fong, stated that he met Lam during the war in China when Lam was a traveling trader and that they again met in 1959 after Lam had become a successful "general." Fong became Lam's personal chauffeur for a short time. Lam was infuriated one day because he found out that his mistress had taken an interest in another man and asked Fong to run her over. When Fong refused, Lam asked Fong to disfigure the mistress's legs with a "chopper." When Fong again refused, Lam tried to persuade Fong to plant heroin in her flat so that she would be arrested. Fong's testimony depicted Lam as a despicable person who would do anything if he felt his dignity was harmed.

The verdicts in many of these deportation cases were not based on solid evidence that a crime was committed, as Fong's testimony suggests. Rather, they relied on general descriptions and evaluations of the defendants' moral character and speculation as to the potential disturbances they might cause to Hong Kong society. On one level, it shows that there was little trust for Hong Kong residents who had strong ties with a political party or were politically active. On another level, it shows that the Hong Kong authorities could remove anyone they wanted without proper evidence or trials. Thus, such deportations reveal much about what the authorities considered to be potential disturbances to society. From Lam's case, we learn that associating with the KMT and the Triad was politically undesirable in 1950s and 1960s Hong Kong. Lam's complaint about the policemen was the last straw for the authorities. By then he had become too much of a nuisance to let him stay, even though he could potentially share information about his KMT network with the authorities.

Lam's loyalty to the KMT was questionable because his identity was fabricated. He had some actual connections to KMT-affiliated Triad members, but there is no sign that he was truly a loyalist who wanted to move to Taiwan. As indicated in some of the reports after he was sent back from Macau, he preferred not to go to Taiwan because of the long distance. This case also shows the double standards in Hong Kong's and Taiwan's immigration policies. It is ironic that Lam was forcibly deported to Taiwan while many inmates at Rennie's Mill Refugee Camp who were eager to be reunited with the KMT applied but were ultimately rejected. What mattered to the Hong Kong government was that the troublemakers in Hong Kong society be sent away. As for the KMT, Lam was likely seen as less threatening than the Rennie's Mill Refugee Camp inmates because the latter could potentially be spies of the CCP or critical of the KMT. While Lam was seen as threatening to social order in Hong Kong, he was not threatening to the ROC regime because he had not expressed publicly any interest in national politics, despite being an impostor as a KMT general.

Lam also would not have been subject to deportation had he been born in Hong Kong, for at the time of his case only people who were in Hong Kong for less than ten years could be deported. He had lived in Hong Kong for seven years but was still classified as an "alien." When one was deported as an "undesirable," it also meant that that he lost the right of abode in Hong Kong permanently. Many such deportees, like Lam, were deported alone. Their spouses and other family members could remain in Hong Kong. At that time, residency in Hong Kong for ten years was required for one to become a Hong Kong "belonger" who could not be deported.[20] Otherwise, people were treated as part of the "transiting" population or as an "alien" in the city.

The deportation process reveals the porousness of the sea borders separating Hong Kong and Macau, Taiwan, and China. Lam was not accepted by Macau. In an article published in *Wah Kiu Yat Pao* on June 3, 1963, the author discussed how Macau did not want to accept deportees from Hong Kong. It contends that most of the deportees from Hong Kong were criminal elements who had brought bad influences to Macau. It urged the police to patrol the harbors more frequently in case people landed in Macau without the consent of the authorities. It also said that one group of deportees from Hong Kong was sent back because of their dubious backgrounds. One of them was said to be a drug seller. Even though the alleged drug dealer had a relative in Macau who could act as a guarantor, he was still not allowed to stay.[21] From these reports, we get the sense that such deportations were not negotiated diplomatically between the Hong Kong and Macau authorities. Rather, they were decided by the Hong Kong authorities and whether the deportees successfully entered Macau was a matter of luck.

When Lam was eventually deported to Taiwan, the local newspaper reported that he was detained for only a short period. This seems to have been standard practice because many other deportees were released soon after they arrived in Taiwan. It is likely that the Hong Kong government and the KMT had a special agreement regarding deportees with KMT backgrounds such that they were to be sent to Taiwan without severe punishment. Most of these cases of deportation were not widely reported in Taiwan either.

The early 1960s in Hong Kong was a time when local identities were in flux. The law targeted people in transit or recent migrants. This case reveals how vulnerable were people in transit residing in Hong Kong. The "suspects" were not given due process and all the proceedings were secret. It also reveals that the colonial administration in Hong Kong was primarily concerned about ethnic conflicts and the influence of the KMT in such conflicts in the late 1950s and 1960s. Of the people who were deported during this period, most were either secret agents for the KMT or were involved in Triad crimes.

After the Cultural Revolution started in 1967, the Hong Kong authorities used the deportation law to mostly target people who were involved in Communist propaganda activities, especially around the 1967 riots. As we will see in the second case, the matter of how to deal with the leaders of the riots became a contentious issue between the Hong Kong government and the mainland authorities.

CASE 2: THE COUPLE—SHEK HWEI AND FU CHE

Shek Hwei (Shi Hui) was born in Nanjing in 1934 and migrated to Hong Kong in the late 1940s. In 1951, she joined the Changcheng (Great Wall) Studio and soon became one of the most popular actresses in the company. Fu Che (Fu Qi) was born in 1929 in Shenyang and grew up in Shanghai. He moved to Hong Kong in 1949 and also joined the Changcheng Studio soon after. Shek and Fu met in the early 1950s while costarring in films. They married in 1954 and were active in the movie industry until the 1970s. At the same time, they were known to be leftist sympathizers.

ARREST

The 1967 riots began in May in Hong Kong and led to fifty-one deaths, 4,500 arrests, and a campaign of bombings that killed and injured many local people. The immediate trigger was a strike at an artificial flower factory. The Communist-influenced Hong Kong Federation of Trade Unions intervened in the strike, and its involvement raised the attention of the PRC Ministry of Foreign Affairs. About the same time, a series of anti-British demonstrations were mobilized across China in major cities such as Beijing and Guangzhou. The Communists in Hong Kong thus framed the riots in the British colony and other protests as anticolonial in nature.

In the PRC's official newspaper distributed in the mainland, *Renmin Ribao*, an article was published on September 30, 1967, a few months after the height of the riots, that glorified them as a strike against British colonialism. The author claims that the struggle in Hong Kong was an extension of the larger, Mao-led Communist Revolution that transcended boundaries and was global in nature. The author explicitly calls the struggle against the colonial administration an achievement in "further expanding the anti-imperialist patriotic united front." According to the article, the Hong Kong activists relied on Maoism to guide them to victory, with Maoism thus "becoming an ideological atomic bomb with which Hong Kong nationalist compatriots engage in the struggle."[22]

On May 16, the leftists formed the Hong Kong and Kowloon Committee for Anti-Colonial Hong Kong Persecution Struggle. The struggle committee took on a multifront approach to attack the colonial government through protests, strikes, and newspaper propaganda. A few days later, protesters formed a rally outside the Governor's House, an event in which both Shek and Fu participated. Hundreds of supporters held up copies of Mao's Little Red Book and chanted Communist slogans.

More protests were triggered in the following weeks. More than twenty trade unions in various industries went on a four-day strike in response to the use of force by the colonial police. An article in *Renmin Ribao* lauded the striking workers for "continuously attacking the military threat posed by the Hong Kong–British colonial administration and the British capitalists." The article also described the workers as appealing to Maoist ideals in trying to achieve their objectives: "To defend Maoist thought, to protect the people's dignity, we must struggle with the evil British imperialists to the very end! Workers now return to their unions, participate in denouncement meetings, and study Chairman Mao's quotes every day."[23] In addition, nine newspapers in Hong Kong, including the pro-Beijing *Da Gong Bao*, were flooded with rhetorical attacks on the colonial government's attempts at repression. Pro-KMT newspapers also reported these incidents, but their commentators and reporters focused on ridiculing or condemning the pro-Mao rhetoric and protests.

Both Fu Che and Shek Hwei belonged to the entertainment industry branch of the struggle committee when they participated in the rally outside the Governor's House. Because of their celebrity status, the police easily identified them. On July 15, 1967, the Hong Kong police went into their house at midnight and arrested them, confiscating their books, scripts, and other materials.[24]

In the 1960s, hundreds of people who were suspected of "plotting to overthrow the British colonial government" or who participated in riots were arrested and detained in the Victoria Road Detention Centre.[25] People who were arrested for disrupting social order, like Lam Yin Chang, were also sometimes detained there. These detainees were mostly politically affiliated with either the CCP or the KMT or had connections with the Triads. They generally were interrogated for their political activities, and the colonial records show that they were not put on open trial but faced hearings within the jail. In 1968, leaders of the 1967 riots were arrested by the Hong Kong Police and then sent to the Victoria Road Detention Centre. Most of these political activists would later be deported to Macau, Taiwan, or mainland China.

Unlike the case of Lam Yin Chang, the record of the couple's hearing cannot be found in the archives of the colonial office. However, their deportation was widely reported and discussed in Hong Kong newspapers, both pro-CCP and pro-KMT, upon which the following is based. Colonial government officials and British government officials also pondered the case. When Fu Che and Shek Hwei were detained, newspapers began to speculate where the authorities would send them. According to a July 19, 1967 report, the couple did not want to be sent to mainland China, so speculation centered on Macau. Two months later, however, the same newspaper predicted a different destination for the actors' pending deportation: "According to reliable sources, [the couple] were disillusioned with the Communists in Hong Kong, and because of their realization, they requested Free China, Taiwan, to be their destination of deportation."[26] Another pro-KMT newspaper stated that they provided precious information to the police about the leftists' activities in Hong Kong, with the implication that this was the reason they were "allowed" to go to Taiwan.[27] Such rumors conjectured that the "real" political identities of the two were suspicious: they could be sincere supporters of the Mao regime, or they could be agents working for the KMT. The implication that Shek and Fu might not be genuinely loyal to the CCP reflects the political atmosphere in Hong Kong at that time, for political activists or people who were vocal about their political beliefs were often distrusted.

As for Macau, the author of the article that speculated where they would be deported showed sympathy toward Fu and Shek, as though they were KMT agents, and expressed his contempt for the Portuguese colony, which he viewed as totally run by the Communists. He doubted Macau's government had the ability to guarantee the safety and freedom of its residents, especially those with controversial political backgrounds. "The Communists in Macau can do whatever they want there," he wrote, "so even if they go to Macau, what kind of protection would they receive? Moreover, Fu Che and Shek Hwei are very talented young artists. Even if they don't have safety concerns, they would be like 'fish in shallow rivers.' They would have a hard time finding a way to excel in a small place like Macau and eventually die."[28]

Such contempt for Macau was not uncommon in pro-KMT newspaper editorials. Even before this period, it was often depicted as inferior to Hong Kong. Especially after the "123 incident" in 1966, Macau was seen as a place that had succumbed to the PRC regime, and residents of Hong Kong were warned not to go there because they might be kidnapped.

OPPOSITION TO DEPORTATION

Both leftist and rightist newspapers reported that there were protests inside and outside the detention center against the deportation of Fu Che and Shek Hwei during the months after their arrest. The two most prominent rightist newspapers, *Wah Kiu Yat Pao* and *Kung Sheung Evening News*, mocked these protests at the detention center. One editorial, titled "Why Are Hong Kong Communists and Triad Members Opposed to Being Deported Back to China? Would the CCP Let Go of These 'Traitors?'" (*Ganggong heibang weihe fandui jiefan dalu? Zhonggong nengfou fangguo zhexie "maiguo hanjian" ma?*), summed up the main critiques:

> According to what is said in leftist newspapers, the mainland is a "happy paradise" where everyone should have more than enough to eat and wear, and that makes everyone so proud, and it is definitely not comparable to the "colonial life" of Hong Kong. For these reasons, all these self-proclaimed leftist "patriots" should love the New China, and there is no reason for them to be afraid of going back. However, the fact is, many of these Hong Kong Communists and Triad members not only are unwilling to go back to the "ultimate happy" mainland to enjoy their happy lives, they are also trembling upon hearing the news of being deported to China, as though they are scared to death... especially the so-called "jailed fighters" (*yuzhong zhanshi*) who are rebelling after they have been detained in camps; their opposition to being sent back to China is the strongest even though they already lost their freedom.

The author continued to explain that many leftist journalists opposed deportation and claimed that "Hong Kong is part of China's sacred territories (*shensheng lingtu*) and that Chinese people have the absolute right to live in Hong Kong (*shensheng buke qinfan de quanli*)." The author criticized the hypocrisy of these leftist writers in glorifying Mao Zedong's thoughts, on the one hand, but objecting to the deportations of jailed Communist activists back to the mainland, on the other. The author added,

> If *Da Gong Bao* doesn't deny that these "jailed comrades" are the followers of Mao Zedong and have repeatedly chanted slogans such as "Long live Mao Zedong!" then their being sent back to China is just returning to be with Chairman Mao. Why do they have to object to this kind of "glorious" action? Wouldn't this be the same as "waving the Communist flag while at the same time sabotaging [the Communist cause]" (*dazhe hongqi fanhongqi*)?

The author then said that the people who were deported were "regaining their freedom and even earning the title of 'honorable release,'" and that they should feel "very blessed" about the opportunity.

The same author then explained what he thought were other "real reasons the Communists in Hong Kong objected to deportation." One was that, because of reporting about what happened to the leftist rioters deported back to China, they feared they too would "not receive a 'triumphant' welcome" and might be seen as "fake labor activists" (*gonggun*) and be "sent to Labor Reform Camps." The author also argued that the activists' "so-called anticolonial struggles" did not receive the blessings of the central government, and thus they would not be protected or acknowledged if they were sent back to China.[29]

Writings as such reflect the uncertainty and disdain residents in Hong Kong felt toward mainland China in the early stages of the Cultural Revolution. The general impression most people had from media reports and relatives' accounts was that everyone's life—including the lives of the activists in the Communist struggle—was at stake and the entire country was out of control.

It was finally decided that the couple would be sent to mainland China on March 14, 1968. According to a report in *Da Gong Bao* on March 15, 1968, Fu and Shek were locked up in a "VIP room" in the immigration office in Lo Wu, and there was a "No Entry" sign on the door. Then, a half-hour past noon, "a group of special agents who looked like wolves and tigers," led by the vice commissioner of police of Hong Kong, grabbed Fu Che and Shek Hwei by the neck, dragged them to the exit of the immigration office on the bridge, and attempted to deport them. This was not successful, and the couple went back to the Hong Kong side of the bridge. A few hours later, in front of the media, the couple made the following statement:

> We protest against the Hong Kong colonial government's fascist treatment, ignoring our rights, illegally deporting us. Hong Kong is part of China, and we have the right to live in Hong Kong. This so-called Vice-Commissioner of Police beat us up this morning, and even threatened us by saying that if we don't want to go back to China, then he would deport us to Taiwan. To protect our pride and rights as Chinese, we will continue our struggle here and not be intimidated. We will just stay here and let the world know about how the colonial fascist state oppresses us.[30]

The report focuses on the resistance of the couple, and their heroism was even highlighted because of the alleged police abuse. Hong Kong represented a battlefront to fight against colonialism. The couple chanted revolutionary songs, including "Daddy and Mommy Are Dear but Not as Dear as Chairman Mao" (*die qin niangqin buru Maozhuxi qin*).

The *Da Gong Bao* report also described the reactions of travelers who were crossing the border: "Facing the righteous condemnation and protests by the couple, the Vice Commissioner of Police in his 40s and other agents were afraid and went into hiding. Many travelers who passed by were touched by their heroic attitude as Chinese people, and they waved to the couple and showed their support to them." After they yelled at the colonial agents, the couple turned to the crowd and shouted, "The colonial government will lose! We will definitely win! Down with Hong Kong–British Fascism! Long Live Chairman Mao!" Then one traveler allegedly took out a Mao button he brought from China and put it on Fu Che. "With tears in their eyes, many travelers went up to shake their hands and showed their respect and concern." Furthermore, when the couple decided to set up a temporary shelter for the night, the people from Shenzhen allegedly brought them "food, tea, fruits and pork buns" and sent them blankets and other materials. Another took out a "dream treasure book" (*mengmei yiqiu de baoshu*)—Chairman Mao's Little Red Book—and presented it to them.[31] It is unclear whether these travelers were merely passers-by or went to Lo Wu intentionally to support the couple.

Da Gong Bao continued to report their conditions two days later on March 17, 1968, and praised the couple's perseverance and mocked the Hong Kong authorities' incompetence: "The special agents and the police were clumsy and chaotically running around (*tuantuan luanzhuan*)." While the couple's activism "won the praises of many fellow citizens," it also "gave the Hong Kong government a real and hard blow." The government officials at the immigration office were described as nervous and beat-up (*langbei jinzhang*) by the process.

The author of the *Da Gong Bao* article also analyzed the couple's psychology. It describes how they were eager to leave Hong Kong and go back to the mainland because the PRC was their real home:

> From this border, we see two different worlds. On the other side, we see a socialist country filled with happiness and brightness. Their children,

Ming Lan, Ming Wei, are learning and growing up in the embrace of the motherland; on this side, this is the Chinese territory governed by British colonialism. What they have [in Hong Kong] is the fascist brutality of colonialism, blood and tears, and the hatred between classes and ethnic groups. How much do they desire to return to be with their family members who are under the guidance of Chairman Mao!

Then it further depicts Shek Hwei's inner struggle between returning to her "homeland" and fighting against British colonialism:

Shek Hwei said before, when she saw the statue of Chairman Mao, she almost could not resist the temptation of stepping across the border. But when she thought of the teachings of Chairman Mao, when she thought of the conspiracy of the British colonials behind the illegal deportation, they were determined to stand firmly in the struggle against the British Hong Kong government until their conspiracy is eliminated.[32]

Overall, reports in *Da Gong Bao* framed Fu and Shek's "refusal" to enter the mainland as a deliberate heroic action against British colonialism. Meanwhile, as if the two actors were living in a parallel universe, the rightist newspapers told a very different version of events. One report in *Kung Sheung Evening News* on March 15, 1968, titled "Fu Che and Shek Hwei Still Dwelling at the Edge of the Den of Monsters," reported that the couple were still stranded because the mainland authorities refused their entry to Shenzhen.[33]

Fu and Shek stayed in Lo Wu for twenty-seven hours and finally were told to return to the detention camp. When it was known that the couple had to return, *Kung Sheung Daily News* began to ridicule them as cowards: "They looked as though they received the biggest pardon, and they happily ran back to Hong Kong, to the hands of the Hong Kong police—even though they still don't have their freedom. But not having freedom in a free atmosphere is better than not having it under the Iron Curtain." Reporters for *Kung Sheung Evening News* emphasized how relieved they were when they were being sent back to the detention camp in Hong Kong. One wrote: "They started to show a smile on their faces when they were brought into a police car." Other writings condemned the CCP for manipulating leftist sympathizers to stage the 1967 riots and then abandoning them: "[The rioters] have been used by the CCP, and they fought hard for them, so they thought that they deserved to be rewarded. But the CCP does not give a damn what they did. Now it's as though they have nowhere to escape while the enemies are right behind them."

Other rightist newspaper columnists chimed in to make fun of their "return" to the camp. One of them wrote a satirical series about the couple in a Cantonese colloquial style. After the couple were not permitted to enter the PRC and were sent back to the Victoria Road Detention Centre, he commented:

> They "should buy a roasted pig and offer it to the gods" because they "regain their lives again" (*jifan tiaoming*). They were eager to pick up all their luggage and volunteer to go back to the Victoria Road Detention Centre. No way would they "fight heroically against the colonial government" on the Lo Wu bridge any longer! Even though the Hong Kong authorities only made them return to the concentration camp, they were happier than picking up a thousand-dollar bill, and they laugh so hard that their eyes cannot be seen.

This author was contemptuous of the couple's hypocrisy for living a luxurious life: "In Hong Kong, they live in Yau Yat Chuen [in Kowloon Tong] with a one hundred fifty thousand-dollar house, sleep on a Simmons mattress, and are only so used to their luxurious lifestyle!"[34] Pointing out the discrepancy between rhetoric and reality is a common criticism by commentators in Hong Kong of Communist activists who claimed to endorse Mao Zedong and the CCP.

In one of his last entries, the same author wrote that Fu and Shek were glad to spend a few nights together because they had been detained separately for so long:

> They were only in tents at the side of the bridge, and they had to face the severe cold and winds, yet, for the couple, being able to meet is something that is worth celebrating. In the concentration camp, even though they could meet, they had to be separated by the barbed wire between them. One could only say, "Good morning, my dear husband," and the other says, "Good morning, my dear wife." Other than that, they could only send their love through their eyes, and they cannot even shake

hands. They should ask the authorities to give them a chance to go to China once a month. So that at least they have a small get-together at Lo Wu. But, it may be dangerous if China may change its mind and let them in, then it would be like surrendering to hell without being asked.[35]

Fu Che and Shek Hwei were sent back to the detention center for a few months before they were released. The reason for their rejection is not known, but some critics speculated that the government in Beijing did not want to have these Communist activists "return" to China because such people who had been enjoying a capitalistic lifestyle in Hong Kong could be a bad influence on Chinese society. One wrote:

> The Chinese Communist were afraid that after they let Fu Che and Shek Hwei return, the Hong Kong authorities would have a precedent and use the opportunity to deport all the detained members of the "struggle committee" who participated in the riot in May. Such "struggle committee" members who are enjoying the benefits of capitalism are actually the most unwelcomed by the CCP.[36]

In a series of official correspondence between the Hong Kong government and the Foreign Office in Britain documenting the political situation of Hong Kong in 1968, a few documents written by the colonial officials in Hong Kong about the Fu and Shek case were included. The documents confirm that the Hong Kong colonial authorities and PRC government interpreted the deportation of Fu and Shek differently. Surprisingly, the Hong Kong government did not portray sending the couple, along with other detainees at the Victoria Road Detention Centre, across the border to mainland China as acts of deportation or political sentences but as acts of release or pardon of detainees who clearly had disrupted the public order of Hong Kong and would otherwise have received severe penalties. One document summarized the recommendations by the Special Branch of the police force, which was in charge of investigating cases of political espionage in the colony, either to release detainees who had committed offenses like those of Shek and Fu in Hong Kong or back to China. Despite the Special Branch's suggestion that the less important Communist detainees be granted unconditional release if so desired by the CCP, the Hong Kong authorities did not release detainees to China because the Chinese foreign ministry in Beijing appeared to have no interest in receiving them. The Special Branch, however, also recommended that a phased release program should be planned so that gradually more detainees could be returned to China if the Chinese government was receptive to this gesture of goodwill. There was one caveat, though: the pace of such release should depend on the political climate at the time and the level of Communist activity the detainee had been involved with as well as the individual's potential threat to security.[37]

It may be the case that the CCP did not allow them to enter the PRC because it was wary of the bourgeois influence that the two actors had had in Hong Kong, but this was not the reason given by the Chinese officials. On the day Shek and Fu were sent back to the Victoria Road Detention Centre, the PRC government wrote a letter to the Hong Kong government stating that the two actors had the "sacred rights" to reside in Hong Kong. The official at the Foreign Affairs Office condemned the deportation: "The Chinese Government provides all Chinese with free movement facilities between Hong Kong and the rest of the motherland but must oppose deportation no matter what." The official explained to the Hong Kong government that any attempt to deport the two film stars was an act of persecution against Chinese compatriots. He also warned that such acts would lead to renewed tension in Hong Kong and on border. The official said, "We must stop these unreasonable practices and guarantee that there would be no recurrence in the future." Beijing demanded that the two film workers be declared innocent and set free and that their safety and freedom from any further persecution be guaranteed such that they would not be sent anywhere outside of Hong Kong against their will. The Hong Kong government responded to the letter denying that the two actors or any other persons were forcibly deported from Hong Kong because the couple "did not express unwillingness to return to China." It held that the action of letting the couple return to China was a friendly gesture "intended to relieve tension" between the two sides. However, the official from the Ministry of Foreign Affairs of the PRC government insisted that the colonial authorities treated the two actors as prisoners and "had used deceptive tactics to lure the two film workers to the border" by telling them that the matter of their return to China had already been arranged.[38] This debate over whether the case was one of deportation or release was unresolved. Only a few Communist activists detained at the Victoria Road Detention Centre were released after that, and none of them received the level of publicity Fu and Shek did.

AFTERMATH

Fu Che and Shek Hwei were sent back to the detention center for a few months before they were released. Despite all the media attention it received, Shek and Fu's deportation was not successful. The reason for the failed attempt was disputable. While the leftist newspaper *Da Gong Bao* portrayed them as patriotic heroes refusing to give in to the colonial regime, pro-KMT newspapers like *Wah Kiu Yat Pao* and *Kung Sheung Evening News* reported that the CCP used the couple as puppets in Hong Kong so that it could accuse the British colonial government of political persecution.

The couple went back to acting and continued to live in Hong Kong until the 1980s, when they immigrated to Canada. During those thirteen years in Hong Kong, they lived with uncertainty of possible deportation. When asked what they thought of their saga at the Lo Wu border decades later, they said, "Everyone has his/her past that is not worth mentioning."[39] None of the reports at that time had asked where the couple truly desired to reside. While the pro-Beijing newspaper claimed that they had an anticommunist mission to carry out in Hong Kong, the pro-KMT newspapers suggested that they desperately wanted to remain in the colony. The story of their deportation has received renewed media attention, as part of the absurdity of the 1967 riots in Hong Kong and the Cultural Revolution in China. Today, the former communist activists in Hong Kong who participated in the 1967 events generally have a negative reputation, and most of them are still ridiculed for their unreasonable rhetoric and behavior at that time. Their experiences were surely very different from those of people who lived through the same period in the PRC. These experiences are properly part of the history of the Cultural Revolution, however, since the actions of the participants in Hong Kong were triggered by events on the other side of the border.

In addition, this story about the couple can shed light on the relationship between the PRC, the KMT, and Hong Kong. Like the stories about dead bodies in chapter 3, the pro-KMT media used this incident to construct an unknown, cruel regime behind the border. The stories about what would happen if the couple entered the PRC's territory were speculations based on hearsay or other similar tales told by travelers. Such reporting and commentary reinforced the fear and repulsion people in Hong Kong felt toward the PRC regime. At the same time, the Hong Kong authorities used this case to showcase its benevolence and goodwill toward the CCP by calling this a "pardon" and "release" rather than deportation, although this gesture was not well received. As for the CCP, it continued to be adamant about the couple's rights in residing in Hong Kong, but the newspapers did not elaborate on the couple's achievements as CCP members. One possibility why the couple was not allowed entry to the mainland is that their forced return by the colonial government, if successful, could make the CCP seem weak and unable to stand up against the British colonial government in Hong Kong. In the reportage on this case, Hong Kong represented a place where Chinese people were under capitalist pollution and colonial oppression in leftist press, but in pro-KMT publications Hong Kong represented a free or even decadent city where even communists could do whatever they want and enjoy luxurious lifestyles compared to what they would have been subject to under the repressive PRC.

CASE 3: THE TEN POWS IN 1975

On June 4, 1975, Zhang Tieshi (Chang Tieh-shih), a sixty-year-old former Nationalist colonel who had been imprisoned for twenty-five years in the PRC after the Civil War, was found dead in a hotel room in Hong Kong. He reportedly had hanged himself.

Zhang had been among the 293 former KMT and Japanese prisoners of war released by the Chinese Communist Party under a special amnesty in early April 1975. Ten of the KMT POWs, including Zhang, chose to join the KMT in Taiwan. In order to go to Taiwan, they had to take a train to Hong Kong and apply for an entry permit. China Travel Services provided them with adequate money and accommodations at a designated hotel in Hong Kong for their stay while waiting for the entry permit.

The mainland government advertised the release of these POWs as an act of the CCP's benevolence, since the party let these former enemies leave and even provided them with travel stipends. Nevertheless, to the KMT at that time, the release of these former KMT soldiers was interpreted as a political act to embarrass the ROC government because the latter would be hesitant to accept them. The CCP's decision was very different from its previous attitude toward KMT soldiers. In 1965, when the Hong Kong–British administration sent four KMT soldiers who had escaped from the PRC to Taiwan, an article appeared in the PRC newspaper, *Renmin Ribao*, describing the Hong Kong government's action as unacceptable and "a clear signal of support of the harassment and sabotage activities conducted by the U.S.-Chiang Kai-shek faction along the Chinese coastline." The author of the article condemned the Hong Kong authorities for not sending the soldiers back to the mainland for prosecution.[40] Because of the drastic difference in the CCP's attitude in 1975, the ROC government worried that the POWs might have been brainwashed after all these years and could be spies working for the CCP.

The leadership of the KMT was also in transition at that moment because Chiang Kai-shek had just died in early April, and there was uncertainty within the regime. Yen Chia-kan, Chiang's successor as president of the Republic of China, said at a press conference that the release of the POWs served only as "a propaganda stunt," and that for security reasons, "no spies or infiltration tools will be welcomed [in Taiwan]," thus rejecting the requests of the ten POWs.[41]

Yen's response was immediately picked up by the mainland authorities. One PRC spokesperson said to the press: "Taiwan has no freedom and lacks basic humanitarianism." A pro-CCP newspaper in Hong Kong also published an article by a former KMT general, who commented, "Taiwan's refusal to let the ten who once fought for the KMT enter the island has caused jitters among political and military personnel in Taiwan. Who else now will be willing to be loyal to, and to give their lives for, Taiwan [if] merely ten men are enough to cause panic among the Taiwan authorities."[42]

The former POWs waited for nearly two more months in Hong Kong, and yet they were not able to obtain entry permits. The KMT then asked them to apply to enter as "refugees" through the Free China Relief Association in Hong Kong, like the inmates in Rennie's Mill. Several of them refused to do so because they took pride in having served as KMT military officers. To them a "refugee" status indicated victimhood from political persecution and a yearning for another state's protection. To these former POWs, their attempt to enter Taiwan was a homecoming, and there should be nothing less than honorable treatment from the party for their past sacrifices as KMT soldiers. As one of them, Duan Kewen (Tuan Kewen), told the press, his "devotion to the KMT is indisputable" and there is "no reason why he should be treated like a refugee."[43] To dispel the worry that these former POWs might be spies, the KMT demanded that they denounce the CCP publicly. This demand was also refused by a few of the POWs since they did not think the CCP had mistreated them.

As explained earlier, loyalty to the KMT was one of the main criteria for migration to Taiwan. Ironically, like many of the Rennie's Mill inmates hoping to go to Taiwan, the loyalty of these KMT POWs—after serving decades in prisons on the mainland—was being questioned not because of what they had said or written but because of their extended detention in the PRC. This reflects the White Terror that was still prevalent in Taiwan's politics in the mid-1970s, in which political activities were suppressed and people who were suspected of being disloyal to the KMT were interrogated and monitored. As we will see in chapter 5, even escapees who succeeded in entering Taiwan were monitored for many years under suspicion of being spies.

After investigation, the Hong Kong police declared that Zhang Tieshi's death was a suicide. Nevertheless, rumors spread in Hong Kong that he might have been assassinated. Some mainstream newspapers in Hong Kong referred to his death as "suspicious." These news reports also described how, according to Zhang's son, who had been phoning him before his death, Zhang had tried to evade the CCP's control by moving to a different hotel from the one designated by the authorities. However, after the move, he thought he was under surveillance.

Zhang's alleged suicide note, published in an AFP report a few days later on June 13, states: "I don't know about the others, but to me, returning to Taiwan is hopeless. It is also not advantageous for us to return and then stir up public sentiments. I know that my son is a grown-up now, and he is living a good life. My wish has been completed. I hope that the KMT government will take care of my children. . . . But if I return to the PRC, I would resent it . . . I hope my comrades would bury me or cremate my body." The note was followed by a comment by the news reporter: "During his last 50 days of freedom the 62-year-old colonel discovered he was a pariah in both societies—unable to adjust to life in China and stigmatized by Taiwan as a brainwashed communist spy."[44] Nevertheless, Zhang's son still did not believe that his father had committed suicide. He said at a press conference: "My father knew his entry permit was going to come down soon and he was confident that he could reunite with his family, so there is no reason for him to commit suicide."[45] Despite the suspicions of Zhang's son, there was no further investigation of Zhang's death.

After the controversy about the cause of Zhang Tieshi's death, his remains became the next item of propaganda disputed between the CCP and KMT. The China Travel Service, an important PRC agency in Hong Kong sponsoring the POWs, announced that it had been instructed by its head office in Beijing to assume responsibility for Zhang's body. A few days later, Zhang's son filed suit against the China Travel Service and the Hong Kong Funeral Home, where the body lay. Hong Kong authorities then issued an injunction forbidding the China Travel Service from carrying out a cremation, denouncing any cremation service without prior approval from the bereaved family. In an interview, Zhang's son said that his father's body had been "snatched by the China Travel Service and used by the Communists for political propaganda."[46] The KMT fully supported the claim of Zhang Tieshi's son, which forced the China Travel Service to finally back down and cancel the cremation service it had arranged. A few days later, Zhang Tieshi's son was able to have his father's body cremated in a different funeral home in Hong Kong and then transport the ashes to Taiwan.

POWS AND SPIES

Political commentators in Hong Kong commented that the China Travel Service's surrender of Zhang's remains in this "battle over a dead body" (*zhengshi'an*) was a setback for the CCP. Some remarked that this should prove that the CCP would not succeed in using these POWs for its propaganda purposes to promote the party's benevolence and that the KMT should now seriously reconsider the permit applications submitted by the rest of the POWs to prevent any further tragedy.

Three more months passed with no sign of these former officers getting entry permits to Taiwan. Three of them—Zhang Haishang (Chang Hai-sheng), Yang Nancun (Yang Nan-Tsun), and Zhao Yixue (Chao Yi-Hsueh)—decided to return to the mainland in early September 1975. Before they left, they held a press conference saying the return trip was a reluctant temporary measure because they were in bad health, but they vowed to return to Hong Kong to apply for a Taiwan entry permit again. The CCP welcomed all three returnees, and they eventually became members of provincial committees of the Chinese People's Political Consultative Conference.[47] They never left mainland China again.

Another four former prisoners—Chen Shizhang (Chen Shih-chang), Duan Kewen (Tuan Ke-wen), Zhou Yanghao (Chou Yang-hao), and Wang Bingyue (Wang Ping-yue)—went to the United States to be reunited with other family members. The remaining two, Wang Yunpei and Cai Xingsan (Tsai Hsin-san), eventually moved out of the hotels and settled in Hong Kong. None of the ten POWs made it to Taiwan.

In October, another sixty-five POWs were released by the PRC, but unlike the previous group, these POWs were former special agents captured between 1962 and 1965 while on "coastal harassment missions." Most of them came from the Chinese Anticommunist National Salvation Army.[48] There were 144 people released in total, but 79 chose to stay in China.[49] Of the 65 people who chose to leave, 60 sailed from Amoy in Fujian to the offshore Taiwan islands Quemoy (Jinmen), Matsu (Dongyin), and Erh Tan, where centers had been set up to receive them. Out of the other five, one reunited with his relatives in Hong Kong; another returned to his native home in Macau; and the remaining three were given permission to enter Taiwan soon after without much trouble. Even though the KMT commented that their release was also a Communist propaganda tactic, unlike the ten who were stuck in Hong Kong, these POWs' cases were processed quickly, and they were admitted into Taiwan within weeks. Why this group of POWs received different treatment remains uncertain, but one possible reason is that their status as former special agents with special knowledge of the KMT could pose a threat to Taiwan if they remained in China or Hong Kong for too long. Or perhaps the ten elderly POWs who had served in the Civil War were deemed useless and thus "undesirable" to the KMT authorities. The differential treatment shows that there was a hierarchy of desirability among released POWs. The older POWs who were out of touch with the KMT for decades were the least "desirable" immigrants to the regime.

LEGACY

In the PRC's official accounts of these POWS, they were written off as victims of the KMT's inhumanity. The China–Hong Kong border played a significant role in this context: the status of living people and dead bodies dramatically changed as they moved across that border. The former KMT officers were prisoners of war on the mainland, but they had to submit themselves to becoming "refugees" to have any possibility of returning "home." Yet when they chose to return to the mainland, they achieved important status in the PRC government. Of the ten POWs who were stuck in Hong Kong, arguably the only one who made it to Taiwan was Zhang Tieshi, because by then he was dead and could no longer pose a threat to the KMT regime. The KMT blamed the China Travel Service and the CCP for holding up the remains of Zhang Tieshi, and some reports suggested that Zhang Tieshi may have been murdered by CCP agents.

But what did this story mean to Hong Kong at that time? The residents in Hong Kong did not protest on behalf of Zhang Tieshi or any of these POWs, nor did the media attention last. While most of the POWs returned to the mainland and a few eventually migrated to the United States, the case of these ten people reveals how Hong Kong served as an "in-between zone" for stateless citizens who could neither fit in nor go back to either Taiwan or the mainland during the Cold War era. One could even say that Hong Kong's being under British colonial rule allowed it to function as a dumping ground for the ROC regime to dispose of undesirables it regarded as unqualified for citizenship.

They were seen as polluted individuals brainwashed by the CCP, so they could not be trusted. There was no way for them to prove their loyalty.

CONCLUSION

All three cases show us how the different regimes in the Southern Periphery engineered their citizenship through denying the rights of the undesirable residents to live in the city. In chapter 1, we saw how the colonial government of Hong Kong and the KMT classified migrants and refugees, only allowing certain individuals to be accepted as permanent residents. Here we see other instruments in the process of citizenship engineering—deportation and denial of permission to enter. The cases also reflect the nature of the ongoing KMT–CCP conflict. Lam Yin Chang, for example, was active in the 1950s and early 1960s, a time when the KMT presence in Hong Kong was significant and a large number of deportations to Taiwan involving people arrested because of KMT political activities or Triad crimes when the Hong Kong government wanted to remain neutral. The key decision in Lam's case was made in 1962, the year the April 4 policy began allowing escapees from China to be immediately transferred to Taiwan. After that, immigration from Hong Kong to Taiwan was tightened. The easy transfer of Lam may mark the end of an era when Taiwan was directly involved in the affairs of the escapees in Hong Kong. Subsequently, the Rennie's Mill Refugee Camp was opened, the Hong Kong government no longer actively managed the camp, and deportations to Taiwan appeared to decrease.

The second case, which happened during the Cultural Revolution, was a response to the 1967 riots. Unlike the 1950s, the mid- to late 1960s was a time that witnessed the increasing impact on Hong Kong of the PRC's political campaigns. The Victoria Road Detention Centre played a central role in deporting "undesirables" in Hong Kong, whether to Taiwan, Macau, or mainland China. The case of Fu Che and Shek Hwei was a response by the colonial government to the infiltration of the CCP in Hong Kong. The politically sensitive people who were deemed "undesirable" were those attempting to carry out the Communist agenda in the colony. The second case illustrates the propaganda warfare between the CCP and KMT in the media in the 1960s that contributed to the distrust that people Hong Kong residents had for both party-states.

As for the last case, it happened in 1975, when Taiwan was still in the midst of the White Terror started by Chiang Kai-shek's regime to inculcate fear of Communist infiltration on the island. The Hong Kong government continued to maintain neutrality between the CCP and the KMT. It provided shelter to some former POWs because, unlike Lam, the KMT agents, or Communist activists like Fu and Shek, the POWs had no intention of staying in Hong Kong to use it as a base for political activities. The Hong Kong and Taiwan governments decided the immigration status of the POWs based not on their political loyalties but on whether they might cause any social disharmony.

These three cases enable us to revisit the image of Hong Kong and Taiwan as part of the so-called Free World for anyone seeking to escape from communism. The cases reveal that although Hong Kong tried to deport its "undesirable" residents, Taiwan, Macau, and even the mainland did not always accept them as expected. These cases show that the authorities in both Hong Kong and Taiwan used deportation as a means to construct citizenship by differentiating people into "desirables" and "undesirables" and removing the latter from their territories.

If we compare the cases of Lam and the POWs, we can see the contradictions in the definition of "loyalty" to the KMT regime. In the case of the POWs, one possibility for their rejection is that the KMT truly feared that Zhang Tieshi and his fellow POWs might in fact have been subject to torture or brainwashing attempts to make them see that the PRC was the *real* China, or to efforts to turn them to spies for the PRC. In other words, their loyalty was put in doubt. To the people who believed that the POWs were loyal subjects of the KMT, it appeared as though serving in the KMT military was not enough to guarantee their entry to Taiwan. The same could be said about Fu Che and Shek Hwei and their loyalty to the PRC. Even though they were registered Communist Party members who were leaders of political campaigns in 1967, they were not "allowed" to reenter the PRC. It is unclear what criteria for citizenship the PRC had at that time, since the reason for the denial of entry remains unknown.

In the cases of Fu and Shek and the POWs, we see how both the pro-PRC and pro-KMT newspapers in Hong Kong used the statuses of these individuals to denounce the inhumanity of the other regime in their propaganda campaigns. Hong Kong served as a stage for political drama, and these individuals were put in the spotlight.

Examining the three cases together, we see that the meaning of Chinese citizenship remained blurry. The PRC claimed that Hong Kong was part of China, so the colonial authorities should not have the rights to deport their citizens; Hong Kong constantly removed people who were active in political organizing out of its borders, but other territories may or may not accept them; the ROC government in Taiwan claimed to be the legitimate Chinese government, but the Chinese who were not loyal to the KMT were not allowed to enter. The fates of these individuals also raise questions about "home" and "belonging." Home was clearly not left to the subjects themselves to define but was imposed by the various political regimes. Their sense of belonging was at odds with where a government determined their place to be. Deportees faced multiple forms of displacement and marginalization during the period from the 1940s to the 1970s.

The three cases also show that the Cold War produced suspicion and doubts about the loyalty and sense of patriotism of those who moved across borders. The propaganda newspapers reveal the fears about political or materialistic "brainwashing" on the other side of the border and the potential for people to be spies or double agents. The experiences of the border crossers and the time they spent in different locations in the Southern Periphery made it hard for the PRC, the ROC in Taiwan, and the Hong Kong government to discern the "true" identities of these individuals and whether they were really desirable.

5

THE THREE ESCAPEES

After the escapees crossed the border of the PRC, where did they go? Did they find what they were yearning for? Where was home to them? Most of the English scholarship about Chinese emigres and exiles of this period has focused on those who eventually settled in North America and how they dealt with the ambivalent identity of being Chinese and an immigrant in their host countries at the same time.[1] This chapter focuses on the journeys of three men who fled the People's Republic in 1962 to the Southern Periphery but who continued to be entangled with Chinese politics. They represent the generations who came of age after the CCP took over China. While their childhood and youth experiences in the PRC were very similar and they shared the same yearnings to leave the PRC, their lives and understanding of China and homeland were very different because of their final destinations and the changing political environment of where they resided. Ip Cheung, Xiao Yujing, and Lao Zhengwu all were born in China in the early 1940s and experienced the Communist takeover and the Land Reform campaign as children in the late 1940s and 1950s, as well as the Great Leap Forward as teenagers. They all were negatively affected by, albeit to different extents, the political campaigns and economic deprivation during the early years of Mao's rule. Because of their family backgrounds, their childhood and youth experiences in mainland China did not give them much hope for the future. These were the foundations of why they harbored negative sentiments toward the CCP throughout their lives.

All three men escaped at about the same time from the Guangdong Province. Ip Cheung represented the typical Chinese escapee who settled in Hong Kong, while Xiao Yujing and Lao Zhengwu had unusual experiences of becoming political celebrities in Taiwan. All three of them demonstrated *fangong* (anti-CCP) feelings at some points in their lives, but the reasons for and the contents of such feelings may be different: while Ip's *fangong* sentiments may have come from his own experiences and the impression he formed from the media coverage of mainland China, Xiao's and Lao's *fangong* sentiments were largely shaped by the KMT after they arrived in Taiwan. Together, they represented the variety of *fangong* sentiments in the political landscape of the Southern Periphery. The favorable impression Xiao and Lao formed after Deng Xiaoping shows that such *fangong* sentiments could also change over time contingent upon the political environment and one's involvement in politics.

Throughout their lives, they traveled within the Guangdong region and across the territories of the Southern Periphery (figure 5.1). In April 1962, when the Guangdong provincial government temporarily opened the border to allow people to leave the PRC, all three of them successfully left China. After much hassle trying to find a new home, they settled down in two destinations: Taiwan and Hong Kong. Their complicated journeys show us the interconnectedness of mainland China to Hong Kong, Macau, and Taiwan—which, together, formed an idea of a homeland called China that was sustained not by administrative borders but by a collective imagination. Yet, each of the territories these three men passed through produced multiple political opportunities that forced them to readjust how they understood and connected with their homeland.

Interviewed between the years of 2015 and 2018, they shared their feelings toward the political parties that ruled over China and Taiwan—the CCP, the KMT and the Democratic Progress Party (DPP)—as well as the meaning of China as a homeland to their past, present, and future. Ip Cheung stayed in Hong Kong permanently. To Ip, Hong Kong may have represented a particular kind of environment that continued the Third Force legacy as a dwelling place where people could observe and be

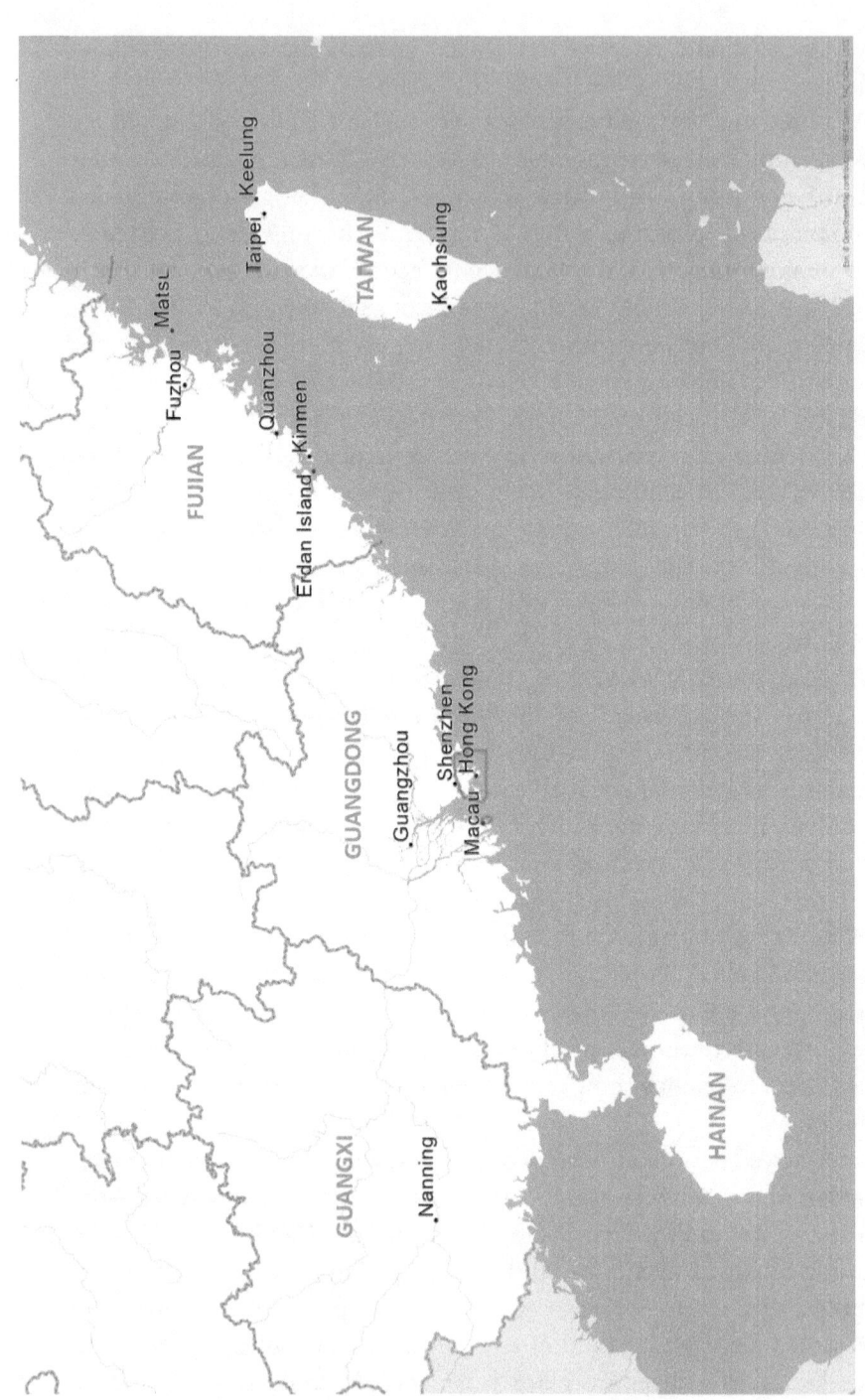

FIGURE 5.1 Taiwan and the southeast coast of mainland China.

Map created by Guoping Huang.

critical of China. Xiao Yujing and Lao Zhengwu intentionally chose Taiwan as their destination. They moved to Taiwan within a few months of each other through the April 4 policy,[2] a special program created by the KMT in 1962 that allowed escapees who arrived in Hong Kong to migrate to Taiwan immediately. After arriving in Taiwan, they were groomed to be "anti-communist fighters" (*fangong yishi*) and later became strong advocates for the Chiang Ching-kuo regime. For Xiao and Lao, Hong Kong's colonial status meant little to them because they saw themselves as engaging strictly in Chinese politics. Yet, until the 1980s, Taiwan was only a temporary home where they could reunite with the KMT—their party-state. They saw their real home as the future China they hoped to build. Taken together, the stories of these three men flesh out the effects of the politicization and depoliticization in the territories where they stayed and reveal the spectrum of political views and historical interpretations across mainland China and the Southern Periphery. Their impressions of China under Mao Zedong were tainted by their painful memories in the Southern Periphery. To them, the history of the Communist Revolution was one of persecution and suffering. The collective memories of migrants like these three men in turn shaped political developments in Hong Kong and Taiwan. Thus, the history of modern China would not be complete without such perspectives from the Southern Periphery.

PART 1: COMING OF AGE IN THE PRC IN THE 1950S AND EARLY 1960S

Xiao Yujing, Lao Zhengwu, and Ip Cheung were born in the early 1940s. Growing up, they all experienced the war with Japan, the Land Reform campaign, the Anti-Rightist Campaign, and the Great Leap Forward. Owing to their family backgrounds, their experiences in the early years of the PRC were difficult. By the time they had become young adults, each was determined to leave the PRC to find a better life elsewhere.

FIGURE 5.2 Xiao Yujing (second from top left) with his mother and siblings in the 1950s. Courtesy of Xiao Yujing.

Xiao Yujing was born in Dabu, Guangdong, in 1941 (figure 5.2). During the war with Japan and the Chinese Civil War, thousands of soldiers would pass through his village at a time.[3] First the KMT came into the village to kill the teenagers who joined the Chinese Communist Party. When the troops came, they occupied the entire village. They entered people's homes and stayed there. Then the Communists came.

In 1950, the CCP enacted the Agrarian Reform Law and started the nationwide Land Reform campaign. During the campaign, work teams would go into villages and confiscate and redistribute the property and lands of rural landlords. In village meetings, crowds would gather and collectively decide the class labels of fellow villagers.[4] Villagers without land were mobilized to fight against the landlords. That traumatic experience left a deep scar on Xiao: "I witnessed the event when I was about eight to ten years old in 1952. The experience ... was the purge of my family by the Communists. All of a sudden, a decent family was degraded to a Black Element."[5]

Xiao's family was labeled "despotic landlords" (*e'ba dizhu*), but Xiao's mother was a concubine. Due to his mother's "exploited" status as a concubine within the family, he was able to claim better status than his half-siblings. To avoid persecution, he even once had to lie to the struggle session committee that the marriage between his father and his mother was nonconsensual and that his mother was raped by his father. Usually, once a person was labeled part of the landlord class, he and his family would be stigmatized and subjected to hard labor. Fortunately, the status Xiao got from his mother's victimized background allowed him to maintain an oppressed-class identity and find work in Fujian later.

As a despotic landlord, Xiao's father suffered through many humiliations during the early 1950s. Xiao witnessed the struggle sessions in 1952 that his father and the rest of his family went through, when the Land Reform campaign reached Dabu. The Communists beheaded his father's brother because of his class status. Xiao related in his interview:

> Ever since the Communists claimed power, there had been no single moment of peace. My parents were extremely terrified, though they did not express their fear explicitly. They hid and moved belongings while waving me off, saying, "Go play outside." Therefore, I knew in my heart that a disaster had befallen my family. As a result, I have deeply experienced the cruel pain that the Communists inflicted upon the landlords. Additionally, I have witnessed Communists arresting lots of people. From the arrests to the struggle sessions (*pidouhui*), I have witnessed them all. It is often said that the mainland then was in a reign of terror (*xingfengxueyu*), and I was an eyewitness to it.

Xiao witnessed his father and other relatives being beaten up and scolded in front of crowds many times. Throughout his life since, Xiao has had nightmares of being caught by the Communists. Xiao's father's life was eventually spared during the struggle sessions because one of the cadres who presided over the village's sessions secretly helped him. Later, Xiao learned that the cadre helped him because Xiao's father had saved his mother's life many years before. Before the Land Reform campaign, each year in each village, farmers had to save much of their earnings to buy offerings to pay tribute to their ancestors. At that time, the cadre's mother, who was already widowed, was given the task by senior village members to buy ancestral offerings. Her fellow villagers gave her one kuai to buy the necessary items. One kuai in the 1940s was enough to feed a dozen people for a day. Unfortunately, the cadre's mother lost the one kuai as she was on her way to purchase the offerings. In despair, she attempted suicide by jumping into the river near Xiao's home. She survived the suicide attempt, and Xiao's father, who was well respected and rich, somehow learned about this incident and decided to help the widow. He gave the woman another kuai so that she had money to buy the offerings. After learning that Xiao's father had given her the money (and because Xiao's father was a prestigious person in the region and it was rare for the rich and poor to have any connection), the villagers began to treat the widow nicely.

Later, when this woman's son became one of the cadres who was in charge of the village's struggle sessions, it is said that she told him that Xiao's father was their family's savior and threatened to kill herself if her son declined to help Xiao's family. The cadre spared Xiao's father's life and even secretly instructed him to hide some of his money and precious belongings so they would not be confiscated. Despite the cadre's help, however, after all the hardship of the struggle sessions, Xiao's father became ill shortly after the Land Reform campaign. Xiao was very close to his father even though he and his mother lived in a separate house. What happened to his father caused Xiao to fall into despair as a teenager. This memory of his family being tortured was reflected in his hatred of Mao: "I want to fight him till death. I want to ask him: 'Why did you hold struggle sessions against my family? Why was I persecuted like this? I will fight it out with you.' Those have been my wishes since youth. I was extremely disgruntled when I saw those executed landlords. 'I want to fight it out with you!'"

Xiao graduated from junior high school in 1958 and decided to move to Fujian. To travel to a different region to work during the 1950s, he first had to obtain a permit from the head of the village. Xiao gave the village head some ration tickets so he would stamp his permit. He was also allowed to leave because of his mother's background as a concubine. The permit stated his name, his educational background, and the reason he wanted to travel. With the permit, he traveled to Fujian and stayed there for a few years. While in Fujian, he first worked in forestry; he also had a job collecting pine resin. Later he became a teacher at an elementary school.

At that time, most people shared the impression that if they were not members of the CCP youth organizations, they would be disadvantaged in competing for opportunities and resources. Even though he was praised as a schoolteacher, Xiao did not try to join the Communist Youth League (Gongqing Tuan) or other party organizations like most of his peers did. He was afraid that his "real" identity as a landlord's son would be discovered as the application process entailed thorough investigation of the applicant's family background. Because of this and his unpromising future as a non-CCP member, even though his job as an elementary school teacher was a stable one, Xiao began to plan for his escape to Hong Kong.

He blamed the CCP for the instability of his life since the Land Reform campaign. "My comfortable life was shattered by the Communists." When Xiao received a letter from his family about his father's ill health, he rushed back to his father's bedside just before his death in 1961. Afterward, Xiao decided there was nothing left for him in his hometown or in Fujian, so he decided it was time to escape from the mainland. However, he did not have a strong understanding about the KMT at that time. "I simply focused on escaping [the mainland] and fleeing the Communists."

During the four interviews in 2016 and 2018, when talking about his father being tortured during the Land Reform campaign in his seventies, he still clenched his teeth and emphasized how much he hated the Communists. Since he went to Fujian and got stable employment as a resin worker and as a teacher, he was not too affected by the famine during the Great Leap Forward. It was the Land Reform campaign and the class label his family received that impacted Xiao the most during his early years in the PRC.

Lao Zhengwu was born in 1944 in Kaiping, Guangdong.[6] Like Xiao, Lao also was born in the countryside, but he did not seem as traumatized by the Land Reform campaign as did Xiao. He once admitted that his family was given the label of "landlords" and that he did not have much opportunity in the countryside, but overall his experiences during the Land Reform campaign did not seem to leave a strong impression. Since he was the eldest son, his father took him to Guangzhou in 1953 when he was eight while his two younger sisters and a younger brother stayed in their hometown with his mother. At that time in China, it was quite common for a parent to take the oldest child to the city and leave the younger ones behind in their hometown with the wife, the grandparents, or other relatives.

Beginning in April 1957, the CCP briefly allowed public discussion of controversial issues and criticism of the government when Mao started a campaign with the slogan "Letting a hundred flowers bloom" in the arts and "a hundred schools of thought contend" in the sciences. During this Hundred Flowers campaign, intellectuals were encouraged to contribute their opinions on national policies. Overwhelmed by criticisms of its leadership and corruption after five weeks, the party-state abruptly decided to abort the Hundred Flowers movement and launched the Anti-Rightist Campaign. The Anti-Rightist movement consisted of purges of alleged rightists within the Communist Party. The term "rightist" was largely used to refer to any intellectual accused of favoring capitalism over collectivization.

Lao was aware of the emerging Anti-Rightist Campaign in 1957 because there were big posters everywhere at school discussing Mao Zedong and the CCP. While many other students were mobilized in political campaigns, Lao was not interested in politics in those days. He only observed what was going on at his school, but he did not have strong feelings against Mao or the CCP.

To him, his most memorable experience was during the Great Famine. In his interview, Lao recalled vividly how the People's Commune was established and people around him started melting iron pots to make steel. It was also a time when people could eat only one meal per day even with a ration ticket:

> The fifty-first year of the Republic, 1962 ... was one of the toughest times. At the time I had just gotten into high school and was still in my third year of middle school in Guangzhou. In the morning on my way to school, I often saw dead people. It was because of Mao Zedong's Three Red Banners and the People's Commune. It was a complete mess—people did not have enough to eat and there were many people starving on the streets.[7]

Lao thought life was relatively easier in Guangzhou than in other cities or the countryside because of the black market where vendors were able to get foodstuffs and other goods from Hong Kong and Macau. Still, the hunger lasted a long time, and it was very hard to bear. Feeling hungry all the time in Guangzhou made him long for a place that could bring him material comfort. In his imagination at that time, Hong Kong and Macau were two such places.

Lao's father worked at a factory and was later sent to jail on charges of making a private profit through repackaging and reselling some of the items produced by the factory. Even though it was only a small profit, his father was sent to a labor camp for several months. Lao was miserable trying to survive on his own. It was around that time that Lao began to seriously consider leaving mainland China for good.

As a young man in his late teens, Lao did not have much political consciousness at that time and knew only that he wanted to have a better life than the one he had in mainland China. Unlike Xiao, his decision to leave was mainly driven by the scarcity of food and other goods. Destination was not an important consideration to him so long as he would be outside of China.

Ip Cheung was born in Xinhui, Guangdong in 1942.[8] His family was not the richest in the village, but he had an abundance of food to eat in his early childhood. He was especially fond of Xinhui, since it was conducive to rice cultivation. As Ip said,

> The Pearl River Delta was considered the most fertile place. At that time, there was a saying that Xinhui and Zhongshan were similar to the USSR's Ukraine. Ukraine had very black soil—very good land for growing wheat and barley—very fertile—so similar to us in the Pearl River Delta, the hub of the He village (*hecun shuniu*), where there were many regions where the cultivation of rice and the breeding of fish flourished (*yumi zhixiang*). It was a good place—even now, it is a good place.

Ip's father had some land before the Land Reform campaign: "The field was divided down from my paternal grandfather. My paternal grandfather had two sons and one daughter. The daughter did not have [a part of the inheritance]. The two sons split it." His father also inherited some land from his maternal grandmother, who bought the land to be the dowry of his mother.

Ip's family was classified as "middle peasants" during the Land Reform campaign, so his mother was not targeted as a class enemy during the struggle sessions. Unlike Xiao Yujing, his family was not too badly affected by the campaign, but he remembered feeling that the treatment of the rich peasants and landlords was not fair. He talked about how in the countryside, the poor were jealous of the rich, and that created a kind of mentality that the rich had to be punished. He referred to the village meetings he witnessed during the Land Reform campaign as a good example of how this mentality works: "Not only rich peasants and landlords were targeted, but even overseas Chinese who had worked hard and brought back capital to help the country were targeted while their hard-earned money was confiscated." Unlike Xiao, his impression of the Land Reform was based on his view of justice at the time.

His negative experience in the PRC came from his background as the son of a KMT soldier. Ip had no memory of his father because he was only a year old when his father went to fight in the war with Japan. As a result of his father's status as a KMT soldier, Ip was stigmatized when he tried to apply for opportunities later in life. For example, while Ip was lucky enough to be able to get into a renowned middle school with teachers who had graduated from Lingnan University and Sun Yat-sen University, he was rejected when he tried to apply to join the Communist Youth League (Gongqing Tuan).[9] The Communist Youth League was a prestigious group for young Communist Party members. Ip said his rejection was because some of his schoolmates knew about Ip's father's role in the KMT and reported that to the school. Since he did not know his father too well and his family did not suffer as much as Xiao's, he did not have the same kind of traumatic experience as Xiao did as a child.

When he was still in the village, life began to change in the mid-1950s with the beginning of the Great Leap Forward. Those were the years when people began to eat in communal dining halls. During that period in Ip's village, "there were just grains, potatoes and taro—all were brought to the commune." People were not allowed to grow vegetables privately, so life was miserable because many did not have enough to eat. The inadequacy of food rations was one reason he moved to the city.

During the 1950s, it was quite difficult for people to move from the countryside to the cities. Yet, Ip was able to go to Guangzhou for postsecondary education because his maternal grandmother and younger sister had already established household registration there. He told local officials in Xinhui that because his grandmother was sick he had to move there to take care of her. He received permission in 1959 and later successfully changed his household registration to Guangzhou. He spent the next three years there at a time when famine was widespread in the country.

There was still a shortage of food in Guangzhou. What was most memorable to Ip as a high school student was the food rationing at that time. Ip remembers that the ration was barely enough for he and his father to have plain congee and two buns (*mantou*) for breakfast every day. However, as Lao said about Guangzhou, despite the low rations conditions were still somewhat better than in Xinhui because people could also take advantage of the black market and buy additional food. The food sold in the black market was not cheap; a butchered chicken went for 0.50 yuan at that time. People sometimes dug out money they had hidden to buy those goods.

In Guangzhou, Ip got into a specialized high school in architecture around 1960. However, after one year, he felt disillusioned and decided to quit. He became a tutor at what used to be the Guangzhou Heavy Machinery Factory before the CCP took over. After the local government decided to send youths down to the countryside, Ip quit the job and took on other part-time jobs instead. Even though the Great Famine had not ended and there was still a shortage of food, Ip was able to survive by eating congee at home almost every day. Ip was not very satisfied with his life and wondered if there were ways for him to continue his studies.

Overall, none of the three men had a pleasant coming-of-age period: All were negatively affected by the political campaigns in the early years of the PRC. Xiao was traumatized because of his father's "despotic landlord" status and the subsequent purge; Ip was stigmatized because his father was a KMT soldier; Lao was left behind when his father was arrested for selling Chinese medicine without the approval of the state. Ip and Lao both fled China because they did not have enough food to eat and did not see any future for themselves in the mainland. There was some qualitative difference in their feelings toward the CCP though. Ip and Lao still did not have a strong impression of the CCP, but Xiao already developed strong hatred because of the death of his father. These experiences echo those of others of their generation who remained in China. Leaving China became a major turning point in these three individuals' lives.

The men were enticed by what they heard about the abundance of food and commodities in Hong Kong and Macau, having all been affected by famine and the failed Great Leap Forward. Lao Zhengwu expressed that the colonies were like a paradise in his imagination before he decided to escape. When Ip Cheung was still living in mainland China, he often received clothes from Hong Kong relatives who visited: "The clothes were newer and more original and those relatives from Hong Kong always wore leather shoes, which was in great contrast to the people in China who did not have shoes, and the most popular clothing for mainland children were the big blue shirts (*da shi lan*) and pants with open crotches (*kai lang ku*)." At the time when Xiao Yujing began to plan his escape to Hong Kong, he envisioned the city as a free and prosperous place but didn't know much about it. He learned about Hong Kong through the relatives who went there, and he had seen residents of Hong Kong who returned to China in nice attire and who seemed to eat well.

PART 2: FIRST STOPS

What led the three men to escape in 1962 was Tao Zhu's open-border policy. As explained in chapter 1, in April 1962, partly because of the Great Famine and the increasing number of people trying to flee to Hong Kong and Macau illegally, Governor Tao Zhu of Guangdong decided to open the borders shared with Macau and Hong Kong and let citizens in the PRC cross over. More than one thousand crossed the Shenzhen border every day during the next two months, amounting to about 150,000 refugees in Hong Kong.[10] The Hong Kong side of the border was still closed, and the unlucky ones were arrested and sent back to Shenzhen. Macau's side of the Gongbei border shared with mainland China was not strictly controlled; henceforth, some escapees, like Lao Zhengwu, went to Macau.

When Ip Cheung was working in Guangzhou, he met some friends who told him rumors that the Guangzhou government was about to let people leave China because of the famine. At that time, Ip also heard that his maternal aunt's father-in-law, who had lived in the United States, had just returned to Hong Kong. Thinking that perhaps he could depend on that relative in Hong Kong, Ip decided to take his chances. The first step was to go to Shenzhen. Ip attempted to sneak into Hong Kong a few days after the open-border policy was announced. Nevertheless, he and his friend were soon arrested by the Gurkha soldiers on the Hong Kong side of the border. They were sent to Sheung Shui Police Training Camp in Hong Kong's New Territories. As Ip recalls,

> At the training camp, we stayed a night; they treated us well—there was food to eat—there was bread. At that time, Hong Kong people were very warmhearted. They knew that the refugees from the mainland were flowing in, so there were a lot of donations—money, bread—there was a lot of bread—at that time I do not know if there was Vitasoy, but there was water and there was bread for you to eat. There were also cakes.

What Ip describes reflects the general sympathy residents in Hong Kong felt toward escapees from China. Many learned about the rush of escapees crossing the border and traveled to the areas near the border to either take them to the city or bring them food.

Ip's friend did not go back to Guangzhou; he stayed near the border and waited for another opportunity to cross. Ip returned to Guangzhou by train after being deported back to Shenzhen, but after four or five days he went again for a second try. This time he took a ship from Guangzhou to Dongguan with a few relatives. They all arrived in Guancheng, where the husband of Ip's aunt (*yizhang*) lived. Another relative found a van, and five relatives went together from Dongguan to Zhang Mu Tou.

After arriving in Zhang Mu Tou, they had to travel on foot to Hong Kong. There were many people walking along the railway because they all had heard about the open border. Sometimes they walked along the railway, but at other times they diverted and walked along the edge of the mountains. They walked all the way to the Shenzhen border after seventeen hours under the moon and the stars (*pixing daiyue*). They then stayed a night at Shenzhen.

The next night, at dusk, they attempted to climb the Wu Tong Mountain. It was a perilous journey for Ip. One of the memorable moments was walking across the river on a ten-inch-wide plank. When they got to the border, they faced a wire fence that separated the two territories. Since many people had tried to escape through this path, Ip easily found a hole at the bottom of the fence and climbed through it. His relatives went their separate ways, leaving Ip by himself. Some Pakistani border guards chased Ip when he climbed through, but he managed to escape. He eventually reached a village in Sheung Shui, a district filled with Hakka people. From Sheung Shui to Kowloon there were seven checkpoints. If caught by the police, escapees would be sent back to China. It was too risky for Ip to travel to Kowloon by himself, so he decided to find a place where he could take refuge in the Sheung Shui area.

Ip reached a house and called for help. A Hakka woman who lived there pointed to a burrow in the grass. As he recalled, she said, "You should hide there!" Ip crawled into the burrow and stayed for the night. The next day, Ip gave his relative's address to the Hakka woman from the village, and she took him to Tai Kok Tsui. His uncle later hired a private detective to fetch Ip on a train from Sheung Shui to the urban area. Once he entered the urban area, he was safe. Since he owed the private detective a fee of HK$700 to take him to the city, Ip had to work for three years to pay off the debt.

Xiao Yujing faced the same Wu Tong Mountain as Ip Cheung when he was trying to get to Hong Kong in 1962. Like Ip, he had to climb it at night to avoid being caught. He escaped with four friends, all men about his age, in their late teens and early twenties. Xiao and his companions escaped through the mountain forests at night. Xiao managed to navigate through the woods of Wu Tong. Behind the mountain was the sea he had to swim across. For some escapees who picked this route, it took several hours to a whole night to cross depending on the tide and their swimming skills. Some drowned and were found by the police patrolling the sea territories. However, this was not too intimidating to Xiao, who had learned to swim at a young age in the rivers near where he grew up. It took him about two hours of swimming to reach the coast of Hong Kong Island. He did not think much about the risk of drowning or being killed because he knew he had no other option but to escape. This was Xiao Yujing's second attempt to cross the border. He had made an earlier attempt a few weeks earlier and succeeded in entering Hong Kong territory, but he was caught near the border, detained, and sent back to Shenzhen.

In the end, only he and two friends were still together at the end. The other two were lost on the way. After crossing the border successfully, they had to be very cautious about asking for help. In the New Territories, they met a young man who oversaw operations at a farm and asked him if he could take them in and allow them to stay until they could figure out how to get in touch with their contacts in Hong Kong. The man agreed and they stayed at the farm for about three months, helping with farm work and raising ducks.

Xiao was then taken in by an older friend from his same hometown who took him to Kowloon. Xiao stayed in Hong Kong at his friend's house for a few months, learning Cantonese and trying to adapt to the new environment.[11] In those few months in Hong Kong, Xiao lived a modest, inconspicuous life, being afraid that he would be caught by the CCP and jailed for escaping the PRC. Xiao worked making deliveries for a shop. However, considering that he had been a teacher in China, this job did not give him much satisfaction. Gradually, he began to question the purpose of staying in Hong Kong because there was no way for him to fight against his enemies from there. "Hong Kong has a free market," he said, "but it's not enough. I planned to fight back, and I needed to join the KMT army." He became convinced that he had to go to Taiwan, because the KMT was the only force that could fight the Communists.

Xiao Yujing discovered the Free China Relief Association (FCRA) by chance one day through reading the newspaper and learned of its focus on destroying the CCP. The FCRA's role in Hong Kong dated back to 1952, when the Social Welfare Office of the Hong Kong government ended food rationing at Rennie's Mill Refugee Camp in an attempt to disperse the camp's inhabitants. The FCRA stepped in and filled the gap providing for the needs of the residents of the camp.¹² It was the main organization operating Rennie's Mill. Besides its relief work at Rennie's Mill, it also was instrumental in processing the immigration applications for escapees who wanted to move to Taiwan as well as sponsoring vocational schools and providing material resources for escapees in Hong Kong. Some escapees went there as soon as they arrived in Hong Kong to seek assistance. The chairperson, Gu Zhenggang, was a respectable figure in the KMT who was very involved in matters related to the refugees at Rennie's Mill and the transfer of Chinese to Taiwan.

When Xiao first heard about the FCRA, he went to check it out and noticed that some people went there to register to go to Taiwan. He went back a few times just to observe. He was cautious for fear he would be followed by Communist agents. When he decided actually to register at the FCRA, he went in discreetly and took only a few belongings and photographs with him.

He told the staff that he was someone who had fled China and wanted to go to Taiwan. They gave him a vaccination and started questioning him in a private setting. He was sent to Rennie's Mill and lived in the camp for a few weeks. He then came to the attention of the CIA because of his former post as a journalist on the mainland. There were not many escapees who came from a landlord background at the time, so the CIA officials were very interested in Xiao's family's experience. They tested him on his knowledge of international political events, such as the Korean War, recent politics in the United States, the work of the CIA, and so on. After getting satisfactory answers, the officials then asked him if he was interested in working for them. They also inquired about what newspaper agency he had worked for, the interviews he had conducted, and the articles he had written. They were satisfied with his knowledge about mainland China and offered him a job in the United States. Xiao rejected their offer, however, and told them his goal was to return to China one day to fight the Communists. When asked why he chose to go to Taiwan instead of staying in Hong Kong, Xiao said,

> At that time, I just wanted the Communist Party decimated. I wanted to find a government that was against the Communists. There was no point staying in Hong Kong! At the time only Taiwan was against the

Communist Party. The purpose [of going to Taiwan] was to fight against the Communist Party. Only in Taiwan was there truly a viable party or army to do that. Hong Kong was more neutral.

Xiao was the only person out of all three who expressed a strong hatred toward the CCP at this stage of their lives. His *fangong* sentiments at the time of his escape mostly like came from the sufferings of his family during the Land Reform. His yearning to fight against the CCP was mainly a personal vendetta during this time. After he arrived in Taiwan, his feelings toward the two parties would evolve to another level.

As a beneficiary of the April 4 policy, Xiao was eligible to take one of the ferries that carried escapees from Hong Kong to Taiwan over the following two months. On the Sichuan ferry he took from Hong Kong to Keelung, he met other people who also had fled to Hong Kong from China and were seeking refuge in Taiwan.[13] He did not tell his relatives in Hong Kong or his family in China about leaving for Taiwan until a few years after he resettled in Taiwan, because he knew it would be dangerous and did not want his relatives to worry.

Lao Zhengwu also twice tried escaping to Hong Kong in the early 1960s but failed both times. Once he walked from Guangzhou, but he was caught on the way before he crossed the border and sent back. He was jailed for about a month, and then the soldiers sent him back to Guangzhou by truck along with other (unsuccessful) escapees.

His choice of Macau over Hong Kong was merely by chance, since he happened to hear a rumor that the police and border guards there were more lenient toward escapees. He had heard that in Hong Kong one was likely to be arrested upon entering Fanling, a town in the New Territories near the border with Hong Kong. Lao said he was lucky to get away during a time when Guangdong governor Tao Zhu was letting people escape. He did not tell his family in advance when he went to Macau. It was not until a few years after he arrived in Taiwan that he informed his mother of his whereabouts.

He went first by bus from Guangzhou to Shiqi. On the day he escaped, it was raining hard. With two other classmates, Lao Zhengwu went uphill and followed the lights of Macau. Unlike in Hong Kong, there was no barbed wire between China and Macau, and Lao swam across a river to get to the rice fields located along the border. There he found some farmers who took him in and called the local police. The police came in a jeep and took him to his friend.

His friend's family in Macau was not able to help him out because they were impoverished. From neighbors he learned about a priest, Father Luis Ruiz Suárez, who ran a center for refugees at Igreja de Santo Agostinho in Macau. Lao went there and stayed for a week. He was told to go to the Macau branch of the FCRA after that. The branch of the FCRA in Macau, which dealt with all refugee-related issues, was a much smaller operation than that in Hong Kong. At first, the FCRA had only a bureau in the Foreign Affairs Office of the ROC. Macau had two refugee camps in the early 1950s, one that could accept around five hundred refugees, and the other, in Rua Dos Pescadores, that was used to accommodate the more than 100 KMT military officers who arrived during the Civil War. Later the Macau FCRA gave HK$80,000 to be the latter camp's main sponsor and then HK$8,000 per month after 1955 in order to use the camps as accommodations for the escapees from mainland China.[14]

Lao stayed at the FCRA Macau office for about a month. The FCRA provided him with a shelter at one of the camps and stipends for food and other essentials. In Macau he was able to use the money to buy bedding and used clothes. He considered this situation luxurious compared to what he had experienced in mainland China.

At the FCRA, Lao learned about the opportunity to go to Taiwan. Lao had much hesitation, though: "At the time [most young people] were very afraid of the KMT because we had received Communist propaganda about the KMT and Chiang—who they said was a thief—which promoted the idea that the KMT was a corrupt, rotten mess. This had a big influence on us." But the impression he got about the KMT through the FCRA turned out to be quite different and more positive: "You are still so young. Do you want to go to Taiwan? If you go to Taiwan you can choose to study or find a job—whatever you want. At this age you should study." Lao was surprised to hear this and was not sure if he should believe the FCRA staff. He had finished only his first year of high school at that point. Since learning was his passion, he leaned toward accepting the offer although he had some hesitation because of the unknowns: "I asked the people with me, 'I have been invited to Taiwan to study. I can't decide. What do you think?' I wanted to find out the opinions of people more mature than I was. Someone responded, 'Don't go there. The KMT will definitely make you into cannon fodder.'"

After gathering people's opinions, Lao thought:

> First, I am desperate right now; second, the CCP had said it would make the people happy but living under it for over ten years proved that it wouldn't. I deduced using basic logic: It is the CCP that said the KMT made people into cannon fodder, and what the CCP said about making people happy was a lie. Obviously, then, this stuff about making people cannon fodder is also a lie! OK, let's go for it then!

Unlike Xiao, Lao did not particularly want to join the KMT at that time. He actually had heard bad things about the KMT from CCP propaganda in China, but he decided to take a leap of faith because based on his past experience he now considered the CCP even more untrustworthy. It was not based on any kind of strong political convictions but on a simple comparison of his impressions of the two parties. More important, the FCRA was giving him an opportunity to be a student again. After staying for a few weeks at the FCRA in Macau, he took the ferry, first to Hong Kong and then to Taiwan in June: "I had good luck. . . . I just barely made it under the April 4 program. After less than six months, the policy ended, so if I had come two or three months earlier, I wouldn't have been able to go to Taiwan; if I had come six months later, I also wouldn't have been able to go. Luckily, it was the right time, and I simply had to enter my name and I was eligible."

After their arrivals in Hong Kong and Macau, respectively, two chose to go to Taiwan and one chose to stay in Hong Kong. The first factor that determined their decisions to stay or leave was their connections with the people and culture of the two cities. Xiao and Lao, because they did not have relatives in either Hong Kong or Macau, had to go to rescue institutions for help. Xiao did not speak Cantonese, which might have added to his sense of alienation in Hong Kong. His and Lao's decisions to go to Taiwan probably were due in part to the difficulties of surviving independently in Hong Kong and Macau. Ip had the advantage of speaking Cantonese and having relatives in Hong Kong.

A second factor that might have affected Xiao's and Lao's decisions to leave for Taiwan was their sentiments toward the two parties. In his 2016 interview, Xiao said he was not interested in Hong Kong because he did not think there was a *fangong* campaign there. When I asked him about whether he had heard about the Third Force, he said he had not. Unlike the readers of Third Force magazines discussed in chapter 2, he was not able to find a community in Hong Kong that shared his beliefs in 1962. He was determined to join the KMT army in Taiwan, even though he had never been to the island. While the term *fangong* may not be a term he actually used at the time he was in Hong Kong, his burning desire to fight against the CCP to avenge his father's death was clear. CCP stood for the enemy who killed his father. In contrast, Lao's reason for accepting the FCRA's offer was more practical—he wanted to continue his studies and the staff at the FCRA in Macau promised to support his education. Ip also wanted to pursue education but the night school opportunities in Hong Kong were sufficient for him. At this time, Lao and Ip had some negative impressions of the CCP because of their childhood and youth experiences, but because their families did not suffer as much as Xiao did, they did not develop deep hatred of the CCP.

PART 3: THE ONE WHO STAYED IN HONG KONG

Compared to Xiao Yujing and Lao Zhengwu, who moved to Taiwan, Ip Cheung led a quite ordinary life in Hong Kong. His story there resembles that of a Lion Rock settler described at the beginning of the book. He worked his way from the bottom stratum of society as an immigrant to become a middle-class Hong Konger. After arriving in Hong Kong, he chose to stay, and the city became his permanent home. It might seem as though he was apolitical; he did not participate in any political organizations, and he fled to Hong Kong mainly for survival.

Shortly after his arrival, he was able to find his relatives to accept him in their flat in the Sham Shui Po district. Ip eventually lived there for more than a year. Unlike Xiao and Lao, Ip did not consider Taiwan to be a viable option because he did not know anyone there, nor did he know much about the KMT. Taiwan was not a familiar place to him: "I did not have enough courage [to go to Taiwan] because there would be no one to give me material assistance. If there is no such financial support, how could I [go to Taiwan?]?" In contrast, Hong Kong was an obvious choice for him because he had relatives to depend on and he could speak Cantonese.

At the beginning, Ip worked at a factory folding cardboard boxes. His uncle and aunt built a loft in the kitchen where he could sleep at night. The whole flat was only a few hundred square feet. Other relatives who also came from China were staying at the same flat. During the 1950s–1970s, it was common for people in Hong Kong, who may be living in a very congested environment themselves, to take in relatives from mainland China. After a year, Ip found a job at a construction site as an unskilled laborer; the company provided dormitories in the Tai Kok Tsui district, so Ip moved there after he switched his job. Because he attended school part-time while working for the construction company, he was able to move up in his career and eventually became a construction site manager.

Even though Ip did not have close connections with the FCRA like Lao and Xiao did, he went to the FCRA office in Hong Kong for information about material assistance and educational opportunities. During the 1960s and 1970s, many adults in Hong Kong who had not attended secondary school began to go to night school. There was also a growing demand for vocational training and education. In his first seven years in Hong Kong, Ip went to night school to study English and then to United College, a postsecondary school, to study architectural engineering. United College was affiliated with the FCRA and the KMT. He received his first degree in 1967. He then pursued another degree at Hong Kong College of Technology, majoring in architectural engineering as well. The Hong Kong College of Technology, unlike Union College, was connected to the Hong Kong Federation of Trade Unions, a pro-Beijing political party.[15] In the 1960s, night education became a contested arena for pro-Beijing and pro-Taipei forces to spread their political ideologies.

Ip did not seem to be bothered by the political strife, nor was he particularly influenced by either side. He viewed architectural engineering was a good career choice since he had some related experience in China and had also worked in construction. His indifference toward politics may have been influenced by the Hong Kong government's restrictions on political activities as well as the limitations placed on KMT- or CCP-affiliated organizations. Nevertheless, the vocational training programs that Ip received shows that the two parties' infiltration in Hong Kong society had an impact even for the settlers in Hong Kong who did not have strong political convictions. Ip did not have a deep connection with the KMT, but he acknowledged that the KMT had done some good deeds in Hong Kong society by funding colleges and other educational opportunities.

In the beginning, Ip's network of friends consisted of people who had migrated or escaped from mainland China. One of the friends who escaped with him from China introduced him to his future wife, an employee in a rice shop where the friend's father worked. They got married in 1972. Since then, Ip has focused on his career and family life: "After getting married, you don't think about other things too much. The most important thing is to keep your job. At that time, I became a supervisor at work." Ip never got involved in politics in Hong Kong though he followed political and social news and would comment on the PRC and Hong Kong governments when he chatted with friends.

Ip's basic feelings toward China were resentment and fear. Until 1982, he did not go back to the mainland at all because he was too afraid he would be punished by the CCP as a former escapee. The first time he did go back, he was disappointed by China's lack of progress even though Deng Xiaoping's economic reform had started: "When I went back to Guangzhou, I felt sad.... It was the same—dilapidated walls and decayed tiles. The people—men, women, and young people—did not have vitality or a youthful spirit—they were quite dull. It was still blue trousers and white shirts and white shoes. It was not like Hong Kong, where the youth had spirit and vitality." Witnessing the differences between the people in the mainland where he visited and the people in Hong Kong confirmed that his decision to go to Hong Kong was correct. He disapproved of the poor material conditions of people's everyday life in China. However, Ip did not have much emotional attachment toward the regime in the two to three decades because he felt quite removed from the mainland. Until the 1980s, Ip had avoided going back to the mainland China as much as he could, even though he had to travel there a few times for development projects. In some ways, his story is more typical of those who settled in Hong Kong in the 1960s and 1970s and moved up the social ladder.

As his career advanced, Ip had opportunities to visit China more often. During the early years of Deng Xiaoping's economic reforms, he began to have opportunities to visit mainland China. In 1983, his company collaborated with the Chinese University of Hong Kong to carry out a project in China. That was Ip's second trip back to China since his escape. He went to Hainan Island and witnessed the economic reform firsthand. His impression of mainland China changed since then. He expressed that economic reform was moving in the right direction. Yet, he was still not very impressed with the CCP's political development then. Like many Hong Kong residents in the 1980s, he felt that the PRC would slowly democratize and slowly catch up with Hong Kong politically. He was not active in political movements, but in the 1980s, with the changes happening in mainland China, he was cautiously optimistic about the handover of Hong Kong to the PRC in 1997.

Although the Tiananmen Square crackdown on June 4, 1989, was a heartbreaking moment for him to see so many Chinese killed, he never joined the annual June 4 vigil held at Victoria Park in Hong Kong. He said that from 1989 to the first few years after the handover, he had faith in Deng Xiaoping's promise of "One Country, Two Systems." Throughout the decades after his escape, he felt somewhat negatively about CCP based on what he heard in the Hong Kong media, but he did not think about fighting against the CCP. Between the 1960s to the late 1980s, he was complacent with his life in Hong Kong and wanted to maintain his lifestyle.

In the late 1990s and early 2000s, the gradual tightening of political grip by the Hong Kong Special Administrative Region government began to make Ip more concerned about Hong Kong's political future. He especially remembered the year of 2003, when the government proposed an antisubversion law titled Article 23 of the Hong Kong Basic Law. Like many fellow Hong Kong residents, Ip feared that the proposal would erode freedom. He said that at that time he only did not want the

CCP to further interfere with Hong Kong's politics because Hong Kong had a different political trajectory after British rule.

Overall, his *fangong* sentiments were quite typical of those who settled and moved up the social ladder in Hong Kong. In the 1960s and 1970s, while he was busying building up his education and employment credentials, he was not very interested in Chinese politics. Because of his past experiences in the PRC, the stories he heard from relatives and what he gathered from the print media and television programs in Hong Kong, he was generally contemptuous of mainland China's chaotic political environment and inferior material conditions, and he felt that the PRC government needed political reform.

This book is mainly about people in transit in Hong Kong, and thus it may seem as though Ip's story does not fit. However, his story shows us that the division between people in transit and settlers may be arbitrary, since both groups shared the experience with Xiao, Lao, and many others of crossing the border and struggling to find a home. One could say that Ip was fortunate to have relatives and cultural familiarity to help him settle down in Hong Kong.

He consciously distanced himself from mainland China and focused on establishing himself in his new home. Nevertheless, he could not help being influenced by stories that he learned about China in the media. Even though his memory of the PRC was fading, his negative attitude toward the CCP did not decrease. Yet, those anti-CCP sentiments were different from those of Xiao and Lao, as we will see in the following sections. In the 1980s and 1990s, as Hong Kong's return to China was approaching, he could not avoid thinking about the politics of China more and more. Therefore, even for settlers who seemingly had a sheltered life in Hong Kong, they would still be forced to confront the reality of reintegration with the PRC. We will return to his view on Deng Xiaoping and national unification.

PART 4: EDUCATIONAL AND WORK OPPORTUNITIES IN TAIPEI

Xiao Yujing and Lao Zhengwu went to Taiwan soon after they arrived in Hong Kong and Macau, respectively, through the April 4 policy. It was their first decade in Taiwan that turned them into members of the KMT. They were the model youths of the program as they took advantage of the educational opportunities and excelled in college. They were also among the few who were accepted at National Chengchi University. Only a minority of youths from the program were able to attend the top national universities in Taiwan at that time, so they were highlighted by the FCRA's propaganda to show how benevolent the KMT was toward the refugees from mainland China. After Xiao and Lao graduated from college, they were able to find civil service jobs through the help of the KMT. They continued to be involved with the FCRA by giving public talks about their experiences leaving the PRC. However, sometimes they also faced obstacles because of their identity as refugees from China, such as being denied opportunities in the military or at work.

Xiao Yujing wanted to start his plan of vengeance against the CCP right away. At first when Xiao arrived in Taiwan, he planned to join the army so that he could fight against the PRC government. He did not expect that the KMT would be suspicious of people like him who had moved from China to Taiwan: "They weren't very clear about their reasoning for not letting me join. They just told me to study. I originally thought I would be able to study at the Political Worker Cadres School (Zhenggong ganxiao)."[16] The Political Worker Cadres School is a military school set up by the KMT for the purpose of preparing for a future war with the PRC. Xiao was not allowed to study there because of his background and instead it was arranged that he attend the National Overseas Student Preparatory School, a special program started at the National Overseas Secondary School in Taipei. It was a one-year course for overseas students who needed remedial education for the entrance exam. The curriculum included the Three People's Principles, the *Analects* of Confucius, and the history of China.

Despite this setback, his attachment toward the KMT grew because of a particular memorable encounter with Chiang Ching-kuo, the son of Chiang Kai-shek, at the National Overseas Secondary School. At that time, the China Youth National Salvation Corps (a.k.a. China Youth Anti-Communist National Salvation Corps) was just established in 1952, and Chiang Ching-kuo was the first chairperson. Chiang Ching-kuo probably visited the Chinese Overseas School as one of his official duties as the chair, and the goal of the China Youth National Salvation Corps at the time was to select youths for military training and conscripting them into the KMT armed forces, as well as providing services for overseas Chinese youths residing in Taiwan. During that visit, Chiang told the students about keeping up the *fangong* spirits. This left a strong impression on Xiao Yujing, as he described that first encounter in 2016:

> The first time I met Chiang Ching-kuo was during his visit to our dormitory at the Chinese Overseas School. It was my first time to shake his hand and converse with him. He expressed words of encouragement and said, "During your study in Taiwan, the government will take good care of you." At that moment, I was so stunned. Here, in front of me, is the son of Chiang Kai-shek—the real, authentic *fangong yishi* [anticommunist hero] who upheld the struggle against Mao Zedong!

To Xiao, his meeting with Chiang Ching-kuo led to the realization that staging an *fangong* counterattack was to be his life mission. At that moment of the first encounter, Chiang Ching-kuo became his lifetime hero. Xiao's relationship with the party was a personal one that derived largely from his admiration for Chiang Ching-kuo. Later in his life, when he participated in far-right political activities, it was also out of his devotion to Chiang Ching-kuo. It was probably after this encounter that the term "*fangong*" became his moto. At this moment, his anticommunist sentiments evolved from one that was founded on the desire of vengeance to one that had grown out of his devotion for his hero, Chiang Ching-kuo.

The student body in the National Overseas Secondary School consisted primarily of refugees from Hong Kong but also included ethnic Chinese who had been living in Thailand, Malaysia, or other places. Those who attended the preparatory course were refugees from the April 4 policy. There were fifty to sixty students in Xiao's class, but at graduation only about half of the students remained because many who had received inferior or insufficient education in mainland China were unable to catch up with their peers.

As explained in chapter 1, the April 4 program created a special quota for applicants to the college entrance exam. Xiao was accepted at National Chengchi University and majored in Chinese. He was eventually conscripted into the army briefly, but he was dismissed after his term was up without a clear reason. Thereafter, the government arranged a job for him, a position at the National Youth Commission (*qingnian fudao hui*), a body created for the purpose of arranging jobs for young people.

As for Lao Zhengwu, although he felt obligated to the KMT, the idea of taking part in a *fangong* counterattack did not really take hold. Lao Zhengwu attended the National Overseas Chinese Secondary School in Taipei when he arrived in Taiwan. Whenever he talked about his education during interviews, he showed gratitude toward the KMT:

> Everything was paid for by the government: tuition, clothes, and a stipend of a few dozen dollars was given out every month. It is amazing that there are things like this in the world—even going so far as to arrange for you to go to school! If you didn't go to school, you would go to government agencies and organizations.... It really was lucky that I got that opportunity. The director was Gu Zhenggang (Ku Cheng-kang) [of the FCRA]. After he died, I wrote something thanking him in one of my memoirs.

In the interviews in 2016 and 2017, Lao showed great gratitude especially to the FCRA for the education opportunity. He also believed that his academic talent was appreciated by the party. Lao worked very hard in the Overseas Chinese High School and was accepted into National Chengchi University College of Law. Then he worked as a teacher at New Taipei Municipal Jui-Fang Industrial High School for two years after graduation in order to prepare for higher-level civil service examinations. His dream at the time was to become a government official. He too the government entrance exam in 1970 and received one of the highest scores. He got a job at the Taipei City Council Legal Department as a legal copy editor. Lao's boss noticed his high score in the examination and recommended he apply to the Executive Yuan in 1971. However, this was also the first time his background was questioned:

> It's pretty good just that you have the chance to go to school, but you'd still have some limitations to what you can do—because the Nationalist

Party fought a decade-long war with the Communist Party, it became afraid of them, very afraid. And this fear affected me too. Because [the head of the Executive Yuan Legal Committee] was timid, he was afraid of causing unnecessary complications. I didn't have any family or other relatives in Taiwan. Unlike now when it would be possible to go to the mainland and do a little investigation, previously it was not allowed—no communication was allowed across the strait.

Because of the legal committee's suspicions about Lao's background, Lao did not get the job at the Executive Yuan. Though disappointed, Lao did not hold a grudge against the KMT. In the interview, he said the KMT's suspicion was unavoidable because of the cross-strait tensions and the fears that the KMT had at the time. Perhaps he did not feel too upset by the decision because he was not actively seeking that post in the first place, or perhaps it was just a small setback compared to all the things he has achieved since then.

After this rejection, Lao continued to work at the Taipei City Council for eight more years. He met and married his first wife after he started working for the Taipei City Council. He also had considered going abroad, but it became increasingly difficult once he had a family.[17] He applied to the National Chengchi University Research Center to be a graduate student instead. Lao was proud of his ability to manage both study and work with ease and graduated in three years, faster than most students who studied full-time. After graduation, he started writing for various newspapers, such as the *Central Daily News* (*Zhongyang Ribao*) and the *China Times* (*Zhongguo Shibao*), on topics related to law and politics. Gradually he began to find law boring and not very useful, so he began to explore the possibilities of publishing magazines on his own.

Xiao and Lao were able to use their educational opportunities to move up the social ladder in Taiwan. Their jobs after graduation were also arranged by the KMT: Xiao worked for the National Youth Commission, and Lao worked for the Taipei Municipal Office. Their career paths were quite smooth overall except for being denied opportunities to serve in the military or fill top-ranking positions in the government due to their backgrounds as mainland escapees. Despite that, they accepted their limitations. It was during this time that both developed loyalty toward the KMT. Xiao's became Chiang Ching-kuo's devoted follower, and this relationship elevated his *fangong* consciousness to a personal level. It was during that time that he slowly developed the identity of becoming a *fangong* fighter, like Chiang Ching-kuo himself claimed to be. Lao Zhengwu did not share the same devotion to Chiang or the KMT as his feelings toward the KMT was that of indebtedness. Yet, because of their backgrounds as mainland escapees, they were actively monitored by special agents deployed by the KMT. It would take them about ten years to gain the party's trust.

PART 5: *FANGONG YISHI*

The term *fangong yishi*—literally, anticommunist fighters—was first coined by the KMT to refer to the POWs from the PRC's People's Volunteer Army who fought in the Korean War but then chose to go to Taiwan after the war. After that, the term was used until the 1980s and was applied to a wide range of defectors from mainland China, including pilots from the People's Liberation Army who flew to Taiwan for political asylum throughout 1960s–1980s and individuals who fled to Taiwan by boat in 1983. The term was also picked up by the FCRA to describe the refugees who went to Taiwan, in particular the beneficiaries of the April 4 policy. They were depicted as anticommunist fighters because they risked their lives to go to Free China—that is, Taiwan. In the commemorative publications that the FCRA put out every few years, there were sections that described the activities of *fangong yishi* in Taiwan.

Although both of Xiao Yujing and Lao Zhengwu were widely known in Taiwan in the 1960s and 1970s as *fangong yishi*, they had very different relationships with this label.

Xiao Yujing only became aware of the term *fangong yishi* when he arrived in Taiwan. It became his primary identity in Taiwan. Xiao recalled that anyone who escaped from China to Taiwan via Hong Kong like he did could be called a *fangong yishi*: "I was born a Kuomintang believer and *fangong* (anti-CCP) because of the political purges and struggle sessions." Reflecting on his past in 2016, he said he had been already deep down a *fangong yishi* as a child even without knowing the term. In his words:

> When I say I'm *fangong*, I'm not saying it out of pride—I just think that's who I am. Even if Deng Xiaoping was in front of me right now, I would say I am an anticommunist. Even if I met Mao Zedong, I would tell him I'm an anticommunist. I swam all the way to Hong Kong, and the moment I reached Hong Kong territory I yelled: "Down with the Communist Party! Obliterate Mao Zedong! Mao Zedong, you're worth nothing, go to hell!" No one taught me these slogans. At the time, I thought of myself as high and mighty. Even with such strict control of the borders by the Communists, I was able overcome the obstacles and escape to Hong Kong. That's how strong my *fangong* determination was.

Xiao believed that the moment he witnessed the struggle sessions and the fate of his relatives at the age of ten, he had developed *fangong* sentiments inside. A decade later, Wang Sheng, one of the top officials at the Ministry of Defense in Taiwan, asked him to write about his experience, with the idea of turning Xiao's experience of fleeing China into a movie. This autobiographical account was published in a series in the *Central Daily News*. The story was mainly about the perilous journey that Xiao took from his hometown to Hong Kong. Even though it was not ultimately made into a movie, Xiao was gratified because of the positive feedback from many readers, some of whom had similar experiences of fleeing the PRC. More important, he believed he had conveyed his *fangong* sentiments well in the series, especially when he recounted screaming, "Down with Mao Zedong!" right after he reached Hong Kong's shore. He was happy to let out his true feelings into the world. From the way he expressed his hatred, it sounded as though he was anti–Mao Zedong rather than anti-CCP. To him, Mao Zedong was the enemy who killed his father.

However, there were also times in his life when he felt he was not fully appreciated by the KMT despite his true anticommunist intentions, such as during the 1960s when Taiwan was in the grip of the White Terror. When martial law was implemented after the 228 Incident in 1947, a large-scale antigovernment uprising ensued, resulting in a KMT crackdown and the killing of an estimated twenty thousand people. Afterward, the KMT suppressed any political organizing critical of the party and imprisoned thousands of people whom the KMT perceived as a threat to its one-party rule. The KMT also sent out agents to surveil people who were suspected of having ties to the CCP. Xiao became a target of surveillance as soon as he arrived in Taiwan.

Shortly after arriving, Xiao was summoned by someone from the KMT. He was told to go to the basement of a building. There he was interrogated for hours. The interrogator even pointed to a puddle of water and said they just shot a spy there not long ago and the water was used to clean off the bloodstains. Xiao protested loudly that he was not a spy and that such scare tactics were of no use employing. He said to his interrogator, "Who do you think Xiao Yujing is? If I really am a spy, then you have done a good job and deserve credit. But if I die here and it's proven that I am innocent, then you are responsible for my death. I am a *fangong yishi*, and I am not sure if you can bear this responsibility." Xiao remembers he had very mixed emotions about his interrogation. He was proud that he was a *fangong yishi* who was committed to fighting against the Communist regime, yet he knew very well that it was his origin that made him a suspect of betraying the party. He knew that the only way to prove his loyalty is to be himself because he had nothing to hide. Yet, he was afraid when the interrogators yelled at him. There were rumors that some suspects had been put in hemp sacks and thrown into the Danshui River. During the first ten years of his stay in Taiwan, Xiao was summoned to talk to the police every time he relocated.

About ten years after his arrival in the early 1970s, the police finally formally invited him to a meal. The officer said: "We're not going to monitor you anymore; you truly are anticommunist." While this was a moment of relief for Xiao, he also expressed that in those first ten years in Taiwan he had many "doubts and hardships." When asked if he felt betrayed by the KMT, he paused and replied, "Well, I guess that was understandable. I am a real *fangong yishi*. I had nothing to hide. That just proved that I am indeed a *fangong yishi*." He seemed to be a bit sad whenever he talked about the way he was surveilled by the KMT. Despite his mixed emotions toward the KMT, he never associated Chiang Ching-kuo with his ill treatment.

FIGURE 5.3 Xiao Yujing giving a speech at a public gathering sponsored by the KMT in the 1960s or 1970s.

Courtesy of Xiao Yujing.

Xiao Yujing fully identified with the *fangong yishi* label, and he mentioned several times that the moment he learned the term, he felt it was the exact description of who he was. He also expressed repeatedly that it was his destiny to be a *fangong yishi* because his father was purged and eventually died under the CCP's rule. The *fangong yishi* label became like a badge of honor for Xiao, and he was satisfied to finally be acknowledged by the KMT as a patriotic hero devoted to the cause of the party (figure 5.3).

Lao Zhengwu was also called a *fangong yishi* as he became more involved with the FCRA while working at the Taipei City Council Legal Department. Lao became the chairperson of the Fangong Yishi

Committee in the late 1970s because of his connection with the FCRA since his days in Hong Kong. However, he disagreed with Xiao on the definition of the term *fangong yishi*. Unlike Xiao, Lao saw *fangong yishi* as only referring to defectors, either PLA pilots who flew to Taiwan and KMT-controlled territories or Korean War veterans who went to Taiwan. Lao denied that he himself was a *fangong yishi* because he belonged to neither group and said he was only a refugee (*nanbao*) or an exiled student (*liuwang xuesheng*). According to his understanding, *yishi* has the connotation of someone who sacrifices their high-ranking position, which he never was in a position to do. Unlike Xiao, he did not rationalize his escape to Macau as an anticommunist act. In other words, Lao simply could not relate to this term. Although he did not spell it out specifically, it sounded as though he did not feel strongly about being *fangong*. He did not like the CCP under Mao's leadership, but he was not eager to join the counterattack militarily to remove the CCP from power.

He explained that he was chosen to chair the meetings of the Fangong Yishi Committee because he had received a very high score on the civil service examination and the KMT wanted someone educated and intelligent to preside over the meetings. He was first asked to chair a meeting when Chiang Ching-kuo came to power in 1978. During that meeting, the well-known *fangong yishi* pilot Fan Yuanyan was invited to speak about his experience. After that, Lao became actively involved in the Fangong Yishi Committee, hosting events and lectures that focused on the propaganda effort against the CCP. He also said that Xiao was in the audience at the meeting where he first presided, opining that Xiao should not be calling himself a *fangong yishi* either because it is a misnomer. To Lao, Xiao was even less qualified as a *fangong yishi* because he was not asked to be on the committee and was simply tagging along as an observer. Even though Lao denied that he was a *fangong yishi*, he sounded quite proud of his role as chairperson of the Fangong Yishi Committee because his leadership talent and academic achievements were recognized by the KMT and its members. He emphasized repeatedly that the FCRA saw him as a role model and thus gave him the important job as the chairperson. Lao felt indebted to the KMT for both educational and job opportunities, so serving on the Fangong Yishi Committee was a way of repaying his debt.

Through participating in the meetings of the Fangong Yishi Committee, both Lao and Xiao developed their identity around the new status of *fangong yishi*. In those meetings and talks, they reiterated their stories about enduring hardship in the PRC and escaping from the authoritarian regime. Years later, both could still describe their childhood and escape routes in detail, indicating that those descriptions were scripts they had repeated many times.

Nevertheless, Xiao Yujing's relationship with the KMT remained complicated. He rationalized how the KMT had monitored him for ten years by saying it was a test to see if he was a true *fangong yishi*. To Xiao, *fangong yishi* was a badge of loyalty, and passing the test of surveillance proved to the party that he was a true loyal subject. As for Lao, his narrative was centered more on himself and how he overcame obstacles and lived up to his full potential as an intellectual. Lao Zhengwu saw his position as the chairperson of the Fangong Yishi Committee as a prestigious position within the KMT and in society.

PART 6: FROM ANTICOMMUNIST TO ANTI-INDEPENDENT TAIWAN

After Taiwan had endured more than two decades of political repression, Chiang Kai-shek's son, Chiang Ching-kuo, wanted to begin democratizing the country. Chiang Ching-kuo's election as president in 1978 was a turning point in Taiwan politics. The KMT had begun to allow elections for a small number of seats in the Legislative Yuan, but opposition parties were still banned. As a result, opponents of the KMT, officially classified as independents, ran only as non-KMT members. This is the origin of the term *dangwai/tangwai* (outside the party). Dangwai was initially a loosely organized group of political activists who challenged and opposed the KMT. In 1978, their coalition Taiwan Dangwai was formed for the elections. It was also the precursor to the Democratic Progressive Party (DPP), launched in 1986. The DPP became the ruling party from 2000 to 2008 under Chen Shui-bien and then again since 2016 with Tsai Ing-wen as president;[18] Tsai was reelected in 2020. From the beginning, the Dangwai movement, and later the DPP, was widely perceived as advocating the Taiwan independence (*Taidu*), and the pro-KMT media depicted members of the movement as propagating a *Taidu* trend in the island.

At about that time, Xiao Yujing and Lao Zhengwu became identified by the media with the far-right (*jiyou*) faction of the KMT in Taiwan.[19] Some rumors say that the far-right faction was secretly paid by members of the KMT leadership to do the dirty work. The far-right faction was often seen publicly attacking Dangwai politicians verbally and sometimes physically. Both Xiao and Lao said later that their objective at the time was to sabotage the political organizing of the Dangwai in order to preserve the unity of China as a nation. In keeping with their intent to uphold the integrity of the KMT, their actions—albeit deemed too extreme by some—were largely justified. Their actions seemed to stem from their own principles, since neither man ever mentioned monetary rewards from the party, and both also claimed that a number of KMT leaders showed their support at the beginning.[20]

On December 5, 1978, the Taiwan Central Elected Representatives (Zhongyang Minyi Daibiao) had a meeting in Zhong Shan Tang as a public forum for the upcoming election. There were about five hundred attendees, including all the leaders of the Taiwan Dangwai coalition. The meeting at Zhong Shan Tang was supposed to begin with the Republic of China's national anthem.[21] A leader from the Dangwai camp proposed to change the lyrics of the national anthem from "The Three Principles is the foundation of our party" (*Sanmin Zhuyi wudang suozong*) to "The Three Principles is the foundation of the people/ citizens" (*Sanmin Zhuyi wumin suozong*), as a way to reclaim the Republic based on Sun Yat-sen's Three Principles and also to decenter the KMT as the focus of the anthem. Infuriated by the Dangwai's announcement to change the lyrics, Xiao Yujing and Lao Zhengwu rushed to the stage and grabbed the microphone to announce that the new lyrics were not legitimate. This led to a clash between the Dangwai politicians and the people in Xiao and Lao's camp. Lao, Xiao, and others were forcibly removed from the meeting after much commotion. A few hours later, Lao and Xiao held a press conference to condemn the actions of the Dangwai camp. This was called the Zhong Shan Tang incident. On December 13, Lao and Xiao sued leaders of the Dangwai camp for "personal assaults, inciting murders, and treason" (*shanghai, jiaosuo sharen ji panguo*), but the court later dismissed the case because of lack of evidence.

Lao Zhengwu still felt agitated by the Dangwai members' actions when he recounted the details of the Zhong Shan Tang incident:

> I was really upset that they were having the elections, so we decided to get three or four friends they notified us of the time to arrive at the Guangfu Auditorium in Zhong Shan Tang—and start the oath-taking ceremony. I was still young then—thirty years old on December 5 in the sixty-seventh year of the Republic [1978]. We went at about one or two in the afternoon, and the three or four of us sat in the front row. When the meeting started—they have records of this—everyone stood and sang the national anthem . . . but they asked everyone to change the words. We were angry and upset about this. Can you change the national anthem? Let alone the fact that we understand the "party" in "our party" isn't necessarily referring to the Nationalist Party—it could refer to fellow villagers and townsmen. . . . But, anyway, how can you change the national anthem as you please? So our group exclaimed: Do not change [the national anthem], get up to sing, and not only sing, but sing loudly. So, we got up and let it out loud: "WUDANG SUOZONG! ([The Three Principles] is the foundation of the KMT)."

Even in the 2010s, four decades after the event, Lao was still somewhat proud of what he had done on that day and the publicity his actions received: "The next day all of the newspapers had my picture in their cover stories saying there was a certain person named Lao Zhengwu, a *fangong yishi*, who came out to protest changing the national anthem." In this context, *fangong yishi* just seems to mean a patriot of China and a loyalist to the KMT. Lao was much more excited when he talked about his activism as an anti-*Taidu* activist than a *fangong yishi* fighting against the CCP during the interviews. Part of the reason may have to do with the fact that fighting against the CCP was no longer on the agenda of the KMT. Or, perhaps, to Lao, his main life mission was to protect the integrity of the Chinese republic rather than fight against the CCP.

When asked why he was so enthusiastic in opposition, he argues that *Taidu* is wrong on moral terms:

> In China we need unified thinking. If we want a grand vision for Chinese civilization, we can't be regionalistic. I know all about regionalism. When I was little in Guangdong, we weren't very accepting of outsiders. For those who came from the North—including people from Jiangsu and Hunan—we screamed "*laotou*" [a derogatory term for an outsider] at them, and we would seldom smile at them in the market. If one jin of pork normally went for one dollar, we would sell it to them for two dollars.... Regionalism—it's a terrible thing to see among Chinese people. Taiwan is also an example of regionalism.

Here Lao associated "separatism" and "regional autonomy" with ethnic discrimination and xenophobia. To him, it is important for Chinese people to promote a single identity—being Chinese—and not emphasize their regional characteristics. He considered the *Taidu* movement an obstacle to the country's strengthening because it is like "one fighting against one's brother": "You could argue with your brother, but in the end, you should not split up with your brother. *Taidu* is about breaking away from your own brother. How can it be acceptable?"

In contrast, he did not bring up similar moralistic arguments about the CCP, even when it was under Mao's leadership. He repeated that Mao made many people suffer because he was a failed politician, but he was not as critical of communist ideologies as he was of regionalism and separatism. Nor was he too concerned about the lack of democracy in the PRC.

His relationship with the KMT began to change. According to Lao, because of a few negative reports in international media about the violent and chaotic nature of the scene in Zhong Shan Tang, the KMT became more cautious in its public stance and began to back away from the far-right activists. Lao was also questioned by the police about the matter. Later, the leadership of the Taipei City Council got a report from the police about his involvement. Under pressure, Lao decided to leave his position on the council and start a career on his own.

Lao Zhengwu did not give up on his anti-*Taidu* activities, however. A few months later, on July 7, 1979, Lao Zhengwu inaugurated *Ji Feng* magazine in response to the growing influence of the Dangwai movement. He asked his friends to help him, and Xiao Yujing served on the magazine's executive committee and as a chief editor. While some writings condemned communism and the CCP, the majority of *Ji Feng*'s editorials and writings focused on vehemently criticizing the Dangwai movement and people who endorsed Taiwan independence. As Xiao Yujing wrote in the inaugural issue of *Ji Feng*:

> *Ji Feng Magazine* has finally been born in the care and attention of the nation.
>
> Our motive in publishing *Ji Feng Magazine* is the difficulties of the country's situation today, with "Black Fist Gang" (*Heiquanbang*) [derogative nickname for Dangwai] running wild on one side of us and the Communist Party on the other. At this moment, we cannot continue in silence! We shall prove our sincere love for the nation with concrete action![22]

Although it closed down a year later in August 1980, *Ji Feng* served as a platform for far-right activists to unite other KMT loyalists against the Dangwai camp. The Mandarina Crown Hotel (Zhongtai Binguan) incident, a major conflict between *Ji Feng* supporters and Dangwai supporters, occurred when the founders of the rival Dangwai magazine *Formosa* (*meili dao*) held its inaugural celebration (figure 5.4). *Formosa* was formed as the voice of the Dangwai movement, and its first issue came out in August 1979 in Kaohsiung, a month after *Ji Feng* was launched. On the afternoon of September 8, some *Ji Feng* supporters, including Lao and Xiao, arrived and protested at the Mandarina Crown Hotel and reportedly threw stones and other objects at the participants of the Dangwai event. Police had to come in to mitigate the incident but did not arrest Lao, Xiao, or other *Ji Feng* supporters. Although the Dangwai participants suffered only minor injuries, the incident was reported in the media as personal assaults committed by *Ji Feng* supporters and the far-right faction of the KMT. A few media outlets even raised the suspicion that the *Ji Feng* supporters were ordered by the authorities to sabotage the event.[23]

Initially, Xiao Yujing did not talk about these events much even though he was also a core member of the far-right camp. When asked about these events during the interview in 2016, Xiao Yujing acknowledged his participation in both the Zhong Shan Tang incident and Mandarina Crown Hotel incidents but did not give any details, because either he did not remember or he may have become a little embarrassed in retrospect

FIGURE 5.4 *Jifeng Magazine* (1979), vol. 1, no. 3. One of the featured articles in this issue is about the Mandarina Crown Hotel incident.

Courtesy of the National Taiwan Library.

about the violent nature of the actions even though he expressed no regrets about fighting against the *Taidu* trend at the time. Another reason he was reticent about this could be the fact that, after this incident, Xiao and others received criticism from within and outside the party that their actions had gone too far. He also faced alienation from colleagues for his association with the far right and was pressured to quit his job. After leaving his job, Xiao believed he had no choice but to go to the United States to continue his studies because he felt "unwelcome" in Taiwan and the political label of "far right" (*jiyou*) had earned a bad reputation after the clashes. Throughout the interviews that spanned over three years in the 2010s, Xiao expressed contempt for the DPP because it goes against the KMT's vision of reunification. Unlike Lao, however, Xiao did not brag about his involvement in these anti-Dangwai movements. He emphasized that he committed those acts because he was loyal to the KMT and its goal of reunification.

Another major incident that targeted the Dangwai party in which Xiao and Lao did not directly take part, but which involved the far-right faction, was the Kaohsiung incident, sometimes called the Melidao incident, when the editors and founder of *Formosa* magazine used Human Rights Day to express their views on the lack of democracy in Taiwan on December 10, 1979. Police encircled the peaceful crowd and started using tear gas. Heavy civilian injuries were ignored in news reports while damages to the police side were played up. The KMT authorities used the incident as a pretext to arrest all well-known opposition leaders.[24] The incident and the subsequent arrests became a rallying point for Dangwai to garner support within Taiwan as well as among Taiwanese communities in North America and Europe.

At that time, Lao believed it was urgent to use publications to stop the *Taidu* movement's momentum in Taiwanese society. After *Ji Feng* was disbanded, he published another magazine called *Long Qi*, which was also anti-*Taidu* in content. Nevertheless, his involvement in politics came to a halt shortly after Lee Teng-hui came to power because Lao knew Lee, who was clearly sympathetic to the idea of *Taidu*, would not support *Long Qi*.

Speaking in an interview in 2018, Xiao Yujing admitted that he did whatever he could as a *fangong yishi* to help the KMT. While in the 1960s and early 1970s he was active in attending propaganda events that condemned the CCP for abusing its citizens, in the late 1970s he became a staunch activist in the far-right faction of the KMT. One would think that since Dangwai and later the DPP also has had a strong anti-CCP stand, *fangong yishi* like Xiao Yujing would be at least amicable toward the DPP. However, Xiao, when asked about the connection, immediately brushed it off saying the *Taidu* movement and the anti-CCP movement were completely different and should not be discussed together. He called his transition from being an anti-CCP activist to being an anti-*Taidu* campaigner a "natural process" (*hen ziran*). To him, anti-communist and anti-*Taidu* activism came from the same root of hoping for the country to become strong and reunited again. He described Dangwai and the *Taidu* movements as "pro-division:" "Pro-division is motivated by private, ulterior motives. The *Taidu* movement is made up of people with parochial interests; it is not a group that belongs to all the citizens. However, if we look at China as a whole, [Taiwan] is only a very small part of it. I don't want to see divisions; I want to see unity."

Xiao Yujing saw himself as very loyal to the KMT, even more so than Lao Zhengwu. Xiao had known Lao for many decades, and the two led anti–Taiwan independence campaigns together, but they did not stay in contact after both went into exile after Lee Teng-hui came to power. During interviews, Xiao showed his low regard for Lao's personality: "I actually had many problems with Lao Zhengwu. He is quite ambitious, enjoys finding faults in others to elevate himself, but yet has not accomplished much. The magazine was his means to realize his political ambition. He wished that the Kuomintang would pay more attention to him and offer him a government position. I have no such intentions." Xiao characterized Lao as always wanting to make a name for himself, whereas he saw himself as single-mindedly loyal to the KMT with no self-interest. Xiao's characterization of Lao Zhengwu seems to be largely accurate. Lao did not express strong political convictions or loyalty toward the KMT throughout the interview. While he did show gratitude toward the KMT for the education, employment, and other opportunities he received over the years, he emphasized his intellectual talents and achievements much more than his political aspirations.

Another difference between Xiao Yujing and Lao Zhengwu was how Xiao framed his anticommunist career around the life of Chiang Ching-kuo. Since their first meeting at the National Overseas Secondary School when Xiao had just arrived in Taiwan, Xiao had written to Chiang Ching-kuo from time to time reporting the changes in his life. According to Xiao, they had meals together two or three times over the next two decades, and Chiang always acted paternally and asked about his well-being. Chiang also allegedly introduced a job at the broadcast company after he returned from the United States. In the 2018 interview, Xiao said that even though the dream of freeing China did not come true, he had no regrets: "Being able to have a few meals with him [Chiang], and getting his help with finding jobs . . . I thought it was sufficient. When he died, all my unification dreams died with him." Even though Chiang Ching-kuo did not publicly discuss the actions of Xiao and other *Ji Feng* supporters at Zhong Shan Tang or the Mandarina Crown Hotel, Xiao had no doubt that Chiang actually did appreciate what Xiao had done for the KMT but just could not express it openly for fear of a political backlash: "Chiang Ching-kuo had his own approach to *Taidu*. Though Chiang would have personally liked seeing the *Taidu* movement go down, he didn't want to provoke *Taidu* [activists]." Xiao appeared to project his own emotions on Chiang Ching-kuo, characterizing Chiang as a generous political leader who did his best to tolerate dissenting viewpoints. According to Xiao, the main life mission for Chiang Ching-kuo was to launch a *fangong* attack and reunite China, but he was not able to do so during his lifetime. The *Taidu* movement was a distraction, like an "unfilial son" in Xiao's word. Xiao probably felt the same way about the Taidu movement. Xiao also expressed his indignance against *Taidu* activists, accusing them of causing Chiang Ching-kuo's death, even though Chiang had been generous to them:

> As Chiang Ching-kuo's death approached, all *Taidu* activists vehemently opposed him. When he was delivering his last speech in the National Assembly (Guomin Dahui), he barely had the energy to speak. . . . These people were holding up banners. Chiang asked Soong Chu-yu [one of his subordinates] about the incident. Soong explained that those who were holding up the banners were advocating *Taidu*.

According to Xiao, what Soong described was too shocking and heartbreaking to Chiang and might have aggravated his illness since he died shortly thereafter. With Chiang Ching-kuo's passing, things grew grim for Xiao as well: "[I felt] hopeless (*juewang*), that there was no hope [for the KMT reuniting China]. I could place my only hope on the proper administration of the CCP." The death of Chiang Ching-kuo and the rise of Lee Teng-hui had a tremendous impact on Xiao. He also mentioned a number of times throughout the interviews that all his dreams died with Chiang Kai-shek. It sounded as though Xiao was heartbroken and faded out of politics after that. While he did participate in a few anti-*Taidu* activities, he lost almost all his motivation after Chiang's death.

PART 7: RETURNING TO TAIWAN FROM EXILE

The political careers of both Lao Zhengwu and Xiao Yujing ended with their temporary departure from Taiwan. The month after Lee Teng-hui was elected president, Lao went to Hong Kong. Upon arriving, he enrolled in a doctoral course at the Muni Institute of Buddhist Studies. Although the reason for his departure was apparently political, Lao claimed that the reason he left at that point was that he had already mastered politics and political theory, so he felt ready to move on and pursue other interests. He decided to study with Nan Huaijin, a philosopher who was well versed in Chinese culture and Buddhism. He also did not find Hong Kong to be home because it is simply too small, too insignificant, and people in Hong Kong "lack cultural sophistication."

After his return to Taiwan in the late 1990s, Lao opened Jingming Cultural Center in Taoyuan, to teach local Taiwanese residents Chinese philosophy and Buddhism. (I conducted the two interviews with Lao at the center.) In the mid-2010s, the center had a storefront selling Chinese medicines and health equipment. The basement had a small hall for Lao to give talks and hold cultural events. Explaining his reason for opening the cultural center, Lao said that despite no longer being affiliated with any political groups, he wanted to continue making contribution to the nationalist cause of reunification through writing. Since setting up the cultural center, he has published books criticizing the Falun Gong and a

FIGURE 5.5 Lao Zhengwu outside a travel agency in Taoyuan in 2017.
Photo by Angelina Y. Chin.

biography of a KMT war veteran, among other works on law and philosophy. He said that even though his cultural center is not explicitly political, he believed it has a mission to transmit Chinese traditions to the public in Taiwan. Lao talked a great deal about Chinese traditions in his interviews, and he viewed mainland China as the center of Chinese culture.

Besides these cultural activities in Taiwan, Lao had become active in Hong Kong and the Guangdong region of China again since the 2000s. Right after the interview in 2017, he had to go to the travel agency to buy a plane ticket to Hong Kong (figure 5.5). He explained that he had been regularly giving talks on philosophy there. He also claimed that he owned a piece of land in Kaiping, Guangdong. In around 2000, a cadre from the mainland had invited him to start a business, and he believed it would be beneficial for himself and people in China to start a farm there. He was a bit vague about the operation of the farm, but he implied that the farm was not very profitable, which led to some legal troubles in the early 2010s when the local government tried to take it back. This upset him because he saw his business in China as a contribution to the cause of national reunification as it recruited volunteers to engage in cross-strait cultural exchanges, whereas the local officials only cared about profit. Despite all the troubles, he still considered himself a public intellectual playing an active role in society by writing books and serving Chinese communities in China, Hong Kong, and Taiwan.

Xiao Yujing, for his part, returned to Taiwan after a few years in the United States and began to work for a radio station sponsored by the KMT. He said that Chiang Ching-kuo helped him with securing the job. He also wrote several books, including collections of essays, novels, poetry, and memoirs. However, he was not very proud of these achievements. He repeated many times in the interviews that his political dream died when he left Taiwan. He described himself as a "person of the past" with no significance in the world of the present. As he discussed his past, he said that his past has no relevance to today's world and expressed puzzlement why anyone would take an interest in his story. Having long since retired from politics, Xiao knew that his active days had passed: "I simply hold both the Kuomintang and my past ambition to be ill-fated and futile. Right now, all I am doing is going with the flow and managing to make ends meet." He also showed regret that his talents were not discovered by the KMT: "If they truly knew and made use of my talents, I wouldn't be writing these lame books today." He held up one of his novels and tossed it on the coffee table as he spoke. When we finished the interview, he took out his er'hu and started playing a melancholic song. He shook his head and smiled wryly, exclaiming in a soft voice, "This has been my life!" (figure 5.6).

Even though the two men went separate ways after leaving Taiwan, they shared the feeling that they were no longer needed by the KMT after Lee Teng-hui came to power. Lee Teng-hui's rise to power was a turning

FIGURE 5.6 Xiao Yujing playing erhu in his apartment after an interview in 2018. Photo by Angelina Y. Chin.

point for Xiao and Lao—a wakeup call that their far-right stance was no longer favored by the regime. They both remained somewhat disillusioned by the fact that they had to flee to other territories.

Disillusionment did not change their minds about what their ideal China should become, nevertheless. Lao believed that he was still contributing to the cause of national strengthening and reunification through his cultural activities. Xiao Yujing's ideal was for the KMT to reunite China under Chiang Kai-shek's, or Chiang Ching-kuo's, rule. "Later on, I realized that the actual situation did not match my ideal. I realized I was dreaming."

PART 8: THREE VIEWS OF DENG XIAOPING

Deng Xiaoping was a figure of contention in each of the personal narratives we have examined in this chapter. While all believed that Deng's economic reforms turned things around in China, the two men who went to Taiwan completely dropped their *fangong* views, while Ip's resentment toward the CCP became stronger after the handover of Hong Kong.

Xiao self-identified as a patriot (*aiguo*). He also strongly believed that leaders of China need to be patriotic. To him, while Mao Zedong was not patriotic because of the suffering he inflicted on the people, Deng Xiaoping could qualify as a patriot because of China's modernization under Deng's economic reforms:

> [My definition of patriotism] is quite straightforward: as long as you govern China well, and the people approve of your leadership, you are a patriot. I evaluate it based on the end result. Now the condition in the mainland is good. By "good," I am talking about mainland China's positive aspects. Are there defects? Certainly. However, if the positives outweigh the negatives, then it is good.

He expressed that it would be best if Chiang Ching-kuo had united China, but since that was impossible, he had to accept the next best option. He believed that the KMT had become weaker after Chiang's death, and at the time of 2018 there did not seem to be a satisfactory leader within the party, which contributes to his adjusted view that a CCP takeover of reunification cause is inevitable.

After his retirement, Xiao started blogging and made occasional trips to mainland China. He went to the Three Gorges Dam and visited the coastal cities and expressed that he had been a witness of the grand changes in China. In his blog posts in the early 2010s, he shared photos of his trip as well as his admiration for the infrastructure in mainland China. In the interviews, Xiao also acknowledged China's economic progress, even stating that the mainland had surpassed Taiwan in modernization. He called China since Deng Xiaoping came to power the "New China." He said: "I had no hope for the CCP until Deng Xiaoping came to power. You know, Mao Zedong was worse than Chiang Kai-shek." As for Deng, Xiao said that he governed the mainland well. "I respected Deng Xiaoping very much. He was patriotic and an outstanding member of the CCP." When he was asked whether he still harbored any anti-communist sentiments after Deng's rise to power, he said:

> You are insane if you mention *fangong* again after Deng Xiaoping [commenced his leadership]. Such a view is still confined to the mentality of Mao or Chiang Kai-shek's era. . . . Deng transcended the notion that the CCP should fight against the Kuomintang and vice versa. Deng focused on empowering the mainland, namely the People's Republic of China, to thrive.

Lao had a similar explanation for his change of direction in his *fangong* stance. He explained his change of mind in one of the interviews:

> Later I discovered Deng Xiaoping's economic reform that has changed China completely. I was extremely delighted. We are the real KMT [members], and we were the most *fangong*, and we hated the CCP. In fact, we all felt that the CCP has reformed and become good, so there is no reason to be anti-CCP. It's like what Confucian said—"Nobody is perfect, nobody makes mistakes (*renfei shengxian shunengwuguo*); to acknowledge one's mistake and to correct it would be the greatest good one can do (*zhicuo nenggai shanmo dayan*)." So, for the CCP, they already corrected their mistake, didn't they? If we continue to stick with our

fangong stance, then it becomes our mistake. That's the right way to act. If someone acts correctly, you have to accept them. Only then can we progress.

Lao used Confucian teachings to rationalize his "forgiveness" of the CCP's past mistakes under Mao. He still followed Confucian teachings in his life. According to him: Mao committed some serious mistakes, especially his Great Leap Forward campaign that brought famine to the countryside. That was why people like him took up a *fangong* stand. Deng Xiaoping, in Lao's view, was a reformer and a national hero who had rectified Mao's mistake. He called Deng Xiaoping a "smart politician with a long-term vision." Lao was no longer *fangong* in the 1980s, especially after he was invited by PRC cadres to visit and invest in China.

Both Xiao's and Lao's rationalization explains they were *fangong* mainly because Mao had made China backward, and since the PRC has been a rising global power, it is not necessary to criticize them. For Xiao, his hatred toward the CCP might have diminished after Mao's death, since he saw Mao as the enemy who killed his father. He was quite neutral about the CCP after Mao's death.

In contrast to Xiao and Lao, Ip did not praise Deng profusely. To Ip, it was not that Deng was particularly far-sighted, but the Chinese leader had no other options at that time other than to implement reforms: "Deng cannot be counted as 'great' (*weida*), but I must say he 'has a lot of guts' (*hao dadan*). At a time of crisis, there needs to be someone who is willing to take on the leadership (*linweishouming*)." Ip agreed that things had improved since Deng Xiaoping's regime, but there were still some fundamental differences between China and Hong Kong: "Of course we have seen development in the transportation network and infrastructure, but the software is no good. What do I mean by software? It is the real strength of the region. In Hong Kong, that means the rule of law, that means freedom." His views are quite typical of the people in Hong Kong who self-identify as Hong Kongers—claiming the superiority of Hong Kong over the PRC in terms of political and judicial systems, as well as everyday efficiency.

Ip Cheung's comment reveals the differences in how each of the three men perceived the PRC. On the one hand, Xiao and Lao contended that since Deng's administration, there has been nothing they disapprove of any longer about the Communist regime; on the other hand, Ip continued to be very critical of other aspects of the PRC because, to him, there are "things that matter more than the economy and reunification," including freedom and democracy. Without them, Ip said, economic progress is not meaningful, and it would not make him feel more patriotic toward China. Ip spoke at a moment when the CCP was tightening its grip on Hong Kong. His views echo those of the mainstream pro-democracy camp in Hong Kong society in the late 2010s, right before the 2019 protests.

PART 9: WHAT IS CHINA? WHERE IS HOME?

As for Taiwan's future, since the late 1980s, Xiao Yujing began to believe that the PRC would take over Taiwan. At the same time, he hoped the KMT would become the ruling party again and reform itself to help with the transition and make China prosperous when reunification happens. His continuing contempt toward the DPP and the *Taidu* movement was exemplified by his comment about Taiwan's worsening under DPP rule: "At this moment, Taiwan is ruled by *Taidu* advocates, so even a Communist takeover is better." During his interviews in 2016 and 2018, he showed strong disapproval of the ruling party, the DPP, and was worried that Taiwan was heading toward a path of destruction: "Currently, the ruling party of *Taidu* besmirched the Kuomintang for the sake of claiming power.... Whenever you turn on the TV, you can see *Taidu* extremism."

In 2018, Xiao remained positive about reunification. He said it is only a matter of time until the CCP will "liberate" Taiwan. In regard to Hong Kong, he criticized the 2014 Umbrella Movement and conceded that it is futile to resist the CCP because reintegration is inevitable given the size and strength of the PRC.

Similarly, Lao Zhengwu strongly expressed his hope for national reunification, but his yearning for a Greater China was stronger than

Xiao's. In the 2016 interview, Lao said that Taiwan, Hong Kong, and the PRC all could complement one another's shortcomings by sharing their strengths; for example, the mainland could learn from Taiwan's preservation of Chinese culture, while Hong Kong's bureaucracy and rule of law could set a good example for the PRC's democratization. With the help of these two territories, the PRC could become a very strong nation: "[After reunification,] you could criticize the mainland for not being democratic enough. Then they must learn from our 'democratic China.' We are an example for the whole of China. Only through learning from one another's strength can we have a bright future." It is worth noting that here he praises the exact democratic fervor that he opposed in an earlier interview. On the one hand, he expressed contempt for *Taidu*'s appeal and called it divisive politics; on the other hand, he viewed democracy as desirable in Chinese society. Ultimately, though, to Lao, building a stronger, united China should trump all ideologies.

With respect to cross-strait relations, Lao is in favor of the "1992 consensus" that acknowledged the coexistence of mainland China and Taiwan but only under the definition of the "one China principle."[25] Like Xiao, Lao also thinks it is impossible to resist a country of such size and power as the PRC:

> Don't talk about the "two states" theory, an independent Taiwan—that way you will definitely lose. Why? Because the strength of the entire PRC is so large. What will you use to resist it? [Tsai Ing-wen] always says things like "Taiwan's public opinion," and "Taiwan is a master of its destiny." Even if, as she says, you are the master of your own destiny, the country only has 23 million people, while the Chinese mainland's population is 1.3 billion, and then there are overseas Chinese. If she gathers all her strength, even if she gets all of her 23 million people together to oppose the mainland, will it be any use? They will vanquish you! She is unaware of the power of the mainland. You cannot fight in this way.

Practically, to Lao, the reason the *Taidu* movement will eventually fail is that Taiwan lacks the strength to resist absorption by the PRC.

Even though by the time he returned to Taiwan he was no longer an active member of the KMT, he still praised the party for having high moral standards: "If the KMT—its ideology and morality—is wrong, then everyone will leave. But it's not wrong; it carries on the spirit of Sun Yat-sen." According to his analysis, the KMT would prevail in the end and could coexist with the CCP after reunification. To him, the future ideal of China is that after reunification the PRC would democratize gradually and learn from the KMT and other positive aspects of Taiwan and Hong Kong. Although both Xiao Yujing and Lao Zhengwu have no plans to move back to China, they now believe that Chinese people in diaspora like themselves will "return home" when the CCP reunifies China.

CONCLUSION

When asked about the future of Hong Kong in the interview in 2018, Ip said that the one country, two systems principle had been eroding. Most people who could afford to emigrate had left Hong Kong because they saw no hope in Hong Kong's future—it would be absorbed by the PRC. The only reason he chose to stay is he did not have sufficient capital to emigrate. As of 2018, Hong Kong was still a unique place where the rule of law was respected. Nevertheless, he also saw that conditions in Hong Kong were deteriorating with the infiltration of Beijing's influence. In his two interviews in 2016 and 2018, he talked about the future of Hong Kong. He sometimes expressed pessimism, stating that the people of Hong Kong had little in the way of bargaining power when facing the government in Beijing. In 2016, he said, "[Hong Kong] is like a piece of pork lying on the cutting board (*rousui zhenban shang*) after the handover." This view resonated with Lao's and Xiao's in that they all feel that Hong Kong resisting the PRC is like David fighting against Goliath.

Then he expressed the view that the "One country, two systems" principle had originally been a sound idea, but that Beijing had violated it:

> Originally under Deng Xiaoping, the Sino-British Joint Declaration guaranteed Hong Kong people a high level of autonomy. If [his successors] had followed this principle, it would have been fine. Even when Hu Jintao was the leader, there was a high level of autonomy.... My ideal would be that they don't change the original form [of "One country, two

systems"]. You know this saying: "river water should not be mixed with well water (*heshui bufan jingshui*)!"

Ip thought the first two chief executives of Hong Kong, Tung Chee-hwa and Donald Tsang, were not bad as compared to their successors, Chun Ying Leung and Carrie Lam. To Ip, the latter two betrayed the Hong Kong people by giving away what was promised to them. In the summer of 2019, during a phone interview, I asked Ip for his perspective on the protests against the Extradition Bill. He replied, "This was just a trigger. [The discontent] had always been there but had been suppressed for twenty-two years, since the handover." He blamed the unrest on the CCP and the Hong Kong government for not honoring Deng's promise to keep Hong Kong unchanged for fifty years.

Ip said that while he felt a certain attachment to Chinese culture and traditions, he had no such feelings for the CCP. As for what an ideal relationship among China, Taiwan, and Hong Kong should look like, he expressed an interest in a political model that resembles a confederation. In Ip's view, the cultures of the three places are too different to be under one political system.

Ip's political views may represent the middle class of his generation who succeeded in advancing socially in the 1960s and 1970s. Unlike those who did not have tertiary education, Ip read a vast amount of political and social commentaries in newspapers since the late 1980s, so he may be more critical of the Hong Kong and PRC governments than most. He also did not regret the decisions to flee China and to settle down in Hong Kong. The Hong Kong government's policy of political neutrality did have an impact on his generation of residents and immigrants. Some Hong Kong residents who fled China during the 1950s–1970s would prefer stability and the benefits from integration with China. One high government official in his sixties expressed in 2018 the view that this was a time of "harvesting" after decades of hard work; thus he could not bear to see all he had been working hard for being sabotaged by the young people who protested and tried to "wreck the system" for democratic changes. Since this politician made his comments, the term "harvesting" has become a popular one to describe the feelings of some of the middle- and upper-class retirees or soon-to-be retirees who condemn any protests that could potentially destabilize Hong Kong society.

Some of Ip Cheung's views on China in the 2010s were influenced by what he had experienced as a child in the PRC. He said that in the PRC, people could be arrested for what they say, and many people were eager to report on one another to the authorities. He strongly condemned such distrustful attitudes, which resembled what he had witnessed when he grew up in Guangdong, saying that they came from the "genes of the peasantry (*nongmin jiyin*)." Ip cited a Hong Kong political commentator's remark that China is a "nation with brain cancer," adding that it is an excellent description of the root of the problem. "In order for it to get better, it would require rigorous educational reform, starting from kindergarten, but it will take a very long time to heal." He believed that because people since his generation had been deprived of proper education, including moral education, their *ren'ge* (human character) was not properly developed.

In sum, Ip Cheung's views about mainland China were influenced by his past experience growing up in China during the Land Reform campaign and the Great Famine, as well as popular media's portrayal of the PRC government as unjust and the citizens as being distrustful of one another. Ip's perception of the PRC as a continuous regime starting with Mao's rule and the political culture he created is quite typical of how some Hong Kong residents tend to view the PRC's history as one continuity. In such view, Deng Xiaoping's economic reform was treated as a mirage rather than a rupture and the PRC's overall plan of integrating Hong Kong, Taiwan, and Macau did not change.

In the late 2010s, he showed pessimism toward the future of Hong Kong, as he saw its reintegration to China as inevitable. He thought Deng Xiaoping offered a tiny sliver of hope in the early 1980s that China would eventually democratize, but that hope was extinguished step by step first by the crackdown in Tiananmen Square in 1989, then the lack of political reform in Hong Kong in the 2000s, and finally China's tightening of political control over its peripheral regions in the 2010s.

The political views of these three men today were largely shaped by their environments after their successful escapes to Hong Kong and Macau. Xiao Yujing and Lao Zhengwu arrived in Hong Kong and Macau, respectively, but these two places made little impact on their lives. On the one hand, the two have very little memory or impressions of their days in those cities. On the other hand, one could argue that Hong Kong and Macau were two "'in-between' places"—as Elizabeth Sinn argues about nineteenth-century Hong Kong's being a place of continuous movement to the rest of the world—because it was those two locations that helped facilitate their journeys to the "Free World."[26] Going to Taiwan was a key point for both men's lives and shaped their views and experiences in ways distinctive from Ip Cheung's. Their status as refugees from China was highly politicized. Lao and Xiao joined the pro-KMT side of Taiwan's political divide between the KMT and the DPP and stayed loyal to the party and its stand on reunification despite being ostracized after their involvement with *Ji Feng* and participation in the clashes with Dangwai.

In contrast, Hong Kong became Ip's permanent home, and he soon adjusted to the lifestyle there. Like many Chinese immigrants, he focused on building a new life in Hong Kong. As a result, he did not share an attachment to the KMT as Xiao and Lao did, although he did gradually develop a strong resentment toward the CCP. He clearly distinguished the CCP as the ruling party from "China" as an ethnic and cultural entity. Despite his love for Chinese culture, he expressed no yearning for reunification between Hong Kong and the mainland.

There was more than one pivotal moment in each of these three men's lives. Their stories show that their escapes to Hong Kong or Macau may have been traumatic experiences that had significant impacts on their lives, but it was what came after those perilous journeys that made them who they are today. The refugee policies and the political culture of Hong Kong and Taiwan not only changed their fates; they also affected their sense of loyalty and created new meanings for them of what "China" is and could be.

All three men were *fangong* at some point in their lives, but the meanings of *fangong* were different based on their experiences and beliefs. Ip Cheung's *fangong* sentiments mostly came from the forced integration of Hong Kong with mainland China by the CCP as well as the lack of democracy under one-party rule; Xiao Yujing's *fangong* consciousness arose from the sufferings of his father as a landlord and his admiration for Chiang Ching-kuo; Lao Zhengwu was *fangong* because he thought Mao Zedong's mistakes in launching the Great Leap Forward made China weak. While Xiao and Lao may seem similar in their political paths and beliefs, their later activism was motivated by different intents: Xiao wanted to prove his personal loyalty to Chiang Ching-kuo and his cause, while Lao was more interested in promoting Chinese ethnic and cultural nationalism. This is especially evident in Xiao's retirement from politics in recent years and Lao's continuation in teaching Chinese philosophy and culture through his cultural center.

Juxtaposing Xiao's and Lao's views on China with Ip's is not meant to suggest that all escapees who ended up in Taiwan are pro-unification or that all those who stayed in Hong Kong are critical of the CCP. One must keep in mind that Xiao's and Lao's experiences as high-profile *fangong yishi* were not typical. They belonged to a very small group of people who were intentionally groomed by the KMT to be propaganda mouthpieces for the party at a particular juncture in history when the KMT was still hoping to take over all of China again. The majority of the people who went to Taiwan under the April 4 policy did not become public figures like they did but lived as ordinary citizens, even though almost all of them benefited from the policy's educational and employment opportunities. They may not have felt obligated to the KMT as Xiao and Lao did.

The deeper meanings of their stories are that they represent a spectrum of political views across the Southern Periphery. They arrived at those viewpoints because of their childhood traumas in the mainland as well as through what they experienced and witnessed since they left the mainland in 1962. For the generation of escapees like them, the Communist Revolution—including the Land Reform campaign and the Great Leap Forward—was personally traumatic and represented the root problems of the CCP regime. One could argue that without those campaigns, the politics of Hong Kong and Taiwan probably would have evolved very differently.

The notion of Chinese national reunification was on all of their minds. Lao and Xiao viewed more favorably the possibility of reunification, but what they foresee in terms of reunification by the CCP seems far from the ideal they once dreamed of. Lao may have tried very hard to be part of the reintegration project by doing business in mainland China, but Xiao had given up on his ambition to be a hero and decided to retire altogether. In contrast, Ip felt reintegration of Hong Kong with the PRC was inevitable but found nothing celebratory about it.

There was a mismatch of state and home for the people who moved to the Southern Periphery. Their feelings toward China and their perspectives on the CCP and the KMT and how they shaped the politics of China changed according to the political development of their respective environments. From these stories we can learn that Chinese history after the Civil War is more than just what happened in mainland China but was deeply connected to the diasporic population in the Southern Periphery. Tracing the routes of people like Xiao Yujing, Lao Zhengwu, and Ip Cheung who crossed the borders allows us to understand how the Cold War was not only a contest between two ideological camps but also a global phenomenon that profoundly transformed individuals' destinies and relationships with their homeland(s).

6

COMMEMORATING THE BIG ESCAPE

The Question of Memories

> *What I retain from these memories is not a history of personal or collective victimization but the sense of immediacy of a particular diasporic reality—of Hong Kong caught, as it always has been since the end of the Second World War, between two dominant cultures, British colonial and Chinese Communist, neither of which takes the welfare of Hong Kong people into account even though both would turn to Hong Kong for financial and other forms of assistance when they needed it. This marginalized position, which is not one chosen by those from Hong Kong but one constructed by history, brings with it a certain privilege of observation and an unwillingness to idealize oppression.*
>
> —REY CHOW, *WRITING DIASPORA*

In *Writing Diaspora*, published in 1993, four years before the handover, Rey Chow talked about the marginalized position and diasporic reality of Hong Kong since the 1940s.[1] She believed that these disadvantageous circumstances provide the people of Hong Kong with a vantage point from which they can critically consider colonialism and Chinese communism. While people in Hong Kong have shown a great deal of resilience and critical thinking, especially in the 2010s, none seemed to be able to offer any solutions as to how residents of Hong Kong could liberate themselves. In 1984, the Sino-British declaration sealed the fate of Hong Kong, asserting, in essence, that it could no longer be a permanent political refuge and that its people had to reestablish their bonds with their nation/homeland (*zuguo*) again. There was a sense of optimism in the following decade among some local intellectuals that Hong Kong's "advancement" in the pursuit of political freedom might help with the process of democratization in China. By the late 1990s and early 2000s, however, when Hong Kong had just been returned to China, most people in Hong Kong became convinced that the territory's peripheral position, as unique as it is, does not portend an alternative political future to that provided by the reigning teleological narrative of the PRC—that is, Hong Kong will inevitably be absorbed by the greater entity of China.

From the mid-1990s, when the 1997 handover from Great Britain to China was approaching, until 2012, when a massive movement opposing the introduction of the Moral and National Education took place, the CCP pressured the Hong Kong government to stress the concept of Greater China through its education curriculum, and to inculcate nationalism and erase local memories. An "imagined community" of a Greater China has been redefined for Hong Kongers through the narrative in Chinese history textbooks, along with state-initiated public commemorations of the founding of the PRC. The CCP's goal is that the successful reintegration of Hong Kong would entice Taiwan to "return home" one day as well.

CONSTRUCTING A FUTURE PEARL RIVER DELTA REGION

In the 1980s and 1990s, the PRC established near the border with Hong Kong and Macau a cluster of special economic zones (SEZs), including Shenzhen and Zhuhai. In these zones, it pursued flexible economic policies and other governmental measures conducive to foreign investment, thus increasing cross-border traffic.[2] The main reasons that the PRC chose Shenzhen and neighboring areas to become SEZs were their proximity to the southern border and their coastal location, both conducive to participation in international trade. Nevertheless, the choice was also a political one: the PRC believed that in order to stop the influx of

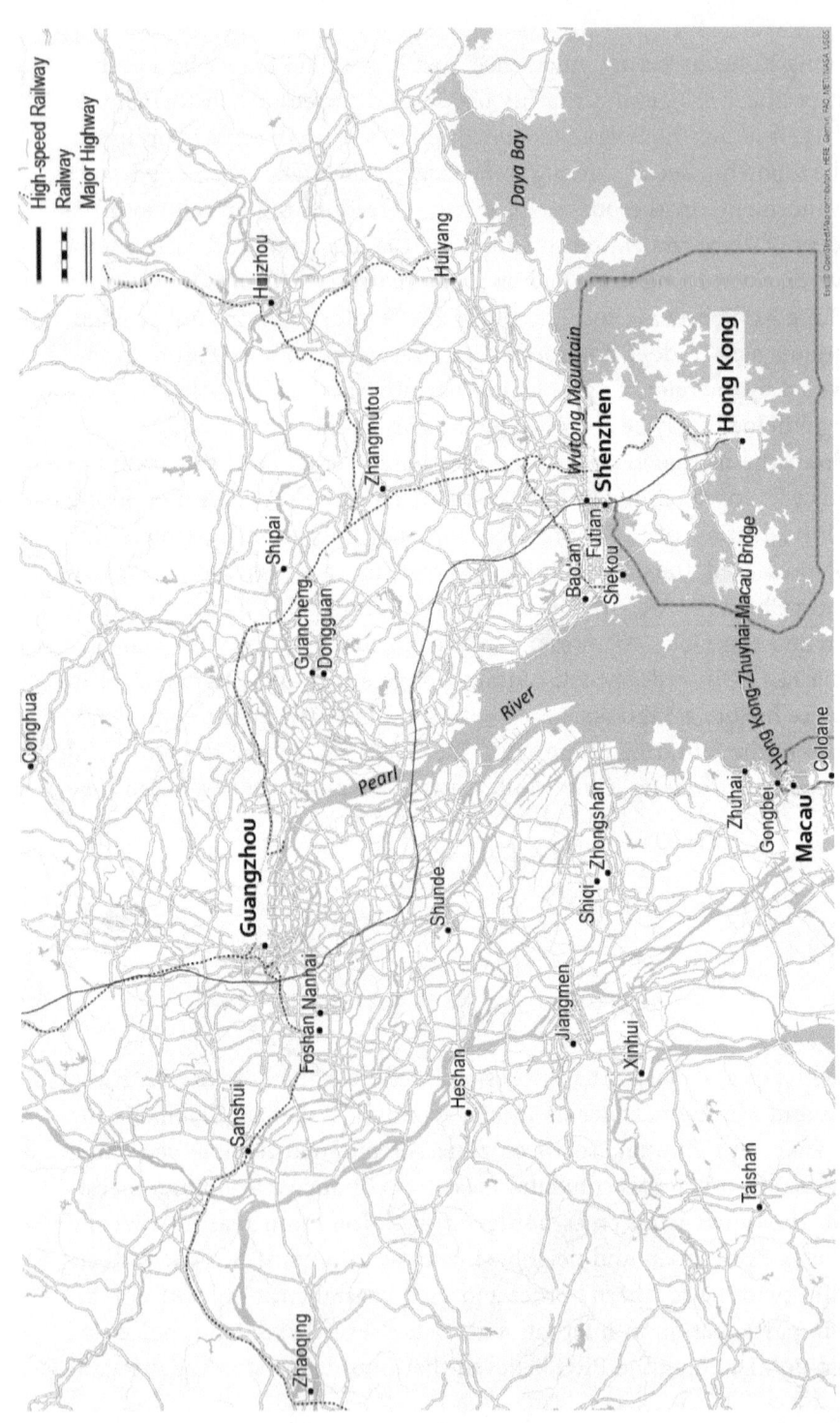

FIGURE 6.1 The Pearl River Delta Region in the 2020s.
Map created by Guoping Huang.

refugees sneaking into Hong Kong and Macau, it was necessary to reduce the economic gap between the two sides of the border and lessen the material incentive for its citizens to leave the nation.

This strategy was effective in raising the standard of living in the Pearl River Delta region (figure 6.1). As a result, illegal immigration began to decrease sharply in the late 1980s. The closing of the economic gap between the two sides of the border also attracted more and more entrepreneurs from Hong Kong and the Southern Periphery to seek business and investment opportunities in the PRC. Since the early 2000s, mainland tourists have become ubiquitous in Hong Kong, Macau, and Taiwan because of the easing of travel restrictions. At the immigration control points between Hong Kong and China, for example, a great number of residents from both sides cross the border every day, from children attending schools to old people visiting their hometowns.

The massive movement of people and capital across these territories has dramatically altered the geopolitical landscape. With the success of the experiment with SEZs, new towns in the Pearl River Delta region witnessed high economic growth and tremendous investments in secondary and tertiary industries. In the 2000s, the local governments and the PRC began to consider a more integrative economic development model that would benefit the SEZs in Guangdong Province by absorbing capital and talent from Hong Kong and Macau as well as encouraging investments from Taiwan.

The strategy for urbanization included a plan to move a great number of people into the cities, creating cities and city clusters with populations ranging from 10 million to 100 million. Beijing expects the metropolis that would encompass most of the SEZs in southern China as well as Hong Kong and Macau to become one of the most important urban clusters in China and to lead the nation's economy forward. It is not the only urban cluster in the country. In the north, the area around Beijing and Tianjin forms another metropolis, known as the Bohai Economic Rim, that focuses on heavy industry, especially automobile production. Another megacity is in the Yangzi Delta, with Shanghai as the center. Establishing a southern megacity in Guangdong was intended to regain competitiveness with these growing urban areas around Beijing and Shanghai so that Hong Kong and Shenzhen will not be completely displaced by the other urban clusters.

The plan to establish a Hong Kong–Shenzhen metropolis was first broached in June 2004, when the two governments signed a memorandum along with other cooperation agreements. The discussions continued until May 2007, when the two governments signed an umbrella agreement known as the Shenzhen–Hong Kong Innovation Circle, under which they would pursue comprehensive technological collaboration. The following August, the Hong Kong think tank Bauhinia Foundation Research Centre revealed a plan to turn the metropolis of Shenzhen–Hong Kong into an economic powerhouse bigger than London, Paris, Chicago, or Los Angeles by the 2020s. In addition, the two governments agreed to create a multiple-entry electronic smart-card system allowing Shenzhen permanent residents to enter Hong Kong and to build a railway line between the two cities' airports; they also initiated a joint program to nurture talent. These plans were intended to make travel across the border between China and Hong Kong easier. Proposals have also been discussed to let 4.1 million Shenzhen residents visit Hong Kong using multiple-entry permits.[3]

The plan expanded in the following years to cover a wider area beyond Shenzhen and Hong Kong. Since 2008, when a draft entitled "Plan for the Reform and Development of the Pearl River Delta (2008–2020)" was promulgated by the PRC State Council, government officials in Hong Kong and Guangdong have been sending signals to local residents that in the coming decades Hong Kong and Macau should merge with the urbanized areas of Guangdong Province. Aside from fostering cooperation among Guangdong, Hong Kong, and Macau, the plan includes ambitious development of the land surrounding the Pearl River estuary. In February 2009, the governments of Guangdong, Hong Kong, and Macau agreed jointly to undertake a "Study on the Action Plan for the Bay Area of the Pearl River Estuary." In the plan, the bay area of the Pearl River Estuary is "defined as comprising all 17 districts abutting the Pearl River Estuary under the administration of Guangzhou, Shenzhen, Zhuhai, Dongguan and Zhongshan, and the whole territory of Hong Kong and Macau Special Administrative Regions." The plan is portrayed as a "general request of the residents of the region," even though there was no consultation with the Hong Kong public before January 2011.[4] The plan covers areas such as financial services, high-tech and high-end research and development, transport, and environmental matters. It aims to foster close communications and movements in a wide range of sectors among Guangdong, Hong Kong, and Macau, such as people and cargo flows, food safety, innovation and technology, information, intellectual-property rights, culture, sports, infectious diseases, social welfare, and emergency management.

Another version of this project appeared in English-language newspapers in early 2011 that featured a futuristic "megacity" larger than other international metropolises such as Los Angeles and Tokyo. On January 24, the *Hong Kong Telegraph* reported that city planners in South China had laid out a plan "to merge together the nine cities that lie around the Pearl River Delta," covering "a large part of China's manufacturing heartland, stretching from Guangzhou to Shenzhen and including Foshan, Dongguan, Zhongshan, Zhuhai, Jiangmen, Huizhou and Zhaoqing. Together, they account for nearly a tenth of the Chinese economy.... An express rail line will also connect the hub with nearby Hong Kong."[5] The core idea is a megacity spreading across all of the urbanizing areas in the Pearl River Delta region and including older cities such as Guangzhou and Foshan. The article also mentioned that Hong Kong will be closely connected to the Chinese cities by high-speed trains. The article quoted Ma Xiangming, the chief planner at the Guangdong Rural and Urban Planning Institute and a senior consultant on the project, on the purpose of the plan: "The idea is that when the cities are integrated, the residents can travel around freely and use the health care and other facilities in the different areas." Ma also stated that twenty-nine rail lines will be added, cutting rail journeys around the urban area to a maximum of one hour between different city centers; residents would be able to use universal rail cards that would allow them to commute around the megacity. Much discussion ensued among the governments in the Pearl River Delta Region as to the infrastructure that would be needed over the next few years to facilitate communications and transportation for the towns and cities that would become part of the megacity. The first phase, connecting Shenzhen North and Guangzhou South, commenced operation in December 2011. It was extended to the city center of Shenzhen in December 2015. The final phase, connecting Futian to Hong Kong, was inaugurated on September 22, 2018. Meanwhile, in other parts of China, the expansion of high-speed rail reached new heights in 2014 with the opening of the Taiyuan–Xi'an line, the Hangzhou–Changsha

FIGURE 6.2 In July 2016, the PRC Development and Reform Commission, Ministry of Transport, and national railroad corporation issued the "mid- to long-term railway network plan" and outlined the grand blueprint of the "eight vertical and eight horizontal" high-speed rail network. The blueprint also includes the Beijing–Hong Kong (Taipei) corridor connecting the mainland and Taiwan.

Courtesy of Li Chao, "China national high speed rail grid," dated February 28, 2022, https://commons.wikimedia.org/wiki/File:China_national_high_speed_rail_grid_8_8_de.svg.

line, the Lanzhou–Urumqi line, the Guiyang–Guangzhou line, and the Nanning–Guangzhou line. By the end of 2014, high-speed rail passenger services had expanded to twenty-eight provinces and regions in total (figure 6.2).[6]

Other related plans include opening up the border areas in the New Territories of Hong Kong near Shenzhen for mainland Chinese tourists and developing new towns in the northwestern New Territories to serve as new business and upper-class residential districts for mainland investors.[7]

The construction of the Hong Kong–Zhuhai–Macau Bridge of the China section and the Hong Kong section began in December 2009 and December 2011 respectively.[8] The main bridge was completed on July 6, 2017, and the entire construction project was finished seven months later.[9]

Many capitalists in Hong Kong and Macau have been in favor of these plans because greater integration and networking would enhance their investments and business opportunities. Real estate developers also have been especially strong advocates of integration because they can make huge profits from such development projects. The common goal is to remake the region into a modernized, commercial hub that would surpass the current status of member cities.

On December 7, 2016, the concept of a Greater Bay Area was first mentioned in the English-language version of China's Thirteenth Five-Year Plan. The concept is a rebranding of the Pearl River Delta region to signify that it will be a rival of California's Bay Area. Soon after that announcement, PRC Premier Li Keqiang revealed a plan for further developing a metropolis in the "Guangdong–Hong Kong–Macau Greater Bay Area," An agreement was signed in July 2017 between the National Development and Reform Commission and the governments of Guangdong, Hong Kong, and Macau that includes an ambitious new initiative that aims to transform the Pearl Delta region by further integrating Hong Kong, Macau, and nine cities in Guangdong Province so that they would become a world-class city cluster. Official materials claim that the region will be transformed from "The Factory of the World" into a dynamic hub of innovation by 2030, as exemplified by the establishment of high-tech companies and research institutes in the Shenzhen area in the 2010s.[10]

The vision is that this integration and development together with that of other megacities inside the PRC and transportation networks will compress the "size" of the country. The citizens, it is envisioned, will feel proud to be members of a modernized nation. A milestone was reached when the Hong Kong–Zhuhai–Macau Bridge opened in 2018.[11] In the same year, Guangdong Province announced a plan for the Guangdong–Hong Kong–Macau region:

> The plan sets out the timetable and tasks for the province and outlines a three-step arrangement for the construction of the Greater Bay Area. The first step is to establish a solid basis for the construction of the

Greater Bay Area by establishing a coordinated, connected and highly efficient construction work mechanism by 2020. The second is to basically build a world[-]leading bay area and world[-]class city cluster framework with enormous vitality, prominent innovation capacity, optimized industrial structure . . . and beautiful environment by 2022. The third step is to completely build an international[-]leading livable as well as business and tourism friendly bay area by 2035.[12]

The plan emphasizes connecting the towns and cities and building an international hub for industry and business. Nothing is mentioned, however, about the characteristics of the original cities or towns, including those of the two former colonies.

In February 2019, the Chinese government also released an outline for economic development, the core of which was to transform the Greater Bay Area from a manufacturing center into a hub of high-end technology. The purpose of the plan was to build a cooperative framework between Hong Kong, Macau, and Guangdong to facilitate their integration.

The benefits of the Greater Bay Area to Hong Kong and Macau are questionable. As a commentator remarked, "The Greater Bay Area has eleven major cities, of which the nine in Guangdong province are the least developed. . . . Almost all the plan's policy ideas relate to Hong Kong or Macau and fit these cities into various kinds of cooperative undertakings with Guangdong."[13]

The idea of building a megacity as a strategy of integrating Hong Kong and Macau has received much criticism. One critic, Chris Devonshire-Ellis, argues that it is unlikely that the Pearl River Delta region can be turned into a real megacity. He describes what a megacity should look like: " 'Mega-city' conjures up images of gleaming spires, steel cathedrals, teeming masses of people, all hurrying to and from, avenues of shopping malls, horrendous traffic jams and air so thick one could stir it. Mexico City, Mumbai, and Chongqing mixed in with a dash of L.A. perhaps. But Jiangmen, Zhaoqing and Foshan?" He says the surrounding areas near the major cities like Guangzhou and Shenzhen are far from urban and will remain backwaters even after the construction of the high-speed railway. "Guangdong's new high-speed rail line interconnecting nine second tier provincial cities surrounded by tea plantations and undulating countryside is rather different than the mental imagery created by the phrase 'mega-city of 42 million.'" Devonshire-Ellis believes the different cities within the Pearl River Delta megacity would not enjoy the same level of modernity. The term "urban sprawl," coined in the 1940s and later made popular by William Gibson in his seminal science fiction novel *Neuromancer*, precisely describes the phenomenon that occurs when urban growth reaches a point at which a city begins to spread outward to lower-density and less-developed areas on its outskirts. In other words, there is bound to be unequal development between the core city and its surroundings.[14] Given the existing geography, critics point out that that a Pearl River Delta region megacity would turn out to be a kind of megacity that invests most of its budget in highways and other transportation to solidify the connections among the primary cities, while letting the rest waste away or play a subordinate role by hosting those people who have a hard time surviving in the most developed areas.[15] The merging of the ex-colonies of Hong Kong and Macau with the Pearl River Delta region would serve the PRC state's political interests in diluting the local identities of the people in Hong Kong and Macau by turning them into megaurbanites of the Pearl River Delta region within China.

Our memories are always subject to manipulation, revision, and reconstruction. The way places are remapped entails processes of hijacking memories and implanting new ones; our associations with the places so altered is also transformed. Locations and landmarks serve as evidence of history. When we demolish them, we are also sabotaging our memories of events that we have experienced in those places. Eventually, people's attachment to the city will be severed because the city they were once familiar with will become remote in time and unidentifiable.

The literary critic Dani Cavallaro's discussion of memory and history in *Cyberpunk and Cyberculture* is relevant to our critique here:

> The idea of history as a synthetic construct with an ultimately unverifiable authenticity suggests that the past may be fantasized about in myriad ways but never retrieved. Relatedly, both individual and collective memories are objects of endless speculation that preclude the possibility of ever ascertaining to what extent the images we recall encapsulate lived experiences and to what extent they embody unfulfilled longings or repressed fears.[16]

In constructing a futuristic landscape, we are expressing our desires and longings while erasing the "undesirable" parts of the landscape that we deem should not belong to the future. If more old landmarks and areas vanish, the old cityscape of Hong Kong and Macau will slowly be replaced by a new one consolidated under the title of the Pearl River Delta megacity. The old memories of Hong Kong and Macau as distinctive Chinese cities with architecture featuring colonial characteristics are expected to become less and less familiar to younger generations and that former cityscapes may one day disappear altogether.

HOMECOMING STORIES

As this economic integration project was underway, the PRC also attempted to inculcate a stronger sense of national belonging among people in Hong Kong and Macau through reinterpreting and overwriting the narrative of the exodus. In the early twenty-first century, the journey of crossing the borders from China to Hong Kong and Macau served as a major source of inspiration for a plethora of PRC government-sponsored documentary and fictional representations, especially around the time the PRC celebrated the tenth and fifteenth anniversary of the handover of Hong Kong and Macau.

One example was a two-part episode of the weekly television documentary program *Xingqi ri dang'an* (Sunday Report) titled "Da Tao Gang" (The great escape to Hong Kong), shown on the Jade Channel of Television Broadcast Limited (TVB) in Hong Kong on November 11 and 18, 2012.[17] The episode features a few residents who are living on one side or the other of the Hong Kong–China border but who share the experience of having tried to cross the border illegally (*toudu*) from Shenzhen to Hong Kong in the 1970s. The episode starts with the well-known history of tens of thousands of people fleeing mainland China in a similar fashion between the 1950s to the 1980s because of social upheavals, including the Great Leap Forward famine and the political persecution of the Cultural Revolution. These border crossers shared an imagination of Hong Kong as a place of political freedom and easy opportunities to get rich (*biandi huangjin*, literally "the entire land covered with gold") under British colonial rule.

However, this classic story of Hong Kong's success is not the central theme of the "Da Tao Gang" episode. Rather, the story broadens to include the ambivalence of many who crossed the border. Between the introduction and the main story, the voice of a middle-aged man introduces this theme: "I still ask myself till this day: did we make the right decision to run away to Hong Kong?"

The first half of the episode concentrates mainly on a former refugee, Cheung Yu Tak, who successfully reached Hong Kong in 1976 at the age of twenty-six. After his arrival, he took up any job he could find: plastics factory worker, printer, mover, hawker, and truck driver. He reunited with his wife when she also escaped to Hong Kong in 1981. They both saved up enough money to buy their first flat in an old building. In the mid-1990s, he and his wife became real estate agents and made a good fortune through buying and selling flats. Unfortunately, their life took a sharp turn during the Asian financial crisis in 1997, which resulted in the loss of all their savings. Cheung had to take up truck driving again. He felt devastated at first but was able to recover from the setback because the rough experience of crossing the border had made him resilient to difficulties in life. Overall, Cheung's narrative aligns with the classic story of Hong Kong that emphasizes the struggle of new immigrants overcoming obstacles and working their way up from the bottom of society during the 1970s and 1980s.

The second half of the episode, broadcast a week later, presents a much more controversial narrative about people living along the border. It focuses on two brothers who had very different life paths even though they both attempted to cross the border. Tam Kam Pui, the older brother, was charged and imprisoned as a "counterrevolutionary" by the CCP at the age of seventeen in 1967. Even though his jail term lasted only a few months, it made him determined to escape. After several years of planning and physical training, in 1972 he finally made a successful entry to Hong Kong at the age of twenty-three by swimming across the sea. His life in Hong Kong was similar to Cheung's. He also started as a low-paid factory worker, but after saving up enough money, he opened his own renovation company.

Beginning in the 1980s, it became possible for him to return to China and visit his family in Xixiang, a town near Shenzhen. "Da Tao Gang" follows Tam Kam Pui on one of his family visits. In a flat in the Xixiang district, Tam Kam Pui celebrates a festival with his siblings. One of his brothers, Tam Kam Hung, a resident of Shenzhen, also had tried to escape to Hong Kong in the 1970s but was caught by the mainland border patrol. Because he had been a CCP member, a demobilized PLA soldier, and a local cadre, he received heavy punishment for the crime of "treason and defection" (*panguo toudi*) and was sentenced to a labor camp for nine months. Life was hard for him even after he was released because he was stigmatized as a traitor to the CCP. However, his life took a dramatic turn in the late 1970s as a result of Deng Xiaoping's economic reforms. Because of the development of Shenzhen as a special economic zone under the economic reforms, Tam Kam Hung was able to start a business, transporting discarded timber from Hong Kong to Shenzhen and selling it to construction companies. He later made enough profit from his timber business to buy land and build manufacturing plants for high-tech investment companies. While purchasing expensive jewelry at a shop in Hong Kong, he says: "I like to shop in Hong Kong and come here often for that purpose, but I would never want to live here. Shenzhen is so much better."

Even when the two brothers walk side by side, the cheerful expression and upright posture of Tam Kam Hung marks a striking contrast with the anxious-looking, slouching Tam Kam Pui. Even though Tam Kam Pui expresses the view that his life in Hong Kong has been satisfactory overall and he has no complaints about it, his presence is overshadowed by Tam Kam Hung's success. The latter indicates that it was a blessing in disguise that he did not cross the border successfully in the 1970s, because the prosperity brought by the economic reform was so much more rewarding. He even exclaims, "[My older brother] made it to Hong Kong and maybe he was a hotshot at that time. But . . . thirty years later, now I dare to say that my life is one hundred times better than his!"

To reinforce this message of economic success brought by Deng Xiaoping's reforms, the program also features another former refugee, Wong Kin Keung, who made his way to Hong Kong but later returned to Shenzhen to open a restaurant in the early 1980s. Because his family had owned farmland that was expropriated by the government for development, he was able to use the monetary compensation to build apartment buildings and collect rent from tenants. Like Tam Kam Hung, Wong belongs to China's nouveau riche as a result of Deng Xiaoping's promotion of the Shenzhen economic zone.

The program ends with Wong saying, "It was so easy to do business and make a lot of money at the beginning of the economic reform [in the SEZs] ... so we had made a wrong decision to leave [for Hong Kong]." Wong is, in fact, the middle-aged man whose voice is heard at the beginning of the episode pondering the decision to leave China.

This two-part episode of *Sunday Report* is one of many variations of a border-crossing narrative genre that has proliferated in documentaries, news reports, journalistic writing, and even in fictional forms such as popular literature and television dramas in both Hong Kong and the Pearl River Delta region since the 2000s. Unlike the previous dominant narrative of border crossing that was popular in Hong Kong from the 1970s to the 1990s, which focused on the struggle of the new immigrant from the bottom of the society, this new genre celebrates the prosperity of the Guangdong region and depicts the return of Hong Kong as a win-win situation for both China and Hong Kong.

Typically, this episode acknowledges the mistakes of state policies and campaigns under Mao Zedong (albeit seldom mentioning Mao himself or the role of the CCP), such as the Great Leap Forward and the Cultural Revolution, and even rationalizes the desires of the people who wanted to go to Hong Kong. Ultimately, however, the decision to stay or the failure of their escape from China is interpreted as a blessing in disguise, because Deng Xiaoping's reforms would eventually bring good fortune to those who stayed behind. It is those who migrated to Hong Kong who have to revisit their decision to leave the homeland (*zuguo*), lamenting their shortsightedness for not foreseeing the rise of China and thus missing out on the opportunity to become rich. Last, in recounting the fortunes of Tam Kam Pui and Wong Kin Keung, postcolonial Hong Kong is also depicted as a "lost" city that inevitably will have to return to the embrace of the prosperous homeland.

Most such popular accounts, like "Da Tao Gang," cite political and economic factors as the main motivation for their decisions. In contrast, for the people who "regretted" trying to escape or for the middle-aged Hong Kongers who lamented their quality of life not being on par with their siblings in China, they only discuss material factors while not mentioning the difference in political freedom between the two territories.

FIGURE 6.3 A view of the high-rise buildings in Shenzhen from the Fanling district of Hong Kong near the Shenzhen–Hong Kong border in 2017.

Photo by Angelina Y. Chin.

The production of "Da Tao Gang" is an effort at historical revisionism, an attempt to introduce a new interpretation of the familiar historical events around illegal border crossing. In this interpretation, such border crossing is not an epic backstory of the Hong Kong economic miracle; rather, it serves as prologue to the story of Deng Xiaoping's wondrous economic reforms. The intent of this particular narrative is to invoke a renewed sense of loyalty to the nation and to downplay the local identity.

Unlike the previous dominant narrative of border crossing popular in Hong Kong before the 2000s, focusing on the struggle of the new immigrant to rise from the bottom of society, the genre that became popular in the 2000s stresses the growing prosperity of Shenzhen and other neighboring SEZs, as well as the ambivalence of the migrants about having left the mainland, a question they reconsider even many years after their departure. This genre still rationalizes the desires of the people who wanted to leave the PRC at a time when most people suffered from poverty and political instability. The main point, however, is that these inadequacies of the "homeland" have been overcome by the strong leadership of the CCP and now the nation is once again capable of welcoming the return of those previously displaced. Here, the state is actively reinventing "homeland" to lure back those who left, ensuring the loyal returnees the benefits of prosperity, comfort, and stability.[18] This narrative is most persuasive to the Chinese residents in Hong Kong and Macau who began to invest or work in the mainland in the 1990s and 2000s and believe that reintegration with China will bring them more economic and career opportunities (figure 6.3).

HONG KONG IDENTITY AND DIASPORIC CONSCIOUSNESS

While Macau had already been under PRC's political influence since the "123 incident" in 1966, and Taiwan had kept the PRC at arm's length since the Cold War, Hong Kong's relationship with the PRC was much more convoluted even before the handover. In the mid- to late 1980s, the democratic discourse of the return of Hong Kong to China was dominated by the view that Hong Kong would influence democratization in China. This view was shared by Ip Cheung in chapter 5. On the one hand, many saw the return of Hong Kong as inevitable after the Sino-British Joint Declaration, so they had hoped that the rule of law in Hong Kong could be maintained through the Basic Law and that the "One country, two systems" framework could become a future model for Taiwan's reunification with China in the future. On the other hand, however, the local identity of "Hong Kongers" solidified. As the scholar Wing Sang Law describes, it was also a time "when Hong Kong's future handover to Chinese sovereignty was being discussed and a 'sense of crisis' emerged as Hong Kong people sought to protect their economic and political systems and way of life."[19]

The 1989 Tiananmen Square incident was a huge blow to Hong Kong residents because it reminded them of past traumatic events they had witnessed in the 1950s–1970s. It also led to the founding of prodemocratic organizations and political parties such as the Hong Kong Alliance in Support of Patriotic Democratic Movements in China (Hong Kong Alliance) as well as the Hong Kong Democratic Party. The majority of the members of these groups were Hong Kong residents who believed at that time that the democratization of Hong Kong would be a first step toward that of the entire nation. Hong Kong's local identity was commonly seen as compatible with and part of the larger Chinese identity. One of the operational goals of the Hong Kong Alliance was to end the dictatorship of one-party rule, but most core members refrained from publicly denouncing the CCP at the time. *Fangong* was not a vocabulary circulated in mainstream Hong Kong politics at that time.

This view slowly became less popular in the early 2000s as the younger generation who grew up after the handover not only did not see the PRC moving toward the direction of democratization, but also experienced firsthand the gradual taking away of many of their own freedoms. As the Hong Kong's government's plans to acquiesce to integration through futuristic planning such as the Pearl River Delta megacity project accelerated, these youths took to the streets and mobilized a countermovement to resist the reintegration trend.

The countermovement first took off after the inception of the Individual Visit Scheme (*ziyou xing*) in July 2003, which allowed travelers from the mainland to visit Hong Kong on an individual basis. Prior to the scheme, most mainlanders could travel to Hong Kong only on business visas or in group tours. The purpose of the scheme was to boost Hong Kong's economy after the SARS crisis in the spring of 2003, and travelers from the mainland did help the city's economy, but negative popular representations of mainlanders also proliferated. Such representations heightened the new anxiety of Hong Kongers that their home was slowly being overtaken by investors and immigrants from the mainland as part of the PRC's plan for reintegration and diluting the local identity. That same year, the Hong Kong government intended to introduce antisubversion legislation, commonly referred to as Article 23, to prohibit treason, secession, and sedition against the Chinese government and to outlaw theft of state secrets. This proposed legislation drew fierce criticism from Hong Kongers who were worried it would infringe on their freedoms under the "One country, two systems" framework, subjecting anyone publicly criticizing China to punishment. This legislation was shelved after more than half a million people marched on July 1, 2003, in opposition to it.

In the late 2000s, the plan to build the Guangdong–Hong Kong high-speed railway again invigorated discussions about the collective memories and identity of Hong Kong. As one critic put it: "After 1997, Hong Kong has quickly fallen into the orbit of mainland China. We have maintained our laws and political freedom, but as we are being economically assimilated into the mainland, so we are also being culturally assimilated, and Hong Kong's identity is in imminent danger. As a symbol, nothing could be a stronger statement than this high rail connecting Hong Kong to Guangzhou and Shenzhen that we are 'just another Chinese city.'"[20]

Through petitions, marches, hunger strikes, and rallies, activists showed their discontent with the government's insistence on pushing through the project. The "anti-high-speed-rail movement" reached its height in January 2010. While prodemocratic legislators questioned the project's rationale within the Legislative Council of Hong Kong, protesters—many of whom were activists born after 1980 (known as the post-1980s)—held a vigil and were active outside the council during the debate. They cited cost, noise pollution, environmental damage, customs and border-control complications, and existing rail links as reasons for their opposition. The most provocative arguments they made stemmed from their uneasiness about the principle behind this type of development, putting Beijing's economic interest above all else and ignoring the cultural and emotional costs to the local people and environment. These costs included the eradication of "collective memories" of the city's residents.

The anti-high-speed-rail movement had close links with protests against the demolition of Queen's Pier and Star Ferry Pier, as well as the heritage conservation movement.[21] The piers had to be demolished to make way for the Central Harborfront Reclamation project, which intended to extend the waterfront for highways, shopping malls, and other commercial buildings.[22] In its rhetoric, the government downplayed the aspect of demolition in development by calling development projects "revitalization initiatives." Both government and financial leaders of the city agreed that Hong Kong needed to prioritize its economy if it was to maintain its edge over the rest of China.

Thereafter, the heritage conservation movement grew in Hong Kong to prevent the local government and real-estate developers from demolishing historical buildings and districts, such as Kwun Tong, Wanchai, and Shum Shui Po. Through participating in such movements, activists claimed that these historical districts and their architecture belonged to the people of Hong Kong who shared "collective memories" and that developers and the government should not have the right to demolish them without citizens' input in the urban-renewal decision-making process.

Meanwhile, another more radical "localist" movement began to take root. Unlike the other trend that was critical of global capitalism as the root of undesired development projects in Hong Kong, the trend directly advocated for Hong Kong autonomy and nationalism. In 2011, a group called the Hong Kong City-State Autonomy Movement was formed with the goal of raising Hong Kongers' support for upholding the city's autonomy and protecting residents' interests and right to rule.[23] Some of its members argued that the Hong Kong government needed to prioritize and defend the interests of Hong Kongers against those of the PRC government and mainland Chinese. At the same time, they believed that Hong Kongers have no right or duty to be critical of the PRC because Hong Kong had been, and in their view should continue to be, under an administration separate from the rest of China. One vocal activist of the movement, Chin Wan, even suggested that there should be a "naturalization" process in Hong Kong for mainland Chinese—only the people with the "correct" values and aspirations should be allowed to obtain permanent residency. Their rhetoric emphasized the peril of mainland Chinese in disrupting everyday life and overwhelming social infrastructure such as hospitals in Hong Kong and the importance for the well-being of the city that Hong Kongers defend themselves against the intrusions of mainlanders.[24] Chin Wan's book became a best-seller popular among Hong Kongers who shared his anti-PRC sentiments. The *Undergrad*, the official publication of the Hong Kong University Students' Union, published a number of articles on the subject of building Hong Kong independence and nationhood. They later became the book *Xianggang Minzu Lun* (Hong Kong Nationalism). The chief executive at that time, Leung Chun-ying, criticized the book in his 2015 New Year's policy address, fanning the controversy over the book—and its sales. At the same time, other individuals and groups began to promote the idea that the only way to stop such grand development schemes was to fundamentally change the political system. Many also became critical of the earlier preservation activists for their "peaceful" approach, which failed to bring about any changes in the government.

On August 31, 2014, the Standing Committee of the National People's Congress rejected an open nomination process for the chief executive of Hong Kong and all of the Legislative Council as promised in the Basic Law, thereby shattering the remaining hopes of the people in Hong Kong for democratization. This was the direct cause of the Umbrella Movement, in which tens of thousands of people, many of whom were students, occupied the street outside the government headquarters and camped in two business districts. Although the movement ultimately failed after more than three months of occupation, it radicalized many Hong Kongers who became convinced that the city needed to strive for a political model that would grant it full autonomy. A poll in July 2016 suggested that nearly 40 percent of respondents aged fifteen to twenty-four supported the territory becoming an independent polity, whereas 17.4 percent of respondents overall supported independence. However, the approach of the Umbrella Movement was deemed unsustainable by many critics, partly because Beijing had no tolerance for secessionism and would suppress any attempt to advance such a cause. The Hong Kong separatist groups were also not armed. Their call for an independent Hong Kong in some way was similar to the Third Force movement in the 1950s and 1960s, which similarly did not have any military means to achieve its idealistic goals.

Nonetheless, local groups became the inspiration for the Anti-Extradition protests in 2019. The popular slogan "Liberate Hong Kong, Revolution of Our Time"—"Guong-fook Heung-gong, Shidoi gak-ming" in Cantonese, "Guangfu Xianggang, Shidaigeming" in Mandarin—was coined by Edward Leung, who founded Hong Kong Indigenous after the Umbrella Movement, and who was later jailed for his role in inciting civil unrest in Mong Kok in 2016. The word *guangfu* is translated as "to liberate," but it also means "recovery," and although its sense as a slogan remains debatable, many people believe that it refers to the prosperous days under British colonial rule when people had more freedom and Hong Kong was not subject to the mainland's interference. It was during the years after the

Umbrella Movement that public slogans or graffiti that say, "Heaven will obliterate the CCP (*tianmie Zhonggong*)!" started popping up in protests and on the streets.

THE LIMITS OF COLONIAL NOSTALGIA AND COLLECTIVE MEMORIES

The localist movements and the emphasis on recovering Hong Kong's collective memories have successfully evoked Hong Kongers' attachment to their city and mobilized many Hong Kong residents of different generations. However, such efforts do not seem to have been effective in garnering empathy from other overseas Chinese communities, with the exception of Taiwan scholars and Uighurs and Tibetan exiles.

For example, the 2019 democratic protests triggered by the Extradition Bill in Hong Kong attracted much international media attention, but they were also criticized by leftist scholars of China. Critiques concluded that Hong Kong protesters were oblivious to racial and class injustice in Hong Kong society and were also disconnecting themselves from the political movements in mainland China.[25] A more severe criticism is that the protesters seemed to want the United States to come to Hong Kong's rescue, thus reinforcing what the critics believe to be an endorsement of U.S. imperialism. This was particularly obvious during the protesters' petition for the United States to pass the Human Rights and Democracy Acts to impose sanctions on Hong Kong and Chinese officials who took part in the drafting of the Extradition Bill or were responsible for the police's violent actions toward the protesters. The sanctions would include freezing these officials' assets in the United States and revoking their U.S. visas. One leftist critic said, "The idea that the United States is a friend of democracy is preposterous. Everywhere Washington has intervened, it has done so to advance and protect the imperialist interests of U.S. big businesses."[26]

Meanwhile, PRC nationalists felt that people in Hong Kong need to be more appreciative of the CCP's effort to build a strong nation and condemned the antigovernment protesters as traitors who had forgotten their roots and betrayed their homeland.[27] Both kinds of criticism see only the PRC and the West—mainly the United States—as the major players on the international playing field. However, the underlying problem with these views is that they overlook the historical role Hong Kong played during the Cold War and the diasporic trauma of the people in the Southern Periphery. The local identity of people in Hong Kong and the negative sentiments toward the PRC regime did not develop overnight.

In order to answer both kinds of criticisms, historians of Hong Kong need to go beyond the conventional story of Hong Kong that emphasizes a distinctive Hong Kong identity devoid of politics until the 1980s. A thorough reevaluation of the history of the city's connection with its neighbors in the Southern Periphery, and of the inclusion of people who moved between the territories in that region, can help us understand why many people in Hong Kong are so resistant to the idea of reintegration, in particular the PRC's imposition of jurisdiction over them. The story of the quest for Hong Kong autonomy today should not just be seen as a response to China's tightening control or blind nostalgia for British colonial rule, but as part of a longer trajectory of how Hong Kong, along with the rest of the Southern Periphery, has been caught between the CCP and anti-CCP forces ever since the end of the Chinese Civil War. The strong sentiments demonstrate that Hong Kong identity is informed not only by the economic prosperity built by immigrants and the lower class, but also by the people and information circulating in the Southern Periphery, and as amplified by the diasporic trauma and sense of abandonment mostly created by the clash of the CCP and KMT.

RECLAIMING "CHINESE DIASPORA" AS A STRATEGY

In recent scholarship, the use of Chinese diaspora as a device to understand Chinese people overseas has received much critique. The common concern about the use of the term diaspora is that, as historian Shelly Chan summarizes, it "essentializes a Chinese identity, flattening variegated practices into sameness" and may risk "portraying Chinese everywhere as perpetually foreign to local societies and potentially loyal to a rising China."[28] Critics are worried that the use of this term may support the PRC's nationalistic propaganda to invoke Chinese nationalism among overseas Chinese.

Some scholars speak of the Chinese diaspora with an alternative term: Sinophone.[29] Shu-mei Shih coined this term to identify the people who engage with the culture of China but have no interest in associating with mainland China. Sinophone studies is "conceived as the study of Sinitic-language cultures on the margins of geopolitical nation-states and their hegemonic productions."[30] It is an important critique of the culturally centered view of diaspora. However, Shih's critique of "Chinese diaspora" and her Sinophone concept work best for people of Chinese descent who can choose not to engage with the PRC or even with their identity as Chinese. In other words, Sinophone might be a useful description of people who have a choice to disengage from the PRC. As for Hong Kong, Shih believes that Sinophone is applicable only to pre-1997 Hong Kongers, as she appraises the local Cantonese movement: "The Sinophone pre-1997 Hong Kong also saw the emergence of a nativist fetishization of Cantonese against the looming hegemony of standard putonghua (Mandarin Chinese)." Unfortunately, however, in Shih's model, there is no hope for post-handover Hong Kong, as she states: "For Hong Kong its incorporation into the Chinese polity in 1997 marked the waning of the Sinophone as its integration into China became inevitable."[31] The political reality is that it is impossible for Hong Kongers to disown China and relinquish their ties with the PRC, even though many would prefer an autonomous Hong Kong independent from Chinese interference. While the Sinophone concept may be useful in thinking about sentiments accenting the local experience, it fails to speak for people in the Southern Periphery and elsewhere who have had to cope with the influence of the PRC, nor is it applicable to the history of those who fled to the margins of China and continued to be traumatized by the CCP.

People who have lived in the Southern Periphery hold diverse views of China today. Some of these views have been shaped by the common diasporic experience of fleeing or living on the margins of the geographic entity of China. After they crossed the borders, they took different journeys. These journeys became their routes, and their destinations became the sites from which they continued to speak. I find the "parallax theory" in astronomy useful in understanding the reconstruction of history through these individual stories. A parallax, the *Random House Unabridged Dictionary* says, is "the apparent displacement of an observed object due to a change in the position of the observer." A parallax shift refers to the apparent motion of an object when it is seen from different perspectives. Using this notion, Slavoj Žižek claims that if we have two vantage points from which to view the object, both are completely incompatible and irreducible. Subject and object are inherently mediated so that an "epistemological" shift in the subject's point of view always reflects an "ontological" shift in the object itself.[32]

When reviewing the game *Kentucky Route Zero*, Laura Hudson said the following about the design that allows to see the surroundings from multiple viewpoints, "Is this perception real, or that one? Is one reality real, or another? There is no right or wrong answer, no single, fixed way of seeing the world. That's the idea behind a parallax—that a more complete version of a story or image is possible when it's experienced through multiple perspectives."[33] This may be what Paul Ricoeur means when he refers to the "composite representations" of historical experience.[34] The theorist Louis Mink also writes that "the significance of past occurrences is understandable only as they are locatable in the ensemble of interrelationships that can be grasped only in the construction of narrative form."[35] Similarly, post-1949 Chinese history is understandable only if we can see the interconnectedness of peripheral positionalities in their relations to the center. In addition to the geographic vantage points of the subjects, we should also pay attention to temporality. Each retelling is not the same depending on how far and how long the subject has traveled. It is similar to astronomy in the sense that the stars we see are light-years "in the past." Similarly, a subject's retelling of an event changes as time passes. Construction of a more "complete" Chinese history would require many of these subjects—individuals who had departed from mainland China and moved to other locations—to tell their histories from multiple perspectives.

In *Diasporic Homeland*, Shelly Chan raises the idea of the temporality of diaspora. She writes: "Situated in time, diaspora is less a collection of communities than a series of moments in which reconnections with a putative homeland take place."[36] To Chan, the concept of "home" can be rearticulated as a form of nostalgia, or as a drawing of social relations with people who have left "home" for common reasons in the past. Overall, the concept of "home" can simply be the result of common experience of running away from the country and yet connecting to the homeland. We can reimagine places like Hong Kong not as a residential city but as a meeting place for people who share the common experience of being in exile. The diaspora of people in transit in the Southern Periphery is specific; it refers to all who were in the space of the Southern Periphery together as an aftermath of the takeover of China by the Communists.

Shu-mei Shih, in her 2011 essay "Against Diaspora," declares that *diaspora has an end date*. She believes that the idea of Chinese diaspora is no longer relevant to the people of Chinese descent who have assimilated to the various "host" countries, and that we cannot impose the term onto these people and try to make them Chinese. I agree that the temporality of migration and crossing a border is important, but it does not mean that we should abandon the concept altogether once people have gained a new consciousness in their new locality. Rather, we should highlight the historicity and spell out the specific political condition that produced a particular kind of diaspora.

Has this particular form of Chinese diaspora ended, and has it become irrelevant to contemporary politics? If diaspora is defined by the longing for the homeland, and the wish to return home, then it may have ended for some who no longer want to return to the geographic entity called "China" or who have developed localized sentiments or assimilated into their host country. Others may feel that they are connected to both China and their new home.

Regardless of whether this form of Chinese diaspora has ended, framing the people in the Southern Periphery as representing a form of Chinese diaspora is useful both for people who endorse a Greater China that encompasses Hong Kong, Taiwan, and Macau and for people who want to advocate for Hong Kong or Taiwanese independence or autonomy. Some nationalists still see mainland China as the only national entity that these ethnic Chinese could possibly identify with. Some of these nationalists may be critics of the CCP and continue to call for the democratization of China, whether through governmental reform within the PRC or the taking over of China by another political party. An example of the Greater China democratic discourse today is the New School of Democracy. It was officially established in Taiwan in 2011 by Chinese, Hong Kong, and foreign academics who shared the hope of ending "one-party rule" in China. One leader of the organization is Wang Dan, the famous political dissident and former student leader at the 1989 Tiananmen Square pro-democracy movement. In its launch, the movement claimed that it has four primary areas of focus: "promoting democratic development in Chinese societies, solidifying the theoretical bases for democratic movements, creating a communications platform for Chinese worldwide and enabling participation in politics beyond the confines of political parties."[37] The organizers also indicated that their goal is to "rise above party politics and transnational borders, while respecting the younger generation and allowing democracy to take root through education." They first registered the organization in Hong Kong, because in the 2000s, there was still political freedom in Hong Kong and certain dissidents could still travel to the city. The idea that Hong Kong was at the center of Chinese politics has been well articulated by Albert Ho, the former chairman of the Hong Kong Democratic Party and a founding board member of the New School. When explaining the special significance of the decision to register the college in Hong Kong, Ho said,

> Hong Kong played a special role in the Xinhai Revolution [in 1911] which led to the formation of the Republic of China 100 years ago.... *Hong Kong had always been the place where revolutionary and reformist ideas in China came from.* ... The demands for democracy and constitutional government that emerged from the Xinhai Revolution a century ago have yet to be met and Hong Kong's duty to history is not yet finished.[38]

His reference to Hong Kong is similar to this book's idea of placing the Southern Periphery back in the center of Chinese and global history, even though he was referring to the early twentieth century. The demands for democracy and constitutional government resonate uncannily with the Third Force and the democratic movement in Hong Kong before the 2010s. Even though the prospect of Hong Kong's fulfilling this role as the critical front has become grim after the imposition of the National Security Laws, and despite the improbability that Hong Kong can any longer be a refuge for political dissidents fleeing China, its history needs to be put in this diasporic perspective. The people in Hong Kong and in the Southern Periphery have always taken part in the political process of China's democratization. The annual diasporic commemorations of the Tiananmen Square incident in Hong Kong and overseas serve as another example of how the history of China may sometimes be better preserved beyond its borders.

As for those who are pursuing a different future, such as Taiwan independence or Hong Kong independence/autonomy, it may seem as though China just stands as another external power colonizing their "homelands." Those who no longer consider China their homeland and do not yearn to return there feel no need to give any valence to the PRC by calling themselves diasporic subjects. To these people who identify with Hong Kong or Taiwan, this history may seem to contradict their claim that people living in these territories have their own distinctive histories since it situates the histories of the Southern Periphery back into Chinese history. Even though current identities may be separate from one another, this book has highlighted their shared, common history of diasporic trauma. Their experiences were intertwined with the events in mainland China as well. This common history may play a useful role in transforming their political frustrations into new forms of solidarity and activism.

After all, the expansion of Greater China has deep implications for Hong Kong, Macau, and Taiwan, all of which have to engage with the PRC in attempts to ensure their survival.[39] These states can be viewed as belonging to the same postcolonial diasporic cluster—having all been colonies for part of the twentieth century. They were then all included in the "One country, two systems" framework proposed by Deng Xiaoping, who suggested that while there could be only one "China," these former colonies could maintain their own capitalistic systems and control over domestic affairs, including immigration, currency, and public finance.[40] In reclaiming "Chinese diaspora," I treat the concept not just as a sociologically descriptive term for people who escaped their "homeland" but also as a heuristic device to raise questions of belonging, continuity, and solidarity in the context of dispersal and transnational networks of connection. Since 2020, many people who resided in Hong Kong have left the city to Taiwan, the United Kingdom, and other countries. While the long-term impact of this newer wave of migration is yet to be seen, it is apparent that the imaginary of the Southern Periphery as a gateway to the "Free World" is gradually fading away and being replaced by a global diasporic reality.

EPILOGUE

On August 23, 2020, twelve people, all under the age of thirty, tried to flee from Hong Kong to Taiwan by speedboat. All had been charged with offenses related to the 2019 protests in Hong Kong. The twelve were captured by the Chinese coast guard and held incommunicado for months. In September, it was found out that these escapees were detained in the southern city of Shenzhen. The main charge against the group was that it sought to cross an international border illegally. After months of detention, in December 2020, the Yantian District People's Court in Shenzhen sentenced two of them, Tang Kai-yin and Quinn Moon, to two and three years of imprisonment respectively for organizing the trip. Two other detainees, who were underaged at the time of the capture, were sent back to the Hong Kong Police for trial.[1] In March 2021, the rest of the eight were sent back to Hong Kong, also to be tried there.

At least two other groups from Hong Kong had reportedly successfully escaped to Taiwan before this incident. In September 2020, a few weeks after the August 23 incident, newspapers in Taiwan and Hong Kong reported a case of five Hong Kongers making it to Taiwan, where the authorities detained them. After these incidents, the Chinese coast guard blocked the maritime routes used by the escapees.[2]

Many people in Hong Kong who participated in the 2019 protests fled to Taiwan beginning late that year. Most of the ones who had not been charged by the Hong Kong authorities at the time of their escape were able to enter legally by plane. The less fortunate ones, like those twelve youths, had had their passports confiscated by the Hong Kong Police after their initial arrests and so had to go by boat or other illegal means, much like the escapees who left China for Hong Kong and Macau in the 1950s–1970s. In addition, the passage of the National Security Law triggered tens of thousands of Hong Kong residents to apply to immigrate to Taiwan and other countries. The ones who left were not just protesters but also included students, academics, professionals, and others who were sympathetic to the protests, as well as parents of young children who wanted their children to grow up in a free and democratic environment.

To many who witnessed the exodus from mainland China to Hong Kong in the 1950s–1970s, the new wave of emigration from Hong Kong may feel like déjà-vu. What is ironic is that what was once considered to be a safe haven for those who left China then has now become a place that is terrorizing many to leave. To the Hong Kong emigrants, Taiwan remained one of the favorite destinations because of its close proximity and its similarity in language and culture to Hong Kong; citizens in Taiwan were likely to be more empathetic toward refugees from Hong Kong because both Taiwan and Hong Kong are claimed by the People's Republic of China (PRC) under the One-China Policy.

Taiwan's political landscape also changed tremendously since the 1970s. The martial law imposed by the autocratic Kuomintang (KMT) government ended in 1987, and it was followed by democratization pushed forward by President Lee Teng-hui. Thereafter the Democratic Progressive Party and other non-KMT political parties were allowed to run in elections. Currently, Taiwan is the only territory in China and the Southern Periphery that has democratic elections for the president and the legislature. If we think about the yearnings of the Third Force and some of the escapees who fled China in the 1950s and the 1970s, it might seem as though their dream of a constitutional democracy has finally been realized, except that it did not happen in mainland China but in a territory whose government no longer claims to represent China as a nation anymore. To the people who were unable to leave Hong Kong, this dream of living under a democracy seems to be out of reach again.

Ironically, since the early 1990s, the KMT has evolved to be a party that is no longer antagonistic toward the Chinese Communist Party

(CCP). In the past two decades, it has maintained a close relationship with the CCP and even acknowledged the future goal of national reunification. Today, the KMT no longer fears the Chinese who came from mainland China; instead, such migrants, especially those who have capital, have been much welcomed because they may improve cross-strait relations. The economic benefits brought by mainland business and tourists are one of the appealing aspects of building closer ties with mainland China that the KMT has emphasized in its political campaigns.

In this new geopolitical context, Taiwan is also the only territory in the Southern Periphery whose residents are temporarily free from the authoritarian rule of the PRC. To the people who have been yearning for democracy in Hong Kong, Taiwan may have replaced it as their new home while they wait for political changes in mainland China and Hong Kong that would allow them to go back to Hong Kong without fear. Nevertheless, with the growing global influence of the PRC, Taiwan's political future remains uncertain. Another ironic development was that in the spring of 2022 Taiwan delayed an immigration scheme that would have made it easier for professionals from Hong Kong and Macau to become permanent residents or citizens, and the reason for that was almost identical to the refusal of entry for the 10 KMT prisoners of war in 1975 (chapter 4)—concerns about possible infiltration by Chinese agents and potential security risk. This time, the concerns over whether the immigrants from Hong Kong and Macau were true "political refugees" were not raised by the KMT, but the Democratic Progressive Party and the New Power Party, two of the main parties that were most antagonistic to the CCP.[3] Xiao Yujing (chapter 5) might find something strangely familiar to his experience during the White Terror if he read about this, except that in the 2020s he would be vehemently condemning these exiles from Hong Kong for not being loyal to China. Even with the democratization of Taiwan, after decades of not being able to settle down, the people in the Southern Periphery continue to be in limbo.

In this book, I have argued that the political identity of people in Hong Kong today was partly constructed on the collective trauma of fleeing mainland China and being on the margin of both Chinese regimes, the People's Republic of China and the Republic of China (ROC). This collective trauma continued in 1997 with the handover, and since the 2019 protests it has been further aggravated by the political crackdown. Most of the pro-democracy politicians and activists are either put in custody or in exile. Many civil society groups, including workers' organizations and the Hong Kong offices of international non-governmental organizations, have been forced to shut down because of political pressures. Like the people who were in limbo in the Southern Periphery in the 1950s–1970s, the people who left Hong Kong for political reasons do not know if there is a home for them and, even if there is, when they can return to it. The diasporic trauma has continued, except that in this latest variation, the KMT has become the CCP's close ally.

In 2019, the song "At the Foot of the Lion Rock," the theme song of the popular drama about lower-class Hong Kongers trying to survive and settle down in the colony, fell out of favor as the most representative song for Hong Kong. It has been replaced by a new Hong Kong anthem, "Glory to Hong Kong."[4] Instead of focusing on the hardworking and persevering qualities of Hong Kong people as "At the Foot of the Lion Rock" does, "Glory to Hong Kong" highlights the importance of "justice," "freedom," and "democracy." The word "freedom" is used four times in the song, and one of the lines reads, "we are gathering and resisting together with all their strengths to defend freedom!" (*han ziyou lai qijizheli lai quanli kangdui*). One reason for discarding the "Lion Rock" song and narrative is that the younger generation in Hong Kong believe that Hong Kong's freedom and democracy had been slowly being eaten away since 1997 because the older generation focused too much on their own financial self-interest and neglected politics. They wanted to revitalize Hong Kong by restoring the elements of democracy that existed during British rule. The most important slogan of the 2019 protest was "Liberate Hong Kong: Revolution of Our Times!" Some protesters believed that the "Lion Rock" narrative belonged to the people who lived through the 1960s–1980s but that it no longer resonated with the desires of the people in Hong Kong in 2019. Both "Glory to Hong Kong" and the revolutionary slogan were banned after the enactment of the National Security Law, and they could no longer be heard publicly in Hong Kong after July 2020.

There is no doubt that 2019 was a turning point in Hong Kong's history. Nevertheless, perhaps the people who criticized the older generations for being complacent have not been aware of a fundamental aspect that has been integral to the identity formation of Hong Kong before their time—the diasporic trauma of statelessness and not having a home. As this book has shown, many people who were in exile or transiting in Hong Kong were traumatized by the political turbulence and their own exile and did not plan to settle down; some of them were deeply entangled with the politics of the two parties in mainland China and the Southern Periphery. Perhaps there are more commonalities across these generations of exiled people than we have imagined.

GLOSSARY OF CHINESE CHARACTERS

aiguo 愛國
aisi jinian ri 哀思紀念日
Bak Lai 白泥
Bao'an 寶安
baodao 寶島
bashihou 八十後
beiming 悲鳴
Bengang yumin mudu qingxing jiwei kongbu
 本港漁民目睹情形極為恐怖
bentuhua 本土化
biandi huangjin 遍地黃金
Bienli Xianggang Diaojingling Nanbao Rujing Banfa 便利香港調景嶺 難胞入境辦法
binansuo 避難所
Cai Xingsan 蔡省三
Cao Lin 曹霖
Chan Yan Lam 陳彥霖
Changcheng 長城
Chen De 陳德
Chen Shizhang 陳士章
Chen Zhengmao 陳正茂
Cheung Yu Tak 張宇德
Chiang Ching-kuo 蔣經國
Chiang Kai-shek 蔣介石
Chin Wan (Chen Yun) 陳雲

Coloane (Lu Huan) 路環
Da Dao 大道
da shi lan 大食藍
Da Tao Gang 大逃港
daji 打擊
Dalu fushi gungunlai 大陸浮屍滾滾來
Dangwai (Tangwai) 黨外
Dabu (PRC) 大埔
Daya Bay (Daya Wan) 大亞灣
dazhe hongqi fanhongqi 打着紅旗反紅旗
Deng Xiaoping 鄧小平
die qin niangqin buru Maozhuxi qin 爹親娘親不如毛主席親
dilei zhengce 抵壘政策
Dong Zhilin 董致麟
Dongfengpai 東風派
Dongguan 東莞
Duan Kewen 段克文
Duli Luntan 獨立論壇
duoluo 墮落
e'ba dizhu 惡霸地主
Fan Yuanyan 范園焱
Fang Chih (Fang Zhi) 方治
fangong fuguo de weiyi jidi 反共復國的唯一基地

fangong yishi 反共義士
Fanling 粉嶺
fenhua 分化
Fu Che (Fu Qi) 傅奇
fuguo jianguo 復國建國
Gongbei 拱北
gonggun 共棍
gonghai 公海
gonghuo 共禍
Gongqing Tuan 共青團
Gu Zhenggang (Ku Cheng-kang) 谷正剛
gualong 刮龍
Guancheng 莞城
Guong-fook Heung-gong, Shidoi gak-ming 光復香港 時代革命
Guangdongsheng Conghua xian pin xia zhong geming zaofanpai lianhe weiyuanhui 廣東省從化縣貧下中革命造反派聯合委員會
Guangzhou Shijiao pin lianmeng 廣州市郊貧聯盟
Guangzhou Shijiaoqu Shipai gongshe pinxia zhongnong geming zaofan weiyuanhui 廣州市郊區石牌公社貧下中農革命造反委員會
guanyu ge dangpai zai Xianggang dou zheng de xiangxi baodao 關於各黨派在香港鬥爭的詳細報導
gudao 孤島
guidi koutou ren tou yu 跪地叩頭認偷魚
Guofang Daxue Zhengzhi Zuozhan Xueyuan 國防大學政治作戰學院
Guomin Dahui 國民大會
haimian fushi diedie canbu rendu 海面浮屍疊疊慘不忍睹
Hainan 海南
Haifeng 海豐
Hang Hau 坑口
hao dadan 好大膽
Hau Hoi Wan 後海灣
hecun shuniu 何村樞紐
Heiquanbang 黑拳幫
Heshan 鶴山
Hu Guang 胡光
Hu Yue 胡越

Huang Yuren 黃宇人
Huiyang 惠陽
Igreja de Santo Agostinho 崗頂聖堂
jiefang zhuang 解放裝
Jiejue Gang'ao nanbao chuli yijian 解決港澳難胞處理意見
jifan tiaoming 執番條命
Jifeng 疾風
Jingming Cultural Center 淨名文化中心
jiyou 極右
jin 斤
jubu fangong 局部反共
juewang 絕望
kai lang ku 開浪褲
Kung Sheung Daily News 工商日報
Kung Sheung Evening News 工商晚報
Kwei Chau (Guizhou) 貴州
Lam Yin Chang 林彥章
langbei jinzhang 狼狽緊張
lansan 懶散
Lao Zhengwu 勞政武
laoshituan 撈屍團
Lau Fau Shan 流浮山
Lee Teng-hui 李登輝
Lei Zhen 雷震
Leung Chun-ying 梁振英
Li Huang 李璜
Li Minde 李民德
Li Qing 李慶
Li Yansheng 李煙生
Li Zongren 李宗仁
lianhe qinggong 聯合清共
Lianhe Pinglun 聯合評論
Liankao 聯考
Liang Qichao 梁啟超
Lin Chih-Yen 林芝諺
Lin Zhaozhen 林照真
linweishouming 臨危受命
Lion Rock 獅子山
Liu Er Da Tao Gang 六二大逃港
Liu Hui 柳惠
Liu Yulue 劉裕略
liuwang xuesheng 流亡學生

GLOSSARY OF CHINESE CHARACTERS 261

lixiang 理想
liyi zhi bang 禮儀之邦
Lo Wu 羅湖
Lü Luo 呂洛
maiguozei 賣國賊
mamu 麻木
mantou 饅頭
Meili dao 美麗島
minzhu zhi chuang 民主之窗
minzhu ziyou de liliang 民主自由的力量
Na lan 納籣
nanbao nanshu 難胞難屬
Nanhai 南海
Nanmin 難民
Nanning 南寧
nongmin jiyin 農民基因
On Shun (Anshun) 安順
Ouyang Fang 歐陽芳
Pak Nai 白泥
pai lau 排樓
panguo toudi 叛國投敵
pidouhui 批鬥會
pixing daiyue 披星戴月
Qi Yilu 齊亦魯
qingnian fudao hui 青年輔導會
Qingnian fudao hui 青年輔導
qushe 屈蛇
Renmin Ribao 人民日報
renmin gongshe 人民公社
renzhen zoujiawutou 認真走夾唔抖
sanminzhuyi, wudangsuozong, yijianminguo, yijindatong 三民主義,吾黨所宗,以建民國,以進大同
Sanshui 三水
Sha Kiu 沙橋
Shanghai 上海
Shek Hwei (Shi Hui) 石慧
Shek Kip-mei 石硤尾
Shekou 蛇口
shensheng buke qinfan de quanli 神聖不可侵犯的權利
shensheng lingtu 神聖領土
Sheung Shui 上水

Shi Yu Wen 時與文
shidai fangxiang de luopanzhen 時代方向的羅盤針
shidai renwu 時代人物
shili 實力
Shiqi 石碁
shiyi yaoren 失意要人
Shizi Shanxia 獅子山下
shiyong Zhujiang kou 屍湧珠江口
Sun Baogang 孫寶鋼
Suárez, Luis Ruiz 陸毅神父
Taishan 台山
Tam Kam Hung 譚錦洪
Tam Kam Pui 譚錦培
Tao Zhu 陶鑄
Tian Xin 田心
tongxingzheng 通行証
toudu 偷渡
Tsang Ngau 曾牛
tuantuan luanzhuan 團團亂轉
Tung Wah Hospital 東華醫院
Waglan 橫欄
Wah Kiu Yih Pao 華僑日報
Wan Lijuan 萬麗鵑
Wang Bingyue 王秉鉞
Wang Qing-quan 王清泉
Wang Yunpei 王云沛
wangxiangtai 望鄉台
weida 偉大
Wen jiaren bei shajin bengang yiwei huaqiao maosi huixiang tanqin 聞家人被殺盡 本港一位華僑冒死回鄉探親
Wong Kin Keung 黃健強
Wuchang 武昌
wudou 武鬥
wuhua dabang 五花大綁
wumin suozhong 吾民所忠
Wuyue dataowang 五月大逃亡
Xianggang danwan zhidi 香港彈丸之地
Xianggang Shibao 香港時報
Xianggang Minzu Lun 香港民族論
Xi Jiping 習近平
Xia Wan Yue 下彎月

xiaodao 小島
Xie Yufa 謝裕發
xingdongxiaozu 行動小組
xingfengxueyu 腥風血雨
Xinhui 新會
Xingqiri dang'an 星期日檔案
xintiandi 新天地
Xiao YuJing 蕭玉井
Xixiang 西鄉
Xu Zhengyan 徐正言
Xu Ziyou 許子由
Yang Nancun 楊南村
yimin 義民
yizhang 姨丈
youjia gui bude 有家歸不得
yumi zhixiang 魚米之鄉
yuzhong zhanshi 獄中戰士
Yuye gongshang zonghui 漁業工商總會
zainan tongbao 災難同胞
Zhang Fakui 張發奎
Zhang Junmai 張君勱
Zhang Kun 張鯤
Zhang Mu Tou 樟木頭
Zhang Tishi 張鐵石
Zhaoqing 肇慶
Zhou Yanghao 周養浩
Zhao Yixue 趙一雪
Zhen Bao 珍報
zhengsi'an 爭屍案

Zhenggong ganxiao 政工幹校
zhengzhi fangong Dalu, minzhugaizao Taiwan 政治反攻大陸民主改造台灣
Zhongguo Minzhu Tongmeng 中國民主同盟
Zhongguo Xinwen 中國新聞
Zhou Yanghao 周養浩
zainan tongbao 災難同胞
Zhonghua minguo 中華民國
Zhongnan Junzheng Daxue Hunan Fenxiao 中南軍政大學湖南分校
Zhongyang Minyi Daibiao 中央民意代表
Zhongshan 中山
Zhong Shan Tang incident 中山堂事件
Zhongguo Zhisheng 中國之聲
Zhongguo Ziyou Minzhu Zhandou Tongmeng 中國自由民主戰鬥同盟
Zhongtai Binguan 中泰賓館
Zhujiang 珠江
zili gengsheng 自力更生
Ziyou luntan 自由論壇
Ziyou Minzhu Da Tongmeng 自由民主大同盟
Ziyouren 自由人
Ziyou Zhegxian 自由陣線
Ziyou Zhongguo 自由中國
zizhi 自治
zounan 走難
zuguo 祖國
Zuo Shunsheng 左舜生

NOTES

INTRODUCTION

1. Hu Guang, "Guanyu ge dangpai zai Xianggang douzheng de xiangxi baodao" (A detailed report on the different political parties and factions in Hong Kong), *Shi Yu Wen* 3, no. 2 (1948).
2. Cao Lin, "Shiyi yaoren zai Xianggang" (Important people of despair in Hong Kong), *Zhongguo Xinwen* 3, no. 8 (1948).
3. See Cathryn Clayton, *Sovereignty at the Edge: Macau & the Question of Chineseness* (Cambridge, MA: Harvard University Asia Center, 2009).
4. For examples of such frameworks, see Roger Cliff and David A. Shlapak, *U.S.-China Relations after Resolution of Taiwan's Status* (Santa Monica, CA: RAND Corporation, 2007); Richard C. Bush, *Uncharted Strait: The Future of China-Taiwan Relations* (Washington, DC: Brookings Institution Press, 2013); Hong Yi Chen, Olaf Unteroberdoerster, and International Monetary Fund, Asia and Pacific Department, *Hong Kong SAR Economic Integration with the Pearl River Delta* (Washington, DC: International Monetary Fund, 2008).
5. See Ien Ang, *On Not Speaking Chinese: Living Between Asia and the West* (New York: Routledge, 2001); Shu-mei Shih, "Against Diaspora: The Sinophone as Places of Cultural Production," in *Global Chinese Literature: Critical Essays*, ed. David Dewei Wang and Jing Tsu (Leiden: Brill, 2010), 29–48; Wang Gungwu, "A Single Chinese Diaspora? Some Historical Reflections," in *Imagining the Chinese Diaspora: Two Australian Perspectives*, ed. Annette Shun Wah and Wang Gungwu (Canberra: Center for the Study of the Chinese Diaspora, Australian National University, 1999), 1–17.
6. This interpretation of diaspora as stateless people living outside the homeland is inspired by Khachig Tölöyan's theorization. See Khachig Tölöyan, "Rethinking Diaspora(s): Stateless Power in the Transnational Moment," *Diaspora* 5, no. 1 (1996): 16.

7. Diaspora theorist William Safran set out some criteria in his essay "Diasporas in Modern Societies: Myths of Homeland and Return," which I found applicable to the situation of the people who fled to the Southern Periphery including these: (1) the group maintains a myth or collective memory of their homeland; (2) they regard their ancestral homeland as their true home to which they will eventually return; (3) they are committed to the restoration or maintenance of that homeland; and (4) they relate "personally or vicariously" to the homeland to a point where it shapes their identity. See William Safran, "Diasporas In Modern Societies: Myths of Homeland and Return," *Diaspora* 1, no. 1 (1991): 83–99.
8. Victor D. Cha, "Powerplay: Origins of the U.S. Alliance in Asia," *International Security* 34, no. 3 (Winter 2009–10): 161–62.
9. Covell F. Meyskens, *Mao's Third Front: The Militarization of Cold War China* (Cambridge: Cambridge University Press, 2020); Jeremy S. Friedman, *Shadow Cold War: The Sino-Soviet Competition for the Third World* (Chapel Hill: University of North Carolina Press, 2015).
10. For Hong Kong's Cold War significance, see Priscilla Roberts and John M. Carroll, eds., *Hong Kong in the Cold War* (Hong Kong: Hong Kong University Press, 2017); Chi-Kwan Mark, *Hong Kong and the Cold War: Anglo-American Relations 1949–1957* (Oxford: Clarendon, 2004).
11. I find Elizabeth Sinn's depiction of Hong Kong as an "in-between" place in the nineteenth century useful in thinking about the role of Hong Kong in the Cold War era. See Elizabeth Sinn, *Pacific Crossing: California Gold, Chinese Migration, and the Making of Hong Kong* (Hong Kong: Hong Kong University Press, 2013).
12. Edvard Hambro, *The Problem of Chinese Refugees in Hong Kong: Report Submitted to the United Nations High Commissioner for Refugees* (London: United Nations Information Center, 1955), 1.

1. "REFUGEES" OR "UNDESIRABLES"

1. Interview with Wang Qing-quan, Taipei, Taiwan, June 10, 2016.
2. Even though many exiled people's first destination was Macau, Dong Zhilin argues that the influence of migrants from mainland China on Macau was not too significant compared to that of Hong Kong. It was only after 1978 that the Macau government felt the pressure of the influx of refugees and immigrants. Thus, this chapter mainly deals with the Hong Kong and ROC governments' attitudes toward refugees and does not include the Portuguese colonial government's immigration and refugee policies in Macau. Dong Zhilin, *Zhongguo Dalu Yimin Zai Aomen Shehui Zhong Shenfen Rentong Zhi Yanjiu 1949–2013* (A Study of Identity Recognition of Mainland China Immigrants in Macau 1949–2013) (Taipei: Tangshan chu ban she, 2015), 7; Agnes Lam and Cathryn Clayton, "Macau One Two Three: Evaluating Macau's 'Cultural Revolution,'" *Modern China Studies* 23, no. 2 (2016): 163–86. See also Cathryn Clayton's forthcoming book on the "123 incident" in Macau, tentatively titled *Macau's 123 Incident: The Cultural Revolution, the Cold War, and China's Global Sixties*.

3. Albert H. Y. Chen, "The Development of Immigration Law and Policy: The Hong Kong Experience," *McGill Law Journal*, 33, no. 4 (1988): 637.
4. Chi-Kwan Mark, "The 'Problem of People': British Colonials, Cold War Powers, and the Chinese Refugees in Hong Kong, 1949–64," *Modern Asian Studies* 41, no. 6 (2007): 2.
5. Madeline Yuan-yin Hsu, *The Good Immigrants: How the Yellow Peril Became the Model Minority* (Princeton, NJ: Princeton University Press, 2015), 225.
6. Dominic Meng-Hsuan Yang, "Humanitarian Assistance and Propaganda War: Repatriation and Relief of the Nationalist Refugees in Hong Kong's Rennie's Mill Camp, 1950–1955," *Journal of Chinese Overseas* 10, no. 2 (2014): 170; Hong Kong Refugees Survey Mission, Edvard Isak Hambro, and Office of the United Nations High Commissioner for Refugees, *The Problem of Chinese Refugees in Hong Kong: Report Submitted to the United Nations High Commissioner for Refugees* (Leiden: A. W. Sijthoff, 1955), 14, table 5.
7. Fujio Mizuoka, "British Colonialism and 'Illegal' Immigration from Mainland China to Hong Kong," *Power Relations, Situated Practices, and the Politics of the Commons: Japanese Contributions to the History of Geographical Thought* (Fukuoka: Institute of Geography, Kyushu University, 2017), 38.
8. Siu-lun Wong, *Emigrant Entrepreneurs: Shanghai Industrialists in Hong Kong* (Hong Kong: Oxford University Press, 1988), 17.
9. Mizuoka, "British Colonialism and 'Illegal' Immigration," 39.
10. One of such figures was Qian Mu, who served as the president of New Asia College from 1949 until 1965. Another cofounder of New Asia College was Tang Chun-I, the son of a wealthy scholar and the firstborn of six children in Sichuan Province. He graduated from National Central University in Nanjing in 1944, then went into exile to Hong Kong in 1949. He helped found the New Asia College, which became part of the Chinese University, Hong Kong in 1963. He and other migrants helped found two publishers: Gaoyuan Chubanshe and Youlian Chubanshe. See Ping-kwan Leung, "Writing Across Borders: Hong Kong's 1950s and the Present," in *Diasporic Histories: Cultural Archives of Chinese Transnationalism*, ed. Andrea Riemenschnitter and Deborah L. Madsen (Hong Kong: Hong Kong University Press, 2009), 23–42.
11. This permit system was also implemented in other provinces as well. People had to carry permits to travel across provincial borders.
12. Mizuoka, "British Colonialism and 'Illegal' Immigration," 41.
13. Laura Madokoro, "Borders Transformed: Sovereign Concerns, Population Movements and the Making of Territorial Frontiers in Hong Kong, 1949–1967," *Journal of Refugee Studies* (2012): 412; Public Record Office (HK): FO 371/83515, April 27, 1950.
14. A. Chen, "The Development of Immigration Law and Policy," 640.
15. For more details of such stories, see Chen Bing'an, *Da Tao Gang* (The great escape) (Hong Kong: Xianggang Zhonghe Chuban She, 2011).
16. Author interview with Ip Cheung, Ip's residence in the New Territories, Hong Kong, July 2016.
17. See chapter 3 for details.
18. Because the definition of "refugees" was controversial and a subject of political debates, I will mostly use the term "escapees" instead to refer to the individuals who fled mainland China to the Southern Periphery in the 1950s–1970s.

19. Meredith Oyen, "Thunder without Rain," *Journal of Cold War Studies* 16, no. 4 (2014): 193.
20. Those who lived in Hong Kong were portrayed by state media as people exercising their rights, and the PRC refused to accept them back when the Hong Kong government wanted to deport them for political reasons. See chapter 4 for details.
21. Laura Madokoro, *Elusive Refuge: Chinese Migrants in the Cold War* (Cambridge, MA: Harvard University Press, 2016), 40.
22. Mark, "The 'Problem of People,'" 10.
23. Quoted in Lin Chih-yen, *Ziyou de Daijia: Zhonghua Min'guo yu Xianggang Diaojingling* (The price of "freedom": The Republic of China and the Chinese refugees at Rennie's Mill Camp in Hong Kong, 1950–1961) (Taipei: Guoshiguan, 2011), 111; "Zhengzhi zuozhan jihua" (Political strategic plans), Minutes of the 240th Central Committee Working Meeting, May 12, 1952, Guoshiguan Archives.
24. Madokoro, *Elusive Refuge*, 63.
25. Glen Peterson, "To Be or Not to Be a Refugee: The International Politics of the Hong Kong Refugee Crisis, 1949–55," *Journal of Imperial and Commonwealth History* 36, no. 2 (2008): 171–95.
26. Leo F. Goodstadt, *Uneasy Partners: The Conflict Between Public Interest and Private Profit in Hong Kong* (Hong Kong: Hong Kong University Press, 2005), quoted in Mark, *Hong Kong*, 7.
27. Peterson, "To Be or Not to Be a Refugee," 182.
28. Peterson, "To Be or Not to Be a Refugee," 174.
29. Peterson, "To Be or Not to Be a Refugee," 173–74.
30. The United States allowed only 3,000 Chinese refugees (nonquota refugees) and 105 Chinese immigrants (quota immigrants) each year. See Louise W. Holborn, Philip Chartrand, and Rita Chartrand, *Refugees: A Problem of Our Time* (Metuchen, NJ: Scarecrow Press), 688–90, quoted in Mark, "The 'Problem of People,'" 22.
31. Peterson, "To Be or Not to Be a Refugee," 184.
32. Glen Peterson, "Crisis and Opportunity," in *Hong Kong in the Cold War*, ed. Priscilla Mary Roberts and John M. Carroll (Hong Kong: HKU Press, 2016), 141–59.
33. Oyen, "Thunder without Rain," 198.
34. Peterson, "To Be or Not to Be a Refugee," 177; Mark, "The 'Problem of People,'" 13.
35. Peterson, "To Be or Not to Be a Refugee," 178.
36. Hsu, *Good Immigrants*, 141.
37. Peterson, "To Be or Not to Be a Refugee," 180.
38. Peterson, "To Be or Not to Be a Refugee," 180.
39. Hsu, *Good Immigrants*, 140, 142.
40. Hsu, *Good Immigrants*, 146.
41. Hsu, *Good Immigrants*, 146.
42. Hsu, *Good Immigrants*, 146.
43. Hsu, *Good Immigrants*, 132.
44. Hsu, *Good Immigrants*, 132. The Displaced Persons Act expired in 1953.
45. Hsu, *Good Immigrants*, 132.

1. "REFUGEES" OR "UNDESIRABLES" 267

46. Norman Yao immigration document, 1950, Norman Gan Chao and Anne Lee Yao Papers (H.Mss.1106), box 2, folders 1–5, Special Collections, The Claremont Colleges Library, Claremont, CA.
47. Norman Yao immigration document.
48. Hsu, *Good Immigrants*, 140.
49. Hsu, *Good Immigrants*, 133, 160.
50. Hsu, *Good Immigrants*, 160.
51. Hsu, *Good Immigrants*, 133, 148.
52. Madokoro, "Borders Transformed," 67.
53. Yang, "Humanitarian Assistance and Propaganda War," 172.
54. Liang Jialin, *Fuyin yu Mianbao: Jidujiao zai wushi niandai de Diaojingling* (Gospel and Bread: Christianity at the 1950s Rennie's Mill) (Hong Kong: Jiandao Shenxueyuan, 2000), 30–32.
55. Yang, "Humanitarian Assistance and Propaganda War," 173.
56. On-Wai Kenneth Lan, "Rennie's Mill: The Origin and Evolution of a Special Enclave in Hong Kong" (University of Hong Kong, 2006), 76, http://sunzi.lib.hku.hk/hkuto/view/B36777766/ft.pdf.
57. Hong Kong Record Series 156/1/2876: 1:1–1:2, Hong Kong Public Records Office.
58. Yang, "Humanitarian Assistance and Propaganda War," 172.
59. Yang, "Humanitarian Assistance and Propaganda War," 165; Hong Kong Refugees Survey Mission, Edvard Isak Hambro, and Office of the United Nations High Commissioner for Refugees, *Problem of Chinese Refugees*, 73–74.
60. Of the 946 Chinese Nationalist soldiers and their families transported in the SS *Kweiyang*, which arrived in Taiwan, only 34 who held individual entry permits were permitted to land.
61. Lan, "Rennie's Mill," 82–83.
62. Lin Chih-yen, *Ziyou de Daijia*, 33.
63. Lan, "Rennie's Mill," 83–86.
64. Liu Yizhang, "Xuan jiaoshi zai Diaojingling nanminying de yiliao fuwu" (The medical services of the missionaries in Rennie's Mill), *Xianggang Shehui Yu Wenhua Lunji: An Anthology of Hong Kong Social and Cultural History* (Hong Kong: Hong Kong Chinese University Press, 2002), 11.
65. Chen Bo, *Xianggang Diaojingling Nanminying Diaocha Baogao* (An investigative report of Hong Kong Rennie's Mill) (Hong Kong: Xianggang da zhuan she hui wen ti yan jiu she, 1961), 15.
66. Lin Chih-yen, *Ziyou de Daijia*, 24.
67. Hong Kong Record Series 156/1/2876:2–3, 5.
68. Hong Kong Record Series 160/3/39:4–5; Yang, "Humanitarian Assistance and Propaganda War," 180; Lin Chih-yen, *Ziyou de Daijia*, 38.
69. Lan, "Rennie's Mill," 77.
70. Hu Chunhui, *Xianggang Diaojinglingying de Dansheng yu Xiaoshi: Zhang Hansong de Fangtan Lu* (The birth and disappearance of Hong Kong Rennie's Mill Camp: Interviews with Zhang Hangsong and others) (Taipei: Guoshiguan 1997), 289.

71. Lin Chih-yen, *Ziyou de Daijia*, 98.
72. "Gu Zhenggang he bu ziji zhaozhao jingzi?" (Why doesn't Gu Zhenggang look at himself in the mirror?), *Lianhe Pinglun* (United Voice Weekly), April 20, 1962; "Wei youjia bin you guo nan tou de zaibao qingming" (Speaking for the refugees who are fleeing because of disasters in their home country), *Lianhe Pinglun*, April 27, 1962; "Wei tao Gang nanbao huyu" (A public appeal for refugees who escaped to Hong Kong), *Lianhe Pinglun*, May 25, 1962.
73. According to the Constitution of the Republic of China and its Additional Articles, the Control Yuan is empowered to exercise the powers of impeachment, censure, and audit. It may also take corrective measures against government organizations. To fulfill this duty, members of the Control Yuan handle people's complaints, inspect central and local governments, conduct investigations, and supervise civil service examinations.
74. Lin Chih-yen, *Ziyou de Daijia*, 93.
75. Lin Chih-yen, *Ziyou de Daijia*. Material in this paragraph is taken, respectively, from 99, 86, 101, 95, and 48n81.
76. See chapter 2.
77. Disabled people were also unwanted by the KMT. In 1955, disabled veterans and their families were relocated to Lantau Island. Many protested by starting a hunger strike. The KMT later let them be transferred to Taiwan, mainly because of the international media coverage of this protest and the likelihood a further delay would hurt the KMT's reputation. See Xianggang Zhongguo Lüxingshe (Hong Kong China Travel Service), "Xianggang yiminju yewu de yanjiu" (Research on the work of the Hong Kong Immigration Department), 106. Foreign Ministry Files 11EAP03175, Jindaishi Yanjiusuo Dang'an Guan (Archives of the Institute of Modern History), Academia Sinica, Taipei, Taiwan.
78. Letter from Ku Cheng Kang (Gu Zhenggang) to James Campbell, Far East refugee advisor of Foreign Operations Administration, April 1, 1955, 58, Foreign Ministry Files 11EAP03247, Archives of the Institute of Modern History.
79. Lin Chih-yen, *Ziyou de Daijia* 137; Chen Bo, Xianggang Diaojingling Nanminying Diaocha Baogao (1960), 36–37.
80. Lin Chih-yen, *Ziyou de Daijia*, 96.
81. Lin Chih-yen, *Ziyou de Daijia*, 332.
82. Mizuoka, "British Colonialism and 'Illegal' Immigration," 43.
83. Mizuoka, "British Colonialism and 'Illegal' Immigration," 49.
84. Burns, "Immigration from China and the Future of Hong Kong," *Asian Survey* 27, no. 6 (June 1987): 664, citing Hong Kong Government Annual Report, 1962, 213.
85. Burns, "Immigration from China," 663, citing data from the Immigration Department.
86. Wang Zhun, "Minguo liushisi nian Chenggong Ling dazhaun jixun ban shengya huiyi" (Recollection of the training course for higher education students at Chenggong Ling in the 64th year of the Republic), July 5, 2015, http://www.4thgrader.net/vault/files/MemoryOfChengKungRidgeIn1975.doc.
87. Wu Yue, *Taowang Chao Laitai Yibao Anzhi Gongzuo* (The work of settling escapees who moved to Taiwan from Hong Kong) (Hong Kong: Zhongguo Dalu Zaibao Jiuji zonghui, 1964).

88. Mizuoka, "British Colonialism and 'Illegal' Immigration," 47.
89. *Common Sitting Hong Kong (Immigrants), May 15, 1964*, Hansard, 1803–2005 Dec 15 May 1964 vol. 695 cc819–37, House of Commons Archives, UK Parliament.
90. UK Colonial Office CO 1023/117. Also quoted in Mark, *Hong Kong*, 1149.
91. Laura Madokoro, *Elusive Refuge*, 42. For a detailed study on the impact of the Shek Kip Mei fire, see also Alan Smart, *Shek Kip Mei Myth: Squatters, Fires and Colonial Rule in Hong Kong, 1950–1963* (Hong Kong: Hong Kong University Press, 2006).
92. Alan Smart, *Shek Kip Mei Myth*, chapters 2 and 3.
93. Political Allegiance of Hong Kong citizens, UK Colonial Office, CO 1030/326 1954–56. The colonial government read a paper written by the Civil Aeronautics Board in Washington, in which the U.S. government claimed that Hong Kong at that time was "composed of largely Chinese Nationalists." Members of Parliament believed the claim was inaccurate, but they showed concern by writing to the Hong Kong government to see whether the claim needed to be corrected. The Hong Kong government responded by saying that Fitzmaurice's claim should be corrected to: Hong Kong is "composed largely of persons of Chinese race." It made no comment on the political loyalties of Hong Kong citizens but stated that it was possible the majority population was neutral and concerned more about safety than politics.
94. Mark, *Hong Kong*, 2.
95. UK Colonial Office CO 1023/117; CO 1013/1313, also in Agnes Ku, "Immigration Policies, Discourses, and the Politics of Local Belonging in Hong Kong (1950–1980), *Modern China* 30, no. 3 (July 2004): 355–56.
96. Mark, "The 'Problem of People,'" n4.
97. Mark, *Hong Kong*, 338.
98. Ku, "Immigration Policies, Discourses, and the Politics of Local Belonging in Hong Kong (1950–1980)," 356n7.
99. A. Chen, "Immigration Law in Hong Kong," 642.
100. After June 30, 1987, the black stamp was later replaced by three stars printed on the permanent ID.
101. For a detailed analysis of this policy, see Florence Mok, "Chinese Illicit Immigration into Colonial Hong Kong, c. 1970–1980," *Journal of Imperial and Commonwealth History* 49, no. 2 (2021): 339–67.
102. Burns, "Immigration from China," 666.
103. It would seem as though those who arrived in the late 1970s were mainly escaping for economic reasons. This was not always the case. Some had experienced the Cultural Revolution and still wanted to go to Hong Kong because they believed that they did not have political freedom in China.

2. THE THIRD FORCE AND THE CULTURE OF DISSENT IN HONG KONG

1. I would like to thank Kathy Lu for her organizing a large number of primary and secondary materials and for translating some of the magazine articles.

2. Chen Zhengmao, *Wushi Niandai Xianggang Disan Shili Yundong Shiliao Soumi* (Historical materials on the Third Force in 1950s Hong Kong) (Taipei: Xiuwei Zixun, 2011), 15.
3. Ming Sing, *Hong Kong's Tortuous Democratization: A Comparative Analysis* (London: Routledge Curzon, 2004), 62.
4. Ming Sing, *Hong Kong's Tortuous Democratization*, 60.
5. Edmund S. K. Fung, "The Alternative of Loyal Opposition: The Chinese Youth Party and Chinese Democracy, 1937–1949," *Modern China* 17, no. 2 (April 1991): 262–63.
6. Roger B. Jeans, ed., *Roads Not Taken. The Struggle of Opposition Parties in Twentieth Century China* (Boulder, CO: Westview Press, 1992), 38, 41.
7. Wan Lijuan, "Yijiu Wuning Niandai de Zhongguo Disan Shili Yundong" (The Third Force movement in 1950s China), PhD diss., Taiwan National Chengchi University, 2001, 2–4.
8. Ko-wu Huang did a very detailed study of another leader, Gu Mengyu, and why the Third Force was seen as a potential alternative to the two parties. See Ko-wu Huang, "Gu Mengyu yu disanshili de shengshuai" (Gu Mengyu and the rise and fall of the Third Force), *Ershiyi Shiji* (Twenty-First Century) 162 (August 2017): 47–63.
9. Ko-wu Huang, *Gu Mengyu yu disanshili de shengshuai*, 30.
10. Chen Zhengmao, *Wushi Niandai Xianggang Disan Shili Yundong Shiliao Soumi*, i.
11. Chen Zhengmao, *Wushi Niandai Xianggang Disan Shili Yundong Shiliao Soumi*, ii; Tianshi Yang, "The Third Force in Hong Kong and North America During the 1950s," in Jeans, ed., *Roads Not Taken*, 269.
12. Tianshi Yang, "Third Force," 270. The group promoted five basic principles: (1) freedom is the most fundamental of all human objectives; (2) pluralism allows progress of human thought and culture, while control of culture and thought can only freeze human creativity; (3) democracy has become the main political trend of mankind, and thus dictatorship should not be allowed; (4) private property is a part of human civilization and should be allowed; and (5) the responsibilities of a government are to reconcile the people's interests and protect their well-being as well as to maintain national interests and friendly international relations.
13. Wan, "Yijiu Wuning Niandai de Zhongguo Disan Shili Yundong," 40.
14. Between 1949 and 1964, more than a dozen Third Force periodicals were published, including *Zhongguo Zhisheng* (Voices of China), *Zaisheng*, *Zhongshengribao*, *Zhongsheng Wanbao*, *Minzhu yu Ziyou*, *Zhuliu Yuekan*, *Ziyou Zhenxian* (Freedom Front), *Zhuguo*, and *Lianhe Pinglun* (United Voice Weekly).
15. Chen Zhengmao, *Wushi Niandai Xianggang Disan Shili Yundong Shiliao Soumi*, 10.
16. The first English-language article on the Third Force, "The Third Force in Hong Kong and North America During the 1950s," written by Zhang Junmai, provides some useful information about the movement's failure. Zhang also wrote a book about the Third Force, mainly focusing on the actors in China during the years of the Chinese Civil War and strongly emphasizing the importance of U.S. aid.
17. Chen Zhengmao, *Wushi Niandai Xianggang Disan Shili Yundong Shiliao Soumi*, ii; Wan, "Third Force Movement," 149.
18. Chen Zhengmao, *Wushi Niandai Xianggang Disan Shili Yundong Shiliao Soumi*, 18.

2. THE THIRD FORCE AND THE CULTURE OF DISSENT 271

19. Wan, "Yijiu Wuning Niandai de Zhongguo Disan Shili Yundong," 28.
20. Zhang Yi, "Di san shili de lishi shiming" (The historical mission of the Third Force), *Ziyou Zhenxian* (Freedom Front) 2, no. 2.
21. "Du shiping Ziyou Zhenxian hou de wojian" (My opinions after reading "A critique of *Ziyou Zhenxian*"), *Ziyou Zhenxian*, August 10, 1951.
22. "Women yao xiang shinsheng de dadao maijin" (We have to march toward the path toward a new life), *Ziyou Zhenxian*, April 16, 1950.
23. "Sheme shi di san shili?" (What is the Third Force?), *Ziyou Zhenxian*, May 16, 1950.
24. "Benkan de dongxiang Minzhuzhengzhi, gongpingjingji, ziyouwenhua" (The trend of this magazine: Democratic politics, economic equity, cultural freedom), *Ziyou Zhenxian*, September 16, 1950.
25. Lang Xuan, "Ruhe xianshen disanshiri?" (How to strengthen the Third Force movement?), *Ziyou Zhenxian*, December 26, 1951.
26. Wan, "Yijiu Wuning Niandai de Zhongguo Disan Shili Yundong," 161.
27. Lin Chih-yen, *Ziyou de Daijia*, 117; originally from Central Reform Committee meetings, April 30–July 4, 1950, 6.4-2/93; 6.4-2/175, KMT Dangshi archives.
28. Fang Wen, "Minzhu Yundong de yaolan" (Hong Kong, the cradle of the democratic movement), *Ziyou Zhenxian* 7, no. 2 (July 16, 1950).
29. Only a few hundred of the nearly seven thousand refugees at Rennie's Mill were repatriated. Many were left in the camp, which was turned into an enclave for pro-KMT migrants from mainland China in the 1960s.
30. Li Minde, "You Tiaojingling kan Taiwan de 'minzhu' "(Taiwan's "democracy" from the view of Rennie's Mill), *Zhongguo Zhi Sheng* (Voices of China) 2, no. 6 (February 7, 1952). Most of the nonelite writers did not write in detail about governance and constitutional democracy as elaborated by the Third Force leaders. They were much more affected by the social circumstances of being marginalized by Hong Kong society.
31. Li Minde, "You Tiaojingling kan Taiwan de 'minzhu.' "
32. Dominic Meng-Hsuan Yang, "Tiaojingling: Xianggang 'Xiao Taiwan' de qiyuan yu bianqian, 1950s–1970s" (Rennie's Mill: Origin and transformation of "Little Taiwan" in Hong Kong, 1950s–1970s), *Journal of Taiwan Studies* 18, no. 1 (March 1, 2011): 155–56.
33. Zhang Kun, "Kanyi—Wo likai le Diaojingling" (Protest—I have left Rennie's Mill!), *Zhongguo Zhi Sheng* 2, no. 8 (February 21, 1952).
34. "Cong Moxingling dao Diaojingling" (From Moxingling to Rennie's Mill), *Ziyou Zhenxian*, December 12, 1952.
35. Bei Ming, "Yige guojia shuangchong tiemu" (One country has two iron curtains), *Zhongguo Zhi Sheng* 2, no. 10 (March 6, 1952[?]).
36. Liu Hui, "San nian Xianggang" (My three years in Hong Kong), *Ziyou Zhenxian*, December 12, 1952.
37. Liu Hui, "San nian Xianggang."
38. Yi Ming (anonymous), "San nian lai de shenghuo yu guangan" (My life and thoughts in the past three years), *Ziyou Zhenxian*, December 5, 1952.
39. Li Hao, "Rang huyu biancheng shishi" (Let my request become reality), *Zhongguo Zhi Sheng* 2, no. 8 (February 21, 1952).

272   2. THE THIRD FORCE AND THE CULTURE OF DISSENT

40. Lü Luo, "Qilai—Xianggang nü qingnian" (Stand up, young women in Hong Kong), *Zhongguo Zhi Sheng* 2, no. 9 (February 28, 1952).
41. Chen Zhengmao, *Wushi Niandai Xianggang Disan Shili Yundong Shiliao Soumi*, 5.
42. Grace Ai-Ling Chou, *Confucianism, Colonialism, and the Cold War: Chinese Cultural Education at Hong Kong's New Asia College, 1949–76* (Leiden: Brill, 2012), 54, 57.
43. Roger B. Jeans, *The CIA and Third Force Movements in China During the Early Cold War* (Lanham, MD: Lexington Books, 2018), 191.
44. Wan, "Third Force Movement," 30.
45. Wan, "Third Force Movement," 59.
46. Chen Zhengmao, *Wushi Niandai Xianggang Disan Shili Yundong Shiliao Soumi*, 9.
47. "Fa kan ci" (Introductory Remarks), *Lianhe Pinglun*, August 1, 1958.
48. "Dalu qingnian xiaochen beiguan" (Mainland youth are disappointed and pessimistic), *Lianhe Pinglun*, March 16 [?], 1960.
49. Na Lan, "Zhonggong fanyou qing zouru si hutong" (The CCP Anti-Rightist Campaign is going toward a dead end), *Lianhe Pinglun*, March 16, 1960.
50. Tian Xin, "Luetan Zhonggong zhengquan de bu wending" (A brief summary of the instability of the CCP regime), *Lianhe Pinglun*, September 9, 1960.
51. "Ba san ge yundong lian qilai" (Linking the three movements together), *Lianhe Pinglun*, August 15, 1958.
52. Xie Fuya studied abroad not only in Japan but also in the United States at the University of Chicago and Harvard University. Like his Third Force compatriots, he left the mainland for Hong Kong in 1949, but he moved to New York in 1958 and was granted U.S. citizenship in 1964. The writings in *Lianhe Pinglun* showed his hope to lead a Third Force movement from the United States.
53. Xie Fuya, "Haiwai yizhi chujin fangong de shihou dao le" (The time for overseas Chinese to fight back has come), *Lianhe Pinglun*, April 21, 1961.
54. Xie Fuya, "Yige shili, Yige Zhongguo" (One force, one China), *Lianhe Pinglun*, August 31, 1962.
55. Ouyang Fang, "Geixun Di San Shili tongzhimen de yi feng gongkai xin" (An open letter to the comrades in the Third Force), *Lianhe Pinglun*, July 13, 1962.
56. Huang Yuren, "Liumei xuesheng kaishi dongle" (The students studying abroad in the United States have taken actions), *Lianhe Pinglun*, September 28, 1962.
57. Xu Ziyou, "Taiwan gai shishi yu Zhonggong jiaoshou" (Taiwan should try to fight with the CCP), *Lianhe Pinglun*, February 2, 1962.
58. "Meixian yu fangong" (U.S. aid and anticommunism), *Lianhe Pinglun*, June 22, 1962.
59. Wan Lijuan, "Yijiu wuning niandai de Zhongguo Disan Shili Yundong," 124.
60. Wan Lijuan, "Yijiu wuning niandai de Zhongguo Disan Shili Yundong," 56.
61. Xu Zhengyan, "Qing Dajia qilai yanjiu fangong fuguo fang'an!" (Let's stand up and think about fighting against the Communists and restoring China together!), *Lianhe Pinglun*, April 15, 1960.
62. Liu Yulue, "Bai zai Taiwan mianqian de jitiao lu" (The paths in front of Taiwan), *Lianhe Pinglun*, February 5, 1960.
63. Liu Yulue, "Taiwan ying jin xian jinxing jubu fangong" (Taiwan should think about a partial attack), *Lianhe Pinglun*, January 19, 1962.

2. THE THIRD FORCE AND THE CULTURE OF DISSENT   273

64. Liu Yulue, "Lun Shaoshu minzu zai fangong douzheng zhong de zhongyaoxing" (Regarding the importance of ethnic minorities in the fight against the CCP), *Lianhe Pinglun*, September 9, 1960.
65. "Du 'Taiwan de san ren zhengzhi' " (Studying Taiwan's "three people politics"), *Lianhe Pinglun*, August 26, 1960.
66. Li Huang, "Renzhi aiguo shui bu ru wo!" (No one is as patriotic as me!), *Lianhe Pinglun*, March 31, 1961.
67. Lianhe Pinglun eds., "Hai neiwai minzhu fangongzhe ying ji yousuo nuli" (The effort that anticommunists in China and abroad should acquire), *Lianhe Pinglun*, March 31, 1960.
68. Li Yansheng, "Tan fangong dalu de xin wenti bing zhonggao Jiang Jingguo" (Discussing the new question of counterattacking the mainland and warning Chiang Kai-shek), *Lianhe Pinglun*, May 13, 1960.
69. Zuo Shunsheng, "Jiang xiansheng neng buneng chuguo yi xing?" (Can't Mr. Chiang take a tour abroad?), *Lianhe Pinglun*, January 1, 1960.
70. Li Jinye, "Wei minzhu zhengzhu you zhu fangong fuguo" (Only in a democratic political system would counterattack and reunification be possible), *Lianhe Pinglun*, December 2 [?], 1960.
71. "Tuanjie fangong yu minzhu zhi zheng" (A struggle between unity against the CCP and democracy), *Lianhe Pinglun*, March 11, 1960.
72. Qi Yilu, "Taibei dangju yu minzhu wei di" (The ROC regime is determined to be the enemy of democracy), *Lianhe Pinglun*, September 16, 1960; Li Huang, "Lei an yu fangong jianguo lianmeng" (The Lei Zhen case and the anti-CCP reunification alliance), *Lianhe Pinglun*, December 3, 1963.
73. Li Qing, "Ping xin jing qi tan Lei an" (Let's rationally discuss Lei Zhen's case), *Lianhe Pinglun*, September 16, 1960.
74. Zuo Shunsheng, "Lei an yu tuanjie" (Lei Zhen's case and unity), *Lianhe Pinglun*, December 2, 1960.
75. Li Huang, "Yi wei gaoya zhengce you hai fangong qiantu" (A heavy-handed top-down policy is jeopardizing the future of the anti-CCP movement), *Lianhe Pinglun*, February 2, 1962.
76. Li Huang, "Lei an yu fangong jianguo lianmeng."
77. Hu Yue, "Qiuzhu liuwang xuesheng buke zai tuo" (Helping exiled students should not be delayed), *Lianhe Pinglun*, October 3, 1958.
78. Hu Yue, "Jiyu liuwang qingnian pengyou" (Some advice for exiled youth), *Lianhe Pinglun*, January 18, 1963.
79. "Minzhu yu aiguo" (Democracy and patriotism), *Lianhe Pinglun*, September 9, 1960.
80. Zhang Zhengwen, "Dalu taogang xuesheng kongsu zhi yi: Wo cengshi nuli" (The outcry by a student escapee, part 1: I was once a slave), *Lianhe Pinglun*, September 19, 1958.
81. Hu Yue, "Qiuzhu liuwang xuesheng buke zai tuo."
82. Chen De, "Wo zai dalu lishou pohai ji tuoxian digang de jingguo" (The story about my persecution and escape in mainland China), *Lianhe Pinglun*, August 3, 1962.
83. "Xianggang yi mianlin yanzhong guantou" (Hong Kong is facing a very dire situation), *Lianhe Pinglun*, May 18, 1962.

274   2. THE THIRD FORCE AND THE CULTURE OF DISSENT

84. "Taowang ren su dalu shi" (Stories about mainland China as told by escapees), *Lianhe Pinglun*, May 25, 1962.
85. "Xianggang yi mianlin yanzhong guantou."
86. Li Huang, "Gu Zhenggang he bu ziji zhao jingzi?" (Why doesn't Gu Zhenggang take a look at the mirror?), *Lianhe Pinglun*, April 20, 1962.
87. Li Huang, "Wei you jia nan ben you guo nan tou de zaibao qingming" (Voicing my concern for the refugees who could not find a home country to turn to), *Lianhe Pinglun*, April 27, 1962.
88. Although there is little online information available on Huang Yuren, secondary Third Force literature features him heavily as one of the earliest and most active figures within the movement. Not only was he head of printing and occasionally contributed to Third Force publications, but Huang Yuren was also a leader in one of the earliest Third Force organizations, the Great Alliance for Freedom and Democracy (Ziyou Minzhu Da Tongmeng), established in 1938. Furthermore, Huang Yuren also acted as an editor for another prominent Third Force periodical, *Ziyou luntan* (Independent Forum). See Chen Zhengmao, *Wushi Niandai Xianggang Disan Shili Yundong Shiliao Soumi*, chap. 1, for the details.
89. Huang Yuren, "Liumei xuesheng kaishi dongle."
90. Colonial Office (CO) 1030/324, 288–325, 1955, British National Archives.
91. Sun Baogang, "Minzhu yu zizhi de xingjue" (Awareness for democracy and self-rule), *Lianhe Pinglun*, June 7, 1963.
92. Sun Baogang, "Tan Xianggangde minzhu zizhi" (Let's talk about Hong Kong's democracy and self-rule), *Lianhe Pinglun*, May 22, 1964.
93. See Kenneth Yung, *Chinese Émigré Intellectuals and Their Quest for Liberal Values in the Cold War, 1949–1969* (Leiden: Brill, 2021) for the crossovers between the Third Force Movement and the political and intellectual discourses in Hong Kong.
94. "Gei xun disan shili tongzhimen de yifeng gongkai xin" (An open letter to the comrades of the Third Force), *Lianhe Pinglun*, July 13, 1962.
95. "Zhi di san shili de yifeng gongkaixin" (An open letter to the Third Force), *Lianhe Pinglun*, August 3, 1962.
96. Hu Yue, "Jiyu liuwang qingnian pengyou" (A few words for the youth in exile abroad), *Lianhe Pinglun*, January 18, 1963.
97. Liu Yulue, "Xiang liuwang qingnian zhishi gongxian jidian yijian" (Some advice for the exiled youth), *Lianhe Pinglun*, March 29, 1963.
98. "Wo wei she me zancheng benbao tingkan?" (Why do I agree to disband the publication?), *Lianhe Pinglun*, October 23, 1964.
99. Chen Zhengmao, *Wushi Niandai Xianggang Disan Shili Yundong Shiliao Soumi*, 38.
100. Chen Zhengmao, *Wushi Niandai Xianggang Disan Shili Yundong Shiliao Soumi*, 41.

3. CULTURAL REVOLUTION AT SEA

1. "Huaiyi zisha pinsheng: kao siyinting xunzhao zhenxiang" (Suspicious "suicide" cases rampant: Relying on the Coroners' Court to find out the truth?), *Apple Daily*, September 19, 2019.

3. CULTURAL REVOLUTION AT SEA   275

2. Niu Mama/Madam N, "Zhichi de qing tui: jingcha shahai beibu renshi huishimieji zhuijiu daodi" (Please spread if you support: Police murdering the arrested and destroying all the evidence; we must hold them accountable), *Zhong Xinwen* (Citizen News), October 13, 2019.
3. People's communes were large rural organizational units introduced in China in 1958. They began as amalgamations of collective farms but evolved to become multipurpose organizations that handled local government and managed all economic and social activities of local residents.
4. *Wah Kiu Yih Pao*, March 9, 1952.
5. *Wah Kiu Yih Pao*, July 29, 1956.
6. *Wah Kiu Yat Pao*, August 23, 1957.
7. *Kung Sheung Daily News*, November 29, 1962.
8. Interview with Xiao Yujing, Beitou, Taipei, 2017; interview with Zhou Qingjun in Ximen, Taipei, 2017.
9. *Wah Kiu Yih Pao*, December 2, 1962.
10. *Kung Sheung Evening News*, December 3, 1964.
11. The few interviewees who went to Macau and stayed there did not seem to have such recollections. This may be a result of the differences in influence of KMT on the local newspapers. Macau's newspapers were mostly pro-CCP.
12. Yang Su, *Collective Killings in Rural China During the Cultural Revolution* (New York: Cambridge University Press, 2011), 2.
13. Yang Su, *Collective Killings*, 5.
14. Free China Relief Association (FCRA), *Fushi, Taowang, Renquan* (Dead bodies, escape, and human rights) (Hong Kong: FCRA, 1971), 3.
15. Yongyi Song, "Chronology of Mass Killings During the Chinese Cultural Revolution (1966–1976)," Online Encyclopedia of Mass Violence, August 25, 2011.
16. Ruoyu Wu, "Wenge Guangxi datusha" (Guangxi massacre during the Cultural Revolution), *Beijing Zhi Chun* (Beijing Spring) 123 (2003): 46–47.
17. Yongyi Song, "Chronology of Mass Killings."
18. "A letter addressed to the Taiwan Foreign Office (*waijiaobu*) in Hong Kong" July 10, 1968, FMF 11EAP03171 60–64, Institute of Modern History Archives.
19. "You Xiangang kan Dalu wang Taiwan (Observing Mainland China and Taiwan from Hong Kong)," *Kung Sheung Daily News*, October 15, 1968.
20. *Kung Sheung Evening News*, June 25, 1968.
21. Internal political situation in Hong Kong: Disturbances and Communist agitation, February–September 1968, 97–98, FCO 21/194, Foreign Office, British National Archives.
22. *Zhen Bao*, July 5, 1968.
23. *Kung Sheung Evening News*, June 25, 1968.
24. "Dead Bodies Rolling in from the Mainland (*Dalu fushi gungunlai*)," *Kung Sheung Daily News*, June 27, 1968.
25. *Singtao Daily*, June 26, 1968.
26. *Kung Sheung Daily News*, June 29, 1968.
27. *Kung Sheung Evening News*, June 25, 1968; *Singtao Daily*, June 26, 1968.
28. *Kung Sheung Evening News*, June 25, 1968.

29. *Kung Sheung Evening News*, June 27, 1968.
30. *Kung Sheung Evening News*, June 27, 1968.
31. *Kung Sheung Evening News*, June 27, 1968.
32. *Kung Sheung Daily News*, June 29, 1968.
33. *Zhen Bao*, June 29, 1968.
34. *Kung Sheung Evening News*, November 9, 1979.
35. *Kung Sheung Evening News*, June 27, 1968.
36. FCRA, *Fushi, Taowang, Renyuan*, 10.
37. *Kung Sheung Evening News*, November 8, 1970.
38. *Kung Sheung Evening News*, June 27, 1968.
39. *Kung Sheung Evening News*, November 3, 1970.
40. *Kung Sheung Evening News*, November 4, 1970.
41. *Kung Sheung Evening News*, November 4, 1970.
42. *Xianggang Shibao*, July 5, 1968.
43. *Kung Sheung Evening News*, June 27, 1968.
44. *Zhen Bao*, June 29, 1968.
45. Denise Ho has written about the relationship between oystermen and refugees in her paper "Oysterman, Refugee, Coast Guard: Hong Kong and China Between the Tides, 1949–1997," working paper presented at the Association of Asian Studies Annual Conference, 2021 (online).
46. *Zhen Bao*, June 29, 1968.
47. "Women ningyuan si zai Xianggang—qing ting taoben ziyou yumin de xuelei sushu" (We would rather die in Hong Kong! Please listen to the outcry of the fishermen who fled for freedom), *Kung Sheung Daily News*, August 30, 1968.
48. *Kung Sheung Daily News*, August 8, 1968.
49. *Zhen Bao*, August 9, 1968.
50. *Kung Sheung Evening News*, July 1, 1968.
51. *Xianggang Shibao*, July 12, 1968.
52. "Di liu zu baogao diyiqijiuci huiyi" (A report from the sixth division, the 179th meeting), July 15, 1968, FMF 11EAP03171 38, Institute of Modern History Archives.
53. *Zhen Bao*, July 8, 1968.
54. *Zhen Bao*, July 8, 1968.
55. *Xianggang Shibao*, July 5, 1968.
56. Internal political situation in Hong Kong: Disturbances and Communist agitation, February–September 1968, 76–77, "From 'the relevant Kwangtung authorities' in reply," telegram addressed to Commonwealth Office, July 27, 1968. FCO 21/194, Foreign Office, British National Archives.
57. "Dalu Tongbao Kunan" (The sufferings of the mainland compatriots), *Lianghe Pinglun*, June 10, 1963.
58. *Kung Sheung Daily News*, July 2, 1968.
59. *Xianggang Shibao*, March 9, 1970; FMF 11EAP03171 71, Institute of Modern History Archives.
60. *South China Morning Post*, September 2, 1970.
61. *South China Morning Post*, September 3, 1970.

62. *South China Morning Post*, October 8, 1970.
63. "A visit to Hang Hau village yesterday disclosed that they had not yet demolished a wooden shack covered with Communist slogans as ordered by the police and the Yuen Long District Officer two days earlier." See *South China Morning Post*, September 6, 1970.
64. *South China Morning Post*, September 4, 1970.
65. *South China Morning Post*, September 4, 1970.
66. Several newspapers were cited in an article in *South China Morning Post*, September 9, 1970.
67. *South China Morning Post*, October 10, 1970.
68. *South China Morning Post*, October 15, 1970. Tang suggested that the border should be defined in Deep Bay. Tang also disclosed that the manager of the Yau kung Tong, a family concern operating the number one oyster farm in Deep Bay, had lodged a complaint with the Ha Tsuen Rural Committee against members of a Chinese commune from across the bay who had taken over more than one-third of the farm. Tang said it was three months ago when Communists came over and planted their oysters for fattening.
69. *South China Morning Post*, October 15, 1970.
70. *South China Morning Post*, September 9, 1970.

4. THE UNWANTED IN LIMBO

1. Speech by Margaret Ng, "After the Amendment to the Fugitive Ordinance Is Passed, You Are NO Longer Safe!" Rice Post Facebook page, video, April 19, 2019, https://www.facebook.com/RicePost.org/videos/388047708713174/.
2. Deportation of Aliens (Amendment) Bill of 1949, Hansard, 1948: 286, *Hong Kong Hansard (Reports of the Meetings of the Legislative Council)*.
3. Expulsion of Undesirables Ordinance 1949, CO129/624/8 1950 Immigration Control, British National Archives.
4. Deportation of Aliens Ordinance (CH 240), Hong Kong Legislation, https://www.legislation.gov.hk/hk/cap115.
5. Those who stayed in Hong Kong for a lesser period of time were allowed to remain, but only if they did not demonstrate any "undesirable" characteristics.
6. The content of Lam Yin Chang's case comes from the Colonial Records: CO 159 Deportation and Expulsion 1963, British National Archives.
7. CO 159 Deportation and Expulsion 1963.
8. CO 159 Deportation and Expulsion 1963.
9. In the 1940s, the KMT government set up new Triads to help fight the Communists. When the Communists won, the founder, General Kot Siu Wong of the KMT army, fled to Hong Kong with his followers. For details, see James O. Finckenauer and Ko-lin Chin, *Asian Transnational Organized Crime and Its Impact on the U.S.: Developing a Transnational Crime Research Agenda* (Newark, NJ: School of Criminal Justice, Rutgers University, 2004).
10. It was later noted in the police record that Lam had not worn the badges and other medals correctly in the photo.

11. Lam asked a scrap merchant to give him HK$20,000 to be part of a taxi business venture in 1957. Tang Sze Lim, a scrap merchant, stated that he met Lam in 1958 at a party. Lam later showed Tang letters addressed to him signed by General Festing, one of which indicated promised support of Lam's endeavor to obtain fifty Kowloon taxi licenses. Lam said he could obtain army surplus contracts for Tang. He then asked Tang to deposit HK$20,000 or HK$30,000 in his account for the purpose of entertaining high government officials. Tang agreed initially but later decided to withdraw from the scheme because he was informed by another general that Lam was "unreliable."
12. It was noted in the record of the hearing that the monks at the monastery were duly impressed by Lam Yin Chang's claims of rank and influence and accepted a copy of his photograph in military uniform, which they hung in the visitors' hall.
13. In September 1962, Li Hong Sang, a resident of Fanling, planned to sell a piece of land of 300,000 square feet that belonged to him and his siblings at $0.80 per square foot. Lam heard of this and persuaded a wealthy businessman of his acquaintance to give him a HK$25,000 deposit to buy the land at HK$1.10 per square foot for the construction of the "Festing New Village." Lam then approached Li Hong Sang and talked him into selling the land at HK$0.50 per square foot. The deal was canceled when the Li family began to suspect Lam's double-dealing.
14. In November–December 1962, Tung Kei, a resident of Fanling who had known Lam Yin Chang since Lam first came to Hong Kong, asked Lam to obtain on his behalf a contract from the organizers to operate gambling stalls at the New Year's Fair and gave Lam, at his request, HK$5,000 for expense money. Lam never obtained the contract or returned the money.
15. *Kung Sheung Evening News*, August 25, 1963.
16. *Da Gong Bao*, August 25, 1963.
17. *Kung Sheung Evening News*, October 13, 1963.
18. Lam was deported with two homicide suspects, Li Cai Fa and Hong Jiaren. *Da Gong Bao*, October 15, 1963.
19. *Kung Sheung Evening News*, April 13, 1962; *Wah Kiu Yat Pao*, July 28, 1962.
20. The required time to become a permanent resident was later reduced to seven years in the 1970s.
21. *Wah Kiu Yat Pao*, June 3, 1963.
22. *Renmin Ribao*, June 30, 1967.
23. *Renmin Ribao*, June 30, 1967.
24. *Da Gong Bao*, July 16, 1967.
25. The deportation ordinance reads: "The Governor in Council may in his absolute discretion establish camps for the purpose of accommodating undesirables prior to their expulsion from the Colony and of accommodating suspected undesirables."
26. *Wah Kiu Yat Pao*, July 19, 1967.
27. *Kung Sheung Evening News*, September 19, 1967.
28. *Wah Kiu Yat Pao*, September 20, 1967.
29. "Ganggong heibang weihe fandui jiefan dalu? Zhonggong nengfou fangguo zhexie 'maiguo hanjian' ma?" (Why are Hong Kong Communists and Triad members opposed to

being deported back to China? Would the CCP let go of these "traitors"?)], *Wah Kiu Yat Pao*, September 20, 1967.
30. *Da Gong Bao*, March 15, 1968.
31. *Da Gong Bao*, March 15, 1968.
32. *Da Gong Bao*, March 17, 1968.
33. *Kung Sheung Evening News*, March 15, 1968.
34. *Kung Sheung Evening News*, March 16, 1968.
35. *Kung Sheung Evening News*, March 26, 1968.
36. *Kung Sheung Evening News*, March 16, 1968.
37. "Internal political situation in Hong Kong: Disturbances and Communist agitation," February–September 1968, 57, FCO 21/194, Foreign Office, British National Archives.
38. "Internal political situation in Hong Kong."
39. "Shi Hui yu Fu Qi: Xianggang yingtan de geming fufu cengjing yiqi zuolao enai 66 nian" (Shek Hwei and Fu Che: A revolutionary couple in the movie industry; they have gone to jail together and have been together for 66 years), *Kuai Zixun*, April 19, 2020, https://www.360kuai.com/pc/968edb32226db2702.
40. *Renmin Ribao*, August 27, 1965.
41. Associated Press report, April 21, 1975.
42. Associated Press report, April 29, 1975.
43. Agence France-Presse report, April 22, 1975.
44. Agence France-Presse report, June 13, 1975.
45. *South China Morning Post*, June 11, 1975.
46. *South China Morning Post*, June 12, 1975.
47. The PRC welcomed all KMT defectors moving to the mainland. An article published in 1965 in *Renmin Ribao* reported the following about KMT officials working as secret agents who decided to change sides: "All patriotic people, regardless of the level of their employment positions or how many crimes they have committed, and as long as they forsake darkness for light, are all welcomed by the People's government, forgiven for past misdeeds and given reward and property commensurate to their contributions." *Renmin Ribao*, December 17, 1965.
48. The Anticommunist National Salvation Army was established in 1949 with the assistance of the U.S. Central Intelligence Agency to raid the southeastern coast of China. When the Chinese Communist Party established the People's Republic of China on the Chinese mainland in 1949, the ROC government, led by the Kuomintang, relocated to Taiwan, where it maintained jurisdiction over Taiwan, Penghu, Kinmen, Matsu, and numerous other islets.
49. Agence France-Presse report, October 12, 1975.

5. THE THREE ESCAPEES

1. See Madeline Y. Hsu, *The Good Immigrants: How the Yellow Peril Became the Model Minority* (Princeton, NJ: Princeton University Press, 2015), and Laura Madokoro, *Elusive*

Refuge: Chinese Migrants in the Cold War (Cambridge, MA: Harvard University Press, 2016).
2. See chapter 1.
3. Content of this section comes from interviews conducted with Xiao Yujing on May 23 and May 30, 2016, and August 8 and 9, 2018. The last interview was transcribed with the help of Jacob Wang.
4. Class labels had tremendous influence for decades in the lives of the individuals and their families, as opportunities were often determined by one's class label. See Donald J. Treiman and Andrew G. Walder, "The Impact of Class Labels on Life Chances in China," *American Journal of Sociology* 124, no. 4 (January 2019): 1125–63.
5. The Five Black Elements included landlords, rich peasants, counterrevolutionaries, "bad elements," and rightists. However, this is anachronistic, since "rightist" was not a category then. The Five Black Elements was a term invented during the Cultural Revolution. Xiao conflated the two periods and mixed up the bad categories in the two purges.
6. The interviews with Lao Zhengwu were conducted on May 24, 2016, and June 14, 2017, at Jingming Cultural Center in Taoyuan, Taiwan. Sections of the transcript were translated with the help of Jacob Waldor.
7. "The Three Red Banners" was a CCP national policy inaugurated in 1958 to speed up land collectivization and farm production. The Three Red Banners comprise the general line of socialist construction, the Great Leap Forward, and the rural people's communes.
8. Interviews with Ip Cheung were conducted on August 12, 2016, and December 23, 2018, at his home in the New Territories, Hong Kong. Part of the transcript was transcribed with the help of Justin Lee.
9. The Chinese Communist Youth League (CCYL) was known to be a cradle for Chinese leaders, many of whom got their political start there and eventually rose through the CCYL into the high ranks of the party.
10. See chapter 1.
11. Xiao's native language is Hakka, so he did not speak Cantonese even though he came from Guangdong Province. He learned some Cantonese in Hong Kong but was not fluent.
12. The FCRA also functions as an organization that brought relief to escapees from mainland China. See chapter 1 for details.
13. Keelung is a port city in northern Taiwan.
14. Ma Youshi, "Bei'xiaoshi de Taiwan zai ao jiuji tuan" (The Taiwan-sponsored charity organization that was made to disappear: The Macau FCRA), *Medium*, July 18, 2019, https://medium.com/@horsehavehistory.
15. The Hong Kong College of Technology was originally founded as Mongkong Workers' Night School by the Hong Kong Kowloon Labour Education Association in 1957. Chui Shan Lau, "Portrayals of Pro-Beijing Workers' Night Schools in Hong Kong from 1946 to Post-1997," *Educational Research for Policy and Practice* 10, no. 3 (October 2011): 135–47.
16. In April 1950, the Ministry of National Defense set up the Defense Political Department (Guofangbu Zhengzhibu) to deal with issues related to cross-strait relations. In May 1951,

Fu Hsing Kang College was established, which later became the National Defense University War College. Most graduates of the college served in Taiwan's military forces.
17. By the time of the interview, Lao was with his second wife, a woman from Guangdong who was also his student. He was interviewed in the presence of his second wife and did not seem comfortable talking about his first marriage.
18. Throughout the 1970s and 1980s, there was a widespread political and cultural movement across the spheres of literature, language, education, and politics that was critical of the KMT and the ROC government. Some of the regime's opponents were subject to political persecution. It was a widespread movement referred to as Taiwanization or Taiwanese localization (*bentuhua*). It later evolved into the Dangwai movement in politics.
19. The far-right wing of the KMT was not a specific organization. It was label given by mainstream media to some individuals after they publicly attacked Dangwai members. Throughout the interviews, Xiao and Lao would sometimes self-identify as "far-right activists" of the KMT.
20. Xiao and Lao were generally vague about who their supporters within the KMT were. They did not give any names.
21. The words of the Republic of China's national anthem were first delivered as an exhortation at the opening ceremony of the Whampoa Military Academy on June 16, 1924, by Sun Yat-sen. The song was designated as the KMT's party song in 1928. The anthem begins, "Three Principles of the People is the foundation of our party, and through that we have great unity" (*sanminzhuyi, wudangsuzong, yijianminguo, yijindatong*).
22. Xiao Yujing, "Introductory Remarks," *Ji Feng*, July 7, 1979.
23. Pan Rongli, "*Meilidao* chuangkan jiuhui qingzhidanwei liyong *Ji Feng* jituan jiaoxiao" (The inauguration party of *Meilidao*: The intelligence agency deployed *Ji Feng* to make a scene), *Minbao*, August 7, 2018.
24. Lin Zhaozhen, "Chengken miandui lishi kuishou zouchu beiqing" (Sincerely face history and walk out of sadness together), *Zhongguo Shibao* (China Times), December 10, 1998.
25. The "1992 consensus" refers to talks held in Hong Kong that year, when representatives of the mainland-based Association for Relations Across the Taiwan Strait met with delegates of Taiwan's Straits Exchange Foundation to discuss cross-strait commercial relationships. At the end of the meeting, they issued a joint document acknowledging that there is only one Chinese nation comprising all of mainland China, Taiwan, Penghu, and other offshore islands.
26. For Hong Kong's being an "in-between zone," see Elizabeth Sinn, *Pacific Crossing: California Gold, Chinese Migration, and the Making of Hong Kong* (Hong Kong: Hong Kong University Press, 2013).

6. COMMEMORATING THE BIG ESCAPE

1. Rey Chow, *Writing Diaspora: Tactics of Intervention in Contemporary Cultural Studies* (Bloomington: Indiana University Press, 1993). The opening quotation is at 22.

2. The Third Plenum of the Eleventh Congress of the Chinese Communist Party adopted the Open Door Policy, and in July 1979, the Party Central Committee decided that Guangdong and Fujian Provinces should take the lead in conducting economic exchanges with other countries and implementing more flexible policies toward investments. By August 1980, Shenzhen, Zhuhai, and Shantou within Guangdong Province were designated as special economic zones, followed by Xiamen in Fujian Province in October.
3. Hong Kong's former chief executive announced on September 8, 2012, that this plan "will not be implemented until the city has examined its capacity to receive more visitors." See "Leung Chun-ying Gets Shenzhen to Delay Issuing Multi-Entry Permits," *South China Morning Post*, September 8, 2012.
4. National Development and Reform Commission, "The Outline of the Plan for the Reform and Development of the Pearl River Delta (2008–2020)," December 2008.
5. "China to Create Largest Mega City in the World with 42 Million People," *The Telegraph*, January 24, 2011.
6. "Zhongguo Gaotie bantu zaikuangrong: Lanxin, Guiguang, Nanguang Gaotie jinri kaitong" (The further expansion of Chinese high-speed rail), *Zhongguo Xinwen Wang* (China Net), December 26, 2014, http://district.ce.cn/newarea/roll/201412/26/t20141226_4208852.shtml.
7. "HK Developers Retain Appetite for Land Banks," *South China Morning Post*, September 6, 2012.
8. "HK-Zhuhai-Macao Bridge About to Open to Traffic," *People's Daily Online*, June 3, 2016.
9. "World's Longest Cross-Sea Bridge Opens, Integrating China's Greater Bay Area," *Xinhua Net*, October 23, 2018.
10. "'Greater Bay Area' Could Cool Hong Kong's Property Market," *South China Morning Post*, May 8, 2018.
11. The bridge was originally expected to be completed by 2016. The opening was postponed until October 23, 2018.
12. "Greater Bay Area Three-Year Action Plan Released," updated July 8, 2019, *China Daily*, http://govt.chinadaily.com.cn.
13. "The Greater Bay Area and 2047: Death or New Life for Hong Kong?" *China Briefing*, May 23, 2019, https://www.china-briefing.com/news/the-greater-bay-area-2047-death-or-new-life-hong-kong/.
14. William Gibson, *Neuromancer* (New York: Ace Publishing, 1984).
15. For a more detailed critique, see Mike Davies, *Planet of Slums* (New York: Verso, 2017).
16. Dani Cavallaro, *Cyberpunk and Cyberculture: Science Fiction and the Work of William Gibson* (London: Continuum, 2007), 208.
17. "Da Tao Gang" (The great escape to Hong Kong), *Xingqi ri dang'an* (Sunday Report), November 11 and 18, 2012. The title of the episode is taken from a book written by a Chinese journalist in 2011. The book's author was also interviewed in the documentary.
18. Similar narratives exist among overseas Chinese. They too have been encouraged to go back to seek their roots and invest in their homeland.

19. Minnie Wong, Howard Yang, and Vivienne Tsang, "From Local Identity to the Pursuit of Independence: The Changing Face of Hong Kong Localism," *Varsity*, November 11, 2016.
20. See In Media, a website formed by Hong Kong activists, http://www.inmediahk.net/, comments.
21. The Queen's Pier was built in late 1957, following a major wide-ranging land reclamation project on the two sides of Victoria Harbor. The original Star Ferry Pier in Hong Kong's Central District was officially closed down by the government in order to facilitate land reclamation. The move was met with fierce opposition by conservation activists, who continued their campaign to preserve the landmark. The pier was modified and reconstructed a few times in its history. It was the central flashpoint of the Hong Kong 1966 riots. Ferry service from the pier was suspended on November 11, 2006.
22. For details, see Joan Henderson, "Conserving Hong Kong's Heritage: The Case of Queen's Pier," *International Journal of Heritage Studies* 14, no. 6 (2008): 540–54.
23. The Basic Law of Hong Kong guarantees that the city enjoys a high degree of autonomy except in matters of defense and foreign affairs; however, government officials in Hong Kong have not actively used the Basic Law to protect the rights of Hong Kongers.
24. Mainlanders are often referred to as "locusts" (*huangchong*) by the Hong Kong public. See Chin Wan, *Xianggang Chengbang Lun* (The discourse of Hong Kong city-state) (Hong Kong: Tianchuang Chubbanshe, 2011).
25. Laignee Barron, "The Coronavirus Has Brought Out the Ugly Side of Hong Kong's Protest Movement," *Time*, February 19, 2020, https://time.com/5784258/hong-kong-democracy-separatism-coronavirus-covid-19/; Promise Li, "Localism Contradictions in Hong Kong," *Solidarity*, August 1, 2019, https://solidarity-us.org/localisms-contradictions-in-hong-kong/.
26. Daniel Morley, "The USA Is No Friend of Hong Kong," *In Defense of Marxism*, September 19, 2019, https://www.marxist.com/the-usa-is-no-friend-of-hong-kong.htm.
27. "Reping: Shouzhu gen, buwangben, gongtong hehu Xianggang anning" (Editorial: Preserve our roots and don't forget our origin—nurturing the peace in Hong Kong), CCTV News, September 14, 2019, http://m.news.cctv.com/2019/09/14/ARTIFTdf7XCUxfVldccJ5Ue7190914.shtml.
28. Shelly Chan, "The Case for Diaspora: A Temporal Approach to the Chinese Experience," *Journal of Asian Studies* 74, no. 1 (2015): 107.
29. Howard Chiang, "Sinophone," *Transgender Studies Quarterly* 1, nos. 1–2 (2014): 184–87; Shu-mei Shih, "Against Diaspora: The Sinophone as Places of Cultural Production," in *Globalizing Modern Chinese Literature: A Critical Reader on Sinophone and Diasporic Writing*, ed. Jing Tsu and David Wang (Leiden: Brill, 2010), 29–48; Shu-mei Shih, *Visuality and Identity: Sinophone Articulations Across the Pacific* (Berkeley: University of California Press, 2007).
30. Shih, "Against Diaspora," 29–48.
31. Shih, *Visuality and Identity*, 31, 34.
32. Slavoj Žižek, *The Parallax View* (Cambridge, MA: MIT Press, 2006).

33. Laura Hudson, "The Tragedy and Mystery of the 'Best Game of the Decade,'" *Wired*, January 29, 2020, https://www.wired.com/story/kentucky-route-zero-5/.
34. Paul Ricoeur, *Time and Narrative* (Chicago: University of Chicago Press), 173.
35. Louis O. Mink, "Narrative Form as a Cognitive Instrument," in *The Writing of History: Literary Form and Historical Understanding*, ed. Robert H. Canary and Henry Kozicki (Madison: University of Wisconsin Press, 1978), 148.
36. Chan, "Case for Diaspora," 107.
37. "Democracy School Opens in Taiwan," *Taipei Times*, June 1, 2011.
38. "Democracy School Opens in Taiwan," *Taipei Times*, June 1, 2011.
39. Many people argue that Macau already had succumbed to the pressure of the PRC since its handover, or after the 123 Incident in 1967.
40. While this framework is implemented in Hong Kong and Macau through the Basic Law, Taiwan rejected it from the beginning.

EPILOGUE

1. Jessie Lau, "Sentences for 'Hong Kong 12' spark outrage from pro-democrats: The case served as a flashpoint for Hong Kong's beleaguered pro-democracy movement," *The Diplomat*, January 4, 2021, https://thediplomat.com/2021/01/sentences-for-hong-krage-from-pro-democrats/.
2. "Taiwan holding five Hong Kongers picked up at sea," Reuters, September 13, 2020, https://www.reuters.com/article/uk-hongkong-security-taiwan/taiwan-holding-five-hong-kongers-picked-up-at-sea-sources-idUKKBN2650J.
3. Erin Hale, "Taiwan delays scheme to help Hong Kongers over spying fears," *Aljazeera*, May 20, 2022, https://www.aljazeera.com/news/2022/5/20/taiwan-delays-scheme-to-help-hong-kongers-over-spying-fears.
4. "Glory to Hong Kong" has been called the anthem of Hong Kong, and it was sung by the masses in shopping malls and public places during the 2019 protests. The Hong Kong government banned it after the enactment of the National Security Law.

BIBLIOGRAPHY

ARCHIVES AND LIBRARY COLLECTIONS

British National Archives, London, England
Chinese University of Hong Kong Special Collections
Chinese University of Hong Kong Universities Service Centre for China Studies
Claremont Colleges Library Special Collections
Guoshiguan (Academia Historica) Archives, Taipei, Taiwan
Hong Kong Public Records Office
Hong Kong University Special Collections
House of Commons Archives, UK Parliament
Jindaishi Yanjiusuo Dang'an, Institute of Modern History Archives, Academia Sinica, Taipei, Taiwan
Kuomintang (KMT) Dangshi (Party History) archives

BOOKS AND ARTICLES

Ang, Ien. *On Not Speaking Chinese: Living Between Asia and the West*. London: Routledge, 2001.
Au, Ka-lun Allan. *A Tale of Two Cities: A Comparative Study of the 1966 Riots in Macau and the 1967 Riots in Hong Kong and Their Consequences*. Hong Kong: University of Hong Kong, 2001. http://sunzi.lib.hku.hk/hkuto/view/B31952902/ft.pdf.
Barron, Laignee. "The Coronavirus Has Brought Out the Ugly Side of Hong Kong's Protest Movement." *Time*, February 19, 2020. https://time.com/5784258/hong-kong-democracy-separatism-coronavirus-covid-19/.

Bernards, Brian, Shumei Shi, and Chien-hsin Tsai. *Sinophone Studies: A Critical Reader.* New York: Columbia University Press, 2013. http://site.ebrary.com/id/10766050.

Bickers, Robert A., and Ray Yep. *May Days in Hong Kong: Riot and Emergency in 1967.* Hong Kong: Hong Kong University Press, 2009.

Burns, John P. "Immigration from China and the Future of Hong Kong." *Asian Survey* 27, no. 6 (1987): 661–82.

Bush, Richard C. *Uncharted Strait: The Future of China-Taiwan Relations.* Washington, DC: Brookings Institution Press, 2013.

Cao Lin. "Shiyi yaoren zai Xianggang" (Important people of despair in Hong Kong). *Zhongguo Xinwen* 3, no. 8 (1948).

Carroll, John Mark. *A Concise History of Hong Kong.* Lanham, MD: Rowman & Littlefield, 2007.

Cavallaro, Dani. *Cyberpunk and Cyberculture: Science Fiction and the Work of William Gibson.* London: Continuum, 2007.

Cha, Victor D. "Powerplay: Origins of the U.S. Alliance in Asia." *International Security* 34, no. 3 (Winter 2009–10): 158–96.

Chan, Shelly. "The Case for Diaspora: A Temporal Approach to the Chinese Experience." *Journal of Asian Studies* 74, no. 1 (2015): 107–28.

Chang, Sung-sheng Yvonne. *Literary Culture in Taiwan: Martial Law to Market Law.* New York: Columbia University Press, 2004.

Chen, Albert H. Y. "The Development of Immigration Law and Policy: The Hong Kong Experience." *McGill Law Journal*, 33, no. 4 (1988): 631–75.

Chen Bing'an. *Da Tao Gang* (The great escape). Hong Kong: Xianggang Zhonghe Chuban she, 2011.

Chen Bo. *Xianggang Diaojingling Nanmin Ying Diao Cha baogao: Wei Xiang Ying Shijie Nanmin Nian Zuo 1951–1960* (An investigative report of Hong Kong Rennie's Mill 1951–1960). Xianggang: Xianggang da zhuan she hui wen ti yan jiu she, 1961.

Chen, Hongyi, Olaf Unteroberdoerster, and International Monetary Fund, Asia and Pacific Department. *Hong Kong SAR Economic Integration with the Pearl River Delta.* Washington, DC: International Monetary Fund, 2008.

Chen Yun (Chin Wan). *Xianggang Chengbang Lun* (The discourse of the Hong Kong city-state). Hong Kong: Tianchuang Chubbanshe, 2011.

Chen Zhengmao. *Wushi Niandai Xianggang Disan Shili Yundong Shiliao Soumi* (Historical materials on the Third Force in 1950s Hong Kong). Taipei: Xiuwei Zixun, 2011.

Chiang, Howard. "Gender Transformations in Sinophone Taiwan." *Positions* 25, no. 3 (2017): 527–64.

———. "Sinophone." *Transgender Studies Quarterly* 1–2 (2014): 184–87. https://doi.org/10.1215/23289252-2399974.

Chin, Angelina. "Diasporic Memories and Conceptual Geography in Post-Colonial Hong Kong." *Modern Asian Studies* 48, no. 6 (2014): 1566–93.

Chou, Grace Ai-Ling. *Confucianism, Colonialism, and the Cold War: Chinese Cultural Education at Hong Kong's New Asia College, 1949–76.* Leiden: Brill, 2012.

Chow, Rey. *Writing Diaspora: Tactics of Intervention in Contemporary Cultural Studies.* Bloomington: Indiana University Press, 1993.

Cliff, Roger, and David A Shlapak. *U.S.-China Relations After Resolution of Taiwan's Status*. Santa Monica, CA: RAND Corporation, 2007.

Clayton, Cathryn H. *Sovereignty at the Edge: Macau and the Question of Chineseness*. Cambridge, MA: Harvard University Press, 2010.

Corcuff, Stephane. "The Last Days of Rennie's Mill." *China Perspectives* 4 (1996): 42–44.

"Da Tao Gang" (The great escape to Hong Kong). *Xingqi ri dang'an* (Sunday Report), November 11 and 18, 2012.

Davidson, Helen. "Save 12 HK Youths: Campaign to Free Boat Detainees Goes Global." *The Guardian*, October 11, 2020.

Davis, Mike. *Planet of Slums*. New York: Verso, 2017.

Deportation of Aliens Ordinance (CH 240). Hong Kong Legislation. https://www.elegislation.gov.hk/hk/cap115.

Dong Zhilin. *Zhongguo Dalu Yimin Zai Aomen Shehui Zhong Shenfen Rentong Zhi Yanjiu 1949-2013* (A study of identity recognition of Mainland China immigrants in Macau 1949–2013). Taipei: Tangshan chu ban she, 2015.

Feng, Chien-san. "The Dissident Media in Post-War Taiwan: From Political Magazine to 'Underground Radio.'" *Taiwan: A Radical Quarterly in Social Studies* 20 (1995): 177–234.

Finckenauer, James O., and Ko-lin Chin. *Asian Transnational Organized Crime and Its Impact on the U.S.: Developing a Transnational Crime Research Agenda*. Newark, NJ: School of Criminal Justice, Rutgers University, 2004.

Free China Relief Association (FCRA). *FCRA Relief Work in Hongkong and Macao*. Hong Kong: FCRA, 1965.

———. *Dead Bodies, Escape, and Human Rights*. Hong Kong: FCRA, 1971.

———. *Free China Relief Association and the Problem of the Chinese Refugees in Hong Kong*. Taipei, Taiwan: FCRA, 1958.

———. *Relief Activities of the Free China Relief Association in Hongkong since 1950*. Hong Kong: FCRA, 1961.

———. *Resettlement of War Disabled Refugees*. Taipei: FCRA, 1956.

Friedman, Jeremy Scott. *Shadow Cold War: The Sino-Soviet Competition for the Third World*. Chapel Hill: University of North Carolina Press, 2015.

Fung, Edmund S. K. "The Alternative of Loyal Opposition: The Chinese Youth Party and Chinese Democracy, 1937–1949." *Modern China* 17, no. 2 (April 1991): 260–89.

Gibson, William. *Neuromancer*. New York: Ace Publishing, 1984.

Goodstadt, Leo F. *Uneasy Partners: The Conflict Between Public Interest and Private Profit in Hong Kong*. Hong Kong: Hong Kong University Press, 2005.

Hambro, Edvard. "Chinese Refugees in Hong Kong." *The Phylon Quarterly* 18, no. 1 (1957): 69–81.

———. *The Problem of Chinese Refugees in Hong Kong: The Problem of Chinese Refugees in Hong Kong; Report Submitted to the United Nations High Commissioner for Refugees*. London: United Nations Information Center, 1955.

Hamilton, Peter E. *Made in Hong Kong: Transpacific Networks and a New History of Globalization*. New York: Columbia University Press, 2021.

Henderson, Joan. "Conserving Hong Kong's Heritage: The Case of Queen's Pier." *International Journal of Heritage Studies* 14, no. 6 (2008): 540–54.

Ho, Denise. "Oysterman, Refugee, Coast Guard: Hong Kong and China Between the Tides, 1949–1997." Paper presented at the Association of Asian Studies Annual Conference, 2021.

Holborn, Louise W., Philip Chartrand, and Rita Chartrand. *Refugees, a Problem of Our Time: The Work of the United Nations High Commissioner for Refugees, 1951–1972*. Metuchen, NJ: Scarecrow Press, 1975.

Hong Kong Government Annual Report 1962. Hong Kong: Hong Kong Government Publisher, 1963.

Hong Kong Hansard (Reports of the Meetings of the Legislative Council) 1950–1980. Hong Kong: Hong Kong Government Publisher, 1981.

Hong Kong Refugees Survey Mission, Edvard Isak Hambro, and Office of the United Nations High Commissioner for Refugees. *The Problem of Chinese Refugees in Hong Kong: Report Submitted to the United Nations High Commissioner for Refugees*. Leyden: A. W. Sijthoff, 1955.

Hsu, Madeline Y. "Aid Refugee Chinese Intellectuals, Inc. and the Political Uses of Humanitarian Relief, 1952–1962." *Journal of Chinese Overseas* 10, no. 2 (2014): 137–64.

———. *The Good Immigrants: How the Yellow Peril Became the Model Minority*. Princeton, NJ: Princeton University Press, 2015.

Hu Chunhui. *Xianggang Diaojingling ying de Dansheng yu xiaoshi: Zhang Hansong de fangtan lu* (The birth and disappearance of Hong Kong Rennie's Mill Camp: Interviews with Zhang Hangsong and others). Taipei: Guoshiguan 1997.

Hu Guang. "Guanyu ge dangpai zai Xianggang douzheng de xiangxi baodao" (A detailed report on the different political parties and factions in Hong Kong). *Shi Yu Wen* 3, no. 2 (1948).

Huang Ko-wu (Kewu). "Gu Mengyu yu disanshili de shengshuai" (Gu Mengyu and the rise and fall of the Third Force). *Ershiyi Shiji* (Twenty-first century) 162 (August 2017).

Hudson, Laura. "The Tragedy and Mystery of the 'Best Game of the Decade.'" *Wired*, January 29, 2020. https://www.wired.com/story/kentucky-route-zero-5/.

Jeans, Roger B. *The CIA and Third Force Movements in China During the Early Cold War: The Great American Dream*. Lanham, MD: Lexington 2018.

———. *Democracy and Socialism in Republican China: The Politics of Zhang Junmai (Carsun Chang), 1906–1941*. Lanham, MD: Rowman & Littlefield, 1997.

———. "Opposition Party Intellectuals in the 1920s and 1930s." In *Roads Not Taken: The Struggle of Opposition Parties in Twentieth-Century China*, ed. Roger B. Jeans, 331–38. Boulder, CO: Westview Press, 1992.

———, ed. *Roads Not Taken: The Struggle of Opposition Parties in Twentieth-Century China*. Boulder, CO: Westview Press, 1992.

Ku, Agnes S. "Immigration Policies, Discourses, and the Politics of Local Belonging in Hong Kong (1950–1980)." *Modern China* 30, no. 3 (2004): 326–60.

Lam, Agnes I. F, and Cathryn H. Clayton. "One, Two, Three: Evaluating 'Macau's Cultural Revolution.'" *Modern China Studies* 23, no. 2 (2016): 163–86.

Lam, Wai-man. *Understanding the Political Culture of Hong Kong: The Paradox of Activism and Depoliticization: The Paradox of Activism and Depoliticization*. New York: Routledge, 2004.

Lan, On-wai, Kenneth. "Rennie's Mill: The Origin and Evolution of a Special Enclave in Hong Kong." Hong Kong: University of Hong Kong, 2006. http://sunzi.lib.hku.hk/hkuto/view/B36777766/ft.pdf.

Lau, Chui Shan. "Portrayals of Pro-Beijing Workers' Night Schools in Hong Kong from 1946 to Post-1997." *Educational Research for Policy and Practice* 10, no. 3 (October 2011): 135–47.

Leung, Ping-kwan. "Writing Across Borders: Hong Kong's 1950s and the Present." In *Diasporic Histories: Cultural Archives of Chinese Transnationalism*, ed. Andrea Riemenschnitter and Deborah L. Madsen, 23–42. Hong Kong: Hong Kong University Press, 2009.

Li, Promise. "Localism Contradictions in Hong Kong." *Solidarity*, August 1, 2019. https://solidarity-us.org/localisms-contradictions-in-hong-kong/.

Liang Jialin. *Fuyin yu Mianbao: Jidujiao zai wushi niandai de Diaojingling* (Gospel and bread: Christianity at the 1950s Rennie's Mill). Hong Kong: Jiandao Shenxueyuan, 2000.

Lin Chih-yen. *Ziyou de Daijia: Zhonghua Minguo yu Xianggang Tiaojingling* (The price of "freedom": The Republic of China and the Chinese refugees at Rennie's Mill Camp in Hong Kong, 1950–1961). Taipei: Guoshiguan, 2011.

Liu Yizhang. "Xuan jiaoshi zai Diaojingling nanminying de yiliao fuwu" (The medical services of the missionaries in Rennie's Mill). In *Xianggang Shehui Yu Wenhua Shi Lunji* (An anthology of Hong Kong social and cultural history), ed. Liu Yizhang and Huang Wenjiang, 113–29. Hong Kong: Hong Kong Chinese University Press, 2002.

"Localism's Contradictions in Hong Kong." *New Politics*, June 29, 2019. https://newpol.org/localisms-contradictions-in-hong-kong/.

Ma Youshi. "Bei'xiaoshi de Taiwan zai ao jiuji tuan" (The Taiwan-sponsored charity organization that was made to disappear: The Macau FCRA). *Medium*, July 18, 2019. https://medium.com/@horsehavehistory.

Madokoro, Laura. "Borders Transformed : Sovereign Concerns, Population Movements and the Making of Territorial Frontiers in Hong Kong, 1949–1967." *Journal of Refugee Studies* 25, no. 3 (2012): 407–27.

——. *Elusive Refuge: Chinese Migrants in the Cold War*. Cambridge, MA: Harvard University Press, 2016.

Mark, Chi-Kwan. *China and the World since 1945: An International History*. New York: Routledge, 2012.

——. *Hong Kong and the Cold War: Anglo-American Relations 1949–1957*. Oxford: Clarendon: 2004.

——. "The 'Problem of People': British Colonials, Cold War Powers, and the Chinese Refugees in Hong Kong, 1949–62." *Modern Asian Studies* 41, no. 6 (2007).

Meyskens, Covell F. *Mao's Third Front: The Militarization of Cold War China*. Cambridge: Cambridge University Press, 2020.

Mink, Louis O. "Narrative Form as a Cognitive Instrument." In *The Writing of History: Literary Form and Historical Understanding*, ed. Robert H. Canary and Henry Kozicki, 129–50. Madison: University of Wisconsin Press, 1978.

Mizuoka, Fujio. "British Colonialism and 'Illegal' Immigration from Mainland China to Hong Kong." In *Power Relations, Situated Practices, and the Politics of the Commons: Japanese Contributions to the History of Geographical Thought (11)*, ed. Akio Onjo, 33–66. Fukuoka: Institute of Geography, Kyushu University, 2017.

Mok, Florence. "Chinese Illicit Immigration into Colonial Hong Kong, c. 1970–1980." *Journal of Imperial and Commonwealth History* 49, no. 2 (2021): 339–67.

Morley, Daniel. "The USA Is No Friend of Hong Kong." *In Defence of Marxism*. https://www.marxist.com/the-usa-is-no-friend-of-hong-kong.htm.

National Development and Reform Commission. "The Outline of the Plan for the Reform and Development of the Pearl River Delta (2008–2020)." December 2008.

Oyen, Meredith. *The Diplomacy of Migration: Transnational Lives and the Making of U.S.-Chinese Relations in the Cold War*. Ithaca, NY: Cornell University Press, 2015.

——. "Thunder without Rain:" ARCI, the Far East Refugee Program, and the U.S. Response to Hong Kong Refugees." *Journal of Cold War Studies* 16, no. 4 (2014): 189–221.

Peterson, Glen. "Crisis and Opportunity." In *Hong Kong in the Cold War*, ed. Priscilla Mary Roberts and John M. Carroll, 141–59. Hong Kong: HKU Press, 2016.

——. *Overseas Chinese in the People's Republic of China*. New York: Routledge, 2014.

——. "To Be or Not to Be a Refugee: The International Politics of the Hong Kong Refugee Crisis, 1949–55." *The Journal of Imperial and Commonwealth History* 36, no. 2 (2008): 171–95.

Ricoeur, Paul. *Time and Narrative*. Chicago: University of Chicago Press, 1984.

Safran, William. "Diasporas in Modern Societies: Myths of Homeland and Return." *Diaspora* 1, no. 1 (1991): 83–99.

Shih, Shumei. "Against Diaspora: The Sinophone as Places of Cultural Production." In *Globalizing Modern Chinese Literature: A Critical Reader on Sinophone and Diasporic Writing*, ed. Jing Tsu and David Wang, 29–48. Leiden: Brill, 2010.

——. "The Concept of the Sinophone." *PMLA* 126, no. 3 (2011): 709–18.

——. *Visuality and Identity: Sinophone Articulations Across the Pacific*. Berkeley: University of California Press, 2007.

Sing, Ming. *Hong Kong's Tortuous Democratization: A Comparative Analysis*. London: Routledge Curzon, 2004.

Sinn, Elizabeth. *Pacific Crossing: California Gold, Chinese Migration, and the Making of Hong Kong*. Hong Kong: Hong Kong University Press, 2013.

Smart, Alan. *The Shek Kip Mei Myth: Squatters, Fires and Colonial Rule in Hong Kong, 1950–1963*. Hong Kong: Hong Kong University Press, 2006.

Song, Yongyi. "Chronology of Mass Killings During the Chinese Cultural Revolution (1966–1976)." Online Encyclopedia of Mass Violence. https://www.sciences-po.fr/mass-violence-war-massacre-resistance/en/document/chronology-mass-killings-during-chinese-cultural-revolution-1966-1976.html.

Su, Yang. *Collective Killings in Rural China During the Cultural Revolution*. New York: Cambridge University Press, 2011.

Tölöyan, Khachig. "Rethinking Diaspora(s): Stateless Power in the Transnational Moment." *Diaspora* 5, no. 1 (1996): 3–36.

Treiman, Donald J., and Andrew G. Walder. "The Impact of Class Labels on Life Chances in China." *American Journal of Sociology* 124, no. 4 (January 1, 2019): 1125–63.

Tucker, Nancy Bernkopf. *Security Challenges for the United States, China, and Taiwan at the Dawn of the New Millennium*. Alexandria, VA: CNA Corp., 2000.

——. *Strait Talk: United States-Taiwan Relations and the Crisis with China*. Cambridge, MA: Harvard University Press, 2011.

——. *Taiwan, Hong Kong, and the United States, 1945–1992: Uncertain Friendships*. New York: Twayne, 1994.

Wan Lijuan. "Yijiu Wuning Niandai de Zhongguo Disan Shili Yundong" (The Third Force movement in 1950s China). PhD dissertation, Taiwan National Chengchi University, 2001. https://ndltd.ncl.edu.tw/cgi-bin/gs32/gsweb.cgi/ccd=kx4ULn/record?r1=1&h1=1.

Wang, Gungwu, and Annette Shun Wah. *Imagining the Chinese Diaspora: Two Australian Perspectives*. Canberra: Centre for the Study of the Chinese Diaspora, Australian National University, 1999.

Wang Zhun. "Minguo liushisi nian Chenggong Ling dazhaun jixun ban shengya huiyi" (Recollection of the training course for higher education students at Chenggong Ling in the 64th year of the Republic). July 5, 2015. http://www.4thgrader.net/vault/files/MemoryOfChengKungRidgeIn1975.doc.

Watson, James L. 2004. "Living Ghosts: Long-Haired Destitutes in Colonial Hong Kong." In *Village Life in Hong Kong: Politics, Gender, and Ritual in the New Territories*, ed. James L. Watson and Rubie S. Watson, 453–69. Hong Kong: The Chinese Univ. Press, 2004.

Wong, Minnie, Howard Yang, and Vivienne Tsang. "From Local Identity to the Pursuit of Independence: The Changing Face of Hong Kong Localism." *Varsity*, November 11, 2016.

Wong, Siu-lun. *Emigrant Entrepreneurs: Shanghai Industrialists in Hong Kong*. Hong Kong: Oxford University Press, 1988.

Wu, Ruoyu. "Wenge Guangxi Da Tu Sha" (The Guangxi Massacre during the Cultural Revolution). *Beijing Spring* 123 (2003): 46–57.

Wu Yue. *Taowang Chao Laitai Yibao Anzhi Gongzuo* (The work of settling escapees who moved to Taiwan from Hong Kong). Hong Kong: Zhongguo Dalu Zaibbao Jiuji zonghui, 1964.

Yang, Dominic Meng-Hsuan. *The Great Exodus from China: Trauma, Memory, and Identity in Modern Taiwan*. New York: Cambridge University Press, 2021.

———. "Humanitarian Assistance and Propaganda War: Repatriation and Relief of the Nationalist Refugees in Hong Kong's Rennie's Mill Camp, 1950–1955." *Journal of Chinese Overseas* 10, no. 2 (2014): 165–96.

———. "Tiaojingling: Xianggang 'Xiao Taiwan' de qiyuan yu bianqian, 1950s–1970s" (Rennie's Mill: Origin and transformation of "Little Taiwan" in Hong Kong, 1950s–1970s). *Taiwan Historical Research* 18, no.1 (March 1, 2011): 133–83.

Yang, Tianshi. "The Third Force in Hong Kong and North America During the 1950s." In *Roads Not Taken: The Struggle of Opposition Parties in Twentieth-Century China*, ed Roger B. Jeans, 269–74. Boulder, CO: Westview Press, 1992.

Yep, Ray. *May Days in Hong Kong*. Hong Kong: Hong Kong University Press, 2010.

Yu, Wai-lu, Alan. "The Clearance of Rennie's Mill Squatter Area." MA thesis, University of Leicester, 1997.

Yung, Kenneth Kai-chung. *Chinese Émigré Intellectuals and Their Quest for Liberal Values in the Cold War, 1949–1969*. Leiden: Brill, 2021.

Zheng Yi. *Hong Se Ji Nian Bei* (The Red Monument). Taipei: Hua shi wen hua gongshi, 1993.

Žižek, Slavoj. *The Parallax View*. Cambridge, MA: MIT Press, 2006.

INDEX

abduction. *See* kidnapping
Agrarian Reform Law. *See* Land Reform
Aid Refugee Chinese Intellectuals (ARCI), 21, 32–34, 38, 40, 46; formation, 32; goals, 32–33; resettlement, 33
Ang, Ien, 8–9
anticommunist (or anti-CCP): activities, 75, 82, 123; background, 36, 56; discourse(s), 22, 100; fighters (*yishi*), 17, 19, 46, 171, 194, 197–202, 209; force(s), 9, 58, 68, 247; ideologies, 26; insurgency, 12; media, 101; movement, 61, 65, 71, 82, 87, 92, 95, 209, 273n75; propaganda, 9, 33, 35, 42, 131; qualities, 44; refugees, 28, 33; rhetoric, 31, sentiments, 11–12, 23, 34–35, 58, 98, 169, 192, 194, 216
anti-Dangwai movement, 208
Anti-Extradition Bill protests (2019), 16–17, 24, 97–98, 134, 218, 221, 245, 246, 253, 255, 284n4
anti-high-speed-rail movement, 243
anti-colonialism, 148, 152–54
anti-independent Taiwan (anti-*Taidu*), 58, 80, 82, 202, 204–5, 208–9, 211
anti-KMT, 58

anti-Mao faction, 110, 115
Anti-Rightist campaign, 29, 79–80, 85, 88, 98, 171, 176, 272n49
Application Guidelines for the Refugees of Rennie's Mill to Enter Taiwan (*Bianli Xianggang Diaojingling Nanbao Rujing Banfa*), 42
April 4 policy, 19, 28, 44–48, 185, 187, 192, 197, 224, 294
Article 23 of the Hong Kong Basic Law, 191, 242
Association for the Study of Democratic Socialism in Hong Kong, 92

Bamboo Curtain, 3, 12, 76, 100, 136
Bao'an County, 45
baodao, 74
Basic Law of Hong Kong. *See* Hong Kong, Basic Law
Bauhinia Foundation Research Centre (Hong Kong), 230
Beijing–Hong Kong railway, 21
belonging: conflicted, 6, 26, 71, 96, 167, 252; local, 12, 19, 53, 55, 59, 96, 269n95, 269n98; national, 8, 236

Bianli Xianggang Diaojingling nanbao rujing banfa. See Application Guidelines for the Refugees of Rennie's Mill to Enter Taiwan
Black Element, 172, 280n5
Bohai Economic Rim, 229
border(s): crossing, 5, 14–16, 23–25, 29–30, 46, 96, 98–99, 124, 153–54, 183, 230, 236–40; definitions, 14–17; enforcement, 5, 25, 238; Macau–Gongbei, 181; policies, 23–24, 27, 45–46, 48, 98, 169, 180–81; of People's Republic of China (PRC), 6–7, 9–10, 14, 96, 99, 115; provincial, 265nn11–12; sea, 8, 16, 103, 115, 121, 126, 130, 146, 277n68; Shenzhen–Hong Kong, 1, 14–15, 21, 23, 28, 98, 116, 158, 164, 182, 227, 229–30, 240
Britain. See United Kingdom
Burgess, Claude Bramall, 52

Cai Xingsan (Tsai Hsin-san), 163
Cao Lin, 4, 263n2
Carroll, John, 12, 264n10
Causeway Bay Bookstore, 16
Cavallaro, Dani, 235, 282n16
CCP. See Chinese Communist Party
Central Harborfront Reclamation Project (Hong Kong), 243
Central Intelligence Agency (CIA), 13, 46, 184, 272n43, 279n48
Chan, Shelly, 9, 247, 249, 283n28
Changcheng Studio, 147
Chan Yan Lam, 97
Chen Cheng, 47
Chen Shizhang (Chen Shih-chang), 163
Chen Shui-bien, 202
Chen Zhengmao, 58, 95–96, 270n2, 270nn10–11, 270n15, 270n17–18, 272n41
Cheung Yu Tak, 237,
Chiang Ching-kuo, 19, 193–94, 197, 199, 201–2, 209–11, 213, 223
Chiang Kai-shek, 33, 61, 64, 85, 87, 160, 165, 171, 215–16; alliance with the United States, 126, 160; criticism(s) of, 12, 65, 70, 85, 86

China: as homeland, 8–10, 61, 169; history before 1949, 6–8; mainland, 4–5, 9, 12, 15; political imaginary of, 6, 209. See also Chinese Civil War; Greater China; People's Republic of China; Republic of China
China Democratic League, 62–63
China Democratic Party, 86
China Democratic Socialist Party, 61–62, 64, 68
China Travel Services, 159
China Youth National Salvation Corps, 193–94, 279n48
China Youth Party, 61–62, 64–65, 68, 86
Chinese Civil War, 1, 3, 7, 10, 14–15, 19, 22, 39, 59, 75, 85, 159, 163, 172, 186, 225, 247, 270n16
Chinese Communist Party (CCP): and Cold War, 10–13, 58; criticisms of, 11, 31, 79–81, 88–91, 94, 104–5, 118, 180, 221, 224; and dead bodies, 111, 115; and Greater China, 8; and kidnapping, 123–24, 127, 131; and Macau, 123; and 1967 riots, 154–56; and POWs, 19, 159–64, 279n47; propaganda, 13, 27, 115, 187; and Taiwan, 81; taking over China, 23, 28, 60, 63, 76, 168; treatment of escapees, 12, 27, 38, 101. See also anticommunist; border(s), policies; China; Chinese Civil War; People's Republic of China
Chinese diaspora. See diaspora
Chinese People's Political Consultative Conference, 163
Chinese Republic (Zhonghua Minguo), 4, 204
Chin Wan (Chen Yun), 244, 283n24. See also Hong Kong, City-State Autonomy Movement
Chow, Rey: *Writing Diaspora*, 226, 281n1
Chuk Lam Monastery, 139, 278n12
Clayton, Cathryn, 263n3, 264n2
Cold War, 5–8, 10–14, 19, 22, 26, 31, 38, 54, 56, 58, 71, 77, 83, 87, 95–96, 100, 111, 133–34, 164, 167, 225, 247
colonialism, 6, 27; British (Hong Kong), 6–7, 9, 13, 27, 148, 153–54, 226; Japanese (Taiwan), 7; influence, 7; Portuguese (Macau), 7, 9, 27

Communist Youth League, 175, 178
Convention of Peking (second) (1898), 6
counterrevolutionary, 27, 35, 237
cross-strait relations, 7, 196, 213, 219, 255, 280n16, 281n25
Cultural China, 9
Cultural Revolution, 11, 13, 18, 55, 99–10, 105–15, 118, 121, 124, 130–31, 147, 152, 158, 264n2, 269n103, 280n5

Da Dao, 64, 65
Da Tao Gang (book), 265n15
"Da Tao Gang" (television program), 236–239, 240
Dabu, 172, 173
Daya Bay, 101
Deep Bay (Hong Kong), 127–29, 277n68
democracy, 59–62, 64–66, 68, 70–71, 76, 80, 84, 87, 92–93, 202, 205, 208, 218–19, 223, 241, 251, 256. *See also* window of democracy; democratization
democratic China, 58, 219
Democratic China Forum, 65
Democratic Progressive Party (DPP), 169, 202
democratization: of China, 68, 76, 77, 92, 219, 227, 241–42, 250–51; of Hong Kong, 59, 242, 245, 270n2; of Kuomintang, 61, 86–87; of Taiwan, 254–55
Deng Xiaoping, 55, 169, 190–92, 198, 238–40; opinions about, 215–17, 220, 222
deportation, 1, 5, 11, 14, 17, 54, 134, 140–47, 149–59, 165–66; ordinances, 133–36, 142, 277nn2–5, 278n25
Diaojingling (Tiaojingling). *See* Rennie's Mill Refugee Camp
diaspora: Chinese, 220, 247–252, 263n5; concept of, 9, 263nn6–7
diasporic consciousness, 60, 71, 74, 96, 100, 241
Displaced Persons Act (1948), 35
Dongfeng faction (*Dongfeng pai*), 110
Dongguang County, 45, 108, 181, 228, 230–31
Duan Kewen (Tuan Ke-wen), 161, 163
Duli Luntan (Independent Forum), 65, 73

Erh Tan, 163
exiled Chinese, 3, 12, 17, 71, 96, 137, 257, 264n2; intellectuals, 9, 24, 32–33, 54, 60–61, 63, 80; Kuomintang government, 9; student(s), 88–90, 201; youth, 75, 94–95
Extradition Bill (2019), 134. *See also* Anti-Extradition Bill Protest
Exodus of 1962. *See* Great Exodus of 1962

factional struggles (*wudou*), 99, 106, 110–12. *See also* anti-Mao faction
fangong. *See* anticommunist
fangong yishi. *See* anticommunist, fighters
Fanling, 140–42, 144, 185, 240, 278nn13–14; Rural Committee, 140
Fang Zhi (Fang Chih), 48
FCRA. *See* Free China Relief Association
Festing, Francis: the story of, 138–39, 144, 278n11
fishermen, 98–99, 100–101, 103, 105, 107–8, 119–29, 131
floating corpses (*fushi*), 11, 18, 97–112, 115, 117–121, 131, 164
Ford Foundation, 29, 78
Foshan, 231, 234
Free China, 10, 28, 87, 96, 121, 133, 150, 197. *See also* Free World
Free China Relief Association (FCRA), 27–28, 43–48, 72, 101, 106, 116, 160, 183–84, 189, 193, 195, 197, 200–201, 280n12
Freedom Front. *See Ziyou Zhenxian*
Freedom Press, 66
Free World, 3, 8, 10, 12, 22, 56, 71, 82, 89–90, 119, 133, 166, 223, 252. *See also* Free China
Frontier Closed Area (FCA), 24
Fu Che, 136, 147–58, 165–66
Fujian, 163, 173–75, 282n2
fushi. *See* floating corpses

Geneva, Switzerland. *See* United Nations High Commissioner for Refugees
Gibson, William: *Neuromancer*, 235
"Glory to Hong Kong," 256, 284n4

Grantham, Alexander, 39–40, 50
Greater Bay Area. *See* Guangdong–Hong Kong–Macau Greater Bay Area
Greater China, 8, 218, 227, 250, 252
Great Exodus of 1962, 44–6, 53, 91, 107
Great Famine, 15, 176, 179, 180, 222
Great Freedom and Democracy Alliance, 64
Great Leap Forward, 11, 45, 168, 171, 175, 178, 180, 217, 224, 236, 239, 280n7
Green Gang, 140, 144
Guancheng, 181
Guangdong–Hong Kong–Macau Greater Bay Area, 230, 233–34
Guangdong Province, 1, 13, 23, 45, 100, 105–6, 108, 110–11, 114–15, 137, 212, 222, 229–234, 239, 243, 282n2; migration from, 23, 46, 49, 55, 169; provincial government, 169. *See also* Pearl Delta Region
Guangxi, 100, 105–6, 110
Guangzhou, 21–22, 35, 39, 46, 64, 68, 90, 108, 110, 114, 138, 148, 176–77, 179, 181, 185, 190, 230–32, 234, 243
gudao, 74–75, 96
Gurkha soldiers, 2, 181
Gu Zhenggang, 91, 184, 195

Hakka: ethnic conflict in Fanling, 144; language, 280n11; residents in Fanling district, 140, 182
Hambro, Edvard, 31; mission, 29–30; *Problems of the Chinese Refugees in Hong Kong*, 14–15
Hau Hoi Wan, 124, 126, 127
Henry, James McClure, 64
high-speed rail, 231–32, 234, 243
Ho, Albert, 251
home. *See* belonging
Hong Kong: Basic Law of, 17, 191, 241, 245, 283n23, 284n40; chief executive of, 245, 282n3; City-State Autonomy Movement, 244; and Cold War, 12–14, 134, 247, 264nn10–11; collective memories of, 246; Democratic Party, 251; emigration from, 253–56; and migrants from China, 1, 4, 15, 24–26, 28–29, 45–56, 69–70, 72, 87–91; and Greater China, 252; government, 14–16, 28–29, 38–40, 52, 72, 244; identity, 13–14, 147, 247, 252; identity card, 15, 54–56; Immigration Office, 24; Legislative Council, 92, 125, 243, 245; as "in-between" place, 223; National Security Law, 17; permanent residency, 54–55; political neutrality, 4, 33, 39, 78, 135, 137, 144, 165, 221; restrictions on political organizations, 60; Secratariat for Chinese Affairs, 140; Social Welfare Office, 40–41, 43; Special Branch, 156–57; and Southern Periphery, 6–8; and Third Force, 74–77, 91–93, 96. *See also* immigration policies; population of Hong Kong
Hong Kong Alliance in Support of Patriotic Democratic Movements in China, 242
Hong Kong and Kowloon Committee for Anti-Colonial Hong Kong Persecution Struggle, 148
Hong Kong Nationalism, 244
Hong Kong–Shenzhen metropolis, 230
Hong Kong–Zhuhai–Macau Bridge, 233
Hsu, Madeline, 34–35
Hu Guang, 3
Hu Yue, 88–90, 94
Huang Yuren, 78, 82, 92, 274n88
Hundred Flowers Campaign, 79, 176
Hung Fat Shan Chung Yee Tong, 138

illegal migrants in Hong Kong, 49, 52–56, 125, 229
immigration (and refugee) policies: of Hong Kong, 1, 15, 17, 22–24, 35, 39, 53–57, 133–34, 145–46, 165; of Republic of China (Taiwan), 32, 34, 38–39, 41–44, 56, 91, 133, 145, 165; touch-base policy of Hong Kong (1974), 15, 32, 54–56; of United States, 32–38. *See also* Displaced Persons Act of 1948; Refugee Act of 1953
Independent China Movement, 65
Independent Commission Against Corruption, 140

Independent Forum. See Duli Luntan
Individual Visit Scheme, 242
international waters (*gonghai*), 102
Ip Cheung, 19, 168–69, 171–92, 218, 222–23, 225, 241

Japan: occupation of Hong Kong, 22–23; war with China, 22, 59, 171–72, 178. *See also* colonialism; World War II
Jessup, Phillip, 68
Jiangmen, 231, 234
Ji Feng, 205–6, 208, 210, 223
Jubilee Fort, 40,
Judd, Walter, 32
June 4 massacre. *See* Tiananmen Square crackdown
Junk Bay, 40, 97

Kaiping, 175, 212
Kentucky Route Zero (game), 249
kidnapping(s), 11, 13, 16–18, 99, 101, 123–127, 129–31
KMT. *See* Kuomintang
Kong Wing Wah, 140
Korean War, 11, 65, 197, 201
Kuomintang (KMT): affiliates, 57, 137, 139–40, 144; Central Reform Committee, 43; and China Democratic League, 63; and China Youth Party, 62; and Chinese Civil War, 172; and Cold War, 10–13, 58; criticisms of, 42–43, 63–64, 74–75, 77, 81, 84, 95, 186; far-right faction, 203–6, 209, 281n18; loyalists, 9–10, 54; loyalty to, 40, 44, 48, 72, 145, 161, 164, 166, 193, 197, 204, 208–10, 223; military, 39–40, 49, 61, 84–87, 138, 161, 178, 183, 194; network in Hong Kong, 136, 138, 140, 144–45, 147, 149; occupying Taiwan, 6; prisoners of war (POWs), 159–161, 163–164, 255; propaganda, 11, 115, 119, 133, 162, 165, 224; and refugees in Hong Kong, 27, 38–44; and Third Force, 70, 77–91, 96. *See also* democratization, of Kuomintang; Republic of China

Kweiyang Ferry, 40, 267n60
Kwun Tong, 244

Lam, Carrie, 134, 221
Lam Yin Chang, 18, 136–47, 149, 165, 277nn6–10, 278nn11–19
landlords (class label), 35–36, 172–75, 178–79, 184, 223, 280n5
Land Reform (China), 79, 168, 171–75, 177–78, 185, 222, 224
Lantau Island (Hong Kong), 41, 104, 107, 268n77
Lao Zhengwu, 175–88, 195–97, 200–213, 215–20, 222–25
Lau Fau Shan, 16, 18, 98, 100, 107–8, 118, 122–30
League of Democratic Political Groups. *See* China Democratic League
Lee Bo, 16. *See also* Causeway Bay Bookstore
Legislative Council (Hong Kong). *See* Hong Kong, Legislative Council
Legislative Yuan (Taiwan). *See* Taiwan, Legislative Yuan
Lei Zhen (Lei Chen), 42, 63, 70, 86–87
Leng Jingji, 78
Leung, Edward, 245
Leung Chun-ying, 221, 244
Lianhe Bao (newspaper), 48
Lianhe Pinglun (United Voice Weekly), 65, 67, 77–95
"Liberate Hong Kong, Revolution of Our Time" (*Guong-fook Heung-gong, Shidoi gak-ming /Guangfu Xianggang, Shidaigeming*), 245, 256
Li Huang, 61, 63, 64, 78, 85, 87, 91
Li Jinye, 86
Li Keqiang, 233
Li Minde, 72, 271n30
Lin, Chih-Yen: *The Price of Freedom*, 44, 266n3
Lion Rock (Mountain), 1, 3, 188; "At the foot of", 256; myth, 5; narrative, 5; Spirit, 1
Liu Yulue, 78, 84, 94–95

Li Yansheng, 85–86
Li Zongren, 64, 68
localist movement(s), 244, 246
lonely island. *See gudao*
Long Qi, 208
Lo Wu. *See* border; Shenzhen
Lo Wu Bridge, 23, 40, 150–57, 158
Luo Yongyang, 78

Macau: and escapees, 10, 16, 46, 98–99, 102, 104, 177, 180, 229, 254, 264n2; and deportation, 136, 143, 146, 149–50, 165–66; and Greater Bay Area, 233–36; and Greater China, 222, 250–52; immigration policies, 264n2; as "in-between" place, 223; kidnapping, 123–24, 131, 150; Lao Zhengwu in, 185–88, 201; Marine and Water Bureau, 103; 123 incident (1966), 150; and Pearl River Delta, 228–31; reports of dead bodies, 99, 102, 105, 107–8, 111, 113, 119, 131; and Southern Periphery, 6, 7; and Taiwan, 255
Madokoro, Laura, 38
mainland China. *See* People's Republic of China
mainland transit pass, 25, 103
Mandarina Crown Hotel (Zhongtai Binguan) Incident, 206–7, 210
Mao Zedong: condemnations of, 105, 112, 174, 176, 205–16, 223; death, 217; influence in Hong Kong, 148; Little Red Book, 118, 125, 129, 148–49; mentioning of, 112, 118, 151, 153–54, 176, 196, 198, 215–17, 239. *See also* Cultural Revolution; Land Reform
Mark, Chi-Kwan, 12, 52
mass killing during Cultural Revolution, 13, 105–6
Matsu (Dongyin), 163, 279n48
Ma Xiangming, 231
middle peasants (class label), 110, 178
migration studies, 8–9. *See also* Sinophone studies; diaspora
Mink, Louis, 249
missionary school(s), 35–36

Mong Kok, 245; Kaifong Association, 140
Moral and National Education, 227
Mount Davis, 40, 49
Moy, Ernest, 32, 36

Na Lan, 80
nanbao, 27–28, 42–43, 47, 201. *See also zainan tongbao/zaibao*.
nanshu. See nanbao; zainan tongbao/zaibao
Nan Huaijin, 211
National Chengchi University, 47, 193–96
National Chenggong University, 47
National Overseas Student Preparatory School (National Overseas Secondary School), 47, 193, 195, 209
Nationalist Party. *See* Kuomintang
national reunification, 8, 58, 68, 79, 83–86, 88, 92, 94–95, 192, 213, 215, 218, 224, 255
National Security Law (Hong Kong). *See* Hong Kong, National Security Law
National Youth Commission, 195–96
New Power Party, 255
New Territories, 24–25, 46, 54–55, 107, 128–29, 139–41, 181, 183, 185, 232. *See also* Fanling
Ng, Margaret, 134
1967 riots, 148–49, 154, 158, 165–66

One Country, Two Systems, 191, 220–21, 241–42, 252
Opium War(s), 6, 8
Ouyang Fang, 82
overseas resettlements of refugees, 32–38
Overseas Chinese Preparation School. *See* National Overseas Student Preparatory School
overseas Chinese intellectuals and students, 62, 79, 81–83
oystermen/oyster farmers, 98–101, 122–23, 127–30

Pak Nai, 118
parallax theory, 248–49

Pearl River (Zhujiang), 99, 105, 107–8, 111, 120; estuary, 110; Delta, 177, 227–36, 239, 242
people's commune (*renmin gongshe*), 101, 125, 176, 275n3, 280n7
People's Political Council, 62
People's Republic of China: as "center" of China, 9; and Cold War, 12, 96; deportation policies of, 14; founding, 12; Ministry of Foreign Affairs, 24, 148, 157; Ministry of Public Security, 24; migration policies of, 14–15, 48; leaving, 5, 8, 10–11, 21–22, 28, 75; and Southern Periphery, 5–6
People's Volunteer Army, 197
political refugees. *See* refugees, political
Political Worker Cadres School (Zhenggong Ganxiao), 193
population of Hong Kong: in 1930, 22; in 1941, 22–23; in 1947, 23; in 1951, 22, 24
Portugal. *See* colonialism, Portuguese (Macau)
PRC. *See* People's Republic of China
prisoners of war. *See* Kuomintang (KMT), prisoners of war (POWs)
Problem of the Chinese Refugees in Hong Kong. See Hambro
pro-CCP newspaper(s), 13, 149, 152–54, 158, 166
pro-KMT newspaper(s), 11–12, 98, 100–102, 104, 108, 119, 127, 131, 149, 150–52, 154–56, 158–59, 166, 203. *See also* Kuomintang, propaganda.
Public Law 85-316 (U.S.), 36

Qian Mu, 265n10
Qinghai, 40
Queen's Pier, 243, 283n21
Quemoy (Jinmen), 163

Red Guards, 100, 107, 115
Refugee Act of 1953 (U.S.), 35–38, 56
Refugee Relief Program (U.S.), 34, 52
refugee(s): and FCRA, 27–28; definition of, 26–31; labels, 5, 22, 54; policies, 22; political, 21, 32, 38–41; pro-KMT, 41–42; statuses in Hong Kong, 31; and United Nations, 26–31. *See also* immigration policies
Renmin Ribao, 148, 160, 279n47
Rennie, Alfred Herbert, 41
Rennie's Mill Refugee Camp, 22, 41–44, 57, 72–73, 183–84; censorship and political suppression, 72–73; population of, 44, 271n29
repatriation, 46, 55–56
Republic of China (ROC): as "center" of China, 9; Central Reform Committee, 43; and Cold War, 12; Control Yuan, 268n73; deportation policies of, 14; Executive Yuan, 47; Legislative Yuan, 39, 42–43, 202; Ministry of Foreign Affairs, 106, 124; national anthem, 203–4; National Assembly, 210; and refugees in Hong Kong, 5, 41–45; Security Bureau, 34; and Southern Periphery, 6. *See also* China; immigration (and refugee policies), Republic of China (Taiwan); Kuomintang (KMT); Taiwan
Ricoeur, Paul, 249, 284n1
Roberts, Priscilla, 12, 264n10, 266n32
ROC. *See* Republic of China

Safran, William, 264n7
Sai Kung, 98, 107
sampans, 25, 128
Sanmin Zhuyi wudang suozong, 203, 281n21
San Uk Leng, 97
Second World War. *See* World War II
self-governance (*zizhi*), 92–93. *See also* Hong Kong, City-State Autonomy Movement
Sha Ling, 116–17
Shanghai, 23–24, 74, 229, 265n8
Shek Hwei, 136, 147–58, 165–66, 279n39
Shek Kip Mei, 50–52; fire, 50–52, 269nn91–92; Low-Cost Housing Estate, 51
Shekou, 123–126, 129
Shenzhen, 15, 21, 24–25, 180, 230–34, 282n2; Shenzhen–Hong Kong Innovation Circle, 230. *See also* border
Sheung Shui, 182

Shih, Shu-mei, 8–9, 248, 250, 263n5, 283nn29–31
Shiqi, 185
Shum Shui Po, 244
Sichuan ferries, 47, 185
Silver Mine Bay, 41
Sing, Ming, 59, 270nn3–4
Sinn, Elizabeth, 223, 264n11
Sino-American Mutual Defense Treaty (1954), 83
Sino-British Joint Agreement (1984), 7, 59, 220, 226
Sinocentrism, 9
Sinophone studies, 8–9, 283n29. See also diaspora
Smart, Alan, 52, 269nn91–92
Social Welfare Office. See Hong Kong, Social Welfare Office
Song, Yongyi, 106, 275n15, 275n17
Soong Chu-yu, 210
South China Morning Post (*SCMP*), 128–29
Southeast Asia, 34, 38, 56, 78
Southern Periphery (China), 5–8, 12–15, 98–99, 123, 137, 171, 224–25, 247–48, 250–51, 264n7
Soviet Union (USSR), 11
special economic zone(s) (SEZ), 227, 238, 282n2
squatters, 32, 49–52, 54, 269n91
Star Ferry Pier, 243, 283n21
Struggle for Freedom and Democracy Alliance (*Zhongguo Ziyou Minzhu Zhandou Tongmeng*), 64–65
Su, Yang, 105–6, 275nn12–13
Suen Koon Ching, 140
Sun Baogang, 92, 274nn91–92
Sun Yat-sen, 94, 203, 281n21

Taidu (Taiwan independence movement), 203, 205, 208–10, 218–19. See also anti-independent Taiwan
Tai Kok Tsui, 182, 189
Taipei City Council, 195–96, 205; Legal Department of, 195

Taiwan, 7–9, 11–13, 15–17, 19, 22, 27, 33–34, 38–39, 45; as base of the Third Force movement, 81; colonial influence, 6–7; as deportation destination, 143, 145, 147; intellectuals, 40–41; perception of, 107–8. See also Republic of China
Taiwan Central Elected Representatives (1978), 203
Tam Kam Hung, 238
Tam Kam Pui, 237–39
Tao Zhu, 46, 180, 185
Television Broadcast Limited (TVB), 236
Teng Chai On, 125
Third Force, 9, 13, 18, 24, 43, 56; counterattack on the CCP, 60, 81, 83–85; first stage, 60, 61–77; formation of, 61–96; and Hong Kong, 59–61, 64–65, 71–77, 91–93, 96; ideals, 68; intellectuals, 9; and Kuomintang (KMT), 70, 82–87; leaders/core members, 60–61, 63, 270n8, 274n88; legacy, 96; magazines/publications, 13, 24, 59, 60, 65–66, 78–80, 270n14; non-elite writers, 70–77; and political parties, 61–64; second stage, 65, 77–95. See also United States, and Third Force.
Tiananmen Square crackdown, 191, 222
Tian Xin, 80, 272n50
touch-base policy (1974). See immigration (and refugee) policies, touch-base policy (1974)
toudu, 28, 236
Treaty of Nanjing (Nanking) (1842), 6
Treaty of Peking (1887), 7
Treaty of Shimonoseki (1895), 6
Triad(s), 136, 144, 149; connections with Kuomintang, 140, 144, 277n9; 14(K) society, 144. See also Green Gang
Tsang, Donald, 221
Tsang, Ngau, 128, 130
Tseung Kwan O, 41, 97
Tsim Bei Shan, 118
Tung Chee-hwa, 221
Tung Kei, 141, 278n14
Tung Wah Hospital, 39, 117

Umbrella Movement (2014), 3, 59, 218, 245–46
Undergrad, 244
UNHCR. *See* United Nations High Commissioner for Refugees
Union Press, 63, 66, 78
United College (Hong Kong), 76, 189
United Kingdom, 28, 252; Colonial Office, 108, 149, 269n90, 269n93, 269n95, 274n90; diplomatic relations with the PRC, 12, 17; Foreign Office, 156, 276n56, 279n37
United Nations, 17, 27, 30; Refugee Fund Executive Committee, 31; General Assembly, 29, 31; rhetoric of refugees, 26–31. *See also* Hambro
United Nations High Commissioner for Refugees (UNHCR), 22, 26, 28–31, 52, 264n12, 265n6, 267n39
United States: and Anti-Extradition Bill protests (2019), 246; and ARCI, 32–33; as a base for the Third Force movement, 59, 81–83; and Chiang Kai-shek, 33; and Cold War, 11, 26; Consulate General of Hong Kong, 33, 35, 79; criteria of citizenship, 38, 54; diplomatic ties with the ROC, 11, 18, 83–84, 95; and FCRA, 46; Information Services (USIS), 35; and KMT POWs, 163–64, Refugee relief program, 34–38, 52–53, 56; settlements of Chinese refugees, 5, 22, 33–36, 49, 59, 266n30; State Department, 13, 22, 35, 65–66, 78–79; and Third Force, 60, 63–66, 70, 77–78, 81–83, 272n52; and UNHCR, 30–31. *See also* Aid Refugee Chinese Intellectuals (ARCI); immigration (and refugee) policies, United States
U.S.-Taiwan Security Treaty (1954), 11, 83, 95

Victoria Park, 191
Victoria Road Detention Centre, 142, 149, 155–56, 158, 165
Voices of China (*Zhongguo Zhisheng*). See *Zhongguo Zhisheng*

Waglan Island, 102–3
Wah Kiu Yih Pao, 102, 275nn4–6, 275n9
Wanchai, 244
Wang Bingyue (Wang Ping-yue), 163
Wang Gungwu, 8–9, 263n5
Wang Qing-quan, 21, 43, 264n1
Wang Sheng, 198
Wang Yunpei, 163
Wan Lijuan, 63, 270n7, 272nn59–60
White Terror (Taiwan), 12, 161, 165, 198, 255
window of democracy (*minzhu de chuangkou*), 72, 75, 93
World War II, 4, 22–23, 60, 65, 140, 144
Wuchang, 21
Wu Ruoyu, 106, 275n16
Wu Tong Mountain, 182

Xianggang Minzu Lun (Hong Kong Nationalism), 244
Xianggang Shibao, 72, 276n42
Xiao Yujing, 19, 47, 168–75, 180–85, 187–88, 192–225, 255, 275n8, 280n3, 281n19
Xie Yufa, 81, 272n52
Xingqi ri dang'an (Sunday Report), 236, 239, 282n17
Xinhai Revolution, 251
Xinhui, 108, 177, 179, 228
Xixiang, 237
Xu Ziyou, 83

Yang, Dominic, 39, 73, 265n6, 271n32
Yang Nancun (Yang Nan-Tsun), 163
Yangzi Delta, 229
Yao, Norman, 35–37, 50–51, 120, 267nn46–47
Yau Tong, 97
Yen Chia-kan, 160

zaibao/zainan tongbao, 27, 101. *See also nanbao*
Zhang Fakui, 64, 78
Zhang Haishang (Chang Hai-sheng), 163
Zhang Junmai (Carson Chang), 61–64, 270n16
Zhang Kun, 73, 271n33
Zhang Mu Tou, 181

Zhang Tieshi (Chang Tieh-shih), 159–162, 164, 166
Zhang Yizhi, 68
Zhaoqing, 108, 110, 231, 234
Zhao Yixue (Chao Yi-Hsueh), 163
Zhongguo Zhisheng (Voices of China), 65, 71–73, 76, 88, 270n14
Zhongshan, 108, 121, 177, 230–31
Zhong Shan Tang, 203–6, 210
Zhou Yanghao (Chou Yang-hao), 163

Zhuhai, 227, 230–31, 233, 282n2, 282n8
Ziyouren, 72
Ziyou Zhenxian (Freedom Front), 65, 66, 68–71, 73, 78, 88, 270n14, 271n20, 271nn21–25, 271n28, 271n34, 271n36, 271n38
Ziyou Zhongguo, 84
Žižek, Slavoj, 249, 283n32
Zounun, 28
Zuo Shunsheng, 61, 63–64, 78, 86, 91, 95, 273n74

GPSR Authorized Representative: Easy Access System Europe, Mustamäe tee 50, 10621 Tallinn, Estonia, gpsr.requests@easproject.com

www.ingramcontent.com/pod-product-compliance
Lightning Source LLC
Chambersburg PA
CBHW032335300426
44109CB00041B/856